MW01194837

THE FOURTEENTH DALAI LAMA'S STAGES OF THE PATH

Publisher's Acknowledgment

The publisher gratefully acknowledges the generous help of the Hershey Family Foundation in sponsoring the production of this book.

The Fourteenth Dalai Lama's
Stages of the Path

VOL. 1: GUIDANCE FOR THE MODERN PRACTITIONER

HIS HOLINESS THE DALAI LAMA

COMPILED AND EDITED BY HIS EMINENCE
Dagyab Kyabgön Rinpoché

Translated by Gavin Kilty

Wisdom

Wisdom Publications
199 Elm Street
Somerville, MA 02144 USA
wisdomexperience.org

Library of Congress Cataloging-in-Publication Data
Names: Bstan-'dzin-rgya-mtsho, Dalai Lama XIV, 1935– author. |
Dagyab, Loden Sherab, editor. | Kilty, Gavin, translator.
Title: The Fourteenth Dalai Lama's stages of the path. Volume 1: Guidance for
the modern practitioner / His Holiness the Dalai Lama; compiled and edited
by his eminence Dagyab Kyabgön Rinpoché; translated by Gavin Kilty.
Description: First. | Somerville: Wisdom Publications, 2022. |
Includes bibliographical references and index.
Identifiers: LCCN 2021054566 (print) | LCCN 2021054567 (ebook) |
ISBN 9781614297932 (hardcover) | ISBN 9781614298175 (ebook)
Subjects: LCSH: Buddhism—Doctrines. | Mādhyamika (Buddhism) |
Spiritual life—Buddhism. | Happiness—Religious aspects—Buddhism.
Classification: LCC BQ7935.B774 F683 2022 (print) | LCC BQ7935.B774 (ebook) |
DDC 294.3/42—dc23/eng/20220223
LC record available at https://lccn.loc.gov/2021054566
LC ebook record available at https://lccn.loc.gov/2021054567

ISBN 978-1-61429-793-2   ebook ISBN 978-1-61429-817-5

26 25 24 23 22   5 4 3 2 1

Cover and interior design by Gopa & Ted 2.
Cover Photo by Olivier Adam. The excerpts from *Stories of Tibetan Women* on pages
385–450 are courtesy of Resa Könchok Gyatso.

Printed on acid-free paper that meets the guidelines for permanence and durability of
the Production Guidelines for Book Longevity of the Council on Library Resources.

Printed in Canada.

Contents

Preface by
His Holiness the Fourteenth Dalai Lama

THE FIRST VOLUME OF this work is a fairly detailed explanation of general points related to Buddhist concepts. It includes an introduction for today's Buddhists on the important and fundamental points of the philosophical tenets of Śākyamuni Buddha, explanations on the reality of base existence presented by Buddhism and modern science, and ways to integrate the essence of Buddhism into daily life.

The second volume, composed by way of analysis of modern-day realities, consists of supplementary annotations to the wonderful work *Oral Transmission of Mañjuśrī*—an exegesis on the Lamrim, or stages of the path treatise, by the Great Fifth Dalai Lama, which is included in the classification known as the eight great works on the stages of the path.

I would like to talk a little about the reasons for this approach. In this twenty-first century the ongoing economic betterment of conditions for the peoples of this world has meant the overcoming of various immediate difficulties. By means of our human intellectual capabilities, alliances have been forged, great strides have been made in education, and, with the huge efforts expended by scientific research, great advances have been made in measurable understandings of the workings of the quantifiable external world. However, up to now, similar quantifiable understandings of the workings of the inner world of mind and experience have not been possible. Nevertheless, the ongoing search for ways to do so, fueled by an increasing interest in these areas, is an excellent sign.

However, at the same time there is the unprecedented phenomenon of climate change, epidemics, environmental problems, health issues, and so on. Moreover, new troubles, such as terrorism, are continuing to beset the world. The reality is that these problems are manmade. Many governments, communities, and individuals, driven by the energy of anger, desire, and wrong concepts, focus on their immediate needs without any thought for the long-term damage that might arise. Additionally, beset by intense sectarianism, they focus shortsightedly on the benefits to the individual or their own groups, not thinking of the effect their actions will have on the global community. There is no other way of resolving and improving these situations than to transform human thinking and conduct.

For such a transformation to take place, we can engage in the trainings of the views and conducts existing in religious traditions. In particular, we should work to benefit others by wholesome secular acts not necessarily linked with religious traditions, such as love, mindfulness, consideration, contentment, and patience, which are the basic attitudes for a conduct of accepting and discarding. These wholesome ways of behavior are found within all religious traditions, but they do not depend upon a particular religion for their existence, nor do they arise from those religions. In general, they arise by virtue of their being the very foundations of society. [viii] For example, abandoning the ten unvirtuous acts was adopted into Buddhist practice because these ten actions—such as killing and lying—did not bring about peace, harmony, and happiness within society. They were not newly decreed by the Buddha as being harmful. Therefore, abandoning these can be categorized as wholesome acts not specifically linked with any religious tradition. There are many such activities, and it is helpful to recognize them as such.

Whether we follow a religious tradition or not, I see it as incumbent upon us all to recognize the common goal of short and long-term happiness and to see that this is our common responsibility as individuals and communities. Many people have no liking for religious traditions and tend to shun a particular training as if it were a contagious disease simply because it comes from a religious tradition. These people, when working for their own happiness, should try to recognize these fundamental trainings as practical methods for bringing about peace and happiness and apply them to their minds. If these trainings are allowed to disappear, ultimately it will be a loss to humanity. It is worth experimenting to see if this is true or not.

Human beings of all kinds, without differentiation, whether they have faith in religion or not, are young or old, traditional or progressive, whether they believe in change or not, are all united in wanting to live happy lives in a well-ordered and decent society. And, keeping in mind that working for the benefit of all beings is essential for this endeavor, we should consider it our responsibility to help as best we can all those who show an interest. Therefore, because we hold that the teachings of the Buddha are reality-based and verifiable by experience, a general introduction to Buddhism in eight chapters has been included in this two-volume work.

VOLUME 1

For many years, wherever I am in the world, I have worked hard to promote three beneficial commitments to be of benefit. The first of these commitments is to attempt to develop the intrinsic and fundamental qualities of goodness that exist in human beings. The second commitment is to increase harmony among world religions. The third is the commitment to the welfare of Tibet. These three are the focus of the first volume, and are the context of the presentation of the general and specific points of Buddhism together with various historical narratives. In this general explanation are chapters on Buddhist philosophy on the reality of base existence, the relation between Buddhism and modern science, and how certain Buddhist trainings can be put into practice in tune with the necessities of daily life.

I will explain briefly the fundamental issues on which the contents of these eight chapters are based. [ix] The conditions that give rise to our manmade troubles are due to the failure to value the wholesome qualities such as love and kindness, which are innate in human beings, and to not recognize them as being fundamental for the welfare of humanity. Not valuing these qualities, we make no effort to develop their potential.

These qualities are like seeds. If seeds of flowers are provided with the right external conditions of soil, fertilizer, warmth, water, and so on, and are nurtured and cared for, the full glory of the flowers' beauty, with their wonderful aromas, can blossom. If not, those seeds remain as potential only, unable to produce their results. Similarly, in order to manifest the potential of the love and kindness innate in each of us, we must nurture the right inner conditions of our attitudes, such as being compassionate, content, disciplined, and conscientious. Our happiness depends solely on others being happy, and therefore, if we alleviate the suffering of others, our own happiness will naturally and inevitably arise. When we understand this, these attitudes of love and kindness will develop unhindered and the innate potential within human beings can emerge.

We must recognize that among the numerous troubles that have occurred in the world over the past thousand years or so, some have involved groups that follow religious traditions. These followers have shown little interest in taming their minds through reliance upon their religion, and they hold their religious views to be supreme and misuse their religion so that it becomes a cause for increasing anger and desire. This is such a tragic situation and it continues today.

The result of such abuse of religious teachings has been a widespread opinion that no religion can be effective in real-world situations.

Followers of the major religious traditions that teach practices for taming the unruly mind have a responsibility to counter this unfortunate situation and to bring about the short- and long-term welfare of individuals and communities. A single religious tradition lacks the methods for fulfilling all the hopes and wishes of all living beings, because such hopes are as numerous as the varied dispositions of living beings. I believe that followers of diverse religious traditions should willingly act to shed any resentment, apprehension, expectation, and competitiveness between them, fueled by attachment or dislike. Setting aside their history of hostility and distrust, they should work to foster harmonious relations by cultivating respect and a genuine appreciation of other religions.

Furthermore, it is important that we Tibetans who have faith in Buddhism understand that all the philosophical positions of the Tibetan Buddhist traditions and their subsects are ultimately of one intent. If we had some familiarity with the historical accounts of where and how these traditions developed, it would without doubt act as nourishment for the respect and pure perception of each of them. [x] Therefore, it is worth having some interest in studying their histories.

The philosophical view of Buddhism is dependent origination, and its conduct is one of nonharming. Relying upon Buddhism can exert a beneficial influence on the way we spend our lives. In Buddhism we recognize that all actions operate solely within the process of cause and effect. On that basis, we devote ourselves to the antidotes to karma and mental affliction, which are phenomena to be abandoned, and we strive for the resultant phenomena, which are factors to be adopted and which bring happiness now and in the long term. To begin we need an introduction to the essence of Buddhism by way of a presentation on the four truths.

In this book it is possible that there is some repetition over the two volumes, but this is because of the particular emphasis of the way of explaining the subject matter.

It is not necessary to become a Buddhist in order to put the fundamental philosophy of Buddhism and its stages of training into practice. All can comprehend these worthy qualities and use them to enjoy a good life blessed with short- and long-term happiness for oneself and others; this is something we all have to do. This does not mean that you should have faith in Buddhism or that you must definitely practice it. We should respect the individual's right to have or not have faith in a religion. It goes without saying that it is acceptable to practice religion and also acceptable not to. However, given that we desire happiness and have no desire for suffering, if a religious tradition's practices for taming the mind and abandoning hurting others are sincerely brought into daily life, they will definitely be beneficial in bringing happiness to oneself and others. I consider it important to try to show that.

Concerning an actual practice of Buddhism, at the very heart of the Dharma of the Buddha is a presentation of karma, or cause and effect. The proposition that "if this is done, that arises" is held to be a fundamental truth. By adhering to the reality of all phenomena existing in a state of mutual dependence, Buddhism must be practiced in harmony with the principle of seeking truth from facts. Buddhism is not a tradition that adheres solely to scripture; it is one in which reason is paramount. Any doctrine that contradicts evidence or sound reasoning, or that contradicts that which is validated by direct experience, should not be accepted and should be discarded. New ways of explaining phenomena that emerge from the investigative skills of modern research and do not accord with traditional explanations found in Buddhist texts of the past should be willingly accepted.

Even the words of Śākyamuni Buddha himself should be practiced having first examined them as one would examine the purity of gold through burning, cutting, and polishing. [xi] This the Buddha himself advised us to do. His instructions are not to be held as objects of veneration, nor followed simply because they are the words of our teacher. This independence of thought decreed by the mighty Buddha is the central pillar and peerless feature of this tradition. Those religions that determine what is and what is not allowed on the basis of the controlling decrees of a creator or of a founding saint, do not accord, in this aspect, with this fundamental tenet of Buddhism. Therefore, when we actually apply ourselves to religious practice, except in those areas of working to benefit others, we cannot simultaneously engage in different traditions, like having a foot in each camp, because of these fundamental differences in the path. Nor would it be of any benefit.

These days, in the conspicuous race of the human intellect to investigate fields of knowledge, competitiveness has increased accordingly. Because of this, many open-minded people, including those who propound modern scientific views, are convinced that Buddhist philosophy and its related trainings stand up to scrutiny. Non-Buddhists are recognizing that Buddhism can provide practices for developing happiness and eradicating suffering, practices that are therefore effective in bringing peace and well-being to society. Such voices are becoming more pronounced. For those who seek out new fields of knowledge and who have taken on the responsibility of promoting the welfare of our human society, Buddhism has become a new area of interest. This clearly illustrates the unique prestige of this tradition. It continues to receive much praise from all quarters that not only is it not a poison, but it can be substantiated by verifiable evidence and experience that it is medicine. This inspires limitless and joyous confidence.

VOLUME 2

Volume 2 is a translation of *Oral Transmission of Mañjuśrī: Instructions on the Stages of the Path,* a Buddhist presentation comprising, for a person who seeks liberation, the essential ways to practice in a single meditation session. It is an example of the stages of the path genre, one of the many condensed and extensive stages of the path works composed by the great masters of the past. It was composed by the

Great Fifth Dalai Lama, whose work was an unparalleled kindness for both the modern religious and secular systems of Tibet and for its people. He was genuinely a great being endowed with learning and accomplishment. This text takes as its foundation the unrivaled work *Extensive Exposition of the Stages of the Path*, composed by the all-knowing Tsongkhapa Losang Drakpa (1357–1419), [xii] and excellently summarizes the main points of practice.

I have taken *Oral Transmission of Mañjuśrī*, which was held in great esteem by many masters of the past, as a basis for the teachings in volume 2 and I have provided, with great respect and service, a somewhat expanded explanation in the form of a supplement.

The explanation in these volumes does not just follow the traditional modes of the past. It is in accordance with these changing times and follows the great ocean waves of beliefs and dispositions of the beings of this world, however they live. It is aimed at those who have a liking for religion in general, or specifically for Buddhism, and at those who are monks and nuns, lay men and women, Tibetan and non-Tibetan, who out of faith have entered this doctrine. It is also for those who have hostility toward religion, or have no particular feeling toward it, and for those who hold various political views. It is a work compiling the wisdom of different valuable philosophies and the great ways of the bodhisattvas.

This work is a small gift for the discerning people of this vast world and is offered with the pure motivation that it will reveal the excellent path of immediate and permanent happiness by opening new eyes of wisdom in all those of unbiased minds.

The Buddhist monk and propounder, the Fourteenth Dalai Lama, Tenzin Gyatso, Thekchen Chöling, Dharamsala, India, the sixth day of the tenth month of fire monkey year of the seventeenth cycle, corresponding to December 5, 2016.

Compiler's Introduction

[XIII] I WOULD LIKE TO SET OUT the thinking and background to the wonderful opportunity I have had in compiling the two volumes of *The Fourteenth Dalai Lama's Stages of the Path* from the teachings of the great and all-knowing Fourteenth Dalai Lama.

On October 7, 1991, while His Holiness the Dalai Lama was giving teachings in Hamburg, Germany, I experienced the great fortune of being deemed worthy to be in his presence during the lunch that was offered to him in his residence at the Rabten Jangchup Chöling Dharma Center. In keeping the thought that we should receive his forever meaningful instructions wherever possible, I expressed a doubt concerning the manner in which texts primarily of the stages of the path genre were being commentated on, wondering whether some were not in tune with the dispositions of the changing times in this world, and I requested his advice on this matter.

It was His Holiness's opinion also that it was certainly the case that some of the more traditional ways of commenting were not appropriate, and that it was important for such commentaries to not fundamentally be in contradiction with progressive modern education and reasoning, and to be in harmony with practical reality

Therefore, with a view of not wanting Buddhism to be regarded as anachronistic, and still be relevant today, I requested that he might compose a work on the stages of the path that would suit the mental dispositions of numerous students. [xiv] This great treasure of compassion agreed that such a work was necessary and was of the opinion that it would be excellent if such a stages of the path compilation were based upon the four truths. However, because of the pressure of his busy schedule and increasing workload, it would have been difficult for him to give time to composing a text with his own hand, and so he said, "I will teach it and you, Rinpoché, will write it down. That would be good."

He had blessed me with a joyous festival of priceless words, and I experienced a feeling of faith, devotion, and happiness beyond description. However, because of his increasing activity in working for the welfare of the world, bringing harmony among the world's religions, and striving for the welfare of Tibet, the project did not immediately begin, and I did not have the confidence to ask him again and so left it as it was.

However, on June 5, 2006, after four days of teachings His Holiness had given in Brussels, Belgium, as he was preparing to leave, I was suddenly asked to see him in his room. His Holiness said that it would be worthwhile to compose a supplement to *Oral Transmission of Mañjuśrī* by the Great Fifth, and because I had received many teachings from His Holiness and was very familiar with his way of thinking, it was appropriate that I should compile the draft of this supplement. There would also be a general explanation consisting of an introduction to Buddhism, and so on, as a preliminary, and therefore I should organize the production of "The Fourteenth Dalai Lama's Stages of the Path."

This was a kindness beyond measure and an unparalleled caring for me with an optimism that regarded a clod of earth as gold. [xv] There was no time to think about whether I could accomplish this task, or to ask his thoughts on how to proceed to carry it out. No sooner had I taken his command to the crown of my head I just uttered the one word, "Yes," and was lost for anything else to say.

Gradually, after this surprising turn of events became a little clearer, I thought about it and realized that it was connected to what His Holiness had said previously at lunch in Hamburg. Although I had no confidence in myself having the knowledge or capability of carrying out such a service, I thought that by the power of the blessings of compassion from the lama, such an accomplishment might be possible. This uplifted up my mind and gave me encouragement.

At the same time, from the Gaden Phodrang Private Office I requested and received CDs and other materials on His Holiness's introductory discourses on Buddhism, as well as his stages of the path teachings primarily on *Oral Transmission of Mañjuśrī*. These I used as a basis. Over time I collected the many published books of his teachings and compiled the various notes I had taken. From Tibetan language newspapers, journals, and the internet, I collected even the smallest teachings that had been published, as well as the various talks that were regularly given. In this way I set about the preparations for the compilation.

On December 18, 2006, at Varanasi, India, while His Holiness was giving a teaching, I had my first opportunity to ask for his opinion and advice on the notes I had made for this composition and on its content being in accord with modern thinking.

[xvi] From August 16 to 20, 2008, at Nantes in France, while His Holiness was giving teachings there, I was able show him a basic compilation of the draft I had completed thus far and I received some profound advice. After that, as suggested by His Holiness, I went to Switzerland to meet with the academic scholar and geshé Thupten Jinpa, the interpreter for His Holiness. In informal and very helpful conversations on diverse topics, he suggested various improvements and put forward many ideas. On that basis I revised the draft.

Generally, the outlines to explanations of the stages of the path are straightforward. However, here, while it was perfectly acceptable to use the outlines established by the *Extensive Exposition on the Stages of the Path*, these were not copied verbatim but at times were abridged, and so the numbering only roughly corresponds.

General explanations of Buddhism have no outlines. Using the suggestions of Geshé Thupten Jinpa and others, I looked into laying out chapters and setting up a new structure, in particular making sure that there would not be much repetition of material and that everything would fit into its appropriate classification. Doing so meant that I was providing the opportunity for criticism from all quarters for my woeful lack of knowledge and ability. However, I have proceeded with whatever my mind was capable of understanding. Nevertheless, I remain doubtful that it conforms to the intentions of His Holiness, and while that is so, I cannot do other than to ask for tolerance of my errors.

[xvii] His Holiness's discourses are delivered in a phrasing that is easy to understand and their meanings are clear. They are timely, of profound potential, contain great counsel, are in tune with the developments of time and place, and are completely in accord with the beliefs, inclinations, attitudes, faculties, latent dispositions, and so on of listeners from different cultures. It is evident to everyone that they are enthusiastically regarded as unparalleled objects of praise and reverence.

When putting these discourses into writing so that the splendor and brilliance of His Holiness's profound words are clearly manifest, I maintained as best I could the prime importance of bringing out those elements that clarify his thought with no degeneration of the written language, and in the first volume especially, by supplementing with relevant material.

Discourses of His Holiness such as these are of great importance, and when writing the draft, I did not shy away from the amount of writing. However, whenever it was shown to His Holiness for his perusal, so as not to tire him from reading too much, those sections that definitely required his attention were written in blue ink. After his scrutiny, any advice he gave was recorded or noted down, and revision made accordingly.

For three days that ran between July 31 and August 9, 2010, at the

Gaden Phodrang in Dharamsala I specially convened with Professor Samdhong Rinpoché, Geshé Thupten Jinpa, and the interpreter Geshé Dramdul. [xviii] Together with His Holiness we discussed the draft text, and I revised the draft based on the advice and suggestions given at that time.

On December 22, 2012, I went to see Samdhong Rinpoché at Ashram, his private residence in Dharamsala. There for seventeen full days, uninterrupted by any of his other duties or functions and with a great sense of responsibility, he gave his full attention to all the notes that had so far been roughly compiled into the two volumes of the stages of the path and preliminary general explanation. In return I received peerless advice and suggestions from him. I improved the draft where necessary and over time sent sections to Rinpoché for review.

In 2015, over three days from May 19 to 21, in the Gaden Phodrang at Dharamsala, I met with Samdhong Rinpoché as well as with Sera Mé Monastery Lharampa Geshé Yangteng Rinpoché, who is the Private Office under-secretary. At that time His Holiness provided us with the pleasing reassurance of looking over the whole of stages of the path section. Taking the advice that we received from him on those parts still in need of improvement and of supplementing, I consulted with Samdhong Rinpoché and amended accordingly. With this, a draft of the second volume of *The Fourteenth Dalai Lama's Stages of the Path*, on the stages of the path, was complete.

Toward the end of December 2015, while His Holiness was teaching in South India, I consulted Samdhong Rinpoché on the first volume dealing with the general teachings and made revisions in accordance with his advice. On April 2, 2016, I came to Dharamsala to present the draft to His Holiness for his perusal.

This precious work, *The Fourteenth Dalai Lama's Stages of the Path*, reviewed and assessed by Samdhong Rinpoché and Yangteng Rin-poché, is a collection of teachings that bring out the very essence of the thoughts of His Holiness. It is an excellent teaching created from his actual words, from words that have his assent, and from words that he has blessed.[1] It is a contribution to a new-moon, authentic literary tradition that reveals a path to benefit all beings of this world equally without discrimination, and now the opportunity to present it to the people of this world, as a gift to ease their pain, had arrived.

His Holiness the Dalai Lama especially gave me this precious opportunity to gather the excellent merit of performing this act of devotion by preparing a draft of the two volumes of *The Fourteenth Dalai Lama's Stages of the Path*. It brings joy to my heart, and with gladness, faith, and devotion I prostrate before him and remember his kindness that knows no end.

As a key to open the vast door to His Holiness' profound collection of teachings, I compiled from these two volumes a summary, *Essence of Thought*, which contains the most succinct statements. The two sections of the summary are included as an appendix in each of the two volumes.

ACKNOWLEDGMENTS

To Professor Samdhong Rinpoché, who from beginning to end scrutinized the various drafts and constantly gave me peerless, abundant advice and guidance, I express gratitude that is beyond measure.

To the academic scholar and interpreter for His Holiness, Geshé Thupten Jinpa; to the director of Tibet House Delhi and interpreter for His Holiness, Geshé Dorjé Dramdul; [xx] and to Gaden Phodrang Private Office under-secretary, Sera Mé Lharampa Geshé Yangteng Rinpoché: for their peerless assistance by way of many gifts of ideas, guidance and discussion given over a long period, I rejoice from the depth of my heart.

To the Gaden Phodrang Private Office also, who provided much needed assistance for this undertaking and who granted us joint copyright to publish in Tibetan, English, German, and Chinese languages these two volumes of His Holiness's book *The Fourteenth Dalai Lama's Stages of the Path,* thereby fulfilling the aspirations of the Tibetan Cultural and Educational Institute, known as Tibet House Germany, which is sustained by the compassion of its honorary patron, His Holiness the Dalai Lama, I offer sincere thanks and gratitude.

Respectfully,
Dagyab Loden Sherab
Compiler
March 15, 2016

Foreword and Acknowledgments by Tibet House Germany (Tibethaus Deutschland)

IT IS REPORTED OF GREAT INVENTORS that they suddenly had a brilliant inspiration, as if from nowhere, during a banal activity such as brushing their teeth. The fact that these inventions were preceded by many years of thought, one-pointed motivation, and intensive work is often glossed over. The idea for writing *The Fourteenth Dalai Lama's Stages of the Path* arose in a similar situation:

> More than a decade ago, during a short audience in Brussels, H. H. the Dalai Lama tasked me by the by—he was preparing to leave and was tying his shoelaces—to compile a contemporary Lamrim on his behalf, based on his own teachings. It was to be his own commentary on the Lamrim by the V. Dalai Lama. In addition, I was to compile a detailed introduction to Buddhism.

With these words, our revered spiritual director H. E. Dagyab Rinpoché described with a chuckle the moment of the "initial spark" for the creation of the two-volume work, the Tibetan title of which is *Gyälwäi Gongsel* (*Rgyal ba'i dgongs gsal*).

As a result, Rinpoché, who had just retired after thirty-eight years at the University of Bonn, worked intensively on these books for more than ten years. What an impressive achievement! In this connection he traveled three times to Dharamsala to review and correct the text in detail with His Holiness. Professor Samdhong Rinpoché, Geshé Thubten Jinpa, and Yangteng Rinpoché were also present at these meetings. The Tibetan edition was then jointly published by the Dalai Lama Trust and Tibet House Germany in December 2016 and presented to the public in the presence of His Holiness, Dagyab Rinpoché, and Mr. Phuntsok Tsering Düchung at a Book Lounge in India.

In this work, His Holiness has pointed out a number of new paths that Tibetan Buddhists in particular are encouraged to follow. For instance, the *geshé lharampa* title, introduced by the Fourth Panchen Lama, Losang Chökyi Gyaltsen (1570–1662), was only given to monks until just a few years ago. The Fourteenth Dalai Lama has initiated that this title be conferred to nuns as well. The first female geshé in the academic history of Tibetan Buddhism is the German nun Kelsang Wangmo, who earned her title in 2011. In addition, he has now directed that in the future this academic title be awarded to all graduates of Buddhist philosophy studies—regardless of ordination, gender, or race.

According to Dagyab Rinpoché, we can regard this work, comparable to the constitution of a country, as something we can always rely on. It is forward looking and of great importance for not only Buddhists but also for people without a spiritual background as well as for researchers.

The work has been translated into English, German, and Chinese under the direction of our Tibet House publishing house. And hopefully this is just the beginning...

Why does Tibet House Germany hold the copyright together with the Gaden Phodrang Foundation of the Dalai Lama? To answer this, we must briefly explain some of the history and orientation of our organization: Tibet House has been under the patronage of H. H. the Dalai Lama since 2005. It is a cultural and educational institute in the middle of the open multiethnic and multireligious cosmopolitan city of Frankfurt. It arose from a Buddhist predecessor organization that had already been working with Dagyab Rinpoché for over twenty years. Our institute has had the honor of inviting His Holiness to Frankfurt a total of four times in recent years, enabling him to present to the public his heartfelt concerns (which are also ours): intercultural and interreligious dialogue, study, and the cultivation of Tibetan culture, and the cultivation of the global, nonreligious ethics he has developed. Particularly important and touching for us were his encounters with sometimes up to two thousand pupils as well as dialogue encounters on inter-religious and secular topics.

Tibet House Germany builds bridges in both directions to create a connection between Tibetan culture and all those interested in it, and to create the necessary basis for this—for instance, by deepening communication with other Tibetan institutions in and outside Tibet, likewise with Western, Tibetan, and Chinese artists and scholars. The purpose is to support people in attaining happiness by providing differentiated information, study, and practice and to impart crucial core values.

According to the Dalai Lama's succinct formulation, these core values are the following:

1. The view is dependent origination.
2. The conduct is to do no harm.

Tibet, Tibetans, and Tibetan culture are the origin and source of the contents and concerns of Tibet House. The supporting pillars of Tibet House are Tibetans and Germans/Westerners alike. Undiluted study of Buddhist texts, application of the teachings in everyday life, and appreciation of all traditions and the overcoming of stereotyped thinking are all a matter of course for us. We also promote the connection between Buddhist knowledge and science. A good example of this is our Cultural Foundation's Phuntsok Tsering Scholarship project, which enables young Tibetans to study at the University of Hamburg under the guidance of Professor Dorje Wangchug. Another concern is the overdue equality of Tibetan women scholars and practitioners, for many years a goal of the Dagyab Benefit Society (Dagyab Hilfsverein) and of our foundation. Just one more focal point should be mentioned: providing specific support for children and young people, who are, after all, our future.

Our School for Tibetan Children, or Sherab Ling ("Garden of Knowledge") follows the secular SEE Learning Method for teachers, which was initiated by the Dalai Lama (we have been a cooperation partner of Emory University/USA since 2016). We also host numerous visits by school classes and student groups, which are a great pleasure for us.

In this way we endeavor to put into practice as many of the important themes and thought-provoking ideas of this great two-volume work as possible.

Our special thanks go to the Gaden Phodrang Foundation of the Dalai Lama, which has financed a large part of the English translation from its endowment funds. The translation into English would not have been possible without this support. We would also like to thank them for entrusting us with the planning and coordination of the English, German, and Chinese translations. We would like to take this opportunity to express our gratitude to Mr. Kungo Tseten Chhökyapa and Mr. Tenzin Sewo for their outstanding cooperation.

Also, we wish to offer our thanks to Geshe Thupten Jinpa, who gave his precious advice at different stages of this publication.

With their outstanding linguistic and philosophical skills, Gavin Kilty and Sophie McGrath have produced translations that are both accurate and inspiring, making this extremely important work accessible to English readers. We wish to express our highest appreciation and deepest gratitude to them. We would also like to give our heartfelt thanks to Rebecca Hufen and Jürgen Manshardt, the German translators of the second volume, who contributed to the quality of the English translation by way of analyzing and comparing difficult parts of their translation with the English edition, and to Franziska Örtle, who compared the English and German translations of the second volume word for word with the Tibetan original.

We would very much like to thank Chandra Chiara Ehm for her inspiring tranlation of the summary, *Essence of Thought*, which can be found in the appendix of the two volumes.

The cooperation with the publication team of Wisdom Publications was always very pleasant and characterized by a high level of professionalism. We are very happy to know that this work is in good hands with this excellent publishing house. We would especially like to thank Laura Cunningham and Daniel Aitken for their excellent project management. In addition, as editor, Alex Gardner has made a great contribution through his careful and meticulous work. Our sincere thanks!

At Tibet House we would like to express our special thanks to Phuntsok Tsering. He accompanied this project as codirector with great commitment before his all-too-early death. A big thank you goes to Claudia Heilmann for her support from the Tibet House Cultural Foundation, as well as to Judith Fries, who was able to collect a large number of donations for these translations with extraordinary dedication. Our heartfelt thanks also go to Matthias Atrott for his generous and professional legal advice. We would also like to thank from the bottom of our hearts all the people who, through their small and large donations, helped to make this translation possible.

Our wish is that many people will personally benefit from this work and contribute thereby to a better world.

Elke Hessel, Director, Tibet House Germany
Andreas Ansmann, Manager, Tibet House Publishing

Translator's Introduction

NO ORDINARY DALAI LAMA

NGAWANG LOSANG YESHÉ TENZIN GYATSO, the Fourteenth Dalai Lama of Tibet, is no ordinary Dalai Lama—if indeed any Dalai Lama can be said to be "ordinary." Sometime in the seventies, when he was in his forties, he remarked that he was not too young to be inexperienced and not too old to be ineffectual in making a difference in this world. And what a difference he has made.

His Holiness was thrust into the modern world in 1959 when he sought refuge in India in the wake of the Communist Chinese occupation of Tibet. The story of these and succeeding events have been related many times. Since that time, from his headquarters in the little hill town of Dharamsala in the foothills of the Himalayas, he has engaged in reestablishing and preserving the religious, cultural, and educational institutions of Tibet in Tibetan settlements in India, while embarking upon a radical approach to the organizing and setup of those same institutions. Never one to maintain tradition for its own sake, he has often set aside well-established Tibetan customs and practices not conducive to the promotion of human values and happiness, or not in tune with modern thinking, and has implemented changes that would have raised eyebrows in Tibetan society had they been suggested by any lesser figure than a Dalai Lama.

However, he is the Dalai Lama—a revered figure and a spiritual leader, whose incarnations go back hundreds of years. He is the fourteenth of this illustrious line, and the first to spend such a long period in exile. Other Dalai Lamas have faced political upheavals in their time, but none have had to adjust to a new and alien way of life alongside thousands of his fellow citizens who fled Tibet with him. On the whole it has been a successful adaptation. Whenever the integration of exiled communities around the world has been evaluated, Tibetan refugees are often held up as glowing exemplars of a culture that has not only found its feet in a foreign land and climate but has even flourished. Those who have prolonged contact with Tibetan communities in India and elsewhere will vouch for that.

Much of this progress in diaspora comes down to the leadership of the Dalai Lama, combined with the unquestioning devotion his people have for him. Very few nations love their leader the way Tibetans do. The radical change of circumstance and living conditions the Tibetan refugees found themselves in when arriving in India meant that he had to reestablish the cultural institutions of Tibet, but not in a way that nostalgically replicated the centuries-old religious and cultural traditions of Tibet. His approach to these issues has been to consider what would be of greatest benefit to those concerned and to the world at large. His Holiness thinks of himself as a Tibetan but also as a citizen of the world. Consequently, he never puts narrow nationalistic considerations first. If what was practiced in old Tibet is beneficial in today's world and is in tune with current thinking, then it should continue. Otherwise, it should be allowed to fade away.

The most striking example of this radical thinking was his giving up of political and administrative rule over Tibetan society in 2011. The political power wielded by the Dalai Lamas had been in place since the seventeenth century, when it was initiated by the Fifth Dalai Lama. Having long understood that democracy was the way of the world, the present Dalai Lama renounced his own power and encouraged the setting up of a democratic system where political power would be determined by the people's will. This was no easy task—not because he had any clinging to the notion of power, but because it was not the stated wish of the Tibetan people. It would be a safe bet that if the

Tibetan people had been consulted on whether His Holiness should renounce political power, the response would have been a resounding "no." However, he explained his decision to them carefully and with reasoning. To have flown in the face of that reasoning and continue the institution of the Dalai Lama just for the sake of tradition would have made no sense to him.

Tibetan society is a conservative society, and it does not take on change willingly or quickly. Nevertheless, such conservatism has been a boon in preserving the scriptural tradition of Buddhism with its huge corpus of Indic and indigenous works. This is now of enormous benefit to the world, especially since Buddhism disappeared in India, the land of its birth, a long time ago. Thousands of pages of Indic texts translated from Sanskrit centuries ago are now only found in the Tibetan Buddhist canon. His Holiness regards such preservation as a gift to the world, and he is at pains to ensure not only that it continues but that these scriptures of Buddhist philosophy and practice are made available to the world in their own languages.

Nevertheless, he sees that not everything that has been preserved and established is necessary or even beneficial for contemporary Tibetans, exposed as they are now to modern thought and modern ways of life. Therefore, he has never shirked from making radical religious and cultural changes. In most cases the Tibetan people acquiesce to any suggestions of change he might make. Nevertheless, it must have taken some courage to go against embedded and well-established habits. Take the Shukden controversy for example.[2] This ritual practice had been widespread among the Tibetan Gelukpa monastic tradition for about sixty years and was propagated by a much-loved lama in Tibet in the 1930s. Tibetans can be quite fierce about their loyalties and devotion. The Dalai Lama was aware of this and even though he had become aware that Dorjé Shukden was not the beneficent protector he was portrayed to be, for a while he made no public proclamations on this matter. However, later the situation became intolerable, and people were being adversely affected. Therefore, he went public, denouncing the practice of this ritual and asking those who refused to give it up to not attend his teachings.

The path he took went against the grain of prevalent Gelukpa practice. There were not many monks in the Gelukpa tradition who did not rely upon Shukden as a protector. His Holiness's pronouncement presented them with the difficult choice of remaining loyal to their own lamas, who had initiated them into the practice, or following the wishes of the Dalai Lama. This was not an easy choice to make, and indeed, some monks refused to give up the practice.

Nevertheless, His Holiness's actions followed sound reasoning, which had led him to realize that Shukden practice was based upon a mistaken perception and was sectarian at heart. He feared that if it continued, it would harm the unity of the Tibetan people. Tibet consisted of different regions and districts, many of which possessed a fierce adherence to their own identity. It was also the home of many Buddhist traditions formed over the centuries by great masters of the past or by the circumstance of time, place, and transmission from India. Unity in the sense of one country and one religion was not always evident in old Tibet. However, in exile, regional and religious unity was essential if Tibetan culture was going to survive. It was this fear that prompted his public denunciation of Shukden. It was a courageous thing to do.

In doctrinal matters too he is forthright, unsentimental, and never hesitates to present truth based upon reasoning and experience. For example, ancient Indian Buddhist scriptures, when describing and referring to the cosmology of the universe, describe our world as consisting of a great central mountain called Meru surrounded by continents and oceans. We humans and animals are said to live on the southern continent. Gods and other divine beings live on or above the higher reaches of Meru, while other supernatural creatures inhabit the subterranean regions of the continents. The perception is geocentric with the sun, moon, planets, and stars revolving around this mountain on a daily basis, and with subtle movements of planetary bodies through the constellations that are measured to record the passage of time. This model of the cosmos is used to create calendars and to make astrological predictions. References to this cosmological arrangement are frequently found in the scriptures, while representations of this world are used in ritual and offering ceremonies. Detailed descriptions, dimensions, and habitats are presented in great detail in Buddhist Abhidharma literature.

Clearly such a presentation is in stark contradiction to modern cosmological explanations. So, who is right? Is it a question of interpretation? The Dalai Lama has looked at the science, examined the Buddhist explanation, and has concluded that the Meru cosmos does not exist in any literal sense of reality. He did not do this to appear modern, to conform with scientific thinking, or because he thought the Buddhist view was old-fashioned, but because solid reasoning and empirical evidence disproves the ancient cosmological presentations found and still studied in the monastic curriculum.

This reasoning involves the claim that the sun moves around Meru on a daily basis, and when the sun is behind Meru in the north, nighttime occurs on the southern continent because the vast form of Meru blocks out its light. This means that Meru has to be a coarse form capable of blocking out light and anything else that moves behind it. Buddhism does accept the existence of a subtle form that is not visible to the naked eye, and which cannot obstruct the sight of other more coarse forms. However, Meru is said to block out light and therefore would have to be coarse form, and not some kind of subtle form, as some have stated. This means that, given its large size, it would be visible to the ordinary naked eye. Yet clearly it is not. Spaceships have traveled far outside our earth, and astronauts and onboard cameras have looked back at our planet, but no Meru is visible.

His Holiness has presented this reasoning many times in public talks and announced that he no longer accepts the Mount Meru cosmos. He goes on to say that he has the greatest of respect for the renowned Indian master Vasubandhu, who authored *Treasury of Abhidharma* in which an entire chapter is dedicated to the presentation of this system, but that he is no longer able to accept this presentation. Vasubandhu's work has formed a major part of the Tibetan monastic curriculum for hundreds of years and is given serious study. Now, the present Dalai Lama totally rejects one of its chapters.

In Buddhism, analyzing the views and tenets of the many Buddhist philosophies of ancient India is commonplace, and much Abhidharma philosophy on the nature of reality, of self, and of ultimate truth is rejected by other Buddhist tenets. Nevertheless, they are still studied as aids to understanding more profound philosophies. However, if His Holiness's assertion is accepted, it can no longer be said that studying Abhidharma cosmology has any practical or theoretical purpose. Therefore, such declarations create great shifts in the monastic curriculum. However, it does not concern him that he is rocking the boat of tradition because these pronouncements are made on the basis of honest investigation and reasoning. He is not an iconoclast for its own sake.

He has also cast doubt on some aspects of the doctrine of karma. In Buddhist philosophy karma is the creator. It is a central doctrine, and all phenomena are said to be the direct or indirect product of the formative process of karma. However, His Holiness has stated that the interaction of the four external elements of earth, water, fire, and air play a part in the creative process, without the need for karmic input. Once he said, "When a leaf falls from a tree, its tip will point in a particular direction as it lands on the ground. Is that direction decided by karma? If so, whose karma?" A strict interpretation of Buddhist philosophy would declare that there is nothing not created by individual or collective karma, but here the Dalai Lama is challenging that.

He also is reluctant to accept some of the more fantastical elements found in Buddhist history, such as great masters living for hundreds of years, saying that we should be realistic and more practical in our assessments of these event, He warns against the dangers of excessive "pure view" in which Tibetan people, driven by their faith, see the divine in the ordinary to an exaggerated degree, and are reluctant to examine in an unbiased way. He stresses that Tibetans should be twenty-first-century Buddhists and combine Buddhist studies with a modern scientific understanding.

In all these radical pronouncements he is pushing against the unexamined and unquestioned elements of Tibetan culture and religious tradition. He loves his people, and it cannot have been easy to do this, but he does what is right, which means doing what makes sense and what is beneficial for Tibetan society as it finds its place in the modern world. To all audiences, he stresses the importance of sound reasoning over mere belief and blind faith. He will often gently chide Tibetan audiences for their adherence to faith and ritual over investigation and analysis. He encourages the Tibetan lay community to take up study as the monastic community have done, saying there is no reason why the study of the scriptures should be restricted to the ordained. Even to some monastic audiences he will stress the importance of study, where he feels the monks and nuns concentrate more on ritual to the detriment of learning. He even encourages debate and discussion in schools on nonreligious subjects. Also, in his promotion of equal rights for women in Tibetan society, and especially in the monastic community, he uses reasoning to back up the points he makes. He does not do it because it is fashionable. The topic of gender equality is dealt with extensively in this book.

DALAI LAMA THE SCIENTIST

Once when I was walking around the temple in Dharamsala, India, I saw an old monk carrying a scripture. While chatting to him, I asked him if he was interested in science. He smiled and waved his hand; "No, no, I stick with the scriptures."

His Holiness is, of course, different. His interest in science is well known and that interest is detailed in this book. But what is it that ignites his interest and how far does he go in accepting its theories?

There is of course his natural curiosity about how things work. This was evident as a small child when he wanted to know how everything functioned. As he grew older he enjoyed taking watches apart and trying to reassemble them. However, as a Buddhist philosopher and practitioner, he has a more serious reason for liking science, or more particularly, scientific thinking. He admires the scientific approach of starting from an unbiased and honest stance in which no one position is favored over another, and facts are not selectively sought in order to support an already determined outcome. He strongly emphasizes that this stance should be applied to Buddhist philosophical investigation. Buddhist arguments should not be circular in the sense of controlling the debate in order to arrive at a desired conclusion. Once, when commenting on a verse in a text that talked about the differences between ordinary people and yogis, he said that maybe scientists were today's yogis because of their desire and drive to understand the unknown. Maybe such a statement affected the sensibilities of those who still imagine a yogi as being a scantily clad, matted-hair meditator in a cave somewhere in the Himalayas. But his statement has logic to it because the genuine yogi seeks to know hidden truths, while much of the world is just concerned with day-to-day living.

He also values science because of its ontological approach to what the Buddhists call the "base realities" of our existence. An understanding of base reality, such as the nature of mind, the measure of happiness and suffering, their causes, and the realities concerning phenomena on a coarse and profound levels, is essential for Buddhism to build its paths and resultant states—that is, liberation from suffering. His Holiness feels that in some areas, especially those concerning matter, scientific understanding of base reality is more detailed and more accurate than Buddhist perceptions, and that therefore, science can be of benefit to Buddhism. In other areas, such as those that focus on consciousness, he believes Buddhism has a lot to offer science. Therefore, he seeks an exchange of views through various conferences and institutions.

Probably, the old monk who prefers scripture to science does so simply because he is too long in the tooth to start studying something new and alien and does not know enough English anyway. However, there are some in the West who see science and religion as enemies. They think that science is powerful and widespread and that it could easily overwhelm Buddhism, consigning it to an irrelevance. His Holiness does not think like this. For him science is a companion, and Buddhism and science working together have a lot to offer the world.

He also regards the old notion that science deals with the material while religion deals with the spiritual as an unnecessary and artificial separation. He equates some areas of science, especially those of quantum physics, where perception plays an important part in determining existence, with particular Buddhist tenets that arose in ancient India. Those ancient tenets had a soteriological purpose of lessening suffering and bringing happiness, and is it not possible that quantum physics and other branches of modern science could serve humanity in the same way?

INTERACTION WITH THE WESTERN WORLD

His Holiness goes out of his way to accommodate requests from Westerners interested in Buddhism. When responding to them, he never sits back and manufactures some spiritual distance between him and the petitioner with an "I am a Buddhist and it is like this" approach, but instead tries to see how best to help them. In doing so, he has no fear of losing his authority, nor does he maintain a reserve in order to protect his "holy stature." He willingly subsumes himself into the genuine desires of his audience. In short, he does not approach the Western world to preach or convert. He has no wish to make Westerners into Buddhists, but only wants to help.

His promotion of secular ethics is well known, and is a topic covered comprehensively in this book. Though he strongly adheres to Buddhist principles and his faith is unshakeable, when talking to Westerners he often sets aside the religion's great tracts of tenet and belief, such as the view of past and future lives, the existence of omniscient buddhas, and so on. In fact, it could be said that it is his understanding and devotion to Buddhism that makes him so willing to be almost non-Buddhist, pragmatic, and here-and-now in his teachings. The central theme of Buddhism is compassion not dogma, reasoning not scripture, and no true Buddhist will ever seek to win over converts.

One thing noticeable in His Holiness's talks is how he always tries to see the good in others. No matter how a person or a community might be viewed in the world, he will seek out any redeeming features. If there are none, he will respond with compassion, never anger. Several years ago he publicly stated that we should feel compassion for Slobodan Milošević, the former Serbian president in Yugoslavia, who was indicted for war crimes and crimes against humanity. For this His Holiness received a great deal of public criticism, but his comments were made on the basis of his own perception of Milošević as an object of compassion, and he separates out the person from the deed. He did not deny the crimes of Milošević or excuse them but looked beyond them to the man, in the steadfast belief that all beings deserve compassion. In this way he achieves the balance of accommodating others without ever pandering to their views in order to win their affection. He does and says what he believes is right.

A few years ago, a Tibetan friend of mine living in the West was in charge of overseeing a large-scale visit of the Dalai Lama. At the end of the visit my friend felt that he had not done that well in organizing the events and went to His Holiness to apologize for the less-than-impressive arrangements. The Dalai Lama replied by saying, "The only person you have to impress is yourself. If you have done your best, that is enough." These words had a strong effect upon my friend. Essentially, the Dalai Lama believes that a kind motivation, honesty, humility, and a thorough analysis of the situation is the best way to proceed. If success follows, good. If not, you have done your best.

COURAGE

Tibetan Buddhists regard the Dalai Lama as a deity and a buddha. In their eyes he can do no wrong. They will fall at his feet in devotion and veneration. He is guarded and protected zealously, and his every need is devotedly waited upon. Many other people too revere him. He is a Nobel laureate and admired around the world. However, it is clear that he deals with this idolization by concentrating on himself as "an ordinary monk" and as "just one of seven billion human beings." These are not just words; his actions show that he genuinely sees himself this way. This humility is a great quality of his. It is further evident from listening to his teachings and talks that he is also very learned, wise, and possessed of great experience. He mentions that he spends most of his meditation hours in thinking and investigating philosophical matters, and this clearly shows when he talks. He has given himself over to the service of others, something that can be seen by the frequent and punishing overseas visits he makes when fit and able to do so. He rarely declines an invitation.

However, of all his commendable qualities, for me as someone who has lived in his close proximity for many years, it is the Dalai Lama's courage that stands out. This is the courage to go where no Dalai Lama has gone before, to implement changes in Tibetan religious and secular society that defy centuries of tradition, to face the challenges posed by being strangers in a strange land since his exile in 1959. It is the courage of not being afraid to say what he truly believes to be right, based upon the path of reason and compassion, regardless of the consequences. It is a courage that is a supreme self-confidence never tainted by pride or arrogance. He is a rare being in this world. We are fortunate to be of his time.

THE TEXT

This book is a compilation of teachings and talks given by the Fourteenth Dalai Lama to lay and monastic Tibetan audiences over many years. At times the content clearly indicates that His Holiness is speaking to a Tibetan audience. This might mean that the message does not seem directly relevant to a Western audience, or that it might even seem outdated. The reader is asked to be mindful of this.

It was compiled over ten years by Dagyab Rinpoché, who is an incarnated lama born in 1940 in Eastern Tibet. All of Dagyab Rinpoché's prior incarnations were spiritual heads of the Dagyab region of Tibet. In 1959 he escaped to India with the Dalai Lama. In 1966 he was invited to Bonn University, Germany, as a Tibetologist, and in 2005 he founded Tibet House Germany in Frankfurt, which published the Tibetan edition of this book together with the Dalai Lama Trust. He lives in Berlin.

This book is the first of two volumes; the second volume is a transcript of His Holiness's commentary and annotations to a work by the Fifth Dalai Lama, called *Oral Transmission of Mañjuśrī,* which describes the stages of the path to enlightenment. How these two volumes arose is described by Dagyab Rinpoché in his introduction.

The Tibetan title of this two-volume work is *Clarifying the Intent of the Conquerors.* Rinpoché explained that "conquerors" refers to the Buddha, the Great Fifth Dalai Lama, and the Fourteenth Dalai Lama.

The book has eight main chapters, each with a different topic. The first chapter is one of the most important. In it the Dalai Lama focuses on kindness and compassion as causes of happiness and the methods to lessen suffering in this world. These causes are our innate love and kindness that can be brought out and developed to the benefit of everyone. His main emphasis is that doing so is not necessarily achieved by recourse only to religion. Instead, he emphasizes that we all intrinsically possess the causes and conditions for a happy life within us from birth. Religion, on the other hand, is something we add to our lives later on. No one is born a religious person. He often cites the example of a mother—especially his own mother—as someone who naturally manifests a deep love and affection for her children. We can know that this is an innate affection because it can be seen in animals too.

To nurture that kindness, it is not necessary to be religious or learned, but it is important to develop our minds in that direction and to shift away from dependence upon sense pleasures as sources of happiness. This requires some contemplation, and in that respect His Holiness stresses the importance of mental consciousness over the five sensory consciousnesses.

Self-confidence is a topic he often mentions, and in the book he stresses that having a sense of self is not necessarily a bad thing. He does recommend, however, having a good and healthy sense of "I" over a negative "I." He does not condemn ambition, or even competitiveness, as long as it is done with this good sense of self, accompanied by a background attitude of kindness. He stresses that in Buddhism, no-self does not mean suppressing or burying any thought of "I." That, he teaches, would leave us with no direction or drive at all.

In the second chapter he talks about religion and its place in the world, stressing that interfaith harmony is essential if religion is to play a positive role in producing the collective happiness of the world. He holds up Buddhism as a religion whose tenets are based upon reason and practicality, stressing that blind faith is not sufficient in these times.

The next chapter is on science, on how he sees Buddhism as a natural ally of science. Following sections are on world philosophies; the importance of the transmission of Buddhism from ancient India; and the value of the preservation in Tibet of the scriptural and practice traditions of this transmission.

The eighth and last chapter, on the essence of Buddhism, includes a lengthy section of almost a hundred and fifty very brief biographies of renowned Tibetan female practitioners. His Holiness had asked Rinpoché to include a section on Tibetan women practitioners. The biographies were excerpted from a Tibetan work called *Stories of Tibetan Women* by Drigung Rasé Könchok Gyatso. This work was composed in Tibetan and has not been translated into English. Most of the biographies in the book appear here.

Not everything in the book is His Holiness's own words. These instances are not many and some are recognizable. Usually, they consist of factual and chronological information, such as the section on Mongolian history. This supplementing was done with the Dalai Lama's approval and was often encouraged by him. The most obvious example of this is the biographies of great women practitioners.

The text is essentially a spoken-word transcript, which presents its own difficulties. Extempore speech, which His Holiness's teachings usually are, invariably means that one thought prompts another which is often vocalized without grammatical connectors to the preceding words. In speech, pauses and tone aid aural understanding. When this is transcribed verbatim, such indicators are absent, and following the thread can be made a little harder. To rectify this Dagyab Rinpoché has inserted connectors, such as conjunctions, to aid the flow. This makes reading easier but can make for very long sentences indeed. I have tried to avoid this and have kept sentence length to an accessible limit.

Although this volume contains some material not directly spoken by His Holiness, and the second volume is a commentary on the work of the Fifth Dalai Lama, the Private Office feels that there is enough of the Dalai Lama's own words here to warrant both volumes being credited as works of the Fourteenth Dalai Lama. The Gaden Phodrang Private Office of the Dalai Lama has often urged groups and individuals who make recordings of His Holiness's teachings around the world to first seek approval before releasing them in order to prevent any unnecessary repetition in the compilations of his teachings, and also to ensure that His Holiness's teachings are accurately presented and are properly attributed.[3]

ACKNOWLEDGMENTS

I was honored to be asked to translate this valuable work, and I would like to thank Professor Thupten Jinpa for suggesting that Tibet House Germany ask me to take on this task. While translating I was able to speak to Dagyab Rinpoché regularly whenever I had a query, as he was instantly contactable over the internet. At all times he was unfailingly patient and completely willing to be of help, to the point that he often called me! I cannot thank him enough for clarifying points I did not understand, especially when facing those long sentences.

There were a few points that Rinpoché felt unable to clarify. These were sent to Professor Samdhong Rinpoché and Yangten Rinpoché of the Gaden Phodrang in Dharamsala, India. I would like to thank them for the time they were able to give me on resolving these queries. I would also like to thank Jeremy Russell for the helpful advice he gave me for this introduction.

We would like to express our gratitude to Resa Könchok Gyatso, the author of *Stories of Tibetan Women,* for granting permission for large excerpts of the book to be reproduced here.

I would also like to thank Alex Gardner, editor at Wisdom Publications, for his skillful editing of the text and his insightful suggestions, which without doubt improved the clarity and accessibility of the text.

Technical Note

THE SHORT TIBETAN TITLE of the two-volume work, of which the first volume is translated here, is *Rgyal ba'i dgongs gsal*, which might be translated as *Clarifying the Intent of the Conquerors*. Bracketed numbers embedded in the text refer to page numbers in the 2016 Tibetan edition published by the Dalai Lama Trust and Tibet House Germany in India (ISBN 978-93-83091-52-2).

The conventions for phonetic transcription of Tibetan words are those developed by the Institute of Tibetan Classics and Wisdom Publications. These reflect approximately the pronunciation of words by a modern Central Tibetan; Tibetan speakers from Ladakh, Kham, or Amdo, not to mention Mongolians, might pronounce the words quite differently. Sanskrit diacritics are used throughout except for Sanskrit terms that have been naturalized into English, such as samsara, nirvana, sutra, stupa, and mandala.

Except in some cases of titles frequently mentioned, works mentioned in the translation have typically had the author's name added by the translator for ease of reference by contemporary readers. It should be noted, therefore, that these names, although appearing without brackets, are not always present in the original Tibetan.

Pronunciation of Tibetan phonetics
ph and *th* are aspirated *p* and *t*, as in *pet* and *tip*.
ö is similar to the *eu* in the French *seul*.
ü is similar to the *ü* in the German *füllen*.
ai is similar to the *e* in *bet*.

é is similar to the *e* in *prey*.

Pronunciation of Sanskrit

Palatal *ś* and retroflex *ṣ* are similar to the English unvoiced *sh*.

c is an unaspirated *ch* similar to the *ch* in *chill*.

The vowel *ṛ* is similar to the American *r* in *pretty*.

ñ is somewhat similar to the nasalized *ny* in *canyon*.

ṃ is similar to the *ng* in *sing* or *anger*.

The Achievements of the Fourteenth Dalai Lama
By H. E. Dagyab Kyabgön Rinpoché

[xxi] IT IS WORTHWHILE and relevant to recall just a few of the accomplishments of His Holiness the Fourteenth Dalai Lama, the great teacher for the beings of this world.

The way in which he is unrivaled by the line of the previous Dalai Lamas, his birth, his recognition and enthronement as the incarnation of the previous Dalai Lama, how he persevered and completed his course of study, contemplation and meditation, how he took upon himself the secular and religious rule of Tibet, his advice and instruction for the protection of Tibet during its times of trouble, his ability to escape without being discovered and to find refuge in India without mishap—accomplished by the good merit of living beings—have all been described in great detail, by year, month, date, and so on, in the many published biographies that list the achievements of the great waves of activities that continue to bring benefit to the religions, politics and economy, and people of this world. The above events can be known from the many such books that continue to be published.

Here, the intention is to present just a fraction of the physical, verbal, and mental activities of this great being in the way that they commonly appear to ordinary beings such as me. All exaggeration and underestimation are abandoned, and it is a natural and uncontrived presentation that even a child could understand. However, even if I had no intention of praising him, there is no way I could have prevented it from becoming praise. As a result, this is a wonderful situation hosting a limitless wealth of wonderful qualities, in which there is no chance of anyone of intelligence and impartiality not having their minds captivated.

[xxii] I have had no need to employ modes of praise such as using those great beings of unrivaled fame within his past incarnations as a support and adornment of his greatness, as is traditionally done; or proclaiming scripture, reasoning, and pure view perceptions, and highlighting various common and exclusive qualities of inconceivable mystery in order to declare supreme spiritual states; or even extoling how his religious and secular status was so esteemed, thereby attempting to eclipse all the great beings of the religious and secular traditions, and so on. All of these are methods of praise assisted by an elaborate compositional style and adorned by devices such as the hyperbole of poetry. Instead, I will speak of the salient points in a natural and informal way.

THE GREATNESS OF HIS DEEDS, WORDS, AND MENTAL QUALITIES

All-knowing and all-seeing conqueror, you took an appropriate birth in a critical and dangerous time so that those disciples who, through the power of karma and prayer, had formed a strong bond with you and would never be apart from such a protector and refuge. You are a ruler revered by all, who had abandoned the jeweled crown[4] but was enthroned as a peerless crown jewel of those who preserve the teachings of the Buddha. However, if there were no vast lotus grove of teaching, composition, and debate flowering in the ground of learning, contemplation, and meditation, then a vital component of a great being—as in the meaning of "guru" being "heavy with excellent qualities"—would be incomplete, and would therefore be compared to a stone covered in brocade.

Therefore, you devoted yourself to incomparable and genuine

tutors such as Reting Rinpoché, Tadrak Rinpoché, Kyabjé Ling Vajra-dhara and Kyabjé Trijang Vajradhara, and became rich with a wealth of learning in sutra, tantra, and the sciences. [xxiii] Not only did you become an incomparable disciple of excellent lamas, but you took on the actuality of "the grandson being more resplendent than the son, the great-grandson being more resplendent than the grandson, and the great-great-grandson being more resplendent than the great-grandson," and in doing so, you became truly a great leader of living beings without discrimination.

Moreover, because of your learning and experience in the religious and secular fields, when irreversible changes occurred in Tibet, it coincided well with you being able to assume the responsibility for the religious and secular rule of Tibet. Consequently, the purpose of the reincarnation of a Dalai Lama appearing, which was to nurture the legacy of the former Dalai Lama, was fulfilled. That such an unrivaled being is alive and with our bulging eyes of hope is the sole focus for we Tibetans, is a glorious fortune for living beings.

Although there is no great lama above you, you are the king who assumes a low standing as if there were no one beneath you. Not even aware of how you have been raised up to high status, you hold to the simple conduct of an ordinary spiritual seeker, clothed in saffron-colored cloth, practicing the four bare necessities,[5] and of a temperament that is serene, tempered, and modest. Yet you outshine those of great power who go to great efforts to pose amid the finery and brocade of gold thrones raised on high. There is no trace of arrogance or fear of losing your reserve, and so whether you are with one person or among many, you talk at ease with a carefree smile, and engage everyone with the relaxed expression of meeting old friends. As a result, even the pompous in high places lose their reserve and their mountain of pride comes crashing to the ground.

Those who have faith in religion, those with no faith, those who hold perverse views toward religion, those of various views and philosophies, politicians, scientists, and so on, whether they are educated or uneducated, high or low, of whatever skin color, [xxiv] as soon as they meet you they are put at ease and experience feelings of closeness. For several days, as many have attested, a joy beyond words naturally arises. Everyone declares unanimously that you possess a splendor and radiance, engendering respect in those who previously had no thought of respect for you, and devotion in those who had no thought of devotion. Others, who by their affection for the Tibetan people and their faith in the teachings of the Buddha, experience a feeling of rapturous joy merely on meeting you, and by their faith the hairs of their body stand on end. Merely seeing, hearing, remembering, and touching you becomes meaningful. How can these deeds of yours ever be measured in this world?

Your activities are many, but without allowing one to interfere with another, you choose whichever is appropriate in a cheerful and easy-going way, and unlike ordinary beings in their hurried and frenzied way, carry them out in a relaxed and unhurried manner. If we look at your activities of a single day, from one point of view it seems as if you spend it solely in a detailed study of sutra and tantra and apply it to your mind. From another perspective it seems that you repeatedly give private audiences to lamas of all traditions, abbots and their students, geshés, monks and nuns, yogis, laymen and laywomen, finding the time to engage in full and meaningful discussions based upon your religious experience.

Similarly, seekers of liberation, those whose minds have been captivated by Buddhism, those who have affection for Tibet and Tibetans, those with an interest in culture, politics, and so on, countless people from the five continents of the world of all walks of life, local and visitors, united by faith, regularly come to meet you in ever-increasing numbers. [xxv] And yet willingly and without fatigue you take on the task of fulfilling the hopes of each of them, showing a special compassion for those in a pitiful state, like a mother toward her only child, caring for them profoundly with the practice of the six perfections such as the giving of the Dharma and the giving of material things, and the practice of the four ways of gathering disciples.[6] This is truly a wonder.

Also, through Indian, Tibetan, and English radio, television, and daily newspapers, you do not miss the opportunity to regularly peruse current events occurring in the world. Thus, you pursue all your everyday and extra activities appropriately and within a timely manner.

For the sake of your health, you are diligent never to neglect dietary rules, walking, exercise, physical activities of gardening, and so on. The way you wear the robes and engage in other everyday essential routines is well-ordered and in a scrupulously clean manner. The care you take in these things is inspiring. You are an incomparable field of merit.

In order to follow an exemplary pursuit of learning without feeling sated, which is the foundation for preserving, nourishing, and disseminating the teachings of the Buddha through the means of speech, you sat in the presence of various spiritual teachers across all traditions and received countless gifts of the precious Dharma. [xxvi] Moreover, in order to stabilize your familiarity with the types of explanation in the literature of the Buddhist traditions of India and Tibet, you made great efforts day and night in the "wheel of learning and contemplation through study."[7] In this way, you became a powerful master of scripture, with a great learning that understands perfectly the vast and profound Dharma. How is it possible not to see you as someone who takes "all the teachings of the Buddha to be without contradiction whereby all four corners can be brought into the path."[8]

With determination and great effort, you engaged in contemplating and meditating upon what you had learned, and you absorbed yourself into the "wheel of the meditative concentration by way of abandoning." As a result, you saw that the individual experiences of the Buddha, his disciples, and the lineage of scholars and practitioners, and the way they taught in accordance with the many dispositions of their disciples, even to the point of bearing the heavy load of seeming contradictions, were actually core instructions and adornments that developed the quintessence of the profound and vast teachings. If this is not a case of "all the teachings of Buddha arising as advice," then what is?

You do not rely merely on the evidence of a particular scripture but will examine the Kangyur and Tengyur of sutra and tantra and come to a determination based on whether or not it withstands reasoning, thereby revealing the very essence of the Buddha's thought clearly and without blemish. If this is not evidence of "being able easily to find the thinking of the Buddha," then what is?

Devoting yourself to the familiarization of experience and practice of that which is to be developed and abandoned, as taught in the literature of the three vehicles, at about the age of fifteen you remarked that, remembering the kindness of Śākyamuni Buddha, a deep faith and respect arose within you. Your bodhicitta and understanding of the correct view gradually increased. and by seeing signs of "the great fault naturally disappearing"[9] you stated that the insights of the Vajra Vehicle increased greatly. Thus, we can infer an experience of secret qualities of body, speech, and mind. If this is not the quality of realization that knows proper practice, then what is?

[xxvii] Although you possess such qualities of wisdom, you consider it improper to be satisfied with your learning, and you studied in detail several works of the seventeen pandits, from Nāgārjuna (c. 150–c. 250), and his main disciple up to the great master, Atiśa (982–1054),[10] thereby opening wide your eyes of wisdom and developing a profound acquaintance with these works. With a complete comprehension of their meanings you put them into practice. Furthermore, all the Buddhas and his disciples agree that of all the deeds of the great beings, those of speech are preeminent. Heeding this, you have reformed the teachings and have appeared as a second Buddha, teaching the excellent path without error.

In order to show the way to practice the points commentated on in the works of many Indian and Tibetan masters, you have mastered the refutation of others' position, the establishment of one's own position, and the dispelling of disputes, by way of the four critiques.[11] In this way, you teach extensively the scriptures of sutra and tantra in general, and in particular, the mind-training topics of love, compassion, and bodhicitta, as well as emptiness as dependent origination showing how mental afflictions and their dormant seeds are to be uprooted, and so on, while emphasizing repeatedly the maxim "I am my own guide."

In your teaching of the tantras also, there are clear signs of your inner proficiency when with just a few words you summarize precisely their profound meanings. No matter how difficult a point may be, the very essence of its meaning is brought out with corresponding ease, and you teach with a clarity that produces an understanding of the synthesis or structure of the scripture. This gives me the certainty that such and such a point could not be other than this.

The profound meanings of sutra and tantra are your own domain, and in places where even the lions of great scholars and practitioners are on shaky legs, [xxviii] you maintain the position of a powerful and mighty lion who quickly finds his feet with a subtle, profound, wide discernment and teaches without any difficulty.

Moreover, lacking the meaningless babble of the arrogant scholar, you are unhindered in explaining to perfection the meanings of the scriptures. Therefore, you follow the Kadampa tradition of engaging simultaneously in the scriptures of all vehicles, high or low. As in the Kadampa saying, "I am the slayer of the great yak of the Dharma,"[12] you explain the many scriptural traditions as all coming down to the same intent of the Buddha. Everyone has witnessed that you possess the incomparable, astonishing, and extraordinary quality of being the only one who can do this.

Over the past thirty years, in the great monastic institutions, scholars capable of propounding hundreds of texts have become great geshés through their efforts in sincere study and contemplation. They have nurtured disciples and are alike in becoming objects of respect and devotion. However, they all lack any comparison to the way that you are able to explain the vast and profound message of the Buddha in such an accessible manner. When it comes to explaining the Dharma, you render the highly capable beings of this world embarrassed to even open their mouths. It is common knowledge to Tibetans, foreigners, the wise and the foolish alike, that there is no greater teacher than you on this earth. These are not just my flattering words.

To sum up, you have vast knowledge of the literature belonging to all the Buddhist traditions of Tibet, and you constantly emphasize the importance of a comparative study in order to understand what these texts teach. You are unhindered in bestowing the gift of wonderfully explained teachings on the meanings of these texts, in which the thinking of the Buddha found in the various sutras and tantras is of one intent. [xxix] This great kindness that makes it easy to develop a pure view across all traditions is something rarely seen in the past and rarely seen these days. Thinking on these great qualities, if this is not a case of the Buddha, the lord of the doctrine, appearing again in human form to flawlessly clarify his own teachings, then what is it?

In particular, you have taught thoroughly, again and again, the topics of the eighteen volumes of the works of Jé Tsongkhapa, who clarified the thought of the Buddha with scripture and reasoning, and you explain how they relate to the thinking of Indian works, such as the tantras. Without a doubt you are the Mañjunātha Lama[13] come again in the form of our spiritual teacher to clarify your tenets and compositions. Moreover, you have emphasized that this Tibetan Buddhist tradition, with its three vehicles and the four classes of tantra, contains the entire thinking of the Buddha, like a hundred rivers converging under one bridge, and is the pure tradition of the pandits of Nālandā Monastery, such as Nāgārjuna and his disciples. Thinking about this, who could possibly deny that this great being is fully entitled to be enthroned as the eighteenth pandit of Nālandā, who has taken birth in the land of Tibet?

In particular, you never dogmatically adhere to traditional assertions and ways of explaining propounded by any particular scriptural tradition where the thinking of the author is distinct from that presented in the text. With a profound intellect you dissect and examine the teachings like gold that has been burned, cut, and rubbed, to remove all superimposition. This Dharma of the Buddha is one that withstands reasoning and one where reasoning is more important than scripture. [xxx] Therefore you teach that not accepting scripture which contradicts pure reasoning opens up great opportunities for his followers and was granted by the Buddha himself.

You put this teaching into practice yourself. Some ways of explaining found in the teachings of Buddha and the later commentaries that are contradicted by the developed elements of direct perception found in modern science, and those that should be repudiated because of time and place, you have kindly taught as being open to dispute and not to be taken literally. Your profound teachings, in which the excellent path of seeking truth from facts is meaningfully explained, uproot wrong ideas and destroy any lack of belief, thereby displaying in all its glory the magnificence of the Buddha and his teachings. You are a peerless object of praise for all who possess wisdom and intelligence. This is a wonder beyond wonder. Emaho![14]

You deliberately seek out renowned scholars in the fields of modern science, psychology, religion, politics, and so on, from various countries, in order to listen to and learn the ancient and modern wisdom of the world. You also continually peruse texts, articles, compositions, journals, newspapers, and so on, on the major issues in the world, and become aware of changes and developments. You maintain an up-to-date understanding of world affairs, such as those of religion, culture, politics, and economy, thereby possessing laudatory confidence and assurance to converse on equal terms with knowledgeable people from all over the world. More than that, you have gained the reputation for engaging in profound discussions that steal the thunder of those speakers. Also, to those who desire the wonderful gift of teachings that relate to views found in Buddhist scriptural traditions, [xxxi] you show joyful interest and attention, thus clearly illustrating the maxim "scholars are beautiful among scholars."[15]

However, the wishes of the living beings of this world with their varying dispositions will not be fulfilled by a single religion. You urge those whose country is not ethnically Buddhist to adhere to the religion of their parents' generation, saying that such a path will be more stable. Never do you zealously promote Buddhism. You say that for certain people, such as we Tibetans, Buddhism is the best, but in general we cannot say that Buddhism is better than all other religions. This is wonderful!

In your discourses and advice, whether in Tibetan or English, you speak appropriately, from the heart, with words that are connected and coherent. The content is free from overcomplication, with one point supporting another, profound yet clear and easy to grasp, like the current of a river flowing gently downstream. It is evident to all that you are unrivaled in the power of speech. When those from other countries talk to you directly in English, you fulfill the hopes of each of them, and without differentiating them as being important or ordinary, intelligent or stupid, you captivate their minds. This too is a powerful act of working for others.

Though you possess confidence in your words, you realize that having skillful means in what you say is indispensable. You are acutely aware of the varying dispositions, attitudes, faculties, and dormant potentials, the changes of time and place, the extra difficulties that arise from a general degeneration, and the various ideas and perceptions brought on by perverse ideas and a lack of faith, and so on. [xxxii] You are extraordinarily wise in focusing on a way of explaining that is to the point and to their liking. For the countless living beings on this planet, you have the power to provide a festival of teachings to please the discerning, the methods to relieve the immediate sufferings of body and mind, and methods for finally reaching the great city of enlightenment. Because of this, the number of foreign disciples that specifically come to Dharamsala in their thousands is always increasing. Also, wherever you give religious teachings, thousands of faithful devotees attend from all over the world.

In the works that you have composed, each word teaches a profound point and there is not a trace of "the leaves hiding the fruit." Using the essence of the deep and vast tenets found in Buddhist works, your compositions are written with an unflagging sense of responsibility based on your experience, faith, and practice, to advise and encourage others to work for others, to bring benefit to society by peaceful means, for a prosperous future, and for stable politics to be of service in this world.

Up to the present time there are about a hundred and ten works published in English that you have composed with the help of others. I have seen about eighty-six books published in Tibetan that compile your teachings and discourses. Together with the many compilations that are yet to be published, this is a powerful literary achievement, as can be understood by browsing bookshops in countries all over the world.

[xxxiii] This way of nurturing disciples through teaching, discussion, and composition is not a case of having to follow the glittering name of "Dalai Lama." Even though you are a simple monk, there is no one who could say that you are not a spiritual teacher whose learning is focused inwardly, whose thinking is to the point, who demonstrates experiences that are signs of accomplishment in meditation, who among a host of pandits with mastery over thousands of texts is a great pandit, a courageous adept in charge of a treasury containing teachings of high attainments.

The praises bestowed upon the peerless Buddha by Jé Tsongkhapa in his *Praise of Dependent Origination* are the very same praises to be bestowed upon you:

It is said, "Others may attack what you teach
but they will never find any weakness."
Such a statement is validated by this.[16]

What need to talk of many teachings.
The simplest conviction in just a single part
brings on the greatest of joy![17]

From such a perspective, if I were to speak of the wonder and marvel of you standing in the midst of a crowd proclaiming again and again with the roar of the fearless lion, how could that be false praise?

You primarily adhere to a mental application of working for others. This is always timely, and focused on vast love and compassion, which is the foundation of the Great Vehicle principle of a peaceful and non-harming attitude, as well as an open mind, great patience, and so on. With these, you carry out your activities with honesty and independence, and in keeping with the spirit of democracy.

Previously, when you were engaged in political activity, you would peruse official petitions requiring approval, and so on, with great scrutiny to see if there should be any amendments. [xxxiv] When engaged in consultations with members of staff, you did so with intelligence and great analysis. As soon as something occurred to you that could be beneficial or harmful, you went to great lengths to investigate every possible avenue. Therefore, officials, whether locally based or coming from afar, would come before you nervous and cowed, with hearts pounding. They would suddenly become unfamiliar with their own duties. Often they could say nothing at all. Those who had neglected or contravened their duties, you subjected to heavy scolding and punishment. To those who had been bearing heavy burdens of hardship and troubles for long periods, and had been without food and sleep, you gave advice that was easy to implement, in a manner of "seeing all with just a glance," where just one word had the ability to gladden the heart.

Such wonderful examples of a vast and profound mind with a wonderful mastery over religious and secular activities are so numerous that they cannot be mentioned here.

A SUMMARY OF
HIS HOLINESS'S KIND ACTIVITIES

1. In order to bring immediate and long-term benefit to the beings of this world through deeds born from these excellent physical, mental, and verbal qualities, His Holiness the Dalai Lama has divided the themes of Buddhist literature into three categories: science, philosophy, and Buddhist practice. The contents of the first two categories are important for everyone regardless of their philosophy, their race, whether they are religious or not, and whether they are monastics, laity, old, or young.

[xxxv] The third category is only for those who have faith in Buddhism. His Holiness has many times given introductory discourses on Buddhism, which begin with the need for Buddhists to know the scriptures well; to practice from a faith that is built on knowledge to ensure that it is a sincere practice and that the Dharma does not succumb to meaningless talk and mere gesture; and to become "twenty-first-century Buddhists," which means to become educated Buddhists.

Because of his kindness in creating the various stages of these introductory practices, these days everyone is familiar with the term "introduction to Buddhism." By establishing a tradition for the practice of these stages, together with their evident results, he has opened a great door to short and long-term happiness in this and future lives, accessible to all beings regardless of their dispositions and beliefs. This is his kindness of creating a glorious and unmatched legacy.

2. His Holiness, with no regard for any physical hardship, has visited sixty-five countries on the five continents of this world—some more than once—promoting the three responsibilities that he has committed to: the promotion of human values, working for religious harmony, and the welfare of the Tibetan religious culture and its environment.

The first of these, the promotion of human values, has as its basis "ethics not depending upon religion" or "ethics that transcend religion"—that is, secular ethics. This is said to be like water, whereas religion is like tea. People can live without tea, but they cannot live without water. He stresses this with great open-mindedness and great kindness. [xxxvi] He gives introductory discourses that stress the importance of putting into practice methods of training in ethical behavior, such as loving kindness, tolerance, and so on, which are values common to the Buddhist scriptural tradition. Through practices found in the Buddhist mind-training tradition, he teaches the methods of developing precious human values. Moreover, he has given wide-ranging guidance for the benefit of the whole of humanity and the environment. This is the kindness of bringing out the positive potential for a new future for the world.

3. In his discourses he has repeatedly emphasized how important it is that the religions of this world forge deep and firm mutual relationships by willingly exchanging the experiences of the valuable elements found within their various philosophies, meditations, and modes of conduct. Specifically, he urges again and again that those who practice Buddhism, and particularly those who follow the Tibetan Buddhist tradition, should work hard to abandon sectarianism and look upon the various traditions as complementary and

not contradictory in order that we all become followers of the same Buddha in name and practice. Moreover, he sets a good example by clearly engaging in activities that bring harmony between religious traditions. This is the second responsibility of promoting harmony between religions.

In connection with this responsibility, he has held a series of discussions on modern science and Buddhist science, or the presentation of basic phenomena, which has proved to be a beneficial exchange, and has even brought about some shift in the positions found in the scientific tradition. This is a remarkable achievement. Moreover, a valuable book, *Compendium of Philosophy*[18]—in which Buddhist science and philosophy have been extracted from Buddhist literature—has been published in Tibetan. His Holiness has advised that this be translated in other languages. [xxxvii] Such ongoing enterprises are also connected with this second responsibility, and the counsel that Buddhism and modern science can be brought together is a kindness that benefits the world in general.

4. The preservation, development, and dissemination of the Buddhist culture, which illustrates the nature of Tibet, together with a Tibetan political system based on nonviolence and honesty, a good economy, and other necessary elements of Tibetan society, has been his third responsibility: the welfare of the Tibetan religious traditions, culture, and environment.

The response to the changes that Tibet has undergone recently has been provided solely by the kindness of His Holiness with his appropriate "hundred ways and a thousand policies" and guidance. In particular, in India many important Tibetan institutions have been set up afresh. Across India, with assistance from private individuals, the government, and the community, schools, children's villages, hospitals and clinics, settlements, homes for the elderly, employment for craft workers, arable and dairy farmers, cultural centers, monasteries, and so on have been set up. These activities, as well as the vast opportunities created by the recent institution of the practices of democratic principles into Tibetan society, are a kindness beyond words.

In 2011 His Holiness freely and magnanimously handed over all political responsibility to a new elected leadership. In doing so, he irreversibly and willingly brought to an end the four-hundred-year-old tradition of successive Dalai Lamas ruling over secular and religious affairs. [xxxviii] The Gaden Phodrang, which had been the labrang[19] of successive Dalai Lamas as well as the seat of government at the time of the Fifth Dalai Lama, was separated from the government and restored to its position at the times of the Dalai Lamas preceding the Fifth. These are excellent and effective deeds completely in tune with modern times and worthy of praise by everyone in the world today.

Nevertheless, governments, individuals, organizations, and countless people in the world today recognize that His Holiness is inescapably revered as "the sole and peerless leader of Tibetans." Indirectly this contributes to the increasing signs of improvement in the welfare of Tibet and again is due to the kindness of this unparalleled leader.

5. Holding firm his attitude of working for happiness of others, he has long cast away any thought that the Gaden Phodrang Labrang is a place of rest and relaxation. When invitations arrive from institutions in the Tibetan exile community and from various countries, whether connected with their governments or not, he responds accordingly and visits them successively. In these places—at conference centers, religious and political functions, education forums, important meetings, Dharma centers—and on topics such as the promotion of human values, religion, the sciences, economy, politics, and so on, he gives suitable speeches, advice, reassurance, praise, [xxxix] opinions, interviews, discussions, and Buddhist teachings. This is a kindness of effortlessly accomplishing the needs of self and others.

6. Following the excellent practice of the Buddha in regarding all beings as equal, irrespective of class and race, he has repeatedly instructed that we should give up the ingrained view and custom that holds men to be superior to women. In particular, he has deemed that the tradition of rewarding those who have completed a study of the great classical texts in the Tibetan Buddhist tradition with the title of "geshé"[20] should not be strictly the preserve of male monastics, and has thereby graciously initiated the wonderful tradition of awarding the title and status of "geshé-ma" to worthy female monastics. Moreover, he is actively pursuing the means by which the lineage of a fully ordained nun will be included in the Tibetan Buddhist tradition. This is the kindness of a great pioneer who illuminates the wonderful path of truth and sincerity.

7. His Holiness urged the thousands of male and female monastics from the Himalayan regions, Tibet, and Mongolia that constitute the monastic communities of the Tibetan Buddhist traditions in the settlements in South India to make efforts to master study, contemplation, and meditation by the learning and practice of the Buddha's words. Also, he has advised that modern science and other subjects be added to the curriculum and stressed the importance of monasteries and nunneries becoming recognized as exceptional centers of learning for Buddhist and non-Buddhist forms of the five classic sciences[21] replete with ancient and modern education. Moreover, monastic communities should see that practice exists in teaching centers and that teaching exists in practice centers, thereby ensuring that study, contemplation, and meditation are inclusive of each other.

[xl] Generally, in the past the qualities of preserving, developing, and disseminating the teachings of the Buddha, as well as those of Buddhist scholarship, ethics, and compassion, were regarded as being those of lamas and geshés. It is His Holiness's position that this is not sufficient, and that these qualities should not be considered to be the

responsibilities of male and female monastics alone. Instead, he has given guidance, urging that this should be the enthusiastic duty of all lay people, young and old, male and female, who have taken an interest in the Dharma. Therefore, irrespective of race, gender, and ordination status, everyone should be able to enter the tradition of study, contemplation, and meditation within the great ocean of the scriptural tradition. The evident results of such compassionate guidance these days can be clearly witnessed, and the ever-expanding arena of knowledge within the Tibetan community is solely due to his kindness.

Similarly, in schools he has introduced the practice of debating various topics, such as modern mathematics and science, that are unconnected with the Dharma. This has increased the overall level of discernment, and consequently even the number of older-generation Tibetans in settlements, for example, discussing logic and taking an interest in debating is increasing. This is his kindness of providing wonderful guidance for eliminating the darkness of ignorance.

8. In gatherings of the Tibetan community, and particularly to monastic assemblies, His Holiness regularly encourages giving up meat and partaking solely of vegetarian food, thereby practicing the peerless giving by which the lives of countless creatures are saved and freed from fear. Such a diet is also good for the health. [xli] Thus, in keeping with time, place, and situation, he has begun a new and accessible custom, properly fulfilling the Buddhist practice of abandoning harm to any sentient being. This is his kindness of setting a peerless example.

9. When giving Buddhist teachings, His Holiness encourages the declaration of any donations given, and always insists that it is improper to accumulate wealth through Dharma. He himself never takes any offerings made for teachings. Moreover, those offerings made by the faithful, whether through a will or by the living, he does not use only for constructing statues, and so on, or for monastic donations. They are

primarily designated toward alleviating disasters in the world, benefiting the poor and deprived, and the effective welfare of the secular and religious communities. This is his kindness of performing wonderful deeds that should be practiced by everyone.

10. If His Holiness held only the banner of practice, the actual practice of working for the many lost beings would be minimal indeed. Therefore, without wavering from the bodhicitta pledge he made at a young age, he understands that the constant application of the bodhisattva practices is of real significance, and through his own and other languages, and with a wisdom that pervades the wisdoms of the past and present, he unceasingly engages in physical, verbal, and mental activities in order to set into motion a vast wheel of activity that promotes this great bodhisattva lifestyle of working for others in keeping with both secular and religious attitudes. Such activities were never undertaken by the Dalai Lamas of the past, nor by the great pandits of India and Tibet. He lives among us in the form of one who in reality is a master of the whole doctrine without distinction, rarely seen these days. This is surely our great good fortune. [xlii]

This has been realized by discerning individuals from Buddhist and non-Buddhist countries alike, and they have consequently bestowed upon him the Nobel Peace Prize, thereby crowning him as a great leader for world peace. Moreover, governments of many countries, educational institutions, and other organizations have commended him over two hundred times with honors, recognition, and awards. In particular, His Holiness has recently been honored as being among the twenty-five most renowned individuals on this planet. *Watkins Mind Body Spirit Magazine*, based in London, and which comes out annually in February, publishes the six hundred most-renowned politicians, religious people, authors, filmmakers, artists, and so on, followed by those voted as the hundred most powerful people in the world. In this category, from 2012 onward, His Holiness has been voted the number-one religious leader of "the spiritually influential people" in the world today. In 2016, the year of this writing, he has again been voted to this position. Moreover, his teaching that if you want to bring happiness to yourself and others, you should practice love and compassion, has been published in the online version of this magazine. [xliii]

With such accomplishments he stands tall like a great mountain in the midst of these great beings, and each of his wonderful and meaningful deeds exceeds by many times even the great deeds performed by previous Dalai Lamas in India, Tibet, China, and Mongolia. He is the medicine of happiness and joy for the teachings and living beings, whether as individuals or communities. Also, he has given the people of Tibet the glory of being able to hold their heads up high among all the peoples of this world. With this, the building of his legacy of wonderful deeds offered for the welfare of the Tibetan people is the greatest kindness.

In 1952 when Kyabjé Trijang Rinpoché gave a teaching on the stages of the path in Drepung Gomang Monastery to about four thousand monastics and laypeople, he predicted, "If it is made possible by the communal karma of Tibet, you should have no doubt that the deeds and qualities of this Fourteenth Dalai Lama will be greater than those of the omniscient First Dalai Lama Gendun Drup, the Great Fifth Ngawang Losang Gyatso, and the Seventh Dalai Lama Kelsang Gyatso combined."

There is no one who can now deny that such a prophecy has not come true in the form of the all-knowing, mighty Fourteenth Dalai Lama, [xliv] a friend to all,[22] who is unanimously revered with affection, faith, and respect by millions of discerning and open-minded people from all walks of life on the five continents of this world. With his teachings on love and compassion, he raises his wonderful activities to limitless heights, nourishing all beings equally like the sun. For Tibetans, whether in exile or in Tibet, he remains their peerless leader, a living symbol and independent spokesman. He is the great teacher and with his qualities of scriptural knowledge and inner realization, he preserves, develops, and disseminates the teachings of the Buddha through teaching and practice, activities in which he is unrivaled.

The above joyful account of the qualities of his physical, verbal, and mental activities, his achievements and kindnesses, spoken truthfully and naturally, are but a drop from a great ocean.

The points of these deeds of His Holiness can be brought out as instructions for practice and concisely summarized into ten categories.

1. Love and compassion is the foundation of happiness for all beings in general and specifically for the long- and short-term happiness of oneself and others. Therefore, training the mind toward the welfare of others should be brought into our daily lives and practiced sincerely.

2. If we practice Buddhism, for the whole day from the morning onward, we should remember bodhicitta, and create its imprints, even in our dreams.

3. [xlv] We should give our attention, even if it is just fleeting, to those who explain directly and in an accessible manner how emptiness appears as dependent origination and dependent origination appears as emptiness, regardless of whether you practice Buddhism or not. Then, beginning with our own private life, we should work to help the community and the country.

4. We should become educated, twenty-first-century Buddhists.

5. We should not regard the teachings of the Buddha and their commentaries as merely objects of prostration and reverence but think of them as study books and learn their meanings.

6. Whatever type of religion they follow, monastics and lay practitioners, male or female, of all traditions, should sincerely practice their tradition in keeping with its precepts.

7. There are no pith or oral instructions separate from the teachings of the great classical Buddhist scriptures. Therefore, without wandering down the wrong path of discarding the trunk and looking for the branches, we should value and train ourselves in the flawless assertions and works of the Nalanda pandits.

8. With the understanding that the various tenets and thinking of the spiritual lineages of the Buddha found in the Tibetan Buddhist tradition ultimately come down to the same intent, we should develop a pure view of them all, and by understanding their different assertions, we should generate an understanding of the doctrine as a whole.

9. Without being distracted by elaborate recitations and making offerings and requests to gods and spirits, we should absorb ourselves correctly in the generation and completion stages of deity yoga embraced by emptiness and the precious bodhicitta.

10. [xlvi] On the foundations of Buddhist practice, we should train ourselves and bring to our experience the understanding of the close relationship between the present consciousness and its gradual progression from coarse to subtle up to the finality of the primordial body and mind, to transform into the four bodies of a buddha.[23]

These ten pieces of valuable advice are just a fraction of the flawless views that arise from the extraordinary experience within the mind of this great protector. Therefore, they can be recognized as the orally transmitted pith instructions of the Fourteenth Dalai Lama. We who wish only good for ourselves should by all means integrate them as practices fit for disciples and followers of the way of the Buddha.

I pray that my longing still to be lovingly cared for by His Holiness for a long time to come, and to relish the wonderful fortune of the unending adornment of his words, is a hope that becomes meaningful, and I pray that through his activities all living beings of this world will enjoy, directly or indirectly, the glories of peace and happiness as they desire.

CHAPTER 1

The Foundation of Happiness

[1] IT IS THE DESIRE OF ALL LIVING BEINGS to be happy and to not suffer. Whether we are rich or poor, educated or uneducated, irrespective of race, religion, and so on, ultimately, each one of us simply wishes the best for ourselves. The right to fulfill our short- and long-term desires, and the right to rely upon various means to accomplish our desired happiness, is the same for all of us. In that sense, it goes without saying that the purpose of our life is to attain happiness.

As a human being, I seek to promote ethics within the human race. This is the first of three commitments I have taken on. It involves recognizing the source from which happiness in individuals, households, and communities arises. In our search for ways to bring happiness for ourselves, if we disregard the freedoms of others and harm others, in the long term we definitely bring harm to ourselves. When we put effort into ways to find happiness and eliminate suffering, it is very important to consider carefully what kind of results they will bring both to ourselves and others. There are immediate results and long-term results, and it is important to understand the differences between the two. When a result brings benefit in the short-term but is harmful in the long-term, it is better not to value that immediate gain, but instead one should consider the long-term effect as being more important and of greater significance, and so refrain from undertaking those deeds that are the foundation for future harm.

[2] When deciding whether an activity is worthwhile, and trying to correctly distinguish its good and bad points, we must first know if it

harms or benefits others. From the starting point of the heartfelt desire to be happy and not to suffer, we should recognize that turning away from harmful activities and their causes, and engaging only in those physical, verbal, and mental acts that benefit others, is the best practice for gaining happiness and alleviating suffering.

For the happiness and the rights, or dignity, of individuals and communities, we definitely need this virtuous way of looking at the world as a whole, and we must bring to an end the thoughtless behavior that ignores the welfare of others. By only working for our own happiness we engage in acts that are in complete dissonance with the fundamental human condition, and by perpetuating the causes of the ongoing oppression and suffering of humans and animals, in the end we and others will surely suffer. For that reason we should work to maintain a mind of compassion.

THE IMPORTANCE OF COMPASSION

The central meaning of compassion is an attitude that wishes to end the sufferings of others and to augment their happiness. In that sense it carries a feeling of affection for others and sense of responsibility. Everyone admires virtues connected with compassion, such as kindness, respect, tolerance, contentment, patience, and generosity, and those endowed with such qualities are held in high regard. On the contrary, anger, intolerance, malice, greed, miserliness, and so on are regarded as faults, [3] and those who carry such mental traits are universally disliked. Nobody is attracted to them. There is good reason why everybody likes someone who turns their mind toward compassion, who tries to develop these excellent qualities and works to rid themselves of the faults of a malicious mind.

Unfortunately, in many communal relationships and in the lives of individuals the power of kindness and compassion is becoming weaker. Sometimes, when the need for helping others and the necessity of love and compassion is spoken about, it is regarded as foolish and irrelevant, or as the speech of religion. This is very sad. Many people mistakenly think that compassion is a practice solely belonging to religion. It is true that compassion is the essential element of the ethical conduct practiced in all the main religious traditions, but compassion itself is not a religious value. Therefore, when it is said that good attitudes such as compassion, tolerance, and so on are important, it is wrong to consider them as religious principles, because no one, whether religious or not, can afford to disregard compassion, affection, and so on. Why? Because kindness and compassion are the main qualities necessary in life. A good mind, enriched by love and compassion, is essential for human beings. Such statements can be understood from experience to be true.

The main destroyers of compassion are anger and hatred. These are powerful feelings and at times they come and take over our minds. [4] However, we do have the ability to move them away. It is never the case that we have no power right now to begin such a practice, or that we can make no progress. If we have a firm basis in our minds, external pressures and inner emotions such as jealousy and anger cannot have much negative influence upon us. We should think hard about whether anger, and so on, is something of value we should hold on to.

Sometimes, when we lose our strength of mind, it seems that anger gives us the ability to be confident and decisive, but if we look carefully, we can see that anger robs the brain of its greatest quality: the ability to think rationally. Anger induces a blind emotion that prevents us from knowing if the result will turn out for the good or not. The power of anger is not to be trusted. It encourages us to act like a madman, doing things that only hurt ourselves and others. We need a state of mind with a power that is equal to or greater than that anger, that will exercise control over the mind, and can be developed. Such an ability arises not only from a compassionate mind but also from reasoning and patience. These are powerful anti-dotes to anger.

Saying that developing love and compassion is important and that we need these qualities does not mean that when faced with those who harm us we should timidly not respond and do nothing. In today's society, where competition to be better than others is rife, there are many instances where we have to stubbornly stand our ground. [5] Moreover, with a pure motivation of love and kindness, and a stand-point of compassion, all for the benefit of others, we can, in practice, be hard-headed at those times where it is necessary to be so. This is a perfectly good perspective.

So, where does love and compassion come from, and how are they produced and developed? Generally, as long as the human mind exists, the seed of compassion exists. Just by being born, the seed of compassion is present as a part of our mind. Moreover, of all the types of mind, the compassionate mind is the most powerful. Recognizing the existence of this fundamental potential of love and compassion, intrinsic within us all, and knowing how to develop it, is of the greatest significance. If we think about this carefully, a heavy responsibility is placed upon our physical, verbal, and mental activities.

Many people think that showing compassion to others will only benefit others and not themselves. This is greatly mistaken. The bene-fit brought to ourselves from having a good mind and helping others depends on many powerful conditions, some of which may not be con-ceivable to us, and the benefits might not be immediate. Nevertheless, the immediate benefit of choosing correctly between a good and a bad attitude will fall on us. Of that there is no doubt.

With compassion we definitely accrue the conditions for the creation of an immediate and tangible happiness. Just as we receive love and affection, it is important that we give it to others. If we have compas-sion or manifest kindness, it is as if we open the gateway of our mind. All narrow-minded thoughts of pursuing self-interest disappear.

Compassion brings strength to our minds by lessening fear, increasing confidence, and so on. [6] Doubts and irrational thinking will decline. As a result, in the company of others the mind is relaxed, there are feelings of closeness, and we have the feeling that life has meaning and purpose. Compassion gives us rest in times of great difficulty. Scientists these days have verified that taking responsibility for others is conducive to our own happiness.

As much as we can have an attitude of working for others, that much will we enjoy a genuine happiness. As all our happiness depends upon others, even if we look at it from the pursuit of our own welfare alone, it is necessary to have good relations with others. To that end, if we can maintain a genuine mind of friendliness in our social relationships, free from envy and malice, and if we interact with honesty, free of deceit and pretense, we will find a state of inner self-confidence and be able to enjoy good relationships.

With an attitude of wanting to help others, no matter with whom we have a relationship, we will have respect for them and a cheerful and open mind. If, on the contrary, we are jealous, proud, competitive, and so on, our minds become tense and we naturally become evasive and deceptive. We cannot help but be secretive and clandestine, with outer deed not matching inner thought. This results in an anxious mind, having to live with the fear of wondering when we are going to be exposed and shamed. Nothing is transparent and others no longer trust us.

For example, some national leaders, when giving press conferences, will only talk and refuse to take questions. This shows that such people are not straightforward. They are devious, with secretive and clandestine ways. [7] Therefore, they are apprehensive and do not have the confidence to be forthright by giving truthful answers to searching questions. Policies designed to bring esteem to oneself, in reality, only bring suffering.

Even within a single household, if the family members live in an anxious atmosphere where there is no mutual trust, each wary of the other, and only irrational attitudes, then even with abundant wealth there will be no joy. If there is trust, then even with only the most basic food and clothing, it is possible to enjoy a happy life in an atmosphere of confidence. Such trust will not be found through money, deceit, power, might, force, and so on, but only through the clear expression of a sincere concern for the welfare of others and a respect for their rights.

In a community of harmonious friends endowed with a natural and genuine trust, you can live in an atmosphere of peace and joy. You are freed from unhappiness such as fear and anxiety, and you can dwell in peace, possessed of the ability and courage to face difficulties when they arise.

Not only in times of difficulty and suffering, but at all times, having someone you can turn to and who will nurture you with love and affection is of great help, whereas those who are angry and thought-less bring nothing but detriment. Such a self-evident truth is clear indication of the need to have love and affection for people.

Always having feelings of closeness to others and maintaining a loving mind is the sole foundation for building everything we wish for. Focusing on small differences in outer appearances to divide and discriminate is nothing but ignorance. In particular, it is often said that the world is becoming smaller, and from the twentieth century onward the people of this world have almost become a single community. This little planet where we humans live is our only home. [8] If we want to protect our home each of us must possess a sense of universal respon-sibility. This alone has the power to negate inconducive traits such as selfishness, deceiving others, abuse, and so on. There will be no need to be afraid. Life becomes meaningful, and households, communities, and nations, large and small, become happier. The key to it all is the development of compassion.

Having compassion, concern, respect, and kindness for others not only benefits society but is the most important factor for our own happiness. Politicians, religious leaders, and businesspeople, or anyone, can strive to become good people with good minds. A single person endowed with the virtues of kindness, compassion, tolerance, and so on can definitely contribute to the happiness of families and society as a whole.

For example, smiling is a natural and wonderful facial expression. Of course, sometimes, even that wonderful expression can be misused by perverse thinking in order to ridicule or to threaten. Some politicians smile out of necessity. But those aside, it can be seen how important it is in daily life to exchange smiles from the heart. Furthermore, when we meet someone, we should be the first to smile. Always waiting for the other to smile first is wrong. There are many similar situations that we should know about, which depend upon our mental attitude and actions.

[9] External progress can provide for physical comfort and to a certain extent can alleviate suffering. However, physical pleasure alone cannot satisfy the needs of human beings. Anyone who lives in dependence upon material factors can be wealthy, have good food and drink, a wonderful home and environment, good friends, and relations. Yet the many effects of a troubled mind, such as being plunged into grief, are not for the lack of conducive external circumstances. These arise from the mind.

Physical comfort cannot eclipse mental suffering, but mental happiness can override physical suffering. This can be understood from the following. If you have an enthusiastic attitude toward achieving a particular goal by way of religion, politics, physical training, competitive sport, and so on, you have the ability to ignore any difficulties connected with that goal, such as pain, the discomfort of illness, physical deprivation, and so on. Moreover, with a joyful mind happily embracing such hardships, no amount of pain is seen as a burden but only as an adornment. At such times not only is there no discouragement or unhappiness in the mind, but such hardships become the causes for increasing our strength of mind and our level of tolerance. Eventually our mental strength reaches new heights and any physical discomfort is no longer felt.

Furthermore, being happy and relaxed, having an open and expansive mind, and other good mental states are preventatives against the onset of illness, whereas an agitated mind and the like can actually bring on sickness. This we all can see. [10] Good and bad states of mind can comfort or discomfort the body. They have the power to bring benefit and harm, and are very important. Physical comfort and discomfort alone are less important than our state of mind, however, and so although we might be undergoing hardship, such as the torment of illness or being bereft of the basic necessities of life, we should nevertheless make the achievement of a peaceful and happy mind our prime objective.

THE IMPORTANCE OF MENTAL COGNITION

Alleviating suffering and pursuing happiness with reliance upon physical feelings is an undertaking we share with animals. However, the unique capacity of the brain ensures that we humans have a special ability. The happiness and suffering produced in reliance upon mental cognition is much greater in humans. Mental feelings of joy and pain brought on by expectations and apprehension, and the great variety of concepts, are also more numerous. These feelings will not be augmented or reduced simply by money, medicine, and so on. It is primarily by sustained practice in our way of thinking that we lessen suffering and develop happiness.

Because human beings possess the faculty and skill of the intellect, by endeavoring to reduce the suffering created by thoughts and to increase our happiness we can definitely steer our minds toward a peaceful, happy, and nonharming state. We can say that such a transformation is the duty of those possessed of human intellect.

So how can humans attain their desired happiness? This involves explaining a little of the underlying philosophy of the above points. Desiring to increase our feelings of happiness and to free ourselves of unhappiness is a desire that naturally arises, which we can understand without resorting to logical proof. It is not confined to humans; even ants have this desire. [11] Moreover, the arising of feelings of happiness and suffering is connected with the thought of "I." On this basis, desire for feelings of happiness and aversion to feelings of suffering is naturally present.

We can analyze these feelings of happiness and suffering in more detail. For example, pleasant feelings, attractive to the mind, are induced through the five sensory consciousnesses, in which the eyes see beautiful form, the ears hear pleasant sounds, the nose experiences delightful aromas, the tongue experiences delicious tastes, the body experiences sensations of softness, and so on. These are all pleasant physical feelings. Through the five sensory objects, unpleasant feelings, or suffering, unattractive to the mind, are also induced. There are also sufferings brought on by illness that are based upon physical feelings.

There is no long-lasting satisfaction in happiness arising from the sensory consciousness alone. Mainly we need happiness in the mind. True happiness is mental happiness, which does not depend upon sensory consciousness feelings. One may accumulate the wonderful conditions for providing pleasant physical feelings, but there is no guarantee that they will eradicate the sufferings within mental cognition. For example, I know someone who is well educated, surrounded by all material needs, with wealth of over a million US dollars. He has no concerns for food and provisions, he is highly regarded, his work situation is excellent, and yet he says he is completely unhappy. I often meet rich people like him.

Suffering associated with mental cognition comes through the causal factor of conceptualization. For example, suffering is conceived as happiness, or the impermanent is held as permanent. These are mistaken ways of mentally apprehending, completely out of tune with reality, and they result in thoughts of hope and expectation, which in turn produce anxiety and fear and other difficult emotions. [12] Pride, jealousy, competitiveness, desire, anger, and so on are mental phenomena, and therefore they must arise from mental cognition.

The suffering that arises by way of mental cognition is more prevalent in humans than in animals. Among humans, those who have lesser intellects, those who are poorly educated, those who are beggars or live in poverty, have less envy, competitiveness, and pride, and in their minds the procession of hopes and fears is probably less. Consequently, it seems as if their mental suffering is less. On the other hand, those who have been well educated, who enjoy excellent living standards can have greater aversion and envy. With competitiveness, pride and so on, they can develop the attitude of "victory for oneself, defeat for others." This leads to a misuse of the power of the intellect, and their suffering created in dependence upon mental cognition is that much stronger.

The search for the remedy to alleviate those sufferings that arise from the intellect and mental cognition must take place in the very mind from which they arise. It will not be found in other humans or external objects. Just thinking "God knows" is also not helpful. Likewise, kindness, compassion, and other qualities of the mind will only arise from within mental cognition and cannot be created by the efforts of external phenomena. If you went to the market and said, "Sell me some love and compassion," everyone would regard that as ridiculous. If you went to a hospital and said, "Give me an injection of love and compassion," people would wonder if you were crazy. Love and compassion cannot be gotten from others. You have to develop them yourself within your own mind. If we turn our attention to that fact, we can know how to bring the mental feelings of peace and happiness to our minds.

THE EFFECT OF LOVE AND COMPASSION UPON HEALTH

[13] Even though the body is suffering, in the mind feelings of peace and happiness can be experienced. On the other hand, even if the body is completely free from any kind of suffering, the mind can still abide in a state of deep unhappiness, and because of that, eventually the body too will come to suffer. Therefore, if we make ourselves unhappy with an angry mind, and so on, then it goes without saying that we need to cultivate a mind of compassion as an antidote. A peaceful and happy feeling in our mind is beneficial for all. It is something we can experience every day. For example, two people who face the same difficulty may have different attitudes toward it. One can face it with a little effort, but the other cannot. Both situations arise from the particular way of looking at the problem.

Whether you are religious, nonreligious, or antireligious, as long as you wish for a healthy body, a happy life, and a long life, you should value attitudes of kindness, affection, tolerance, contentment, and so on, as you would value your life. Compassion and the motivation of helping others, which are innate and fundamental to our human nature, are the foundation of such a development. Recognizing this is crucial, and everyone should take this to heart.

To do that, we should know the workings of our mental cognition, what types of mind bring peace and what types bring trouble and disturbance, and work to lessen the strength of those types of mind that increase suffering, and develop those that have the power to grow a genuine happiness. It is not enough just to know about the wonderful qualities of a peaceful mind; we must make efforts to cultivate them within ourselves.

[14] Those whose minds are troubled can avail themselves of therapists, who are widely accessible these days. The causes of unhappiness are sought, counseling is lovingly provided, the essential points are discussed, and advice and ways for finding a peaceful mind are given. However, the crucial element is to try to change our daily thoughts and habits from those that are in direct opposition to kindness and compassion.

In Tibet, the innate qualities of kindness and compassion were traditionally taught to be a great medicine with beneficial effects on the health of mind and body, and contemporary developments in medicine that point to the value of kindness and compassion for good health bears testimony to that. If a doctor, no matter how skilled they are, administers treatment thinking only of their own benefit, with little feeling of kindness toward the patient, without expressing empathy, patience, consideration, or respect, the beneficial effect will be weak. On the contrary, treatment from those doctors who administer to their patients with kindness and compassion has greater effect. This we can all see.

Moreover, American doctors have told me that about twelve percent of the population of the USA have mental health problems, and that the prime cause of their illness is not a lack of material resources but comes from not receiving love and affection from others. From this too we can see that the greatest happiness comes from kindness and compassion.

THE IMPORTANCE OF THE INTELLECT

It is certainly not necessary for everyone to have faith in a religion or to hold to a particular philosophy, but being determined and aspiring to increase kindness and compassion is definitely necessary. These are the wonderful features of being a human and are jewels of the mind. [15] Buddhist texts state that human beings are a higher species in this world, and that this human form is more precious than the forms of other beings. This is because the potential for kindness and compassion, as well as the seeds of a good character and intellect, are naturally and innately a part of us from the moment of birth, regardless of any societal environment.

We possess the very special and fundamental qualities of being able to bring happiness not only to ourselves but also to others. The seeds of that virtuous human behavior are present in everyone, save possibly for those who have suffered certain forms of brain damage. However, whether or not those seeds produce this happiness depends upon making use of them with the skills of the intellect. Our intellect ought not be a tool for destruction, and we should contemplate and understand that it is not to be misused. Whether we generate the happiness we long for or we create unwanted suffering or mental torment depends on how we use our intellect. Whether the customs, laws, and regulations found in religion, politics, economics, and so on is a force for good or bad depends upon how the individuals who are responsible for these make use of their intellect. Even a good system, when misused, instead of bringing benefit, can become a cause for harm. We can see many examples of this these days.

Religion has potential to help people to live in a state of meaningful happiness even in this life. However, if that religion is misused it too becomes a cause for strife and division. [16] Even in international sports, there are cases of corruption that put the honest endeavor of sport unnecessarily at risk. These all come from the perverse actions of humans.

We can divide up the human species in terms of race, color of skin, language, religion, gender, wealth, and so on, but the reality is that fundamentally we are the same. This is verified by modern science.

In short, the relationships between married couples, friends, households, communities, and even countries depend mainly upon the strength of kindness and compassion, on the level or absence of resentment, on the interest taken in the harm or benefit that occurs to others, on the level of responsibility that puts the welfare of others before oneself, and so on. States of mind such as hostility and suspicion are expressions of the misuse of the intellect. They have no value or good qualities. They will destroy attitudes related to any decent and ethical way of being and are a prime cause of others mistrusting us.

When the ethical qualities of human beings deteriorate, disreputable and opportunistic acts such as corruption, exploitation, intimidation, and deception will automatically arise, even with the laws and regulations of the country or its religion in place. This without doubt brings great difficulties to communities. Therefore, even the thoughts and actions of individuals have a direct connection with the welfare of the community. Calamitous instances of perverse human behavior and activity, however they might arise, only result in greater misfortune such as war. [17] Therefore, with the benefit of such insight, we need to persevere with deep and assured recognition of the necessity of a future that is better than that of animals, where we can have a meaningful life with immediate and long-term well-being.

Again, the main methods for bringing about a meaningful attitude of working for others depend upon the excellent qualities of kindness and compassion that are the innate and fundamental nature of human beings, and promoting their value is a very important responsibility. That is the way I view the world.

The human intellect and the compassionate mind work well together. However, if all the power is concentrated in the intellect and the connection to the compassionate mind is lost, these two become unbalanced, and all kinds of misfortune and tragedies can occur as a result. If we can eliminate faults and develop good qualities, without doubt we will be able to bring about all manner of positive changes in our lives. We need to increase by various methods the precious mind endowed with kindness and compassion. That is not easy, but there is no other way to make human life better in the present and to ensure happiness for self and others in the future. If we think in the long term, those who have compassionate minds will be happy. On the other hand, entertaining nonvirtuous states of mind such as pride, anger, jealousy, and so on may bring a little gain in the short term, but the reality is that they will always result in increasing feelings of dissatisfaction.

THE WORLD SITUATION

[18] In today's society kindness is wanting. We operate under the influence of afflictions such as anger and desire that are precipitated by self-centeredness. This leads to a lack of honesty, to confusion about the nature of reality, and to ways of thinking that lead us to engage in nonvirtuous acts. As a result, we lack contentment and tolerance. The immediate condition of these wrong thoughts and activities is that our regular thoughts and activities are not connected with our innate mind of love and compassion. This causes most of the difficulties and problems of today's world. These problems are not only manmade troubles such as war; from the individual through to a community, from the country and up to the international community, there are many different levels of problems. On top of that, there are natural calamities, such as epidemics and external disasters, difficult to prevent and about which we can do little when we are unprepared.

What is the fundamental cause of these situations? It is possible to believe that they arise from excessive focus on the rapid growth of this century's material culture. With our pursuit of material wealth we give little attention to the actual foundation of human happiness, such as kindness, affection, compassion, and living in harmony. If we cannot see any self-benefit in making a connection with an individual or a particular organization, we simply show no interest in it. These are mistaken attitudes and activities devoid of the common good, and we can see by our own experience how such attitudes give rise to the problems discussed above.

The abilities that come from an education are not sufficient to deal with these problems. Nor do these problems all arise simply as the effects of karma, which is a topic taught in Buddhism and elsewhere. An educated intellect can itself become a cause for the arising of problems. [19] For example, there are educated people who suffer from fear and excessive thinking and have lost confidence, and there those who see how problems arise and how they could end and yet remain indifferent. Such people may be well educated and have specialized intellects, but they hold goals that could bring about negative consequences, and pursue risky enterprises.[24]

Education and intellect on their own are no guarantees of a positive outcome. The way that the human intellect driven by hatred and resentment can misuse technology can be illustrated by the dreadful events in New York on September 11, 2001. Fostering the intellect and education alone can provide no answer for the prevention of such tragedies. Other human qualities are required. This means reacting to the plight of others, including animals, with affection and compassion. Recognizing the importance and necessity of achieving the well-being of society, as well as that of the environment and health, ultimately impacts on our own happiness. We must be able to see how important it is to take on this responsibility.

We should learn lessons from past mistakes made by not properly recognizing the innate human values, and ensure that these mistakes do not continue into the future. To do so the younger generation especially should comprehensively understand how these events arose from wrong thoughts and deeds and should be properly prepared to face up to and prevent them from occurring again in the future.

THE ROLE OF THE MEDIA

[20] These days, in our society, horrific incidents of murder, rape, violent robbery, and so on take place every day. It goes without saying that these depressing occurrences arise from the inability to value ethical behavior. Of course it is the duty of the various media outlets to report them at the time. However, in every country there are those worthy movements who work for the provision of education, who care for the elderly, the young, the chronically sick and the poor. In developed countries there exist excellent opportunities that provide education, good employment prospects, amenities for living a daily life, including hosting sporting competitions for the disabled and those with learning difficulties. These are people and communities who do not look down upon those with adverse physical conditions, but who, with belief and respect, provide the resources for them to be able to live as equals with the rest of society. Yet widespread information on this admirable side of society for any long period of time is lacking. Therefore, the media should give equal time to, and not lose the responsibility of promoting, those exemplary efforts that bring out the good and reduce the bad, and which can prevent those incidents that threaten and harm the stability of society.

Similarly, in some films the portrayal of stealing, robbery, deceit, lust, killing, and bloodshed is extensive, and for many vulnerable people this becomes a corrupting influence that can create the faulty aspiration to engage in those types of acts. It can also create the wrong idea that the nature of human beings is fundamentally bad, thereby producing unhappiness, depression, and lack of self-confidence. There is much discussion about this topic in many countries all over the world. [21] We should take interest in their ideas and, without thinking only of the benefit gained from the immediate accumulation of wealth, we should be suspicious of those harmful and faulty notions that prevent our human society becoming more decent and ethical.

The press and movie industries are important sectors for fulfilling the wishes of human beings. In particular, as methods of putting an end to corruption and of exposing improper practices, it is vital that they become a beneficial force with an independent voice that encourages the growth of kindness and compassion that is so valuable to society.

If we misuse others and manipulate situations solely for our own benefit, no matter how clever, intelligent, and powerful we are, ultimately it will only be a source of great remorse. If each individual, in accordance with their own capabilities and without loss of confidence or courage, develops enthusiasm on the basis of working to create a happier life by way of mutual dependence, peace and happiness in this world will naturally increase. Such confidence is not deluded confidence but arises from recognizing one's capability and potential. This I have seen from my own experience.

There are many states of mind, such as confidence and pride, that share similar characteristics, but when examined can be seen to be of positive and negative types. This is important to know. Confidence, or courage, and pride, for example, are somewhat similar in being experiences that lift up the mind. However, there is a difference in motivation. [22] Confidence, or courage, will produce a positive outcome, whereas pride will produce the opposite.

TWO WAYS OF APPREHENDING "I"

There is something important that should be explained here. To think, "I have this constant thought of I. It is deluded and therefore must be destroyed completely," is wrong thinking. Just as there are two different types of desire, there are two kinds of holding a sense of self. One type of thinking "I" forgets the rights of others or considers them to be of little consequence, while holding self to be more important than others. Such an apprehension of "I" has a desire for personal gain, and thus a strong cherishing of self. It might even have no qualms about trampling thoughtlessly over others. Even the act of killing is possible with such an attitude. This is the apprehension of "I" on the negative side.

The other way of apprehending "I" is connected with a sense of self-respect or thoughtfulness for others that considers, "It is not right that I do not do good." It carries the thoughts, "In order to be of service to others I will willingly bear the responsibility to achieve whatever task I am doing. I can do this. I will accomplish it by all means." This is a good apprehension of "I," and, as an assault upon negative states of minds, it creates a strong basis for countering timidity and laziness. It enables the development of confidence, courage, and self-assurance, leading to the ability to accomplish great things.

This second way of apprehending "I" is present in bodhisattvas described in Buddhist texts, and is one that thinks, "I can accomplish the welfare of others." It is not only more powerful than the former apprehension of "I" but engenders great mental fortitude in the person who has it. [23] It makes no difference whether it takes days, months, years, or eons to achieve the welfare of limitless sentient beings, the enthusiasm and courage continues to grow. Without this firm apprehension of "I" such an unshakeable fortitude will not arise. Therefore, this good way of apprehending "I" is something wonderful, beneficial, meaningful, and very necessary, and is definitely to be developed.

The other way of apprehending "I" disregards and casts away the rights of others. It deceives and is contemptuous. It is a stupid and negative apprehension of self that uses others for its own benefit. Therefore, having such an apprehension will ultimately bring misery to others and result in defeat for oneself and ongoing suffering.

Likewise, uncontrived humility and a timidity may be similar in both being a lowering of the mind, but humility is an asset for increasing one's good qualities. Timidity, on the other hand, is a barrier to that.

Take being competitive for example. With an attitude of competing with others in the field of material development it is possible to generate capabilities that exceed those of others, in order to secure the welfare of the community and the environment. We can learn from others who possess admirable qualities and with great joy make efforts to reach a level that even exceeds that of our teachers. It is this kind of intelligent competitive spirit, where there is no mutual hostility, that we should develop. For example, in the Buddhist practice of going for refuge we take the Jewel of the Sangha as an example, and it is taught that we should have the competitive spirit of wanting to develop in our minds qualities similar to those who have attained the ārya level. [24] Moreover, we should go further by striving to reach the even greater level of Buddhahood. This is an intelligent competitive spirit, and we should try to develop something similar.

TYPES OF COMPASSION

Affection and attachment are similar. Both are focused on others and involve feelings of closeness, but they differ in their results. I always talk about there being a higher and lower compassion. One is innate and arises naturally. This compassion can be one-sided, linked to attachment, and is therefore dependent upon the actions of others. It is a small mind that only embraces those on whom one relies, such as the friends and relations.

The second type of compassion takes the first type as its seed, and through a wisdom that discerns and analyzes, takes great joy in continual improvement. With effort this grows in strength. This compassion is accompanied by wisdom and is therefore limitless. Because it has the power to extend to enemies, and not only to friends and relations, it is a mind of great embrace.

Therefore, the first kind can be said to be a limited kindness and compassion, while the second is limitless.

It is important to know the nature of kindness and compassion and the factors that oppose them. The form of kindness and compassion for friends and relations arises mixed with attachment. Therefore, it mainly arises because of something we need for ourselves, and probably does not arise from an attitude of wanting to help others. This is not true compassion. True compassion does not arise from conditions built on feelings of attachment, but is a responsibility shouldered for the sake of others, built upon genuine reasons. [25] Therefore, such a true compassion motivated by reality and benevolence toward others will not change even if the others are hostile.

To grow and develop such a compassion requires patience and takes a long time, but we can without doubt know that we have the ability to create it. Therefore, first of all we should contemplate the following. All living beings, whether attractive or not, friendly or bad-tempered, are all equal in wanting to be happy and not wanting to suffer, just as we do. Moreover, they all have the same right to experience happiness and be free of suffering. Therefore, there are no genuine reasons to create divisions by way of attachment and hostility to our side and their side. Even if someone does something bad to us, if we can understand that it is not logical to alter our altruistic thinking toward them, then feelings of affection, compassion, and kindness will effortlessly and naturally arise. If we can integrate in our minds this altruistic motivation that encompasses all beings generally, a sense of responsibility focused on others will grow, and with the strong aspiration to be of benefit to all, we will help others to free themselves from hardships. Such a wonderful aspiration is without question good and fruitful for ourselves and others, and we should definitely try to achieve it.

It is excellent to contemplate compassion, patience, and other virtues, but that alone is definitely not sufficient for making progress. I want to stress that when we meet difficulties and hardships, we must try to put these qualities into practice right away. [26] Our friends will always find many ways to help us, but it is not friends who truly provide the opportunities to generate those precious minds of compassion and patience. Those difficult and important challenges are posed by our enemies. The occasions when those who we hold as our enemies cause us great difficulties are opportunities for facing and bearing adversity, practicing patience, and generating compassion. These opportunities only arise when faced with enemies, and we should think about their kindness.

If we want to train our minds in compassion we should regard our enemies as our best teachers. Christianity teaches that if our enemy strikes us on one cheek then we should offer them the other cheek. This is very moving advice. In Buddhist philosophy and practice there are similar teachings. If the proper application of such teachings leads our training in patience to firm levels, attacks by our enemies only serve as conditions to increase our practice. If we are free of anger and vengeful thoughts toward our enemy, we can clearly see with a peaceful state of mind that the actions that caused us hurt and pain arose from our enemy being under the control of mental afflictions. Moreover, if we contemplate that this person's behavior will have a terrible karmic effect for them, we will hold them even more as objects of genuine compassion. This is a fundamental teaching of Buddhism. The truth that our enemy can become our friend, and that even our greatest friend can become our enemy, is visible to all.

[27] It is the kindness of our enemies that enables us to engage in training our minds in kindness and compassion, and in them we find the most helpful friends for increasing our peace of mind. This is a worthwhile change of perception for society and individuals, and at the same time, those we hold as enemies become friends.

Our need and desire for friends is a right and natural human desire. Therefore, if we want to cherish ourselves, we should develop a strong sense of altruism and, with strong empathy for their happiness and suffering, cultivate a loving respect for others. If we do this, we will be happy. It is only by means of kindness and compassion that we can find true friends. Fighting, anger, envy, competitiveness, and so on cannot possibly produce friends. Wealth and power may bring people near, but we will doubt whether they will be truly reliable, and when our situation deteriorates we may be left on our own. We would be better off developing altruism in order to find friends.

Individuals in human society possess different dispositions and beliefs, giving rise to different economic and political systems. Whatever kind of dispute arises in those communities, kindness, compassion, and altruism are indispensable methods for solving such problems. Such attitudes are not only for religious leaders, medical professionals, and public servants; they are necessary for all sections of society, communities, or individuals.

Kindness and compassion are the foundation to all good things. Our happiness at all stages of life, from a baby drinking her mother's milk to our youth, middle age, and elder years; the certainty of our being able to trust others, whether they are loved ones or not; [28] even the development of world peace: all these depend upon the existence of kindness and compassion. Therefore, even common sense can tell us that, ultimately, achieving happiness and dispelling suffering arises from kindness and compassion.

I see efforts being made to begin engaging in this kind of ethical behavior, which can encompass the whole world and is unconnected with any religious path, as wholly achievable and worthwhile. The possibility arises from having certainty about the innate attitude of wishing for good. I have the firm belief that a way of building a solid foundation of values, which in no way contradicts religious traditions, and definitely does not need to depend upon a religious path, is within our comprehension.

ETHICAL CONDUCT IS LIKE WATER; RELIGION IS LIKE TEA

Human beings can manage their affairs without religion, but without inner values we cannot manage any activities that will result in happiness. I am not uncomfortable at all in saying that ethical behavior does not depend upon religion.

Generally, when discussing the goal of happiness, in terms of psychology, I believe there are two paths. The first relies upon thought and experience in equal measure and concerns those who do not depend upon a religious tradition but nevertheless naturally turn to compassion, a kind heart, and caring for others, which are, as discussed above, fundamental to the nature of human beings. [29] The second type is a psychology that has a religious tradition as its basis. It derives from the culture and the place where the individual grew up, and involves specific practices combined with faith.

I see inner values and ethical conduct unconnected with religious thinking as being like water, and inner values and ethical conduct embedded in a religious tradition like tea. The main component of the tea we drink comes from water. Therefore, we can live without the tea but not without the water. Likewise, we can live without religion, but we cannot live without those inner values such as secular kindness and compassion. From the time we were born we may have had no connection with religion, but there can be no progress from birth to adulthood without kindness, love, and so on. Therefore, inner values are more important than religion.

The precious inner value of concern for the general welfare of humanity, induced by those seminal qualities intrinsic within us, is the very basis of all world religions. The fundamental practices of all religious traditions have their roots in secular ethical conduct. For example, the ten nonvirtuous acts as defined in Buddhism cause harm to others, and therefore contravene the standards of worldly ethical behavior. Also, they cause damage to ourselves, and are therefore naturally wrong acts. Therefore, seeing that these harmful acts are to be abandoned, the Buddha included them in Buddhist practice. [30] It is not that he thought of them anew and then taught them.

It is certainly possible to turn the mind toward kindness and compassion without depending upon a religious framework. We are sentient beings and from that perspective such an act is biological in nature, and arises from the need to live in an environment of caring for others, empathy, kindness, and compassion.

No one can exist without happiness. I often say that the Buddhist expression "the glories of a higher existence"[25] does not refer solely to future lives; we need the glories of happiness with the bodies of this human existence also. In order to gain the excellent human form of a higher existence in future lives we need to accumulate the right causes. Therefore, the source and foundation of happiness and suffering is the body that is connected with outer phenomena, and the mind that is connected with inner feelings. We should know that happiness and suffering arise solely in connection with body and mind.

The inner factor brings about feelings of happiness and suffering. It is important to know this. Mental feelings of happiness and suffering follow from one's own concepts, or arise from the way such conceptualization views the world, and a method for genuine happiness must be sought from within that conceptual process and not elsewhere. It is within this process that we should develop a practice of creating and destroying the causes and conditions for happiness and suffering. Happiness cannot be bought from the outside, nor can it be created by machines. It arises only from developing understanding and kindness and compassion within our minds. [31]

Therefore, inner values such as caring for others, respect, kindness, treating others compassionately, and so on are the most important factors for bringing happiness to ourselves. The reasons why they are called "inner values" is that all living beings appreciate these attributes of the mind and people are naturally drawn to them. Moreover, other mental qualities and all the good things we wish for arise solely from these mental attributes. Therefore, they possess "value." These values are not gained from a particular religious tradition but are the innate and natural virtues of all sentient beings.

Religion has benefited many millions of people in the past. It continues to do so and, without doubt, will bring benefit in the future also. However, no matter how helpful religious traditions are in making human life meaningful and in giving advice on how to live our lives, they are insufficient as guides for increasing an ethical way of life in today's world, which is so dissociated from religion. This is because there are many people who do not follow any particular religion. Moreover, the modes of ethical conduct embedded in any one religious tradition are suited for those of certain dispositions only and cannot possibly have universal appeal. Therefore, there can be no one religion that is meaningful for all. What is more necessary is a system of secular ethics divorced from religion, which can be accepted by all, religious or not. It is important to know this.

I am someone who has worn robes, the mark of a monk, since I was a child, and it is quite possible that when I say these things, some will be astonished. [32] However, there is no contradiction here. On the basis of my religious faith I go beyond my own tradition to work as best I can for the welfare of those who practice other religions, those without religion, and all sentient beings, encouraging myself to expand the boundaries of my mind. I continually seek to reinforce that.

We should hold our shared human intellect and experience as the main provision for any exposition of ways to achieve happiness without relying upon religion. This should then be determined by science with conclusions arrived at through analysis. As for empirical evidence, we should take as examples those people in this world who are not religious and yet have developed a high level of ethical conduct with great qualities of kindness and compassion, and point out the way to find happiness by practicing as they did.

These methods could also be beneficial for the many people who have faith in a religion but who do not follow a daily practice of prayer, study, contemplation, and meditation. Other than that, just saying that you must practice a religious path of prayer, and so forth, cannot possibly express a genuine and complete method for finding happiness. That is very clear.

Many people in this world who find it difficult to have faith in religion also find no satisfaction with material progress. Those who seek a third way are increasing. In discussions and interactions in many parts of the world I regularly say that when we work to develop our intrinsic qualities of kindness and compassion for the sake of the happiness of humanity, [33] it is not necessary to depend upon religious faith or religious philosophies, but that a third way is definitely needed. I am heartened to see that those who support this method for developing this precious and beneficial quality are increasing in number.

MOTHER AND CHILD

Being cared for and nurtured with love and compassion is important for all beings at all times throughout their lives, but it is not the case that this will not occur without some recourse to religion. The importance of such a love and compassion can be gauged from looking at the relationship between parents and child at the time of infancy, which is an experience common to us all. This has profound connection to the welfare of body and mind throughout life and is something essential.

From the moment of birth, the provision of food, clothing, bedding, and every element of the child's physical and mental well-being depends upon the mother. That bond is created by love and compassion, and a mother's love is at the very root of the child's life and its well-being.

Even from a scientific perspective it has been established that the bond of the mother caring for her child, and of the child feeling closest to its mother, is one that arises from love. If the mother's love is not strong enough, or anger is present in the mother, and so on, this can lead to all kinds of difficulties, both emotional and physical, such as the mother's milk not flowing. The first three or four years after birth is the most formative time for the brain's development [34] and is a period in which a healthy physical experience of love and compassion is essential for the child. During those years, if the parents and others do not have a loving physical contact with the child, if they do not hold it, sit it on their laps, and play with it, and if the mother especially does not devote a lot of her time to the child, that can become a hindrance to the development of the brain.

Providing for the happiness of the child, protecting it from fear, instilling it with confidence, and so on, all done with love and affection, is directly connected with the mental and physical health of the child. Without the help and protection that stems from the love and compassion of others, children do not survive. Love, therefore, is the greatest nourishment a child could have.

I always say that the first person to teach me about love and affection was my mother. If a mother lacked this great and unique love she would not work day and night for her child with no concern for her own hardship. From the child's side also, if it lacked a profound love for its mother, the crucial unquestioning trust would not be there. Therefore, in order to live, the necessity of having affection for each other in a physical sense is instinctive. To survive physically we need to rely upon others. Therefore, we need a strength of mind, with strong feelings, that willingly takes on the difficulties of physically caring for others. The courage of such a strength of mind is love, and even if it is mixed with attachment, it is important to us. It is clearly a biological element. Therefore, [35] I usually say that advancement in this aspect of human behavior, which arises from love, is of prime importance.

If a child has not received nurturing kindness and love as an infant, in the future they will find it difficult to show love to others, including their own parents. Moreover, being deprived of this kind of love is a condition for an unbalanced mind, an unruly nature, a bad personality, and so on throughout their life. They are angry not only with others but also with themselves and may even want to end their own life. Their only recourse is to an experienced mental health specialist, as any other method will be difficult to find. This is tragic.

In contrast, those who grow up in a healthy environment where they receive the nurturing love of their parents or other caring adults will naturally have good minds, a gentle nature, quick mental development, and so on. We can understand that these worthy values and admirable qualities have a connection to fundamental biology or physical development. With life born from the womb, love and compassion is indispensable.

For those children brought up in children's homes it is essential that they are looked after with love and affection by their foster mothers. Likewise, during the time a child spends in school, it is important that the teachers treat them in a kindly way and teach them with the hope that they will be of benefit to individuals and society in the future. If they lay the foundation for developing excellent prospects in life, and regularly teach them with kindness and affection, [36] the students will happily embrace the opportunity to study while having respect and admiration for the teacher. They will listen to the teacher's words and take to mind whatever they teach. Anything other than that and we can see that the relationship between students and teacher will not be a good one, and the educational prospects for the students in the future will be adversely affected.

On the basis of the experience of a life lived with such love and compassion, if we can be convinced, with a knowledge that discerns the facts, that this compassion is necessary for living a good life, that our own happiness depends upon others and our community, and that the greatest profit for oneself is to work for the welfare of others, it will without doubt bring great benefit for us all.

To sum up, if there is someone to give us love from the day we were born, it brings us a deep joy. To live our lives we need compassion in a physical way. The creation of decent individuals and a decent society begins with the love and nurture given by parents, and continues into adulthood under the kind and loving behavior of teachers, and so on. This topic is dear to my heart and is the subject of one of my books, *Beyond Religion.*[26] [37]

MUTUAL DEPENDENCE

In the past individual communities with fundamentally different ways of thinking could have little to do with each other. However, generally speaking, in this world we are all born as part of one large human family, and as individuals we must live together. We are not creatures that live alone and nor could we exist that way. Otherwise, there would be no need to build towns and cities. For human beings to be able to live together, love and compassion is an indispensable foundation for fulfilling our aspirations. Such a necessity arises from the deep and interdependent relationship that we all share.

Our human intelligence allows us to understand this relationship of dependence, and taking a long-term view, we will be able to accept the responsibility of ensuring the well-being of self and others. On the other hand, some, using their intelligence and ability as a means to achieve only their own welfare, presume that their wonderful life needs nothing from anyone else, that it was created solely by themselves, and that they are totally independent beings. [38] The reality is that none of the good things of our life, such as education, reputation, power, wealth, and so forth, arrived with us at the time of our birth. We all came into this world naked, empty-handed, not knowing anything. In childhood, when preparing our prospects for public and private life, and in those times when we experience the sufferings of illness and the depredations of old age, we are totally dependent on the love, concern, company, and assistance of others, such as our parents, relatives, friends, and strangers. There is no one who does not depend on others, who is self-sufficient and not needing to connect with others. If we had to live alone, we would not survive. This is not unique to us, but is common to all animals as well. Even insects have to live in communities where they depend upon each other. This dependence is not ordained by religion or law but is the actual way of things.

PROTECTING THE ENVIRONMENT

There is no need to state why we need happiness. It is evident to everyone. And it is very clear that to achieve that goal, we must also protect the natural environment. The subtle phenomena of the external world all exist in a mutual dependence. On this earth where we live, the oceans, clouds, and forests, the sun and moon and other planetary bodies, all exist through the potential of a subtle interdependence. The world as a container and its inhabitants as the contents exist as support and supported. In that sense, the general and specific arrangement of that container—such as its wonders, its space, its rivers, the passages of the sun and moon, [39] the climate, the flowers and the trees, the aromas of the forests, its sources of energy, the plants and grass, the fruits, and all that is produced from the earth—are clearly indispensable provisions for a happy life. All these aspects of this container earth are the supports that we sentient creatures depend upon. As such, one could say that even the insentient inhabitants of the world—the forests and ecosystems that are so vital to us—have the right to exist. Therefore, we should have the strong feeling that it is worth cherishing.

If at any time, the relationship of this mutual dependence is not in harmony, there will be degradation and decline. Therefore, protecting the environment for the welfare of all creatures, and not just for humans, is the responsibility of the entire world. If there is no awareness, understanding, or belief that those living on this planet are friends, or brothers and sisters, and no awareness of the need for environmental protection, not only would world peace and happiness be out of the question but survival itself would be in danger. Therefore, mutual kindness and understanding are the very foundations of living for all of us, and it is a responsibility we cannot afford to ignore.

THE ONENESS OF HUMANITY

In recent times, the force of globalization has brought about change on this planet. Now, if some great disaster occurs in one place, the entire world is concerned. In this new age of mutual dependence, thinking about benefiting others is the best attitude to have for our own sake. [40] All destructive activities, from harming our immediate neighbors up through to destroying a neighboring country, are in reality cases of us causing harm to our own communities. Therefore, we should work to develop ethical behavior by way of compassion and kindness, and cultivate the understanding of the close dependence between all of us, adhering to the broad-minded perception of belonging to one large family.

It is wrong to neglect this awareness of our basic oneness and the innate qualities present in all of us and to create trouble on the basis of a few minor contrasting points of religion or political systems. It should be remembered that religions and political systems exist as ways to accomplish the welfare of humanity. It should not be forgotten that this is their fundamental aim, and the other goals should never be placed above this. It is always important to put consideration and respect for humanity before material progress and philosophies.

More than in the past, the nations of this world have to rely upon each other economically. In order to bring about a good understanding between the peoples of this world, our breadth of mind should transcend national boundaries and reach out into the international community. Until we can create an environment where there is no cause to resort to terrorism and violence, where there is genuine understanding, world problems will increase and not lessen. If there is no respect for the beliefs and hopes of the peoples of less-developed nations, eventually the wealthy countries will suffer.

[41] I believe that to face the difficulties ahead of us, we have to develop an altruistic mind that takes on a universal responsibility. Each of us as individuals should train our minds to work not only for ourselves, our family, our community, and our country but also for the whole of humanity on this earth. Adopting this altruistic universal responsibility is the wonderful magic key that will enable humanity to live happily. It is the best foundation for bringing world peace, for a balanced and sensible use of natural resources, and for ensuring the welfare of future generations.

The conditions of every single person in the region or country where we live is directly or indirectly linked to the conditions of every other, even if they live on another continent. Religious, cultural, political, and economic communities are also intimately linked. The concept of "us and them" is not that important. If we look at the differences, it is true that in terms of races, customs, and religions there is much that differentiates us. However, insofar as we all share this little globe together, we do so as one people. [42] Therefore, if we cause others suffering, ultimately we too will face hardship. If we are happy, that will benefit others too. Therefore, a universal responsibility is something humanity should desire.

Throughout our lives we will meet with various hardships, but that is not something special that happens only to us. It happens to everyone. Losing hope and becoming discouraged will only reduce our ability to face up to difficulties; recognizing this will strengthen our ability to deal with hardships. Then, when we meet a new and difficult situation, we will discover in it a valuable opportunity to develop our minds. Moreover, an uncontrived empathy for the sufferings of others, with a compassion that wishes to free them from their suffering, will grow and become stronger. As a result, in our own minds too we will find peace and a special strength of mind.

Our hardships cannot be dispelled by a single person. Therefore, each one of us must carry our share of the responsibility of universal concern. If a single person with this universal responsibility is multiplied to become ten people, ten become a hundred, a hundred become a thousand, and so on, to many hundreds of thousands, the general situation in society will definitely develop for the better.

If you think, "The problems of the world are great. A single person of little significance, no matter how much they try, can have no influence at all in solving them," such thinking is not correct. No matter how great the problems are, if each person from their own side attempts to solve them, [43] then by the power of dependence and the strength of unity, the negative influences can gradually be reduced. Therefore, it is important to work to realize that even as individuals we have the power to unite for the common good. Otherwise, if we become discouraged, it is possible that we will not be able to accomplish the easiest of goals. If we are determined and we work with sustained effort, the most difficult of goals can be reached. Even if we see that our efforts do not immediately produce good results we should persevere. If we work with great confidence in what we are doing but no satisfactory result is forthcoming, our efforts still have purpose, and although they do not produce the desired result, we will see that there is no point in being dismayed, and at least there is no cause for regret. If we give up and never accomplish anything, that is pitiful and nothing more than a cause of regret.

When working together for the common good, to the extent that our minds are peaceful and clear, to that extent we will be able to solve the problems with little difficulty. On the other hand, if we fall under the power of unruly anger, or into the pursuit of profit for ourselves, envy, competitiveness, and so on, the faculty of intelligence that separates good from bad will become blurred, and from within this confusion of mind, under the sway of delusion, all manner of violence can ensue. Therefore, practicing love and compassion with the accompaniment of intelligence is an important responsibility to be carried by all living' beings, especially by those leaders of communities and nations who have the power to create world peace.

[44] If we examine the lack of cooperative effort within communities, it can be seen to be caused by not understanding how we exist in a state of mutual dependence. This can be summed up by looking at insects such as bees or ants, which can be quite stimulating. These insects have to live and work together, and they adhere to a seemingly natural law, the result of which is a very acute sense of communal responsibility and awareness. They lack the restraints of any formalized constitution, a system of law and order, organized control, or religion, and yet instinctively they engage tirelessly in a cooperative effort in order to live together in harmony. We can all see this. Humans not only have laws and norms; they also have an astonishing intelligence and the potential to develop kindness and compassion for each other. Nevertheless, in terms of communal behavior we lag behind these little creatures. That makes me very sad.

We need to develop a profound and vast attitude of responsibility encompassing the whole of humanity, for the sake of all beings, in order to accomplish our and others' goals through cooperation and reliance, without dividing people up by way of gender, ancestry, religion, race, and so on. If we can do this, accompanied by compassionate and loving thoughts, our inner peace, levels of tolerance, and contentment will grow, and I believe that world peace, exemplified by happiness here and now and in the long term, is definitely achievable. I hold this as a source of hope.

To ensure that humanity is endowed with all the potential and benefit that arises from cooperation we must cultivate our understanding of our mutual dependence. Our innate uncontrived kindness and compassion are excellent qualities that arise from familiarization, and are the main foundation for the peace and stability of the world. [45] Both human beings and animals naturally value honesty and affection. If animals, such as dogs or cats, are treated with affection, they respond to those people with affection and loyalty. Conversely, toward people who display threatening gestures or who deceive them, animals will respond with aversion. This we can all see. Humans too need relationships built on sincerity and kindness. Everyone, rich or poor, religious or not, will respond negatively toward those who are insincere and hold wrong attitudes. Not only is it wrong to regard others as unworthy, but we should see them as having the right to be happy, just as we do.

Society and the environment exist in mutual dependence, and there is no better way to build the firm bridges to cultivate the links of that dependence than through thoughts of kindness, compassion, sincerity, and so on.

Whether it is explained through modern science or from the logical arguments of dialecticians, from a personal perspective it is evident that we need to rely upon each other. Moreover, in this day and age of information and increasing global economics, this state of dependency is a reality we cannot fail to accept, even more than before. [46] Looking at things from the perspective of this actuality of interdependence, if we want long-lasting peace and happiness for ourselves, there is no way we cannot think about others. Whatever we have done in the past with an altruistic intention, we can be sure it will indirectly benefit us.

Beginning with the recognition that humanity exists in mutual dependence, if we work to develop our altruism even within a context of mutual competitiveness, then many necessary provisions for a happy life, such as physical and mental well-being, a long life, a sufficient standard of living, good friends, and so on will arise incidentally.

These days many countries are experiencing difficulties arising from a weakening of ethical behavior. This comes from an unawareness of the reality of dependence and is detrimental to the causes for happiness. Some countries may increase security and expand policing in order to ensure the stability of society and look into ways of improving the power of technology for security purposes, but until people are able to successfully transform their own way of thinking, it will be difficult to forcefully control others by external force. Persuading others what is good and bad with kindness and compassion is more effective.

The protagonists here are we humans, and as individuals and communities we have to live in mutual dependence. If future generations are of good character with a strong sense of peace and happiness, it will be of benefit to all. There is a responsibility on each of us to engage in good works designed to bring happiness to oneself, one's community, and humanity as a whole. It is worthwhile to try to understand these things.

CHAPTER 2

Religion

[47] DUE TO THE VARIETY of types and dispositions of living beings many different religions have arisen and blossomed over the past several thousand years. These religions have brought comfort and happiness for thousands of years, and they will continue to have a necessary role in the future.

When we look at the evolution of religious traditions and consider both the types and dispositions of living beings and the changes in the times, we can agree that no one religious tradition has been able to accomplish everything necessary to suit the dispositions of all beings, and moreover, no single religion can substitute for all others. Those who adhere to religious traditions carry a great responsibility toward world peace and toward developing the excellent qualities innate in human beings. Many people regard activities such as praying to God as being the main path to achieving the happiness they long for, but such an activity alone will not fulfill the hopes of human beings. [48] The true potential of religion should reach into the daily lives of individuals and encompass the whole of one's existence.

Whether the majority of people have faith in religion or not, there are still many who show an interest in religious practice these days. Such people will be won over not by obligation or law, but naturally, by seeing the benefits for humanity. Throughout history many religions have spread and prospered, and certainly each religious tradition has had a connection with the cultures and needs of its time and place. Nowadays we have huge growth in material progress and yet at the same time the difficulties that we have to face are increasing. In societies all over the world a special potential for bringing help and happiness to living beings still exists within the major religions.

Different religious traditions hold different philosophical views and tenets, but they all hold the development of genuine kindness and compassion as a central part of their goal. In terms of practice, they all preach the importance of developing the excellent intrinsic human qualities in order to negate the self-centered thoughts that arise from an uncontrolled mind and that lead to all sorts of suffering. They teach techniques for taming the mind in order to turn their followers away from the wrong thinking that brings about the pursuit of improper physical, verbal, and mental deeds, such as killing, stealing, lying, and so on, and which bring them to the right path. With the goal of guiding their followers in becoming good human beings they all teach the excellent and universally valued qualities of human behavior such as love, compassion, altruism, sincerity, nonviolence, patience, contentment, ethical behavior, and so on. [49] Because of this, religions too have the ability to lead beings on the path of happiness. In order to cultivate the thinking that brings about inner peace, which is the foundation of happiness, we who follow a religious tradition must teach within our own traditions those methods to improve, through mindfulness, awareness, and conscientiousness, the mind possessed of essential human values. As we do so, we should not lose sight of the responsibility that our activity is solely for the welfare of others.

INTERFAITH HARMONY

The different religious traditions of the world preach different tenets and have different methods for putting these into practice. What is asserted by one will not necessarily be accepted by another. There are significant differences, many of which are necessary. They arose at different times, in different places, for people of different dispositions. In the Buddhist tradition too different vehicles and tenets arose because of the varying types and dispositions of disciples. If we examine the purpose of these views or what they are establishing, we see they are united in emphasizing kindness and compassion. This shows that once you have found faith in a particular religious tradition, you should put into practice the teachings found in its literature.

[50] If we look at this from a practical perspective the ideas and notions of individuals are limitless. It is very important that religious adherents find ways of bringing their tradition's teachings on an ethical life into daily practices without quarreling with members of other traditions simply on the basis of a few differences in their doctrine or methodology. If we religious people who hold to distinct tenets cannot work together willingly, and precipitate argument and trouble, our communal relations will inevitably be damaged. In today's troubled world it is increasingly important to be broad-minded and to respect other customs and religions.

It is not enough just to read the literature of other religious traditions. We must engage in exchanges and discussions with practitioners of other religions in order to fully appreciate the qualities of these traditions. Doing so will increase our respect for them. There is great benefit in developing such a pure perception of other customs, cultures, and, particularly, religions through worthwhile and meaningful exchange. The people of the world, their mental makeup, their attitudes arising out of differing cognitive faculties, their inclinations, desires, needs, and so on, are many and diverse. Based on that fact, approaches to peace and happiness must also be diverse. This is without doubt essential for strengthening the well-being and prosperity of the world. The more religious traditions there are, the more means there are for fulfilling the hopes of the various peoples of the world. On that basis all religions of the world share this fundamental value, even as it must be said that no one religion can serve for all.

[51] If all religions were to take on the responsibility of ensuring the growth of happiness among humanity, the communal effort of coming together for the good of humanity would be accomplished with little difficulty. This is a worthy goal, but it should be understood that this cannot be achieved in a short time. It is a long-term goal.

Religious practitioners who share a concern for world peace have two fundamental responsibilities to the global community. One is to work to build harmonious relationships between religious communities by increasing mutual understanding and learning the essential messages of each tradition. The second responsibility is to promote fundamental religious values that inspire followers to work for the general good. With these two approaches, it will be possible through individual and communal efforts to accumulate the provisions necessary for religion to promote peace throughout the world.

In this changing modern world, progressive attempts to promote nonsectarian religious views are worthy. There are those who are making systematic efforts toward eradicating religious traditions, but there remain huge numbers of people with faith in their particular religion. Religious attitudes can even be seen in regimes that do not otherwise accept religion, which shows the power of religion. There is no respect for national boundaries within religious traditions. If any kind of religion is beneficial to any group of people, it is perfectly acceptable to make use of it and practice it. [52] For people to choose the religious practice they are attracted to is very important. However, once a religious path is chosen it is not necessary to cast out other traditions from one's community with the excuse that they can no longer be accepted. Instead, with cordiality and friendliness we should allow other religious followers to remain beside us.

We should always bear in mind that aiming in every way possible to bring happiness and benefit to others lies at the very heart of religion. We should examine our attitudes toward others, and if we slide into a wrong attitude, we should remedy it at once. These two activities are essential.

A cause of religious dissension in this world is the notions of there being one single faith, one true religion, one truth only, and one goal above all others. It is difficult to say that these notions can be accepted. From the perspective of a single individual, it is important that these concepts are applied to their own particular religion. Even on the basis of being a Buddhist, it is taught that we should go for refuge to the Buddhist teachings without acknowledging any other refuge. Similarly, just as it is necessary for a Buddhist to have single-pointed faith in the Buddha's doctrine, followers of other traditions should have a similar single-pointed faith in their own religion.

However, to use that as a reason to criticize other religions is very wrong. Each follower should have strong faith in their own tradition, while at the same time accepting the existence of other religions in the community and respecting them as an essential part of humanity.

[53] It is harmful and outdated to seek to promote a religion with an attitude that it is the sole religion and the sole truth, and to proclaim that others must also follow this line. In the past, societies did not have such close mutual relationships, and they lived in their own fairly isolated localities in the world. In such environments it was perfectly acceptable to promote their own religious traditions. In old Tibet too, it was acceptable to promote Buddhism alone. However, these days nations are linked to each other, and travel between them is so much easier. The old ways have been completely transformed. There is no way that the structures of societies in the past can remain as they were. Therefore, now the term "a small world" is universally used. In large cities the established customs of many peoples and any number of religious traditions can be found. In a land where the ancestral religion is widespread, it is not right to proselytize a new religious tradition. Whatever countries I go to, I always emphasize to my audience how it

is fitting to continue studying and training in the religious traditions established by their ancestors. Even to those who have an interest in Buddhism, I stress that it is not right for them to change their religion without significant consideration.

I once met some Korean Christians who were actively proselytizing Christianity in Mongolia. I told them that since Mongolia was a Buddhist country, they would not find their efforts very effective. [54] Some people are put off by a particular organization or an individual teacher of a religious tradition, and they see this as a fault of the religion. This is a big mistake. There are those who teach religion incorrectly, who corrupt their tradition, who wear the mask of religion and go out in search of money, who manipulate religion to accomplish their own ambition in politics, and so on. These are not the faults of the religion, but of those people assuming the role of religious followers. It is important to distinguish the two.

NO RELIGION IS "THE BEST"

The various views and philosophies of religious traditions cannot be arbitrarily divided up into good and bad. Good should be understood as that which is beneficial. Beneficial and nonbeneficial should be understood as that which is fitting and not fitting, appropriate and inappropriate. Whenever discussions come up on the topic of good and bad religions, I always say that I cannot make judgments. This is because religion is like medicine. Medicine must benefit the patient. Sometimes an illness can be treated with just one small pill. Other illnesses require a course of expensive medication. Therefore, whatever medicine is beneficial for a specific illness, that is the medicine considered to be the best in that situation. Medicine is not determined to be good or bad by way of its price or popular opinion. The dispositions of humans are varied, and whatever religious practice is suitable for a given individual is the best for that person. For someone like me,

Buddhism is the most suitable and therefore the best religious practice, but I never say that it is best for everyone. [55]

Those who believe in God will be able to put their faith in the presentation of a world and its inhabitants created by God. For such people it is right that a religion based upon the tenets of a creator deity is taught to them. If they respect and practice God's precepts of love, compassion, and tolerance it will be unproblematic and very helpful for them, whereas they might find concepts such as past and future lives, karma, and so on, somewhat troublesome. I like to think that those who look for scientific explanations for phenomena and are disposed toward analysis will not so easily dismiss these and other Buddhist concepts. Such people might find it troubling to consider that if the world and all things in it was created by God, then wars and other troubles were also created by him, and even our mental afflictions were his creation. Sometimes I joke that if God has created all this trouble on earth, and is responsible for all this unmanageable hardship, then this God is not one of compassion. Moreover, maybe there is a risk that God himself will say, "I did not think that such troubles would occur." Maybe he will think that his creation was excessive!

It can be said that Buddhism is one of the most vast and profound religions. This is attested to by the fact that although these days many religions are facing a serious challenge from science, [56] to Buddhism—specifically to the tenets and philosophy of the Nalanda tradition—science is becoming a friend rather than a challenge.

This can be illustrated by examining Buddhist training. According to Buddhism, feelings and emotions, the world, its inhabitants, and so on, all arise in dependence upon their own individual causes and conditions. Therefore, happiness and suffering also have their own causes and conditions. Examining those causes and correctly identifying them is the method to achieve happiness and eliminate suffering. The Buddha taught in great depth and detail ways to identify the proper cognitive modes to cultivate and improve these states of mind. These teachings are a foundation of all facets of society, from our personal life to the economy, administration, religion, politics, law, and so on. These abundant and freely available teachings, which not only serve to bring happiness in the long term but are beneficial even for this short life, can be adopted by everyone—individually and communally—regardless of whether they believe in future lives, are religious persons, or are followers of other religions. Relying upon these practices will bring great courage, a strong resilience in the face of fear and a broken spirit. This is attested to by the experience of many individuals.

If we live as good human beings, we will have rapport with others and have many friends. Our lives will be content and those around us will feel happy. [57] If we are not good people, we will have few friends, no rapport with anyone, and will be alone. Our lives will be spent in the dark cave of suffering, and those around us will also suffer.

Our behavior as an individual influences others. Within a community the better the conduct, the happier that community is. The worse the conduct, the more trouble and the less peace and stability there will be.

FAITH BASED ON REASON

There are different kinds of religious faith. In Buddhism for example, the proper kind of faith is not blind faith, but faith based on intelligence. The Buddhist way to understand something is through an investigation of its whole structure, regardless of how complex it is. After a minimum of one or two years of detailed discussion, eradication of doubt, and serious study, if one gains an understanding of these vast tenets of Buddhism, then when the qualities of the Buddha—the ultimate attainment in Buddhism—are being explained, it will be possible to see how such an inconceivable state can be developed in one's own being. In dependence upon this fundamental state of existence, we become convinced through reasoning that by engaging in the relevant practices on the path and perfecting the accumulated experiences, we will be able to produce such exalted qualities. [58] The result of that conviction is an enthusiasm that will allow us to persevere year after year in the methods of improving our mind. This transformation of our attitudes will bring huge benefits for ourselves and others.

Religious faith is a mental attitude that arises subsequently and acts as a condition for nurturing the innate seeds of love and compassion—the foundation of ethical behavior—and should be of great benefit, including that of bringing happiness to everyday life. Following this or that religion by way of lip service does not make one a religious person. Being a religious person depends upon assuming a personal sense of responsibility.

THE ESSENCE OF RELIGION

All religious traditions in this world have the capability to be of service in the sense of developing and increasing the virtuous thoughts of human beings. However, if there is no interest in putting into daily practice the teachings and instructions of these traditions, then nothing will bring about these results. Many people consider religion to be old-fashioned and outdated. Some groups of religious followers assume a study of their religion with great intensity, but with narrow-minded and extreme attitudes, these obstinate and hard-headed people become fundamentalists, adopting the attitude that their views have supremacy over all others. Such people have contempt for other religions and philosophies and adopt views that descend into violence. Although all kinds of thought and actions surface that are in complete contradiction to religion, these people are deceived by a strong adherence to it being their tradition, and are unable to face up to the realities of life and everyday hardships in society. This is an obstacle to the beneficial potential of religion.

[59] Many in Tibetan religious communities lack awareness of the

proper approach to religion and its principles. In the performance of rituals, special importance is often erroneously given to the elaboration of external details, thereby "obscuring the fruit with leaves." This is self-deception, and is like discarding the root and searching for the branches. The effect of this is that the influence of religion and its ability to benefit people is weakened. Regardless of time and place, our religion is necessary. It is crucial that we distinguish the essential teachings of a religion from the cultures that have developed over many centuries. We should hold the essence of the teachings as the most important. This is very important. Those who practice a religious tradition must make well-informed choices that accord with necessity and the situation they are in.

In many places the thoughts and deeds of kindness and compassion for others—the very essence of religion—has been lost. There are Christians, for example, who merely go to church on Sundays, and Muslims who only make prayers and prostrations five times a day. Among Buddhists too there are those for whom practice means performing rituals of daily recitations with eyebrows raised, reading scriptures, making offerings to statues, chanting prayers, reciting mantras with rosary in hand, making regular and additional long-life prayers, and so on. At such times their eyes may be closed in apparent devotion, but when these people come into contact with certain external circumstances, coarse mental afflictions such as pride and anger rise immediately. [60] During both recitations and in daily life a detailed examination of the mind and the imprints of love and compassion are lacking. These Buddhists never go beyond thought and deed aimed at victory for self and defeat for others. This is an indication that the religion has not blended with the mind, and in the practice of religion that is a great mistake.

When we say, "religious practice," it does not refer to pursuing the established norm in the sense of following customs and traditions almost to the point of regarding prostration, offerings, and so on as being of paramount importance. It is not these external activities, but the teachings and instructions of the religion that should become part of our daily life. There will be no improvement to the mind by merely following the spiritual practice of outer behavior. Deity meditation, mantra recitation, practices involving the inner channels, winds, and vital points, the blazing of the inner heat, consciousness transference, and other tantric practices can all be found in non-Buddhist traditions. However, the basis of Buddhism is kindness, compassion, and bodhicitta together with meditation on the view of emptiness, and it is on that foundation that these attainments should be developed.

Meditators who practice a genuine Buddhism enter a meditation session without the need for rosaries. They first examine their minds to cut away mistaken concepts. They then absorb themselves in meditation on the main practice of training according to the common and exclusive paths.[27] This is the way of training through the sequence of learning, contemplation, and meditation. Those who do not know the points of practice will perfunctorily perform a ritual or repeat mantras without any meditation. This is an inadequate way to practice the Dharma.

In the past, there was no organized system of Buddhist studies that was common to the Tibetan monastic and lay communities. [61] This sorry state of affairs meant that the ordinary man and woman had little understanding of the topics of Buddhism. This posed a serious deficiency for lay practitioners.

Whatever hardships we face, we all possess the Sugata essence,[28] and we should know, therefore, that ultimately the attainment of buddhahood is a certainty. This should give us the confidence that all difficulties can be overcome. Buddhists often pray with great devotion whenever some unwanted suffering arises, saying, "I go for refuge. Three Jewels, please hear me. May this suffering disappear." But it is unlikely that the hardship will just vanish. Those who lack faith might, as a result, rebuke the Three Jewels, saying, "I prayed to the Three Jewels, but they were of no help."

Blind faith is the idea that making prayers is sufficient to produce a result, that the Buddha will simply lead us with his compassion.

The statement of the Buddha, "We ourselves are our own protectors," is of great import. Once, in the city of Patna, in the Indian state of Bihar, I attended the consecration of an important new Buddhist temple that had been built. At the opening ceremony the Bihar chief minister gave a speech in which he said he had great hopes that by the compassionate blessings of the Bhagavan Buddha, Bihar would prosper. I replied that if the Buddha was able to bring prosperity to Bihar by way of his blessings, he would have done so by now. Instead, the blessings of the Buddha must come through the hand of the chief minister! There is no other route to prosperity. [62]

Faith alone will not bring about results. The reality is that a method is required. What kind of method? What we need is the actual object of refuge—the Jewel of the Dharma[29]—as a quality of the mind. This is the insight that brings about transformation. If no change is brought to the mind, there is no refuge.

Therefore, we should understand that the way that the Buddha Dharma eradicates suffering and creates happiness is solely by way of a causal process in which we ourselves bring about a transformation of our minds. Some time ago an elderly man who had arrived from Tibet—well versed in Tibetan written language—received the Kālacakra empowerment in Bodhgaya. Later, during the spring teachings in Dharamsala, he listened to a commentary on Śāntideva's *Engaging in Bodhisattva Deeds*. Afterward he said, "Although the *Kālacakra Tantra* is very special and a huge blessing, having received teachings on *Engaging in Bodhisattva Deeds*, I now know the true teachings of the Buddha. I am so happy. This is so beneficial for this and future lives. Previously when I was in Tibet, I regarded Buddhist practice to be rituals, doing prostrations, making offerings, and the like. That is not so. Genuine Buddhist practice is transforming the mind, developing love, compassion, and bodhicitta, and meditating on emptiness."

This is a perfect description and is the kind of practice we should follow. About fifteen or twenty people from various places in Tibet have requested that in the future I give the Kālacakra empowerment in Tibet. Not a single one asked me to give teachings on *Engaging in Bodhisattva Deeds*. In general, for Tibetans to hold that empowerments are special is simply a confused notion. [63] Mostly, they take no interest in talks and discussions about Buddhism, or in any methods of profound study. Moreover, when Buddhist teachings and explanations are being given, they are not inspired and often appear unenthusiastic. This is wrong.

I always say to Buddhists of the Himalayan tradition that Buddhism means to make full use of the human intellect in order to know a way of practice that will benefit the mind, and that just saying "I go for refuge" is not enough. Even if you have extraordinary faith in the Dharma, there is the risk that when you look for what it actually is you will find nothing. This I say until it annoys them!

Signs of attainment displayed by Buddhist practitioners who gain high realization from their practice, such as flying through the sky, traveling underground, and so on—like those described in fables from the past—and which everyone agrees could be clearly seen and were verifiable—are not seen among Buddhist practitioners these days. However, there are those who have understood the Dharma of the Buddha and found faith in it. These people are broad-minded, with a good and kind attitude. They are of benefit to others in this life, while happy in themselves, and live a good life in a state of contentment. Finally, when they face death, they are able to peacefully bring their life to a close. This illustrates a healthy and fitting achievement of study, contemplation, and meditation, together with a confidence of understanding. We clearly see examples of these people and continue to see them. From this we can infer that when anyone practices sincerely, their mental condition will improve. It is not that difficult to find conviction in moving through the stages of the path and the levels of attainment.

[64] The most important responsibility of those who practice any religious tradition is to analyze the thoughts and actions of body, speech, and mind, and transform them to become virtuous and ethical. If you are merely learned in the tenets, meditations, and ethical behavior of your religion, but are unable to implement its practices and tame your mind, not only is that a big mistake, but there is a real risk that you will use the religion to exploit others and deceive them, thereby causing great harm to society. For everyone who follows a religion, examining their minds and their actions in this way should be their first priority.

RELIGION IN SOCIETY

There are those who say that religion is an impediment to progress in society. To understand why some might say this, we should first understand that we can conceive of two ways of fulfilling the desires and aims of human beings: through a culture in which religion and the secular are combined, and one in which there is only secular thinking. The first can be considered by looking at the Buddhist perspective in terms of the present life and future lives. It is important to contemplate ways to accomplish long-term and long-lasting goals. This life is just a life of evident experience, whereas in future lives there are many things we cannot see. Comparing what we can and cannot see, that which is unseen entails a greater responsibility for us. Therefore, for someone who is a genuine practitioner of Buddhism, what happens in this life is not so significant, whereas the concerns of future lives will be given greater significance. Because of that some Buddhists might appear to remain unmoved by the developments and progress of this life. [65] This could possibly contribute to the view that religion hampers the progress of society.

However, the following should be considered. The Buddha said that there were four excellences for the fulfillment of our desires: religion, wealth, pleasure, and liberation. Temporary happiness, in the form of sensory pleasures, is an excellence found in a high rebirth, while ultimate happiness is the excellence of freedom from suffering. The causes needed to fulfill the excellence of a good rebirth are wealth and possessions. The cause needed to bring about the ultimate and permanent freedom is religious practice, as epitomized by the three trainings.[30] Therefore, when practicing Buddhism, the injunction "Give up this life" should be understood as meaning not to become one-sidedly attached to this life alone. It does not mean that we should abandon the excellences of this life.

Although a good rebirth—epitomized by the human form—only constitutes a temporary happiness, it is set forth as something to be achieved. This is because the attainment of the permanent happiness of liberation is gained by way of a good rebirth. Therefore, the high rebirth of a human form together with its associated excellences are important goals as the foundation of liberation.

We speak of the characteristics of a good human rebirth as "the eight ripened qualities."[31] The first two are (1) power and influence, and (2) renown and prestige. These do not refer to power in the ordinary sense, but to the power or ability to be of benefit to others. This is because in order to be of benefit to others it is necessary to be able to attract and captivate the minds of others. For this we need (3) a good complexion—that is, a beautiful form. [66] The presence of this feature means that when seeing such people there is nothing at all unpleasant about their appearance, and they are captivatingly attractive. This quality is described in the teachings on the signs and marks of an enlightened being.[32] It is not to be understood as simply making one-self look beautiful.[33]

(4) Being capable. Here "capable" in Sanskrit is *puruṣa*, which is generally translated as "male" but need not be. It refers to having a strong and fit body or possessing a human form that is able to accomplish great activities. (5) Possessing strength refers to having the strength of faith, effort, mindfulness, concentration, and wisdom—the five strengths listed in the thirty-seven facets of enlightenment.[34] Alternatively, they refer to the five strengths taught in the seven-point mind-training literature:[35] the strength of intention, habituation, eradicating, the white seed, and the strength of prayer.

(6) The perfect status. This refers not only to those groups usually considered to be of high status or class; it can also be understood as referring to the noble ārya class. It includes those whose bodhisattva status has awoken or those who possess the status of being disposed toward training in the deeds of the bodhisattvas for the sake of others. (7) Of trustworthy speech, which means that by speaking truthfully and honestly, they are trusted by everyone. (8) Having a long life, which is necessary in order to be able to work for others for a long time.

Several excellences of a good rebirth have also been taught. They are qualities that have ripened from virtuous deeds accumulated in the past and are to be sought after.

The Buddha said that ordained monastics must avoid the extreme of sensory pleasure and the extreme of austerity and hardship in their lifestyles. The first of these—excessive indulgence in sensory pleasures—can become a cause for the weakening of one's merit[36] and therefore should be abandoned. This applies not only to male and female monastics but to anyone who practices the Dharma. Of course, we have the right to enjoy our individual and necessary provisions of life, but the rich and the poor are alike in the size of their stomachs. Therefore, these things should be enjoyed in moderation. [67] Otherwise, indulging without contentment in the pleasures of food, clothing, home, and so on is the mistake of never being satisfied, and a basis for the growth of unhappiness. It is important that we lessen our desires and be content.

The extreme of austerity and hardship is pursued by some in the Hindu traditions who claim that unvirtuous deeds and obstructions will be cleansed by severe ascetic practices. However, the Buddha said that such purification is accomplished by the mind and not by physical torment. This can also be understood through reasoning.

Whatever the case may be, if from our own side we know how to live with a moderate lifestyle without falling to these two extremes, it can only be for the good. Adhering to Buddhist practices such as sincerity, altruism, compassion, observance of the law of cause and effect, having a sense of responsibility, and so on, in a life with few desires and contentment, can become a major preventative force, even against corruption and degeneration.

The responsibility for improving our well-being through better living conditions, a good economy, and material development lies with us. Knowing this, it becomes very important to work by all means possible to create the right conditions for the welfare of world communities and the environment. This is an altruistic undertaking; it is the action of the powerful bodhisattva. Because religion shows various ways to value improvements in society and individuals, it can be seen that instead of hindering the improvement of the country, it is actually a stimulus and a powerful service that benefits the world and its inhabitants.

[68] The reasons why some see religion as being an impediment to the improvement of life and human progress can be explained with an example. In 1954, while visiting China, I spent about four months in Beijing, where I met the Chinese leader Mao Zedong many times. At that time, I regarded him as a brave revolutionary, and I admired him as a powerful spokesman, concerned not only for the welfare of the Chinese people and the Chinese working classes in particular,

but of all the working classes of the world. In 1955, as I was about to return to Tibet, I met him for the final time. At that meeting he gave me some detailed and important advice on how to conduct affairs in Tibet in the future. At the end he said, "Your mind is well disposed toward science. Having an interest in science is very good. But religion is poison. One reason is because it greatly harms the growth of the human race. Another reason is that it impedes any improvement in this life."

It seems that the first of these—that religion harms the growth of the human race—is not totally without foundation. We can look at our own history for example. In the past, during the time of the three ancestral emperors[37] the population of Tibet was thirty million. Later, during the time of Atiśa's disciple Dromtönpa (1005–65) when the "great census" was conducted, the population was about six million, four hundred thousand. It is not certain whether the area covered by the census was just the central region of Ütsang or if it included the eastern regions Kham and Amdo, but this was the figure mentioned. [69] After that, during the time of the Sakya rule,[38] it was said to be about six million. Whatever the case, if we take the population of Central Tibet, Kham, and Amdo to be ten million at that time, the present population is six million—not more than seven at least.[39] Therefore, the population has decreased by about three million. This decrease is evident from historical documents and can be inferred from the many ancient ruins and empty fields that can be seen everywhere in Tibet. One cause of this decline is probably the high number of men and women who entered the monastic life. Also, a poor system of health care, epidemics, and so on definitely contributed to the population decline.

On this point, I usually say the following. Whether we Tibetans are in Tibet, India, or elsewhere, we have to maintain a virtuous community of monastics. We are happy when the numbers are high and work to ensure that the monastic community is of good quality, which is a cause for rejoicing. Some might argue that we must ever increase the number of monks and nuns, without paying much attention to the quality of those monastics. However, I do not see any need for having many people living in celibacy yet as though they were householders, without any of the higher qualities of being able to adhere to the doctrine and insight through teaching and practice. When monasteries and labrangs are at fault in the way they conduct themselves they will fail to provide proper Dharma and monastic discipline. We will have let slip the "mooring rope" we held on to since the times of our great forefathers and the necessary connection to the Buddha's teaching will be lost.[40]

[70] The statement "Religion is poison" was uttered not only by Mao Zedong but also by Karl Marx before him. Marx mainly had Christianity in mind, but there are plenty of other examples of those using religion to take advantage of people. Such exploitation continues today. Anyone who genuinely practices religion will be motivated to help others and will therefore never exploit others in the name of their religion.

It is true that the practices of some religious groups are backward-looking, bringing sadness and despair to many people. However, to say that all religion hinders progress is simply the talk of those who do not understand the nature of religion. By first understanding a religious tradition thoroughly and then presenting sound arguments backed by reason in order to present a critique, one can bring about a discussion in which "scholars are beautiful in the presence of scholars." Pointing out faults with spurious reasoning and no knowledge of the religion is just senseless and incoherent talk. How can it carry any weight?

If the essential teachings of religions are not properly practiced, it brings great harm not only to the individual practitioner but to the community and the country. Values such as kindness, compassion, honesty, and contentment are the very foundation of all happiness in any land, no matter the type of society or individual. Without kindness and compassion there can be no way to bring happiness to self and others, and the community will experience nothing but trouble.

As stated above, such happiness is not brought about by external means. It must be achieved within the mind. [71] Those who are affluent through conducive circumstances have quite a lot of power in society because of their wealth. However, I have often met such people who said they were not at all happy. Some even commit suicide. This comes from not knowing where to search for happiness. We can see this even in the capitalist system. For example, the founding fathers of America were very profound in their thinking. They laid a democratic system that was based on the human rights of liberty and equal opportunity under the law. However, when it comes to putting that into practice, society remains divided; the affluent have little concern for the poor, and there are serious inequalities in terms of education, race, and so on. Washington is the capital of the most powerful country in the world—where human consumption is at its highest—and yet the gap between rich and poor in that city is huge.

In India too, in Delhi, Mumbai, Bengaluru, Kolkata, and elsewhere, there are many wealthy people who own great houses and expensive restaurants, and at the same time, in the same neighborhood, there are many penniless people searching every day for food. [72] Such people are everywhere in developing countries. Equal rights are enshrined in the law of these countries, and governments list detailed policies for protecting the poor, but they are not implemented. The main reason for that is a lack of compassion in the minds of those individuals who hold power. They think primarily of their own happiness and their own pleasure. They have little empathy for others, often neglecting, exploiting, and using others for their own benefit. Under such a situation these hardships can never be alleviated.

THE RESPONSIBILITY OF SOCIETY

Not harming by way of thought and deed is not just a necessary condition for the happiness of the individual. It is the foundation of wellbeing throughout the world. For example, two people following a conduct of not harming each other will not make a huge contribution toward world peace. However, a sizeable percentage of a population doing the same would deliver a correspondingly significant result. Therefore, it can be seen that if a large number of people were to follow the virtuous conduct of not harming, the potential for society to be blessed with happiness would be huge. Ever since the end of the Cold War of the last century, I have had great hopes that this planet has finally begun to leave behind the ways of violence and to become a world of peace, and that the whole population of the earth can come to live in unity. I have had opportunities to encourage that.

[73] In Europe the influential effects of fostering a great spirit of cooperation have brought about speedy progress toward democratic freedoms and unity there. I have faith that this will serve as an example, even the standard, for bringing about unity, democracy, shared economic progress, equal benefits, and so on throughout the world. I rejoice with delight and emotion at the impact of this worthy transformation of Europe, and I see it as the valuable and wonderful legacy of the deep intelligence and efforts of the authorities and the people. I have great hopes that such a spirit of unity can be fostered in Eastern Europe, and that the former member countries of the USSR will also be able to join the European Union.

Furthermore, the great regions of this world such as the Americas, Africa, the Arab countries of the Middle East, Asia, and others possess the potential for an actual union. Take Asia for example. Some time ago the great Indian acharya Vinoba Bhave (1895–1982) formulated a plan of cooperation between India and three countries he labeled

"ABC" (Afghanistan, Burma, and Ceylon), and urged the formation of an Asian Union.

[74] Now, at the beginning of the twenty-first century, most people in the world have become averse to war and conflict and instead hold hopes for unity, democracy, and the equal distribution of wealth. On this planet that sustains us, the level of interdependence that our living conditions and welfare demand—whether as individuals or communities—is becoming greater than before. This is the trend of the times. In that sense, it is not possible that these efforts made for greater unity will remain an empty hope. Although there are many difficulties in having to deal with the threat of nuclear war, the gap between rich and poor, the damage to the environment, the problem of terrorism, economic competitiveness, the decline in human behavior, and all the other evident changes that have occurred in the world, nevertheless in this twenty-first century the situation is better than that of the last century, and it possesses the precious potential of even greater hopes for the future. In order to actually build a century of lasting peace on our earth, it is the responsibility of us all to perceive the world as one large family and transform the outdated views that concentrate on "victory for self, defeat for others" through atomic weapons, military force, national boundaries, and so forth.

[75] The twentieth century was the most eventful in recent history. If we think about the First and Second World Wars, the internal conflicts in China and Russia, the wars in Korea and Vietnam, the amount of killing and bloodshed in that century was exceptional. Many millions lost their lives. Moreover, the atomic bomb was invented and used over Japan twice. Those two explosions brought about unimaginable destruction in which upward of two hundred thousand people were killed. Because of the excessive number of wars and conflicts in that century, many people have developed an interest in nonviolence and world peace.

As a result of the experiences of the twentieth century, a fundamentally new way of thinking could appear, which asks, "What is truth? How was that just? What is right for humanity?" A special era of clear desires, characterized by strong and resolute aspirations for independence, democracy, and self-determination, has arisen in the people of various countries. Eastern Europe and Mongolia had labored under Communist rule for more than seventy years, and now the wall that divided Berlin is gone, which is an extraordinary change in the world.

In Mongolia, the Baltic countries, and Bulgaria, I saw people—millions of whom had lacked freedom for many decades—now enjoying the happy fruits of independence. It was truly admirable. [76] This proves that although it might take a long time and involve great hardship, the wishes of the people, their aspirations for freedom, can be realized. That such a victory was achieved not through violent means is even more a cause for rejoicing. This is an important point.

There are those who, longing to achieve their unrealized desires, intensify their thoughts and deeds of victory for self and defeat for others. With desire and aversion they generate mutual hostility that becomes a cause for conflict and trouble. Such troubles result from a lack of the essential qualities of compassion and love—the fundamental nature of human beings—and its supports of patience and contentment.

Throughout history dreadful situations have occurred through the name of religion. These days too there are conflicts and bitter divisions in society that stem from religion. These are completely inappropriate and totally contradictory to religious teachings. To be able to live a trouble-free life of peace and happiness is an aim shared equally by everyone. Therefore, there is sufficient opportunity, reason, and basis for developing interfaith harmony and a pure view, which would benefit both the individual and society. This is something we should cherish.

I do not think that these days anger has increased in the minds of human beings. I believe that it is the expression of anger, made more evident by way of the vast armory of dreadful weapons existing now, that has fundamentally increased. [77] In our time we have been witnesses to a tragic history of mass killing by poison and weapons. Everyone, especially religious practitioners, should not forget that. It is of the greatest importance that the powers of the various religions come together and initiate a movement designed to protect us from the dangers of war. This is a very necessary responsibility.

Human life is the most important innate, sovereign right. No human being wants suffering and grief. It is the universal responsibility of the international community to be concerned about the trampling of the rights of people through war and violence. These situations are not those of one particular nation alone; we should concern ourselves with alleviating the sufferings of all our brother and sister human beings, wherever they are. This is a fundamental point.

Military might by its very nature poses the greatest opposition to human rights, and is the main backing for violent tyrants in their murderous pursuits. We should never think beforehand that a particular war is going to produce a good result. Developing a military force in order to keep the peace is only a temporary measure. In reality it is like a bomb waiting to explode.

[78] The greatest danger and fear that human life faces—in fact the greatest danger to all life on this planet—is that of nuclear annihilation. I passionately appeal to the leaders of those nations who possess the might of nuclear weapons in whose hands the future of the world lies, to arms manufacturers, and to all those who hold influence in such matters to dismantle all nuclear weapons and render them nonexistent.

If a nuclear war occurs, the only result is that all beings will die. It is clear that no one could possibly emerge victorious. In that sense, such conduct would be inhumane. Just to think about such merciless destruction brings nothing but fear, and so it is completely right that we should eliminate the causes of our own destruction. Therefore, now, when time and conditions are ripe, we must find a way to free ourselves from this danger. This makes perfect sense.

Generally speaking, in the past, aims were achieved through war and countries gained their freedom. However, not all problems can be completely solved through war. We can all see how acts of violence are met with acts of revenge and will never bring peace. This is inevitable. The power of military force is just a temporary force. It can never destroy the power of truth and right. Knowing this, it is vital that all religious traditions unite against the view that problems can be solved by force. It is not enough just to point out its faults from time to time; we must work to actually implement a method to put an end to military violence. [79] One fundamental way to do that would be to make these weapons nonexistent.

It is clear that those who see a need for these armaments and encourage their production do so because of a wrong attitude and a fundamental hostility toward others, fostered by a strong attachment to their own side. The production of weapons and the preparation for war in reality is preparation for killing people. Anger is an enemy to everyone, and weapons are likewise enemies to everyone. Therefore, it is a particular concern and necessary responsibility of those that follow religious traditions to look into the dangers posed to peace and happiness by the use of these weapons, and the chasm between gloating victory and humiliating defeat.

Some weapons, such as guns, may be beautiful to look at and employ the most up-to-date technological features to accomplish their purpose, but we should recognize that their real use is for taking the lives of living beings.

Some people hold the view that Westerners are fearful of death[41] and that Easterners do not have such a fear. It is difficult to say either way, but many Easterners if they inadvertently kill an insect while walking are in fact filled with remorse. When I lived in Tibet and news came that someone had been murdered, everyone was shocked. Such news was so hard to believe. Looking at these examples it seems that Easterners are more fearful of death than Westerners. However, in both Eastern and Western monarchies, those members of royalty who have the experience of having trained in the armed and naval forces of their countries are held in high regard by the people. [80] There are those countries who spend vast amounts on developing their military strength, while several countries engage in the export of huge quantities of arms. In that sense, it is not possible to determine if Westerners are fearful of death or not.

War and military force are perhaps the greatest source of physical harm and damage in the world. However, soldiers are considered to be in compliance with the law, and the killing of an enemy is not regarded as being a crime of murder. People boast about such acts as being courageous, skillful achievements. Such attitudes come from a wrong way of thinking. In reality, such acts are nothing more than brutal and tragic, bringers of misery. No matter how much we label them as acts of self-protection, they are grave deeds that deprive others of their lives, and religious practitioners cannot just ignore them.

In the way that it spreads, war is like fire. We human beings, living our lives, are like the fuel for that fire. Wars these days are fought by fire in its many different forms but the reality is that we fuel-like human beings are not regarded as being consumed by their flames. Reinforcing an army in order to increase military strength is like throwing living soldiers into a pit of fire. However, because of our perspective we do not think of the suffering of individual soldiers. No soldier wants to be injured or killed, and their relatives and loved ones do not want it either. [81] If an ordinary soldier is killed, it plunges their relatives, and even the people and leaders of that country, into grief and sadness. Seeing this, we should "know the path is wrong and correct it." Yet under the sway of confusion we do not think about the harm it brings for ourselves both now and in the future. We are "sighted people jumping off cliffs."

Nations pour vast sums of money into their armed forces to boost security and defense. It can be understood how that money could provide for extraordinary and significant projects, such as those in the fields of health, education, and so on, for the various inhabitants and environments of this world. Therefore, if the power of religious cooperation could steer matters in such a new and worthwhile direction, we would definitely gain the needed provision for a settled peace and solid progress within the international environment.

Many years ago, when I expressed my hopes that one day this earth of ours would become a world free of weapons, many people, including close friends, remarked that this was an excellent but empty hope. However, some time ago the American president George H. W. Bush and Mikhail Gorbachev, the leader of the Soviet Union, made the historic declaration that they were working toward a time when the world would be free of nuclear weapons. I praised this highly. This new direction gave me support that my hopes could eventually be realized. [82] Of course, such a responsibility will be beset by difficulties and many obstacles, but we should all generate strength of mind and strive as best we can to be of service for such a worthwhile goal yearned for by all humanity.

BELIEVERS AND NONBELIEVERS

When it comes to religion, there are believers, nonbelievers, and those who are indifferent. What are the differences in happiness for these three?

The human population of the world will soon reach eight billion. Concerning the number of believers belonging to the larger world religions, one estimation states that Christianity has 2.4 billion followers, Islam has 1.8 billion, and Hinduism has 1.2 billion.[42]

[85] Those who do not believe in religion and protest against it include Communists, a section of the scientific community, and those

who dislike of the activities of some religious groups. For such people to achieve happiness and alleviate suffering, religion will be of no help. Moreover, they regard religion as ruinous and a cause of problems. In order to arouse opposition and resentment they say such things as "religion is poison."

The third group—those who are indifferent to religion—mostly see religion as unimportant and unnecessary. [86] They are concerned just with the pursuit of their own happiness and can be considered as having no profound spiritual interests.

These three groups are alike in not wanting suffering and wanting happiness. Those who practice a religion and those who oppose religion both seek to be happy and to avoid suffering. If we honestly examine which of these two groups has the greater happiness and the greater suffering, generally speaking, those who have religious faith and who properly practice the teachings are more at peace and have happier lives, whereas those who have abandoned religion find it difficult to achieve genuine happiness simply through the extent of their mental capacity.

Similarly, there are many people who are not motivated by religious faith nor by an active opposition to religion, but who do not understand the nature of religion, and consequently see it as an obstacle— pointing out faults as they see them and making superficial comments about religion. To them I say, first, with an open mind, examine the religion to find out what its teachings are, and with that knowledge, make use of the opportunity to gain some experience. After that, if you then can provide sound reasons why a religion has nothing good about it, it is perfectly acceptable to criticize it. Otherwise, without real knowledge and experience criticism is nothing but meaningless talk. Rejecting or ignoring good advice simply because it comes from a religious tradition is harmful to self and others and nothing but a great loss.

[87] To make life meaningful we should make full use of our human

intellect and special human abilities. If you are happier without religion, then it is perfectly acceptable not to follow a religion. There is nothing wrong at all in having no faith in religion. However, you should be someone with a good mind.

Because of the variety of dispositions and types among humans, not only do people have the right to practice religion, they have the right to regard religion as a mistake and to criticize it. It is not right to regard such people as having wrong views and to ostracize them. Human beings on this planet are as one, living side by side in one global family. Therefore, it is important to get along with each other. If proper attitudes of kindness and compassion exist, there is no need for a connection with a particular religious faith. Many of the crises that occur in our society can be solved by relying upon these innate human values. For that to happen, we need the recognition that these qualities in our minds are essential, and on that foundation we take on the responsibility for the welfare of the whole of society without prejudice.

I believe that these days there are many who, like me, are concerned over the deterioration of human behavior. I hope that in order to build an environment of kindness and compassion, honesty and open-mindedness, their concern for the welfare of humanity will grow even stronger, and I trust that religious followers will join me in this call.

[88] Whether you believe in religion or not, there is no one who does not value and rejoice in a good mind, ethical behavior, kindness, compassion, and so on. Therefore, as I am one human being in this world, I maintain a firm awareness of having the responsibility for contemplating various beneficial undertakings and the welfare of humanity. With this perspective, my way of thinking can be categorized into four main points:

1. Concern for the welfare of the people of this world as a whole is essential for solving the problems on this planet.

2. Compassion is the root of world peace.

3. All religious traditions of this world should be concerned for the welfare of humanity as whole, regardless of what philosophical views they hold.

4. Every individual has a responsibility for the well-being of humanity.

Not only do I not say these things on the pretense of being an international politician, I do not even say them on the basis of being a Buddhist or a Tibetan. I express them just as a human being and as someone who sees the value of being concerned for the welfare of humanity.

All the religious traditions of this world possess aims and objectives for universal benefit and contain many excellent instructions. They continue to be helpful in countless ways to bring happiness in the short and long term for many people. In order to implement those religious instructions in keeping with their fundamental aims, if these religions are able to put aside attachment and partisanship with all sincerity and bring about a united force, it will create harmony within those religions themselves and among all others. If mutual respect and interfaith relations grow and prosper, it will not only be profitable for religion generally and specifically but will be worthwhile for society as a whole.

[234] Therefore, from the standpoint of a religious practitioner, and in order to increase mutual respect among all religions without prejudice, I have been making efforts for many years to promote interfaith harmony and build a genuine bond and better relations between religions for the general good. This is the second of my three responsibilities for this life.[43] To carry out this universal responsibility I have been implementing certain practices and have urged members of other religious traditions to do so. There are four main ways to do this.

1. In the past there was not much connection between the world religions, and by not knowing the facts about other religions there arose all kinds of prejudice, which resulted in conflict. Therefore, to learn about areas of agreement and disagreement between individual religions, there should be doctrinal exchanges through discussion in order to gain a better understanding, and we should look for ways to embrace what is good in each religion.

2. In order to encourage friendship between religions, practitioners should hold discussions to exchange their experiences.

3. As far as it is possible—in keeping with individual meditations and practices—the leaders and devotees of the various religions should pray together. In cases where it is not possible to chant together, the participants, united in an altruistic motivation, should gather together and engage in silent meditation on a particular topic.

4. [235] There should be visits to the places of worship of different religions and through learning their history we should rejoice, pay proper respect, and exchange offerings.

In the opportunities I have had for working to establish good relations between religious traditions through these methods, I have received support and commitment from all quarters. This is now turning into an excellent custom worldwide, and I see this as a positive result of maintaining the attitude of having respect for all religions.

"Faith" and "respect" can be differentiated. Respect, as taught in Buddhist texts, means to think of the kindness of that particular object and develop a sense of humility and esteem. Likewise, by knowing the kindness of other religions that do so much good for so many people, respect should be understood as holding them in high honor and regard, without aversion or desire.

Faith is "a state of mind that takes the form of holding the religious tradition you believe in and its objects of devotion alone as being trustworthy objects and actively holding them as objects of refuge. It is the direct antidote to a lack of faith."[44] Therefore, toward religions that are not one's place of refuge we have respect, but not this "faith."

The Buddhist scriptures establish three kinds of faith: pure faith, trust or belief, and longing faith. Seeing the wonderful qualities of the Three Jewels, and so on, a purity arises in the mind, through which the mind becomes clear and free of troubles, making it suitable for the development of the qualities of insight. This is the first kind of faith.

[236] Seeing the reasons behind the presentations on cause and effect in the teachings of the Buddha, as well as reasons for the existence of past and future lives, and so on, a certainty is generated. This is the faith of belief or trust. In reliance upon such perfect reasoning, suffering and the causes of suffering are ascertained as that which is to be eradicated, and the cessation of suffering and the path are ascertained as that which is to be taken and developed. From that one wishes to become an enlightened buddha—the result of the proper practice of eradication and development. This is the third kind of faith.

Therefore, for someone like me who believes in dependent origination and is a religious follower who propounds no-self, I cannot hold as an object of refuge for the three kinds of faith those religious traditions who adhere to assertions of the existence of a creator, and so on, or those religious practitioners who follow such traditions. However, for me to pay respect in complete sincerity is only right and proper.

Take the ancient Bön tradition of Tibet, for example. It was a very important tradition of our forefathers and is considered a very important source of our culture, worthy of praise, respect, and honor. In some of its texts there are teachings on the view of emptiness and some that are akin to those on bodhicitta, meaning that we have practices in common. Furthermore, it has a vast system of sutra and tantra that has served the people, and therefore I have great respect for it.

Regarding the one doctrine of the Buddha, those Buddhists from countries that follow the Pāli tradition and those Chinese Buddhists who followed the Sanskrit tradition I regard as senior followers and trainees of the Buddha, and I bow down single-pointedly to them with great respect and have faith in them. [237] Likewise, to all those who belong to the Tibetan tradition of Buddhism with its Old and New Tantras that spread also to Mongolia and the Himalayan regions, with high regard for their nonsectarian views held over a long time, I pay great respect to them through the three kinds of faith. I try to practice their teachings and spread them to others as best I can. These small attempts have seen the worthwhile result of an enhancement of experience and a great increase in pure perception.

Therefore, a bond between the different traditions and holders of different lineages that is as unified as milk mixed with water will not develop simply through clever and sweet talk, but by leaving behind desire and anger with sincere and pure thought, and by training in each other's teachings. Those traditions that hold common philosophies should take teachings, empowerments, instructions, and transmissions from each other, practice them, become familiar with them, and promote what is good in each other's traditions. If we can focus on that, harmony and a sincere bond will arise effortlessly.

In order to work for the benefit of all societies in this world with its many religious traditions, it is important to learn as much as possible a nonsectarian presentation of religion. As it says in *Ornament of Realization*, "Those who work for sentient beings should accomplish the welfare of the world by knowledge of the paths."[45] In order to care for others, bodhisattvas have to know the exclusive paths of the śrāvaka and pratyeka practitioners[46] and train in the common path. Therefore, it is customary in Tibet, when studying Buddhism, to study and contemplate, as much as is appropriate, the Buddhist tenets of the higher and lower vehicles, such as the Vaibhāṣika, Sautrāntika, Yogācāra or Cittamātra, and Madhyamaka schools, and to train in their tenets.

Moreover, we have the exemplary custom of studying extensively, not only these four Buddhist tenet systems, but also the assertions of non-Buddhist tenet systems. [238] For example, the Indian master Bhāvaviveka, in the root text and commentary of his work *Essence of Madhyamaka*, lists all Buddhist and non-Buddhist schools. In *Treatise of Valid Cognition* by Dharmakīrti, many non-Buddhist schools are described. It is the tradition to study these.

In India in the past, it was also traditional to study all religious tenets. Mr. L. K. Advani, the former deputy prime minister of India, said that in ancient India there were many religious traditions with different philosophies, and they argued vociferously with each other. For example, the Lokāyata materialist school did not accept past and future lives, liberation, and objects of refuge. Therefore, other traditions derogatorily called them "nihilists." However, the founders of this tradition were respectfully called "rishi."[47] This peaceful coexistence of different religions is an exemplary and wonderful characteristic of India. Therefore, it is very important that we know the views, meditations, and spiritual conduct of other religious traditions. This he told me many times.

If a religious practitioner mixes faith with attachment to their own religion, their mind falls to prejudice. A mind that is one-sided cannot see the complete reality of the situation. In practice, that will lead to difficulties of not being in accord with reality. For example, in the Buddhist texts on epistemology it says that the happy mind we all desire is a result of a validly perceiving cognition, whereas the suffering that we all want to avoid comes from a misperceiving cognition. This is very significant. Knowledge that conforms to reality is valid cognition. Any mode of apprehending that is at odds with reality is a misperception.

[239] A Chilean acquaintance, who is a learned psychologist, explained that if a scientist mixes attachment with science, it damages any observation of the truth and is inappropriate. This is very similar.

Therefore, to be able to have a perfect understanding of any situation surrounding the economy, religion, the environment, and so on, or of complete significance of a person's actions or conduct, it is imperative to know the complete situation. The actual reality of a situation is a product of many circumstances, and so whatever that reality is we should be able to see all of it. If we see that, we will see everything.

Does this mean that we should be able to comprehend every reality that exists in this phenomenal world? This is a difficult question to answer. Hidden phenomena that are beyond thought, beyond words, and beyond expression are found in all religions. God in Christianity, Allah in Islam, the wisdom dharmakaya[48] in Buddhism, and so on are phenomena beyond thought and verbal expression. Therefore, in all traditions, when talking of ultimate truths it proceeds on the basis of them being beyond thought and expression. Can this be comprehended by the valid cognitions of ordinary beings? This is a common difficulty faced by all religions.

There are some excellent instructions, practices, and conduct in other religious traditions, and even if we assert that they are not superior to those found in Buddhism, it is also the case that they are not inferior. We Tibetan Buddhists should hold these up as good examples. [240] I can mention a few. In some Christian monasteries silence is maintained and the monks there live up to the name of "going from home to homelessness."[49] They dwell there with body, speech, and mind pacified and well disciplined, and in a great state of conscientiousness. They are absorbed body and mind into their religious practices, and all food, clothing, and instruction is provided by the monastery. By looking after the monastery and taking care of the poor, and so on, they work solely for the benefit of the local community. Never involving themselves in the business of personal finance, or in the affairs of family and friends, they have few desires and live in contentment, not being allowed to have any luxury possessions. They never lapse into a state of wanton or reckless self-enjoyment. The monks in the monastery are not even allowed to have a mobile phone. They have so few possessions. Many of our monastic disciplines are just left in the books, whereas they actually put into practice their monastic regulations. This is excellent behavior, and whether heard or seen is well worthy of praise. These things can also be understood from the attitude and behavior of Christian monks and nuns everywhere who work in schools and hospitals.

There are a number of Christians who have practiced meditation, for example, from the Buddhist tradition. Therefore, if we can value, respect, and accept the good in each of our religions as best we can, without doubt this will be a contributing factor in increasing good relations between the world religions.

CHAPTER 3

Science

[89] HISTORY TELLS US there was no expression of religion during the very beginning of civilization, and that the formation of the religious traditions as we know them arrived about three or four thousand years ago. The people of ancient times had no power to overcome the difficulties and hardships they faced, and they identified the beneficial powers of the natural world—in which they had placed their trust since the beginning of time—as "gods," and its harmful powers as "demons." Over time people propounded the existence of gods and even a supreme being, which were identified as sources of hope, in contrast to the demonic forces intent on harm. This was the foundation for the reification of these two sides. Some had faith that a supreme being would protect them from difficulties, and so they petitioned and prayed to their gods. Certain beings were identified as sources of destructive power, and rituals were initiated to kill them or drive them out. Perhaps there were those who did not accept these views, but we cannot know whether they had other objects in which they placed their faith.

From the eighteenth century up to the beginning of the twentieth, faith and trust in material progress grew considerably, whereas interest in religion waned. [90] During the second half of the twentieth century, and particularly in the twenty-first century, material development reached unprecedented levels, resulting in an extraordinary increase in our living standards. However, faith in religion, which people had for thousands of years, ceased being given the same level of importance. I have a friend who is a great scholar in economics, and it was considered productive that we wrote a book together. I am no expert in economics and have no experience in that field. We were having a discussion on whether decent human attitudes—living within the law, ethical behavior, and so on—had a place even in the field of economics. I asked him if a fear of God or a sense of shame and modesty in the face of God was beneficial or not. He replied that this was eighteenth-century thinking, a time when there were many who believed in God, but it was not like that in the nineteenth and twentieth centuries.

There is the question of how much religion conforms to science. These are the days not of faith but of investigation and science. In the eighteenth and nineteenth centuries, when modern science was developing, interest in religion declined. This was due to the approach that many religions took of not focusing on the human intellect or engaging in investigation through reasoning but having sole respect for the word of God and relying only on faith as their foundation. For example, some time ago I was having a religious discussion with someone from the religious department of BBC radio, [91] and he said, "Our inability to know the nature of God is created by God himself. That is extraordinary."

Scientists, however, proceed by investigation until they have proof. These are two separate approaches.

In the past, a person who had an interest in science could quite possibly be someone who prayed to God as a way to alleviate any personal suffering. However, for their scientific study and undertakings they probably would not consider any teachings found in the Bible, Koran, and so on. Nor had they come across any other new science. Many Buddhist countries such as Sri Lanka, Myanmar, Thailand, Tibet, and Mongolia, as well as China, Korea, and Vietnam, where the teachings of Buddha were well developed, had built relations with the West for many years, but there were probably no Western scientists who made any efforts to study the philosophy found in Buddhism.

Therefore, during the spread of scientific thought, we can surmise that scientists did not place their hopes in religion and did not make use of its teachings. However, these days some are becoming interested in Buddhism and in the inner science of consciousness as found in the Tibetan Buddhist tradition. Many professional scientists are showing interest in the possibility of adopting new sources of knowledge and of learning new philosophical principles. This is wonderful. [92] They are discovering the taste of something different in the Buddhism of Tibet.

It appears that this new form of interest in religion comes out of new forms of sufferings existing in the mind for which material progress alone brings no relief. For example, one Christian leader said, "In the past fewer people attended church to pray, but recently this number has increased. There has been great material progress in society but no happiness in the mind. Consequently, interest in religion is fundamentally increasing."

Over the past two hundred years or so scientific thought has established itself with discoveries based on investigation. Using the potential of matter, mechanical production was developed, and science and technology have grown enormously. Most of what was only dreamed about for thousands of years has now been created by science. Various medicines for disease and illnesses, wonderful treatments in the field of surgery and elsewhere, and so on have appeared and are continually being improved. Many years ago, Buddhists who lived in faraway countries could only wish that they could visit sacred sites such as Bodhgaya in India. Any journey there would have been difficult. Over time, ships and now air travel have facilitated such journeys. This development of excellent causes and conditions for improving our lives is a worthy cause.

However, I believe that adhering to the attitude that reliance upon technology and material development alone will solve all of humanity's problems is mistaken. [93] The material progress made since the end of the twentieth century cannot by itself produce happiness in the minds of people. It is evident that even the people of materially advanced societies suffer many mental hardships. Living beings are not created from external matter alone, or produced by machinery, and our bodies are not like machines. Putting trust for all our well-being in material progress alone is a mistake. It is very important that we pay great attention to the workings of the mind and not lessen our interest in ethical conduct. We should investigate our origin and nature and think deeply about what we want.

Just having a good motivation of wishing that peace and happiness would flourish in this world will not produce that result. Prayer cannot create happiness. Implementation is needed, and that primarily must come by way of inner feelings. These days many people—especially scientists—are beginning to take an interest in the nature of mind, inner feelings, methods for dealing with adverse conditions, and so on. Those who are investigating ways of producing inner happiness are increasing. This is a wonderful source of hope for the future. Once when I visited the USA I learned that the curricula of Stanford, Wisconsin, and Emory universities included lessons on the mind in their search for ways to accomplish peace and happiness. [94] This is a sign of the harmonious relationship that is developing with great enthusiasm between science and religion. These days biochemical and psychological research has advanced to new levels, and profound questions regarding the ultimate nature of the world and human life are being asked. These questions are also found in religion. Therefore, a common and productive viewpoint, as well as new views on mind and phenomena in particular, are clearly emerging.

I like to think that we Easterners have a greater acquaintance with the inner workings of the mind, while Westerners are more familiar with external phenomena. These days East and West are greatly connected. If presentations on the mind found in Buddhist texts and presentations on the elements of external phenomena found in modern science were brought together, it could form a wonderful gift for humanity.

Science and technology have succeeded in extraordinary accomplishments, and their contribution to the well-being of humanity has been hugely significant. They have made life easier. The benefits that derive from the scientific understanding of the world we live in is undeniable. However, putting aside any ultimate happiness, there are still many immediate problems that science cannot solve. There are far more educated people today than there were in the past, [95] but universal scientific education alone cannot bring about the growth of ethical behavior and, in fact, can become a cause for dissatisfaction and a lack of stability. Not only does nothing change, with no alleviation of suffering, but unhappiness, anxiety, dangers, and so on actually increase instead of lessening. This is a sign that material development is not enough.

One thing we can do is put a stop to harmful and wrong material development. If not, the consequences for the world—with its human and other inhabitants—will without doubt be disastrous. If we pay too much importance to science and technology, to the neglect of moral and ethical issues, we run the risk of moving away from the needed intelligence and understanding that encourage us to work toward honesty, sincerity, and altruism.

These wonders of today's world are no substitutes for values that are taught by religion and that have prevailed for generations and brought so much benefit. The growth of material development and the growth of fundamental human values are of equal importance. For such a balance to come about, a universal sense of responsibility must be restored.

QUALITIES OF SCIENCE

Today's material progress is not without its critics. From one perspective, this progress is the achievement and splendor of Western civilization, and if this expansion of material development is carried out properly, always respecting the rights of others, there is no fault with that. [96] Therefore, I firmly believe that material growth, as a way of alleviating difficulties and hardships, and the development of the excellent qualities of mind should work together as equal partners. Today Western doctors are also recognizing that a peaceful mind is essential for the well-being of both body and mind. Therefore, the determination to restore human values should have a place in science.

In order to live a happy life, every person, whoever they are, should work to develop their mind and their material life. It could be said that the first of these is a religious occupation, but we should make the distinction that this is not to be understood as solely referring to religious development. This development of the mind primarily refers to the growth of ethical behavior that is fundamentally innate in human beings—mutual kindness and compassion motivated by a good mind, a sense of responsibility, sincerity, honesty, good use of the human intellect, and so on. The seeds of these traits have been within us since the time of our birth. They are not newly developed later on. Faith and other qualities associated with religion come later. Religions have distinct levels of philosophies, but when they teach ways of becoming better human beings and of having a kind mind, this is not some new creation of a spirit of ethical behavior, but the development of that behavior we innately possess within us.

[97] From the age of nineteen or twenty I had a great desire to learn about machines. From this I came to be interested in science, and from about 1970 I began to cultivate relationships with scientists. Gradually I started having discussions with scientists on physics—primarily on cosmology, neuroscience, and quantum physics. There was some concern among American Buddhists that scientists would be disrespectful and would not be able to open their minds to Buddhism. Scientists are not supposed to come to conclusions by making judgments based upon their own conceptions. They are trained to thoroughly examine a matter with an open mind, and if evidence points to a conclusion

they will accept it; otherwise they will not. Where an issue is in a state of uncertainty or doubt, questions will arise. When questions arise, there will be investigation. With investigation comes understanding that leads to certainty.

In my experience most scientists are very honest and speak primarily from the perspective of what has been established. They evaluate from that which is evident and explain by way of empirical truths. Something is not accepted as true merely on the basis of one person's investigation and experience, but on the basis of the same result being arrived at by anyone who follows a valid means of investigation. They do not accept as existing or nonexisting, or as being this or that, anything that has not been a subject of investigation. [98] They are not attached to or partial toward an old culture, a philosophy, the citations of scholars, or religious philosophies, but move forward solely in keeping with the developments of science. They will seek out faults in their methods and improve wherever they can. This is an excellent methodology on the great road of progress. They do not assert that something does not exist just because they have not perceived it, but hold to the view that it could be possible; it could exist. This is a special feature of science. Generally, scientists are completely open-minded.

However, sometimes even scientists can be influenced by other philosophies. For example, in 1979 I met some Russian scientists. In discussions on the nature of consciousness one scientist understood "mental cognition" to be the self or type of mind identified with the Christian concept of soul, and, because this was a religious concept, he expressed his disagreement. Those who hold Communist views consider that "religion is poison" and will therefore criticize it. Many scientists refuse to entertain the possibility of past and future lives simply because it is a religious concept, even though they have not ascertained with any reasoned certainty their existence or nonexistence. Such people do not have open minds.

[99] Similarly, when Buddhists investigate the validity of a particular concept, if they rely upon explanations found in Buddhist texts—taking that to be the benchmark of truth—and conduct investigations of what is and what is not valid on that basis, that is also not an open-minded approach. To settle on determined goals from the very outset and declare this is what is to be practiced, this is what is to be abandoned, and then to present reasons to establish these already-determined issues is not the logician's way of investigation or the way to search for what is true. Therefore, with an open mind that does not fall to one side or another—while taking the view that anything could be possible—you search for the reality of the subject under examination. If you establish its validity, with another cognition you examine to see if it is beneficial or not. The cognition that searches for the truth of the matter should not analyze on the basis of wanting from the very outset to establish that it is good or bad, right or wrong. That is not an open-minded approach, and such a way of analyzing cannot discover the actual truth.

In my discussions with Western scientists we use the title "Dialogue between Modern Science and Buddhism," but I think the wording is not right. If the umbrella term "Buddhism" is used, it would include many topics such as the attainment of liberation, the achievement of the state of omniscience, the gaining of a good rebirth in the next life, and so on. It would be a vast topic. This is not what is intended here. In meetings with scientists we do not discuss the existence of past and future lives, the states of liberation and omniscience, and so on. We compare topics such as the workings of the mind, the kinds of methods suitable for resolving mental difficulties, [100] how to prevent the onset of illness, and so on. Science has proven that when illness strikes, the state of mind is very influential as an aid to a quick recovery. Therefore, for bringing about the welfare of people in those common situations, by alleviating the many difficulties of this present life, now we can see that the mind is important. When that is understood, science develops an interest in the presentations on mind explained in the Buddhist tradition, as a way of understanding in detail the process of thought.

The three main topics of Buddhist literature are (1) base reality, (2) the stages of the path to be traveled, and (3) the resultant states to be actualized. The determining and presentation of base reality is Buddhist science. In that topic there are no discussions on what qualities are to be developed, on what are to be abandoned, and on various Buddhist practices. Therefore, these discussions with science do not involve "Buddhism" in the sense of the path and liberation. They are "A Dialogue between Buddhist Science and Modern Science."

During discussion sessions scientists ask me questions about Buddhism, and out of necessity I will give some Buddhist explanations, but I never deliberately seek to establish the validity of Buddhist views. I see that as wrong.

When analyzing, an open mind is essential, as mentioned above. It would be a mistake to wish to establish Buddhist philosophy as valid and search only for a compatible scientific proof to support it. This would be reasoning based on merely seeing what exists in compatible areas and not seeing it in incompatible areas.[50] That is not the way to analyze.

BUDDHIST SCIENCE

[101] Science's main area of investigation is the truth of phenomena existing within coarse manifest form. The object of investigation may have clearly defined specifications, but they will search for the truth within that. Buddhists also search for the truth. As a method of doing that, they employ the four kinds of reason: (1) the reason of the innate characteristics of things, known as reasoning by way of the nature; (2) the reason of what a phenomenon does or is capable of, known as reasoning by way of function; (3) the reason of mutual dependence of

cause and effect on the basis of wanting happiness and not wanting to suffer, known as reasoning by way of dependence; and (4) establishing validity through those three types of reason, known as reason of validity.[51]

Buddhists accept an outcome determined by investigation built on valid reasoning in order to accurately know the object to be comprehended. For this, two kinds of distorted views that misconceive the nature of that object must be eliminated. These two are (1) the distorted view of superimposition, in which conceptualization goes beyond the reality of the object and excessively superimposes; and (2) the distorted view of deprecation, in which the reality is undervalued and deprecated as not existing. Therefore, this clearly shows that Buddhists accept a reality that is devoid of these two distorted views. Because of this, whether through investigation by valid reasoning or the investigative techniques of technology, biochemistry, and so on, if a reality is discovered, it must be accepted by Buddhists.

[102] In Buddhist literature it is with this approach that presentations on the world and its inhabitants are determined. In particular, there are detailed presentations on the nature of mind. Therefore, these days some scholars who show an interest in Buddhism say that Buddhism is not a religion but a science of the mind.

For example, as of now, science has not determined the existence of past and future lives, but neither has it determined their nonexistence. Therefore, it is unable to establish either their existence or nonexistence. Without coming to a conclusion either way, for the majority of scientists it is left as a doubt, because although the existence of past and future lives has not been found, not finding and not existing are not the same. If through their investigations scientists discovered, with complete validity, that past and future lives did not exist, Buddhists would have to accept that. The reason is that Buddhist philosophical texts assert that the definition of existence is "that which is apprehended by a valid cognition." Therefore, any investigation and subsequent conclusion concerning existence and nonexistence proceeds on the basis of being apprehended or not apprehended by a valid cognition. We cannot come to a conclusion by only considering scriptural sources our main support. Therefore, discoveries that are supported by evidence must be accepted, even if they go against scripture. That is the right way for Buddhists in general and is especially compliant with the Great Vehicle of Buddhism. Therefore, investigation with an open mind is very important. Scripture that is contradicted by reasoning is not taken literally but explained as being interpretive. This is one important reason why Buddhism and science are compatible. [103]

Also, they are similar in that the subject of analysis to be determined by way of investigation is base reality. For Buddhism, primarily adhering to certainty induced by the power of reasoning is a fundamental principle. Therefore, if something does not concur with reality—even if it is the words of the Buddha—we have the authority to separate it into that which is provisional as opposed to that which is definitive. In this way we should have a faith that can be trusted as being validly reasoned. That is the foundation of the relationship between Buddhism and science.

Buddhist philosophical works concentrate primarily on the nature of mind and not on external phenomena. Scientists mainly determine the nature of the external world and do not investigate so much the inner workings of the mind. I believe that in the future that will definitely change. Maybe this situation arises from the fact that presentations of mind arise from the various conceptualizations built on our countless types of individual karma, thereby making them complex to analyze. In comparison, external phenomena exist by way of various common processes and are easier to analyze. Whatever the reason, the more connections that Buddhism has with modern science, the more Buddhist science will widen the scope of science. For Buddhists it is important that we link scientific explanations and analysis to our

Buddhist way of determining truths. The more ways there are of analyzing, the more profound and vast our understanding will be, and the result will be one of greater conviction and certainty.

SCIENTIFIC INTEREST IN BUDDHISM

[104] Albert Einstein took some interest in Buddhism—and when the world-renowned modern scientist described his famous theory of relativity, he appeared to be going beyond the bounds of conventional truth and external reality of atoms and so on, and venturing toward the direction of emptiness. However, the principles of dependent origination and emptiness, presented in the Buddhist sources, and which relate to the ultimate mode of being of all phenomena, both outer as well as inner, transcend what current science describes. So, Einstein stated that, if in future science and spirituality can go together hand in hand, it could be science and Buddhism.

In the latter half of the twentieth century, the science of mind began to flourish with advances in cognitive science and neuroscience, and some quantum physicists even began exploring explanations of atoms and so on found in the Buddhist thought. Scientists initially did not understand the Buddhist theory that the existence of any phenomenon is not established from the perspective of the object itself, and that phenomena exist by virtue of dependent origination and are established solely as a names and imputations. When modern quantum physicists search for material phenomena, those phenomena cannot be found, but it is not right to say that these phenomena do not exist. The notion that phenomenon exist solely as names and imputations had previously not occurred to scientists and proved a great difficulty for them. [105] Now, quantum physics posit the existence of phenomena in terms of "subjective designation." This is obviously very similar to the Buddhist approach.

At a scientific congress held about twenty years ago, the great Indian physicist Raja Ramana said that when he read the works composed by the great Indian Buddhist scholar Nāgārjuna he was astonished to find there was much in them that was very similar to the explanations given by modern scientists on their findings in atomic physics.

Similarly, in 2014, Professor S. Bhattacharya, the vice chancellor of Presidency University, Kolkata, said that when he first learned of the concept from atomic physics that nothing exists from its own side, he recognized that it was very similar to the teachings of the Buddhist Cittamātra and Mādhyamika schools,[52] which state that phenomena do not exist by way of their own intrinsic nature. He also noted the similarity to the tenets of Nāgārjuna, who taught that phenomena existed solely as names and imputations.

Just as these two scientists broadened their horizons on the nature of emotions and on different approaches to the understanding of consciousness, we too can learn new ways of investigating the subtle nature of matter. [106]

Many great achievements have come about as a result of Einstein and other intellectually gifted scientists discovering unseen truths in this world. Moreover, generally, the body of work scientists have produced in whatever field they have shown interest in and researched has been truly remarkable.

Everybody possesses a mind or consciousness, but it is difficult to explain its complete nature and function on the basis of neurons alone. The ways that the five sensory consciousnesses know their objects— such as the visual consciousness perceiving form, and how the signals are transmitted to the brain—these are certainly dependent on neurons, but there is more to it. Although the understanding of good and bad, and what is to be developed and what is to be abandoned, likewise arise from the brain, these too become difficult to describe without moving from coarse descriptions of the physical body to subtler investigations of consciousness.

There is a story that has some relevance here. Once, at a conference with scientists in the USA, a participant who was very learned in science and philosophy appeared bored, and gave the impression that she thought there was nothing to be discussed between scientists and religious followers. For example, if we Tibetan Buddhists chanted the mandala offering prayer, beginning, "The ground anointed by incense and strewn with flowers...,"[53] adhering to the literal truth of every word, in the presence of someone who recognizes that the world is a globe, we can imagine that there would be no common basis of discussion. [107] Yet as the conference progressed, and the talk turned to topics taught in Buddhist texts such as the nature of the mind, and particularly the rejection of a creator of the world and of a permanent and independent self, the expression of the participant changed completely. "You clearly stand out from those who assert a soul and a creator of the world," she remarked, as her interest increased. Even in the session breaks she keenly pursued her questioning on the tenets of Buddhism.

In their personal lives it may be the case that some scientists have faith in God and pray to him when they suffer because of their expectations and apprehension or desires and resentments, but within their studies and fields of research they feel that there is probably nothing worthwhile or no new lines of thought to be found in religion. I think the above story illustrates that.

Scientific investigations have employed various techniques to understand the experience of happiness and suffering. For example, brain scans reveal that at times of great affection, love, and compassion, the left side of the brain is very active, and the body's immune system is strengthened. These mental states are considered to be effective for improving health. In contrast, when disturbed states of mind such as anger are manifest, the right side of the brain is clearly active, which in turn weakens the immune system. From these results it can be established that a peaceful and controlled mind is directly beneficial for the welfare of the body, whereas a violent, disturbed, and uncontrolled mind is damaging. [108] Therefore, even if from the perspective of the welfare of body and mind, it can be proven that compassion and a peaceful, controlled mind are necessary.

Similarly, in response to my suggestion, some scientists and Western schoolteachers had their students meditate daily for ten to twenty minutes on love and compassion. When they evaluated the results, after a few weeks they found that the students' personalities had become gentler and kinder, their minds were relaxed, and they felt happier.

It is important to recognize this profound and powerful connection between the innate human values of love, compassion, tolerance, and so on and the alleviation of bodily and mental difficulties.

One difficulty that science faces these days is that any expression and experience of an individual consciousness is by nature subjective. The nature of consciousness has to be understood through meditation— that is, individual investigation into the characteristics of awareness. The individual can talk about their experiences, but another person has no way to evaluate or measure them. They cannot be verified by a third person.

Although scientists have yet to reach an understanding of consciousness, significant scientific investigation into the mind has begun. Gradually, researchers of the brain are pursuing their investigations, and their interest in the nature of consciousness continues to grow. This is a positive step. [109] Prevention of and recovery from illness, the well-being of society and the individual, and many other things will all benefit from the science of the mind. The Buddhist declaration that all physical and verbal movement depend upon mental activity is becoming better accepted. Therefore, investigation into consciousness is extremely important.

The discoveries made by modern science in the field of inanimate matter, as well as scientific explanations of these phenomena, are far more detailed and more clearly presented than those found in Buddhist literature. That is undeniable.

THE COMMON BASIS SHARED BY BUDDHISM AND SCIENCE AND THE VALUE OF AN OPPOSING FORCE

Over the last several decades there have been thirty conferences that have brought together in dialogue Buddhist philosophical scholars from Tibet and modern scientists.[54] Many other similar meetings have been held. One major finding of these discussions is that the science taught in Buddhism and modern Western science are similar to each other in their determining the nature of the truth of suffering. For this the meetings are an aid to the development of the Buddhist theoretical tradition. Many learned scientists these days have shown an increasing interest in Buddhist explanations—primarily in the processes of investigation through reasoning, which include existence and nonexistence; permanence and functioning phenomena; form, consciousness, and nonassociated composite phenomena;[55] valid and nonvalid cognition; continuum; subtle particles; the cause of consciousness; past and future lives; conducive and opposing causes and conditions; and so on. [110] These are becoming starting points or platforms for modern scientific research [110] and they serve as starting points for dialogue.

Three decades have passed since these discussions began. They started out from my private interest and over time have developed into regular discourses between Buddhist philosophical scholars and modern scientists. In recognition of the benefit to those who study the classical texts of Buddhist literature, the study of science was introduced into various monastic curriculums over a decade ago.

In the past we Tibetans took the Indians as our teacher and studied the Buddhist works of great Indian masters. Now we have taken Westerners as our teachers in order to learn modern science. From 2000 onward scientific study programs were initiated in some Tibetan monasteries as monthly intensive modules, and recently students have graduated from Tibetan Buddhist colleges with a major in science. For example, in conjunction with Emory University in the USA, the best students from the Tibetan monasteries are selected to participate in a joint science program. In the future, the most important topics that connect science and Buddhism will be available to the monasteries in both Tibetan and English languages. Textbooks will be part of the science classes in the monasteries and those who have been selected will serve as teachers and assistants in the classroom. This is my hope.

[111] When those who have received a modern education, whether Tibetan or non-Tibetan, are introduced to a Buddhist education, they will be able to verify with modern science not only that it is our mind that controls happiness and suffering, but also that human thinking and conceptions have a direct relation with our physical health and well-being. For some years now, within the Tibetan refugee community we have set up study programs on modern science combined with Buddhist philosophy. This has been primarily an exchange program through which Buddhists can receive the benefits of scientific knowledge, and scientists can be introduced to explanations and experiences of Buddhist knowledge.

The ways that something is explained both from a scientific perspective and in Buddhist texts is unquestionably helpful in coming to understand it. This approach should be developed completely and should involve special in-depth training. It would be excellent if those in possession of a modern education, who have studied Buddhism—and who have experience of partaking in discussions at scientific meetings—could bear the main responsibility for expanding this program.

Scientists and Buddhists have exchanged ideas and insights for many years now. These discussions should not be the specialized interest of a few individuals, but should be something that nonscientific Tibetan institutions should take up as well.

[112] There is much that scientists will be able teach us that will be of enormous benefit to Buddhist psychology, and there is much within

Buddhist psychology that will be helpful to science. The fact that in the twenty-first century, Tibetan Buddhist philosophy can be of benefit to science is something we can be rightly proud of. Not only can it not be concluded that the march of science means that there is no such thing as liberation and omniscience, but many who hold scientific views are becoming more and more interested in Buddhist philosophy, and new attitudes and perspectives are increasing like the swelling lakes of summer. It is very clear that in its classifications of mind, such as conceptual and nonconceptual cognition, primary minds and mental factors, valid and invalid cognitions, Buddhist literature is proving to be a powerful aid to science.

In particular, the understanding of external matter through the reasoned presentations of emptiness and dependent origination, and the conclusions arrived at from the analysis of objects, reveal a great deal of agreement between science and Buddhism. Consequently, many psychologists have lent great support to the concept of there being no self that is separate from the psycho-physical aggregates, as taught in Buddhist texts. These wonderful exchanges are increasing.

It can also be said that science encompasses part of what is constituted as the truth of suffering by Buddhists. In Asaṅga's *Compendium of Abhidharma* when it says, "This is the truth of suffering," the inhabitants of the world and the world itself are included. When the external world is being explained, the makeup of the world, its chronological development, its cosmology, and its physics are all connected. When these topics are expanded, the basis of the mind and the experience of happiness and suffering also become important.

In dialogues between Buddhists and scientists, it is important to discuss the best explanations of our own position for those who find fault with religion, who refute religion by relying upon modern thinking, or who are unable to believe in it. [113] Generally, for any branch of knowledge to arise and flourish in the world, it is necessary that there be an opposing force present. For example, in terms of the stages of Buddhist practice, it is in the face of the apprehension of permanence that we think about impermanence. Also, if the cravings for the experiences of this life are particularly strong, it becomes necessary to seek out special methods to counter that. There are many types and degrees of forces that are in direct contradiction to the practices of the ten levels and five paths, such as the mentally constructed and innate abandonments of the path of seeing and the path of meditation. It is in dependence upon these forces that these remedial powers will inevitably arise.

If there is an opposition and a contradiction to something, it provides a wonderful opportunity for the development of ideas and the understanding of essential points. That is very apparent in assertions of philosophical tenets. When the Buddha was alive the presence of many opposing philosophies greatly helped the development of Buddhist philosophy, and there are accounts of the Buddhist and non-Buddhist philosophies flourishing as a result of debates and arguments between the two.

This is very clear in the following examples. During the time of Ācārya Dignāga (c. 480–c. 540), non-Buddhist epistemological philosophy was dominant, and as a result Dignāga preached Buddhist epistemology, which the non-Buddhists criticized. In response, the great master Dharmakīrti (seventh century) composed new epistemological treatises focusing on refuting and establishing. Also, in response to non-Buddhist critiques of Dharmakīrti's treatises, Ācārya Śāntarakṣita (725–88) composed extensive refutations and assertions in his own works on Buddhist epistemology. [114] Without these critiques between the schools it would have been difficult for the epistemological works of these Buddhist masters to become widespread.

Similarly, with the classification of the philosophical view of Nāgārjuna, the Buddhist master Buddhapālita (c. 470–540) commentated on the actual philosophical intent of Nāgārjuna, against which Ācārya Bhāvaviveka (sixth century) argued strongly. Later, the great Buddhist master Candrakīrti (seventh century) clarified the position, and the intent of Nāgārjuna's works became clearer, resulting in the emergence of the special Madhyamaka Prāsaṅgika school of thought. Also, because the Cittamātra tradition was well developed at that time, Candrakīrti explained the difficult points of the Prāsaṅgika school.

From one perspective, unlike the debates between Buddhist and non-Buddhist philosophical schools in ancient India, and in particular, the debates described above, debates these days between with those who accept religion and those who are indifferent to it are not that significant. However, it is impossible not to think about those who are openly antagonistic toward religion. That should not result in arguing with those who criticize religion in order to defeat them. We should learn thoroughly the various reasons for their refutations and criticisms, and if, on consideration, we find their reasons to be genuine, we should accept them.

During the twentieth century, religious traditions faced many obstacles, and in Asia particularly, Buddhism encountered many difficulties. This hostility was mainly of two kinds. One was the political ideology of Communism that criticized religion, resulting in the persecution of many countries. There were various reasons for this condemnation but mainly it was done in order to hold on to power. [115] However, this criticism cannot harm the theoretical tradition of the religion, and so there is no reason to be startled. These days much is changing, and this issue is not of any great significance anymore.

The other opposition to religion is that which centers on religious doctrines that do not conform to scientific knowledge. If we look at this honestly it is possible to see areas of disagreement between Buddhist tenets and modern science. This is something we should take seriously and be aware of. There are those who hold views similar to the ancient Cārvāka school.[56] Because of the view that as soon as the brain ceases to function the consciousness also ceases, there are still those these days who believe that there is no consciousness separate from the brain's capability, and by this logic they do not accept past and future lives, liberation and omniscience.

In the many years that I have been having discussions with scientists I do not forcefully try to prove the existence of past and future lives. I hold the views of learned scientists to be important, whatever they are. For those who do accept past and future lives it is only right that we attempt to establish their existence. We should not rely on those arguments that have been in existence for thousands of years. New lines of investigation are needed, and there are many perspectives to this that we should think about. [116] Our assertion of past and future lives should not be based on faith alone.

On a practical level, transformation of bad states of mind into good is something we know from experience in this very life. With desire and aversion, for example, we can see that thoughts in keeping with these two mental states will strengthen desire and aversion, while the kind of thinking that opposes them will result in their reduction. Therefore, we need to conclusively establish that by relying upon the antidotes to desire and aversion, the stains of the mind can eventually be eradicated completely. There are many reasonings in Buddhist literature that establish the existence of liberation, but non-Buddhists also can put forward reasonings that prove liberation, and we should express them. Fundamentally, Buddhist and non-Buddhist traditions share the belief in a continuum of consciousness. Consequently, if we research by way of all available reasonings, and if individual philosophies can produce reasons that liberation—the complete eradication of the stains of the mind—is possible, it will be very beneficial.

Modern science, in its production of many new classifications of knowledge, has become like a new friend to Buddhist philosophy, producing a positive broadening of its horizons, and of great benefit to its progress. On that basis, in terms of their logical approaches, I see no contradiction between Buddhism and modern science. We should regard modern scientific knowledge on external phenomena as authoritative, whereas in presentations of consciousness, the experiences of happiness and suffering, dealing with suffering, and so on—in terms of their nature, features, paths, and transformation techniques—ancient Indian wisdom, particularly that of the Nalanda Buddhist tradition, is very profound. [117] This forms the platform for the fundamental relationship between Buddhist philosophy and science.

The happiness we seek and the suffering we dislike are feelings and experience. Experience is consciousness, and the support of consciousness is matter. Therefore, we have to know about matter. The detailed presentations on the external world and the physical aggregates of its inhabitants in Buddhist text constitute one section of the presentation of the truth of suffering. Therefore, this body of work on feelings of pain and pleasure, experience, and the inner consciousness is becoming something to be added to scientific knowledge.

BASE, PATH, AND RESULT IN
BUDDHIST SCRIPTURE

Whenever I talk about to Western scientists about the connection between Buddhist philosophy and science, I speak about three stages: base reality, the path, and the resultant states to be actualized. Base reality refers to the way that the phenomena of happiness and suffering, the world and its inhabitants, and so on actually exist. Changes that naturally occur[57] and changes brought about on the foundation of that base reality determine the paths to be traveled. The transformations that result from the changes made are resultant stages.

Therefore, talking about the stage of base reality is not religious parlance but is the determining of the actuality of basic existence. In that sense, Buddhism and science are united in establishing the nature of this base reality. When base reality is ascertained in Buddhist literature, there is a reliance upon scripture, but reasoning is primarily employed using evident and visible phenomena as a basis. Therefore,

I always explain that, ultimately, we analyze based upon experience. This is one reason why there is a strong consensus between Buddhist scripture and science when using reasoning to understand reality.

[118] The Buddhist way is that the reality of a phenomenon is investigated and analyzed, and if that reality is proven and established, it is accepted. If no such proof is forthcoming, then even the word of the Buddha himself is not taken as literally explicit, but must be explained as having some other intent. This is a fundamental procedure. Therefore, not being able to follow that process, but instead denying that which is clearly evident, and stubbornly holding on to that which goes against reasoning, is a contradiction that does not fit at all with the special feature of Buddhism.

The teachings found in the Buddhist scriptures can be divided into three areas:

1. Buddhist Views: This is the philosophical side and deals with the all-pervading and compositional suffering as one of the three kinds of suffering, and so on; the presentations of karma as an origin of suffering, mental afflictions as an origin of suffering, the stages of the paths to be traveled, and the resultant states to be actualized.

2. Buddhist Science: An explanation of the nature of the truth of suffering and the truth of the origin of suffering in order to determine the base reality. Many areas of dialectics that are primarily epistemological studies in ways of validly cognizing are also included here.

3. Buddhist Practice: This refers to the way to practice as a means of traveling through the stages of the paths, and the way to actualize the resultant states by relying upon those paths.

[119] In short, the truth of suffering and the truth of the origin of suffering are phenomena included in base reality and in Buddhist science. The truth of cessation refers to the method of actualizing the resultant

states and is at the essence of the stages of practice. The truth of the path constitutes the stages of traveling the paths, or the paths themselves, and is also included in Buddhist philosophy.[58]

Whether or not the classical works of Buddhism explicitly use the above terminology and divisions, these topics are nevertheless to be found in the teachings. In tantric texts especially, base reality, the paths, and the resultant states are the main subject matter.

The general procedure of the Great Vehicle can be summarized as the two truths as the base, method and wisdom as the paths, and the two enlightened forms as the result.[59]

It is necessary to make changes for the good and an elimination of faults in dependence upon the good or bad conditions of the base reality. The existence of methods to produce such changes and the results that arise from these methods bring about the division into base, path, and result.

BASE REALITY

[120] The base reality of the external container of the world and its contents of living beings is subject to change. It is created through causes and conditions, is by nature impermanent, and it will ultimately be destroyed. Explaining this comes down to "particles," which exist in dependence upon a base, because we cannot point to anything that has no dependence. When Buddhist texts explain base reality, the dividing line between existence and nonexistence is determined by being apprehended by a cognition, and also whether or not that apprehending cognition is negated by another valid cognition. "Valid cognition" means that the way a cognition comprehends an object is the way it exists in actuality.

Existence and nonexistence are demarcated by the criterion of being apprehended or not apprehended by a valid cognition. An existence created by causes and conditions possesses the nature of constantly changing, while those not created by causes and conditions do not change moment by moment. This is the division into impermanence and permanence. This is not just an arbitrary division. In order to determine the nature of reality, those phenomena that change are posited as impermanent, while those that do not are permanent. There are three types of phenomena that are subject to change. (1) Matter that is visible, touchable, and measurable. (2) Consciousness, a phenomenon whose nature is one of mere experience and devoid of matter. Without a material existence, consciousness reveals happiness and suffering to our minds by way of experience. It cognizes and comprehends an object and so can be described as "experience by way of knowing an object." [121] (3) Phenomena such as time and "I," which are imputed on the psycho-physical aggregates are devoid of material form and do not possess the nature of an experiencing cognition experiencing its own object. This category of phenomena that are subject to change and destruction is known as "nonassociated composite phenomena."

The reason for the different terminologies is to establish the conventional realities of these phenomena. Within this base reality, the desire to avoid suffering and the desire for happiness naturally arise. Therefore, analysis of the causes and conditions that create happiness and suffering—such as whether they are subject to destruction, whether they have the nature of change, and whether they are created purely by causes and do not change by themselves—form the fundamental research in this base reality.

Being created in dependence upon causes and conditions means being subject to material causes and coexisting causes. A material cause refers to that which necessarily exists as a single continuum, the previous instances of which are of a similar type. Such a continuum can be one of type or of substance. A continuum of type requires similar-type continuity. A substance-continuum is not one of similar type but is a continuum of the substance of that phenomenon. For example, the first instant of a fire is the previous similar-type continuum of the second instant, while the second and third instants constitute the succeeding continuum of the first. The fire no longer blazing is still in the nature of fire but is not a similar-type continuum of fire; instead it is a continuum of substance.

[122] Therefore, if we trace back the material forms of this world by way of their substance continuum, we arrive at the very subtle substance particles that existed before the world was formed. I think this is what the Abhidharma texts are referring to when they talk of "form affording visibility." This is very subtle form. It is not a source of visible form but is explained as a source of mental phenomena.[60] The *Kālacakra Tantra* calls them "space particles."

These causes of a given material form arise from a succession of their own previous material causes. The material form's aspects change and even its entity might change, but its substance continuum is one that has been in existence for beginningless time. Any future world will likewise arise from the substance continuum of those very subtle particles—which are form as a source for mental phenomena—and which have abided in empty space after the previous world was destroyed.[61] Whatever the case may be, if we trace back the material causes of material forms, there will always be material forms as material causes. Form cannot be produced from nothing. Consciousness, whose characteristics are fundamentally opposed to form, cannot be the material cause of form.

CONSCIOUSNESS

According to Buddhist theories of mind, consciousness occurs in different forms. An example would be sensory consciousnesses, which can be divided into sensory consciousnesses apprehending visible form, apprehending sound, and so on, depending on the particular sense faculty they are dependent on. The different aspects of sensory consciousnesses depend upon the different objective conditions for these consciousnesses, such as those that apprehend the colors white, blue, red, and so on.

All consciousnesses are produced as entities of mere experience in dependence upon similar-type previous entities of clarity and knowing. [123] As explained previously, when a similar-type continuum, which is the material cause of a material phenomenon, is traced back, it will be seen that it is created from its own similar-type cause; it is not created from nothing, not created from something that is not a cause, nor created from a dissimilar-type cause. Likewise, consciousness with the nature of mere experience is not created from a dissimilar-type cause but in dependence upon a similar-type cause. Therefore, there must be instances of previous, similar-type consciousnesses. This is one of the logical proofs for the existence of past lives. From the position of those traditions who accept past lives this is a base reality and not something conceptualized and made up. Just as we can understand the continuum of external matter, so we can understand the continuum of the inner consciousness.

Nonassociated composite phenomena are imputed phenomena. According to those tenet systems that divide phenomena into imputed and substantially existent, even those that are imputed must be imputed on the basis of substantially existent phenomena. Just as the continuum of something substantially existent can have no beginning, that which is imputed upon substantially existent phenomena must also have existed from beginningless time.

If consciousness were posited as having a beginning, then that first instance of consciousness would either have been created from a cause of a dissimilar type or from no cause at all. If you accept that, this just becomes a dogmatic assertion. You have no other argument, and ultimately you are only saying, "I do not believe that consciousness has no beginning." Therefore, from the assertions that consciousness is born from a dissimilar cause and from a similar cause, we should look to see which has the stronger validity.

[124] If it feels uncomfortable to accept that the continuum of consciousness has existed from beginningless time, it will not be possible to accept that the continuum of "I," or person—which is imputed on the continuum of consciousness—has existed from beginningless time. Therefore, in dependence upon a particular basis of imputation there exists the self of humans, the self of animals, and so on. With human beings, the I that is imputed on our psycho-physical aggregates when we were young is the I of our youth. The I imputed on the psycho-physical aggregates of adulthood is the I of an adult. It is through imputation on those aggregates that we establish different existences of I, in dependence upon the features of those aggregates.

The I of the time when I was born is not the I imputed on the aggregates when I am old. Nevertheless, there is a general I that pervades the I of youth, the I of middle age, the I of old age, and all other instances of I. In that sense, when we talk about the previous I of our youth and at the time of birth, this is neither negated by being contradictory to experience nor is such labeling refuted by valid cognition. Therefore, we can establish an I characterized by place, time, and particularity, as well as a general I that is not characterized in that way. If we trace back the continuum of such a general I—which depends upon the continuum of consciousness—its basis of imputation has to be primarily established as consciousness. That continuum of consciousness has no beginning and therefore the person of the mere I that is imputed upon it can also have no ultimate beginning.

In the tenet systems of ancient India, those who asserted the existence of past and future lives accepted their existence in general terms but asserted that ultimately everything was created by the god Brahma. Therefore, I think that they probably posited consciousness as having a beginning.

Within Buddhist tenet systems there is no assertion that existence has a beginning. [125] The Buddhist Vaibhāṣika school claims that when arhats achieve nirvana without remainder, their continuum of cognition is severed. Therefore, this tradition propounds that consciousness has an end, and that the continuity of a person will be severed. Buddhist tenet systems from the Sautrāntika upward assert that consciousness has no beginning and no end, and that there is no circumstance or condition that can obstruct the abiding of its continuum. If an opposing force to consciousness existed, as that force grew in strength the consciousness would correspondingly weaken and eventually would be destroyed. However, there is no opposing force that can hinder consciousness in its nature of clarity and knowing.[62] This is not to say that there are not powerful remedial forces that hinder the adventitious faults existing within the clarity and knowing. There are indeed such forces that can put an end to those continuums, but there is no opposing force that can counter that nature of clarity and knowing. This refutes the assertions of those who insist that the stream of cognition can be severed. Therefore, the Sautrāntika and all higher Buddhist schools of thought all assert that consciousness can have no end and no beginning, and they do not accept that the continuum of cognition can be severed. Consequently, the I that exists in dependence upon that continuum also has no beginning and no end.

Causes producing results and results being under the control of causes are natural processes. External form is produced in dependence upon similar-type causes and material causes. Every kind of inner consciousness is produced in dependence upon a-similar-type continuum, and although that consciousness will take on different aspects and change its entity because of the number of cooperating causes, its entity of clarity and knowing does not change.[63] There are many different conditions resulting in different changes, and therefore different types of consciousness will naturally arise together with a particular type of condition. [126] Also, within those changes brought on by particular conditions are our inner experiences of suffering or happiness. Such feelings of happiness and suffering are produced in reliance upon causes, and are results because they are phenomena produced in dependence upon their own causes.

The arising of such happiness and suffering is due to a number of different causes. Generally, the arising of feelings—which are of the nature of consciousness—must depend upon a similar-type consciousness as a cause, and specifically, the arising of happiness and suffering comes about by coming into contact with a number of different conditions. Our thinking is one of those conditions—one way of thinking brings joy to the mind and from the condition of another way of thinking comes suffering. Different types of thinking at particular times will bring suffering or happiness. The consciousness of clarity and knowing that experiences suffering or happiness arises through its own cause.

Feelings of happiness and suffering come about in dependence on conditions present at that time. These conditions include the amount of effort exerted at the time of thinking, the type of activity at that time, and the object of that activity. Physical feelings such as coming into contact with pleasurable and painful phenomena also arise by way of many conditions coming together.

Coming into contact with such conditions occurs in dependence upon karma. Generally, composite phenomena undergo various changes in dependence upon causes and conditions. This is natural. Within this process some new activity can take place in conjunction with a particular motivation, through which happiness and suffering occurs. On that basis karma and its results can be explained. "Karma" means "activity," and when we talk about good and bad karma we understand this to refer to the characteristics of that activity. Such an activity is intentionally carried out in connection to the motivation that propelled the action. The results of that action, be it happiness or suffering, arise in dependence upon that intentional cause. 127] That is probably the way that the cause-and-effect process of karma can be explained.

Why do changes occur? Change occurring through causes and conditions is a natural process. What is the reason for the variety of changes? Change occurs due to the existence of an opposing force. If there is no opposing force, there will be no change. With external phenomena—for example, those that exist as mutually opposing elements within the four elements, such as heat and cold—are opposing forces. The strength or decline of one opposing force causes changes in another. Heat and cold cannot remain together as individual continuums because they are opposing continuums. Light and darkness cannot remain together. There are many types of opposing forces.

In analyzing phenomena, we seek to identify these opposing forces. For example, something hot to the touch and something cold to the touch cannot exist together in a single continuum. They are opposing forces. Therefore, when we want to reduce the heat of something, we rely effectively upon something that is cold. Conversely, we rely upon methods of heat in order to destroy cold. In this way we take advantage of phenomena that are naturally opposing to accomplish what we need and to banish adversity.

With consciousness also, we can identify opposing forces and use them for the purposes of eradicating that which is harmful. Consciousness does not have the same kind of opposing forces found in the external world. With consciousness there are the opposing modes of apprehending. For example, one person will conceive of a carpet as being white while another will conceive it to be a collection of different colors. [128] Of these two distinct ways of apprehending, one might be preferred and is labeled good, while the other is disliked and is regarded as not good.

We have no liking for an object of aversion and we turn away from it. The object takes on an unpleasant aspect and we see it as unappealing. An object of affection takes on an aspect of being appealing, and we feel close and affectionate toward it. An angry mind and a loving mind will not be able to coexist toward a single object at the same time. Through opposing forces, changes naturally occur in the external world. Recognizing them will allow us to control that change. In the inner world of thought also, changes occur naturally through this fundamental principle, and by seeking out their opposing forces they can be deliberately controlled.

NEURONS AND MIND

Base reality can be divided into inanimate matter and the categories of mind and cognition. Western science has mainly concentrated on investigation into external phenomena. Recently—initiated by concerns for health, and so on—scientists have begun investigating mind and feelings. However, their investigation has been limited to the nerve cells, under the belief that consciousness is entirely a function of the brain. Consequently, when the functions of the neurons[64] come to an end, they are inclined to regard this as the cessation of consciousness, and if consciousness ceases there is no reason to accept past and future lives.

In my discussions with neurologists sometimes strange things happen. Some scientists clearly understand that changes in the functions of the brain are initiated by the outer five sense consciousnesses. [129] Therefore, I ask them, if there are no outer conditions at all, do not similar changes occur in the brain simply through the conditions of inner thought? Some reply that it seems that way, but because these changes have to occur in dependence upon the brain, it cannot be like that. I think this answer is actually too simple, and I wonder if such an answer is not influenced or tainted by past culture and traditional thinking. Therefore, I say to scientists that there are many kinds of experiencing consciousnesses such as valid and invalid cognition, conceptual and nonconceptual, faulty perception, and doubt, and I suggest that they conduct research on whether or not these phenomena also bring about changes within the neurons. When scientists conduct research on the mind and cognition, they find it very difficult to explain all the workings of consciousness—which we all experience—by way of the neurons alone.

A German neuroscientist, who was learned in the workings of the nervous system, had previously partaken in a scientific conference in the United States. After that, she came to Dharamsala bringing with her diagrams of neurons she herself had drawn. She had explained to that conference that research on neurons revealed that within the brain there was no center or main area that directed the many different consciousnesses, and that therefore the neurons operated collectively to perform the functions of the brain. She also explained in detail how "mind" mostly operated by way of neurons and said that nevertheless, this was one part of the brain's function, and it was not possible to understand everything about it.

[130] Scientists currently cannot distinguish between valid and non-valid cognition on the basis of the brain. For example, suppose that there is a single object and an instance of cognition of this object is wrong in its mode of apprehension. Suppose then that the succeeding instance of cognition of the same object, by relying upon new conditions, realizes that the previous mode of apprehending is mistaken. A valid cognition that then thinks, "It is not like that, it is like this," is created. Therefore, within the same continuum of consciousness, apprehending the same object, a former instance of that continuum is a wrong consciousness and the succeeding instance is a valid cognition. It is difficult to explain this process on the basis of neurons within the brain.

Those scientists who base their explanations on neurons alone say that when someone experiences suffering, the region of the brain that houses the strong feeling that occurs while that suffering is being experienced is the same region of the brain that experiences the feeling of unhappiness that occurs in the mind when strong compassion is aroused with thoughts that wonder, "What can I do, what can I do!" This was voiced at a scientific conference. When I heard of this I said,

"In that case, our neurons are stupid!" Why? The strong and unwanted feelings of unhappiness that arise when we experience suffering and the feelings of unhappiness that arise when we think of the suffering of others are completely different. However, they are both activated within the same brain. Therefore, the experiencer of those feelings of unhappiness and of being upset—arising as a process of the brain—is one set of neurons.

[131] The causes and conditions for the arising of these upset minds are completely different. One is an upset mental state occurring when we are beset by suffering and are unable to bear it, thinking, "What has happened to me! What can I do! I am in a terrible state." We are upset. The mind is low, naturally depressed, and feels defeated. There is a feeling of helplessness and so the mind becomes small. On the other hand, when we think about the suffering of others and our minds become full of compassion, the mind also becomes upset, thinking, "What can I do to help with their suffering!" However, spurred on by the strong desire to help others, there is no feeling of depression and weakness, and the thought "What can I do!" is not all comparable to the above; the mind becomes vaster. This induces courage, confidence, and a strength of spirit. The causes and conditions for these two types of feelings are completely different, but neurons do not recognize that.

Furthermore, feelings that arise as unhappy mental states, and so on, experienced by the mind and body also arise within the same neurons. Take crying, for example. Tears can flow when reuniting with friends, parents, and so on after a long absence, or when feelings of great joy arise. Also, in bad times, times of disasters and catastrophic events, when depressed, in moments of great anxiety, or when thinking about the specific and general sufferings of samsara and about the impermanent nature of life, tears can fall. Sometimes we cry when laughing uncontrollably at something funny, or when we generate great faith. There are many different circumstances that bring on tears, but the physical reaction of tears falling from our eyes is the same in all. [132]

Expressions occurring at times of joy and sadness, by way of the neurons in the brain, are generalized and coarse. The subtle and varied expressions of consciousness produced through the subtle and varied types of cognition are not visible. This is probably because they are not directly apprehended. Consciousness is very subtle, whereas neurons are matter and coarse in comparison. These days a great deal is known about the workings of the brain, but a thorough understanding has not yet been reached. Therefore, much remains unknown. Eventually, with detailed research they will arrive at a detailed understanding. However problematic and troublesome understanding the brain is, it is coarse compared to consciousness.

These days science is taking a new interest in consciousness and emotions. It will be difficult to gain a profound understanding of very subtle feelings and perceptions. Generally, in the classical texts of ancient India, and in Buddhist texts in particular, there is an enormous amount of explanation on the workings of mind. As we have discussed, modern science concentrates on external phenomena in its investigation of base reality and finds it difficult to explain the workings of inner consciousness. Therefore, if we compare Buddhist psychology and Western psychology, the latter is in the process of developing, while the psychology found in the Buddhist works of ancient India is highly developed.

[133] According to neuron theory, desire, anger, and so on have a region of the brain as their place of origin. Let's think about that. It seems than in general we have a strong connection primarily to generating desire. We persistently develop attraction toward the beautiful and material phenomena of form, sound, smell, taste, and touch. These phenomena have a connection with bodily consciousness and therefore they can be recognized on the basis of neurons. I think there should be research into whether there is any difference between the neurons at the time of generating desire toward the five material sense

pleasures and the neurons at the time of generating desire toward an object by way of mental cognition alone.

Also, is it possible for the desire for liberation to be an afflicted desire?[65] If liberation is ascertained by way of valid cognition, then liberation has to be understood as being empty of any intrinsic existence. Such cognition is probably not an afflicted desire. For example, when looking at the peaceful and coarse features of the higher realms of existence,[66] which are mental phenomena and not sense pleasures, the higher existence is regarded as a state of peace, and desire for that is developed within the mental cognition.

Science has experientially established that contemplating kindness and compassion pacifies anger. Therefore, whether or not this can be explained by scientific investigation of neurons is an interesting question. I made the acquaintance of a well-known scientist at a scientific conference. I have spoken to him a lot about kindness and compassion. He told me that when he was young his father scolded him a lot and made him unhappy. As a result, he also had become very bad tempered. However, after our discussions about kindness and compassion he did some research, and after about six or seven months his bad temper completely disappeared, and he experienced great mental peace. [134] He told me that it was experientially evident that this transformation could not be explained by the science of neurons. This is proof that kindness and compassion definitely brings happiness to the human mind.

In Buddhist texts, the understanding of these types of base reality is given great importance. It is determined that suffering and happiness arise from causes and conditions. For any living creature—including animals—the happiness they desire and the suffering they wish to avoid is not inanimate matter but consciousness. Happiness is the feeling of happiness and suffering is the feeling of suffering. Therefore, trees, flowers, stones, and so on are not spoken of as having happiness and suffering. Some plants, such as the "shy plant"[67] that retracts and shrinks at the touch of hand, have no consciousness but by way of a chemical reaction they produce such movements. Fire has no consciousness but when a hand moves toward a flame some chemical force in the hand causes the flame to flicker. This is also a chemical reaction.

For we living beings possessed of consciousness, discernment arises toward objects, thinking this is this and that is that—regardless of whether we know their names or not. If we were to input every piece of information into a computer, it would produce a signal, but it does not operate of its own volition, discerning and recognizing this and that. The operations of the human brain are like those of a computer. Within our small brains there are enough computer-like components that if it were an actual external piece of machinery it would fill a house. [135] In the brain there is discernment as well as the experience of feelings of happiness and suffering associated with that discernment. This is consciousness, and in dependence on that consciousness experience is produced. Experience occurs in a number of ways. It can arise in dependence upon brain matter and in dependence upon the sense faculties. The classical Buddhist texts explain many types of consciousness arising in dependence upon the sense faculties, while those that arise within the mental cognition itself occur in dependence upon mental elements.

Scientists of the past who believed in the existence of a soul asserted that the soul had to exist within the brain, and it was explained through diagrams. However, as the understanding of the workings of the brain developed, no place could be found for the location of the soul. This inability to locate the soul also presented a difficulty for Christians. This was explained to me by scientists at a scientific conference: "You Buddhists only accept a self that is posited entirely upon the aggregates, and do not talk about the existence of a self posited as the entity of consciousness. As you do not accept a self (soul), there are no such problems for Buddhists."

SENSE CONSCIOUSNESS AND CONCEPTUAL COGNITION

At scientific conferences I usually explain that within consciousness there are five sense consciousnesses: the visual, aural, nasal, gustatory, and bodily consciousnesses. These focus upon external phenomena, which act as objective conditions for the creation of many types of consciousness. They have a particularly deep relationship with the brain. For example, when the brain is partitioned, seeing form, hearing sounds, uttering speech, and so on all have their own regions within the brain. Like the citation "As the bodily sense power pervades the body...,"[68] these are probably pervaded by the bodily consciousness. [137] Therefore, the individual sense faculties, such as those of the eye, are pervaded by the bodily sense power. Other divisions of consciousness such as conceptual and nonconceptual cognition are taught in our classical texts, but in modern science it is the bodily consciousness connected to the neurons that is the most evident.

If people look at the face of the Dalai Lama, there is a cognition focused on the person that they see. That cognition will comprehend me moving my hands, and so on, but whether or not it can ascertain those movements or not is another question. If you think that the Dalai Lama's eyes are like such and such, and you mentally focus on them, looking at the color, seeing what I am looking at, how I am looking at it, and so on, these things are clearly seen and ascertained.

Similarly, when looking at a crowd of thousands of people, all those people—in front, to the sides, near or far—are in my field of vision, but it is not possible to ascertain all of them. If I focus on one person's face, I can begin to ascertain them. In these examples there is a consciousness to which the general aspect of form appears in its entirety, and within that, a more specific aspect that is singled out and focused upon. The latter is a mental cognition. When just looking directly ahead, that observing consciousness is a nonconceptual sense consciousness. Generally speaking, there are nonconceptual discerning consciousnesses, but the ascertaining talked about here operates on a mental cognition.

Therefore, someone looks at me and the Dalai Lama's form and expression all appear to the cognition. After that, they close their eyes. The visual consciousness is no longer operating but those images still appear. Previously they were seen by the visual consciousness and are now imprinted on and appear to the mental cognition. [138] That is a conceptual cognition. To that person who has closed their eyes and whose conceptual cognition is focused on the form of the Dalai Lama, my form will still appear. Is that a direct perception? It is not. It is just an image of a previous experience. The previous seeing is no longer there.

Conceptual cognition has a way of appearing in which entities of time, place, and object are mixed together. For example, we think, "I saw this flower last year. Yesterday I saw it in such and such place." If we close our eyes and think about the Dalai Lama that was sitting here two days ago and the Dalai Lama that is here now, we think, "That is the Dalai Lama of yesterday and of the day before." This can precipitate a cognition of permanence, which is an error.

The way that a nonconceptual cognition perceives is in the manner of the present direct perception of the Dalai Lama, where whatever is there at that time is what is seen. A particular time, place, and object is apprehended right now. It is a perception in which former and later times, places, and objects are not mixed.

The inability of science these days to distinguish between conceptual and nonconceptual cognition on the basis of neurons is an indication that to explain consciousness through scientific methods is not sufficient. The inability to distinguish valid and nonvalid cognition, wrong cognition, and so on are also signs of this.

The reason we hold the classical texts on epistemology in great esteem and study them thoroughly is to know these matters precisely. To learn about the physical features of the earth we study geography.

To know about economic processes, we pursue a study in the science of economics. [139] In this way we learn about the reality of each subject. If we do not know the facts and truths, it becomes very difficult to engage in a proper practice.

A doctor's medical treatment of a patient will only be successful if the doctor knows the physical condition of the patient. Similarly, in order to achieve something exactly as we want it to be, we must have a valid cognition that knows its reality without error. That depends upon cognition itself according with reality. I think that knowing the complete reality of that object's mode of existence and engaging with that object accordingly, or knowing how to function correctly with that object, can be called a valid cognition.

Generally, the term "valid" can be applied to a person and to a cognition. Whichever it is applied to, there has to be a presence of nondeceptiveness.[69] Take as an example the troublesome political discussions between the powerful nations of this world. The actual situation might be one that is vast and wide-ranging, but if they do not consider these facts they will fail to comprehend the root truth of the matter. If instead they seize upon one particular point, thinking, "This is what has caused all the trouble, all these problems come from this," they will fall into wrong thinking and the effect will be failure all round.

In our lives, all religious and secular affairs—even down to the activities of our daily routines—should be carried out by way of valid cognition. Whatever the case, dividing consciousness into valid and nonvalid, and valid and wrong cognition, has a definite connection with our daily life.

[140] The scientific view on the material continuity of body and mind is that our parents' bodies are part of a continuum of the physical bodies that goes back many thousands of years. Extending that further, it goes back to four-legged land creatures. Even further, it goes back to sea-dwelling creatures. These too are our ancestors.

How did these ancestors gain their physical forms? In the beginning this world was a ball of fire. The material continuum of our present physical forms must have been in existence from those times. If there was no material continuum, the first cause of our bodies would have to have been created from no cause, or from something that was not a similar-type cause. That would be contradictory to our common sense.

If we go further back, we arrive at the Big Bang—before the world was created and when there was only nothingness. At that time too, there must have been a very subtle continuity of the material continuum responsible for the creation of our present physical form. It is said that the Big Bang occurred about 13.7 billion years ago. There are those who posit a series of multiple big bangs and those who assert there was only one.

Nevertheless, this raises many questions. The Big Bang was an explosion occurring by very powerful material forces coming together. [141] Therefore, we must explain what brought these forces together. To say it was God's work creates many problems, and if it was not God, then some other cause must be put forward. The Buddhist cosmology of the three-thousandfold universe system speaks of limitless worlds, all of which arise through big bang occurrences. It is difficult to say that there were no big bangs occurring before the causes and conditions of these worlds. That is the reason Buddhist texts state that the universe has no beginning.

If we posit a beginning to the universe, questions would arise asking what was the cause for its existence, what were the conditions for it to come into being, was it created from a permanent cause, or from no cause? If we extend the material continuum of our bodies back in time, it existed in the form of subtle particles during the periods of the empty eons before the world was created, and from the time of the causes of the Big Bang. The *Kālacakra Tantra* texts talk of "space particles." These are the building blocks for the formation of all animate and inanimate matter in the world, and we have to assert that they too arise from previous similar-type causes. Therefore, if we look at the material continuum in that light, I think we can say that it has no beginning.

However, there is a problem here. It is explained that the material continuum of flowers, for example, first emerged twelve million years ago, while the material continuum of our bodies existed before the Big Bang. If we say that there was a similar material continuum of that first flower also at that time before the Big Bang, then from similar material continuums of subtle particles, what was it that made one part become a cause of inanimate phenomena devoid of mind and one part to become the cause of the bodies of animate phenomena? If we are pushed, it seems that to say this is the handiwork of God is the easiest explanation. [142] However, I have talked with scientists and said that we need a good reason to explain this. As a result, it seems that the reason was that when matter was mostly similar in type and operating as subtle matter, they were probably equal in potential. Later, matter joined with other matter to form new compound particles, resulting in different potentials, and thereby producing different outcomes, I think.

Contemplating this from the analytical standpoint found in Buddhist texts, this topic is pertinent to the four kinds of reason—those of nature, dependence, function, and validity—which have been mentioned earlier. This is very important. Whatever the case, matter combines to create new potential. For example, when continuums of chemical substances are combined, the makeup of those subtle particles changes and a new potential is formed. From the combination of substances that were capable of forming a support for consciousness, the physical aggregates of the animate, mind-possessing world gradually formed, whereas that matter, which was still incapable of creating a support for consciousness, probably became the material and similar-type causes for the inanimate world. On the basis of that reasoning, when they are all the same in being subtle particles of inanimate form, it is very difficult to say that one such particle can become a support for feelings and experience and one can be a support of something other than that purely on the potential of the particle substance itself.

From the time life was being formed in the universe, when something became capable of supporting consciousness, consciousness would enter it and life would be created. This is the Buddhist explanation. If that is so, then the question arises, "What causes and conditions does that consciousness come from?" [143]

Consciousness changes moment by moment, and like external matter it is created as an entity subject to destruction in dependence upon its causal moments. If it is posited that there is a first causal moment, then that first moment of consciousness would have to be created from a cause of dissimilar type. If that were possible then even now it would be possible for consciousness to be created from dissimilar-type causes. But such a claim is refuted by reason.

In Buddhist texts a sense consciousness requires three conditions for it to come into existence: an objective condition, an empowering condition, and the immediate condition.[70] In terms of mental cognition, the immediate condition is the most important. Consciousness, in its nature of experience, has many different forms. There are the sensory consciousnesses of the eye, ear, and so on. Even in terms of the brain, different consciousnesses arise in dependence upon different regions of the brain. Nevertheless, all of them are created in the nature of experience, clarity, and knowing. This is because of the immediate condition.

It is important that further research be done and that discussions are held with scientists on the divisions of consciousness into coarse and subtle, the kinds of consciousness connected with the brain, and after brain activity has finished, what kind of experience, if any, is possible. When the Buddhist texts put forward the reasoning that the state of knowing that is present as soon as an infant is born must have been preceded by a previous state of knowing because it is knowing, we should not be satisfied with that general understanding alone.

I do not think "knowing" here refers only to the type of knowing found in the categories of cognition, knowing, and consciousness,[71] as was explained previously. Consciousness has many degrees of coarseness and subtlety, and we should also think about subtle consciousness. [144] If we carry out investigations on the basis of a subtle consciousness, it seems that the teachings of Highest Yoga Tantra[72] take on a great significance.

Whatever the case, if you assert that the stream of consciousness has a first moment, you would have to accept that this moment of consciousness was created from a cause of dissimilar type. Then you would have to say that consciousness can be created from no cause.[73] When it is taught that consciousness has always existed and has no beginning, it does not always sit well with the mind. However, whatever you accept, if the mind is uncomfortable with that, you should not just go with whatever the mind is comfortable with, but analyze instead. If one reasoning produces more proof for and less refutation against and another produces less proof for and more refutation against, you should accept the former.

The way that Buddhist science and modern science are in accord with each other in terms of their views is that they set the reasoning of cause and effect as a basis. On top of that is direct experience with inferential reasoning built on that experience, and lastly, the shared necessity of proving propositions. Here there is common ground. For many years I have held several discussions with scientists, and experience has grown on both sides. More details on this can be found in my book *The Universe in a Single Atom*.

CHAPTER 4

The Universe

[145] THERE ARE MANY DIFFERENT ACCOUNTS and myths that describe the formation of the universe. In Tibet, before the spread of Buddhism, various creation myths could be found in the indigenous Bön religion. Their main topics include order from chaos, light from darkness, day arising from night, and the creation of place from emptiness. These events were solely due to the powers of a special being, and therefore they are accounts of new creation of existence. Other myths say that our world was created from a universal egg and is a living organism.

The rich religious tenets and philosophical traditions of ancient India contain several competing accounts of the formation of the world. The Samkhya tradition with its tenet of a universal principle[74] explains that the origin of our world and the life within it are manifestations of a fundamental source that is the self-sustaining foundation of existence. The Vaiśeṣika school does not posit a single self-sustaining root-substance, but asserts a theory of subtle particles that cannot be subdivided. These are asserted as being the fundamental components of reality.

[146] The materialist school known as the Lokāyata[75] claimed the development of the world occurred from the random creation of inanimate matter, without purpose and design. They also assert that mind and states of mind are formed from the coming together and aggregation of matter. They assert that the mind is an entity of nerves and the result of organic chemical processes. These two positions are not

dissimilar to the tenets of scientific materialism that hold these phenomena to be based on physical forces and processes.

In contrast to the above, Buddhism states that the origins and fundamental basis of every kind of existence is built in dependence upon a network of mutually reliant causes and conditions. Because of this, they explain the development of the world solely on the basis of the natural process of dependence. This process encompasses both consciousness and inanimate phenomena.

The two main Buddhist literary traditions that describe the formation of the world are those of the Abhidharma and Kālacakra. The Abhidharma tradition is accepted by many Buddhist tenet systems such as the Theravada found these days in Thailand, Sri Lanka, Myanmar, Cambodia, and Laos. In Tibet the main work of the Abhidharma tradition that describes the formation of the world is the *Treasury of Abhidharma* by the Indian master Vasubandhu. The two sciences of the psychology of mind and cosmology found in the Abhidharma literature are important and prized elements of Tibetan thinking.

[147] According to the literary tradition formed from the compilation of the Kālacakra texts and various important Vajra Vehicle treatises that incorporate its practices, the main Kālacakra texts were taught by the Buddha, but it is difficult to say when the earliest treatises of this tradition appeared. Nevertheless, several Kālacakra texts were translated from Sanskrit into Tibetan in the eleventh century. Since then they are regarded as holding an important place in Tibetan Buddhism.

According to Abhidharma cosmology, the surface of the earth is flat, around which the sun, moon, planets and constellations move through space to complete their orbits. In this presentation, at the very center of the world is Meru, the king of mountains. Around this mountain at the four compass points are four great continents, each of which is bordered by two lesser continents. All intervening spaces are filled by great oceans. The place where we live is the southern continent. It is asserted that the physical forms of these worlds occupy empty space and are supported by the force of winds. In some ancient texts it is stated that the planets and constellations are globular forms scattered throughout empty space. This is not dissimilar to the structure of constellations described in modern cosmology.

The great scholar Vasubandhu described in some detail the dimensions of the sun and the moon and their orbits, as well the distances between them and our southern continent of Jambudvipa. [148] However, these explanations are in contradiction to the direct observations of modern-day astronomy.

When I was about twenty, I saw pictures of the craters on the moon. I had already understood that the earth was a globe and had some understanding that the earth and the moon orbited around the sun. Therefore, when I studied the Abhidharma tradition of the formation of the world, to be honest, I was not particularly taken by Vasubandhu's Abhidharma description of the creation of this world, although generally the *Treasury of Abhidharma* is an extraordinary work.

In the assertions on the cosmology of the world, the structure of atoms, and so on, taught in the *Treasury of Abhidharma*, there are extensive sections on refutation and proof. However, followers of the Buddha should not rely upon scripture alone. In keeping with developments of our time, we must be able to accept and reject assertions by way of powerful and extensive reasoning in order to produce new ideas and new experiences. Because of that, as a follower of the Buddha I cannot accept the presentation of Mount Meru and the four continents taught in Buddhist literature. The Buddha himself said:

> Monks or scholars, as with the burning,
> cutting and rubbing of gold, examine well,
> and accept my words, but not from respect.[76]

The Buddha has emphatically given us, his followers, the right to examine his own words. Also, in the excellent *Essence of the Excellent*

Explanation on the Provisional and Definitive—which is like a treatise on tenets—composed by Tsongkhapa, it says, "Anyone who holds a tenet that contradicts reason is not fit to be called an authoritative person."[77] [149] Therefore, if we hold such teachings from the *Treasury of Abhidharma* to be literally true, not only does that contradict reason, it contradicts direct perception. Then we would have to deny direct perception. Therefore, someone who accepts such tenets cannot be an authoritative person.

In Buddhist texts in general, and especially in the Great Vehicle texts that place great value on epistemology—the Nalanda lineage, as I often call it—that developed within the Sanskrit tradition, the practice is to investigate by logic and analysis, and if something can be proven, it should be accepted. If not, it is not accepted. If it is not only unproven but something completely contradictory is seen instead, the conclusion in the epistemological texts is that it does not exist. Alternatively, if there is something that is visible, it should appear, and if it exists, we should see it. But if we cannot see it, then we can conclude it does not exist.

Therefore, if Mount Meru and its associated phenomena did exist, we should be able to see them. It is said that the shadow of Meru is something we experience. We supposedly see it and experience it.[78] But to explain that Meru itself, which is the cause of that shadow, is something inexpressible is a difficult position. Therefore, accepting that Meru and so on do not exist is nothing surprising.

Phenomena such as the four continents and the lesser continents may seem like very hidden phenomena to us. And in works that describe very hidden phenomena, there should be no direct and indirect contradictions, but there are many discrepancies in such texts.

In a work by the fourth-century Indian master Dharmatrāta called *Treatise of Miscellaneous Abhidharma Works*,[79] which was translated into Hindi and published by the Central Institute of Higher Tibetan Studies, in Sarnath, Uttar Pradesh, India, Abhidharma topics as they exist in the Pāli language—similar to those in *Treasury of Abhidharma*—are reproduced. This work has sections on the aggregates, sensory spheres and sources, the sense faculties, karma, mind and mental factors, and so on, but the chapter on the world is not there.

The fact is that although descriptions of the formation of the world are found in the philosophical works of Buddhism, there are many contradictions in their explanations. Therefore, although you may be a Buddhist, in order to know what you can accept from those explanations, you have no choice but to examine them, even if you do not use science as a support. In my opinion many sections of the formation of the world as described in the Abhidharma tradition should be discarded. Just how much the master Vasubandhu himself believed in those Abhidharma presentations of the cosmology is open to question.

In the 1930s the great Tibetan scholar Gendün Chöphel (1903–51) traveled around India. He expressed the idea that the Abhidharma explanation of the world we inhabit—identified as the southern continent of Jambudvīpa—represented a map of the central region of ancient India. He also put forward the tempting explanation that descriptions of the other three continents were similar to actual parts of modern India described in Indian geography. Whether his views are right or not, or whether those areas of India were named after those continents asserted to surround Mount Meru, is open to question.

[151] The presentation of the formation of the world as found in the Kālacakra tradition describes definite periods of development of the heavenly bodies in our galaxy. After the stars were formed, the orbiting of the sun through the zodiac, and so on, began.

If we take a wider look at the origins of the world presented in the Abhidharma and Kālacakra traditions, we can see that our world is just one of countless worlds. Both traditions speak of countless worlds, using the term "the three-thousandfold universe." I think this is close to ten billion worlds. Whatever it is, both traditions talk of countless worlds. Therefore, my idea is that, in terms of the Buddhist explanation, all those worlds as a whole have no beginning and no end, but individual worlds have a specific duration with a beginning, middle, and an end.

This has just been a brief discussion on this topic.[80]

CHAPTER 5

Philosophies of World Religions

[207] RELIGIONS OF THIS WORLD that propound particular tenets include Christianity, Islam, Hinduism, Buddhism, and Judaism. Apart from those, there are religions that worship the sun and moon, and so on. Among the first group there are two very different types. One group adheres to the theist philosophy of a creator of the world, and the other does not accept a creator but asserts that the world, its inhabitants, and everything else arise and continue to change by way of many inner and outer conditions.

Among the ancient religions of India was the religious tradition that adhered to the Samkhya philosophy. They were divided into theist Samkhya and nontheist Samkhya. The latter, as well as those of the Jain religion, did not accept the existence of a world creator. The Buddhists also are included in those religions who do not accept a creator.

The various branches of Christianity that are widespread throughout the Western world, and the Middle Eastern religions of Judaism, Islam, Zoroastrianism, and so on, assert the existence of a creator.

[208] Generally, among those who accept a world creator there are those who believe in past and future lives and those who do not. For Christianity and Islam, the type of next life is determined by God. Apart from that, they assert that God created one life and that there is no continuity of lives. Of the non-Buddhist Indian religions, those that teach a system of cause and effect, and that ultimately everything is created by Brahma, also accept past and future lives as well as cause

and effect. In India most schools that accept a creator also assert past and future lives. Christians, and so on, believe that God created this very world. That is very significant.

I once had a conversation about Judaism with a man who told me about Jewish mysticism that was practiced in secret. He said that according to its traditional explanation, when the world was created, we sentient beings played an equal part in the creation. God also was a creator. This struck me as similar to what we say in Tibet, that the world is a human-divine creation. The creator of the world was divine and the world was itself created in conjunction with humans. Whether they believe in past lives, I don't know. Maybe it is that the changes in this life are made by humans with the creator in the background, where the work is directly carried out by humans and changes in the world occur by way of a human-divine process. Or, maybe when the world was first created it was a human-divine effort. In that case they would have to accept past lives. But I don't know. It was not clear to me.

[209] I have an acquaintance, a Christian, Father Bede Griffiths, a wonderful old man. One day I asked him, "If Christians were to accept past lives, what would be the problem?"

He replied, "There is no past life. The creator directly created this very life."

I saw this as being very profound. If you believe in a creator, and it is explained how that creator made this actual world, you will generate great devotion. For example, our body was given to us by our parents, and especially our mother. Because of this we feel very close to our mother. Even animals feel this way. As much as we are devoted to our mother, that much we will happily respond to what she says. Except for those with bad minds, usually we happily respect what she says. This comes from our devotion to her.

Likewise, someone who holds the view that a creator God produced this life of ours will have great devotion toward that creator, and the strength of their devotion will determine the strength of their desire to follow that creator. And what is that creator's wish? For us to be kind and compassionate. That is the creator's main instruction. Therefore, I see this assertion as being very profound.

Tantric Buddhist practitioners engage in a retreat practice called "deity approach" in which they devote themselves to and become close to the meditation deity, thereby "accomplishing" that deity.[81] For theists a creator God has directly created this life, and so there is no need for any deity approach practice; the creator of the world has given us this very life, and a natural closeness arises. Therefore, this assertion is very significant.

[210] This type of theist believes that the creator not only created the world and its inhabitants but also created this life. Therefore, I think there is a little difference between these theists and the theists of ancient India. Generally, Christians believe in the existence of a creator and that this creator is of the nature of wisdom and compassion, and they explain that just as they have faith in such a creator, so they should have love and compassion for all sentient beings created by this creator.

Likewise, when I was having a discussion with an Islamic teacher, he told me that in the Islamic teachings and in Islamic tenets also, it is stated that we should have love and compassion to sentient beings who were created by God.

Therefore, the essential instruction of religions in general, and especially those that are based on tenets, can be categorized as bringing out the love and compassion that is innate in sentient beings. Apart from differences such as having or not having an established philosophy and the variety and depth of practices, within their own systems at the very least they all teach methods to develop happiness in people. Moreover, for the great religions of the world, that happiness does not just refer to the pleasures of this life; they emphasize striving for other more profound and essential goals that center on something everlasting.

QUESTIONS ON SELF

When these religions assert the beginning of self, they posit a creator and say that self has a beginning that was not causeless but was produced by the creator. [211] Moreover, they say that the very complex workings of external nature and the inner workings of the brain all arose by way of design, and that it is not possible that they are just randomly created. Therefore, there must be someone who designed them, and thus there is a creator.

We can examine this issue. During interfaith discussions, three big questions arise directly or indirectly: What is the nature of self? Does that self have a beginning? Does that self have an end? These are very important questions, and the way in which they are answered gives rise to views on whether there is a creator or not.

The way I explain it is as follows. The human species on this planet evolved gradually and in doing so created language, and so on. The ability to think and analyze also developed and the investigation of the I—that which experiences feelings of happiness and suffering—began. Animals are the same as humans in wanting to be happy and not wanting to suffer and in striving every day to ensure they do not suffer and are happy. However, animals do not ask what this I is that wants to be happy and does not want to suffer. Humans, on the other hand, are able to investigate and analyze this. [212] Organized systems of doing so seem to have been around for about three or four thousand years. It is said that culture itself began to develop five thousand years ago, and that religious thought also began around that time.

I have some interest in the development of human societies, but I have not been particularly conscientious in reading any books about it. Therefore, when a well-known Egyptian scholar and university professor met me, I asked him some questions, as I usually do with such scholars. He told me within the development of human societies, religious thinking began about five thousand years ago. In India there are so many different assertions on when Hinduism began to flourish, but it is generally agreed it was not less than three thousand years ago.

The Samkhya philosophical school was part of this early propagation, and if we look at their understanding of self or I, it is like the following. From the perspective of our own experience, when we say, "I saw this flower," the seer is the visual consciousness, and therefore it is the visual consciousness that actually sees the flower. However, when that arises as a thought, in dependence on it being seen by the visual consciousness, we think, "I saw it." The actual seeing is done by the visual consciousness, but to our natural understanding the thought "I saw it" arises.

Similarly, with the body, the thought "my body" arises but not the thought "this body is me." Also, "my mind" occurs as a thought, but there is no identification of mind and body being "I." What arises within the mind is that there is an I that owns body and mind and that controls body and mind. [213] We say, "My body and mind," and therefore, the thought arises that there must be an I that is separate from body and mind.

There are many people who remember their past lives. They establish the existence of their own past lives on the basis of their own experience. The body and mind of their past life and the body and mind of this life are completely different. However, they think, "I remember this. It was like that," and are able to verify it. Therefore, they think, "There must be an I that travels from the past life to this one." The outcome of such thinking is that they declare that this I exists as something other than the aggregates of body and mind, and a self that is other than the aggregates of body and mind.

In ancient India, except for the Buddhists and the materialist Lokāyata school, all schools asserted that there is a self existing as something other than the psycho-physical aggregates. The way that this self arises in the understanding is that when talking about the I that travels from the previous life to this one and the I that travels from this life to a future life, there is the appearance of a single I within the cognition. There are many specific and general instances of the psycho-physical aggregates—those of youth, of adulthood, of old age, and so on. The body undergoes many changes, becoming white-haired and wrinkled. Consciousness also changes, as we can clearly see.

The I of infancy, youth, adulthood, and old age always seems as if it is one. No matter how many changes the body and mind undergoes, an I that undergoes no such changes appears to the cognition. Because of this, this unchanging and permanent self, appearing to permeate all instances of I, is known as "permanent, single, and independent." [214] Whether it has that label or not, the reality is that when talking about a self that is other than the aggregates, it appears as permanent, single, and independent.

Religions that originated outside of India such as Judaism, Chris-tianity, Islam, and Zoroastrianism assert the existence of a conscious-ness known as a soul. For example, Christianity does not accept the existence of past and future lives, and yet they assert that after death there is a soul that separates from the aggregates. Those who have followed God and behaved well will take birth in his presence or in Heaven. Those who held wrong views and not heeded his words are born in everlasting hell. In this way the righteous are divided from the sinners.

At the beginning of the sixties, I met a kind-hearted American woman who was touring around Kullu district.[82] She mentioned that the many Tibetans in Kullu were all very humble and moral. This was wonderful and pleased her greatly. The only sad thing, she continued, was that they had no religion! She was coming from a Christian per-spective, in which we Tibetans were holding wrong views, especially the nihilistic view of not believing in God. As a result, there will be no other place for us except hell, and certainly no Heaven!

In that sense, the object that creates the dividing line is this "soul." It is permanent, single, and independent. Although it does not carry that label, in actuality the Hindu *ātman* and the Christian "soul" seem similar.

Islam also asserts something similar. [215] The creator made the self and after the body is discarded, one is born in his presence.

In my opinion, of the various religions in this world, there are about ten that can be considered major religions. Of these, only Buddhism teaches no-self. When examining what constitutes no-self, Buddhist texts generally speak of a self that is established in dependence upon body and mind, or as a dependent imputation. In establishing just what no-self is, there are one or two subsects of the Vaibhāṣika school from the four main Buddhist schools of thought who talk about an inexpressible self, but no-self is still described as the nonexistence of a permanent, single, and independent self.

So is the meaning of no-self the nonexistence of the I that regularly appears to our cognition? Not at all. The I that appears to our cognition definitely exists. It is on the basis of I existing that I do not want suffering and want happiness. With the reason that I want happiness, I say that I have to develop the causes that dispel suffering, that I will eradicate the causes that bring about suffering, and once they are eradicated I will be free from suffering and enjoy happiness. This I is to be accepted.

The self that does not exist in the term "no-self" is one that exists as something other than the aggregates. This does not exist. Within that, the I exists in dependence upon the aggregates. However, as mentioned previously, when it appears to the cognition, it appears as if it had an intrinsic existence, like a master or lord with power over the body and mind who belong to that I. It is as though the body and mind are like servants or slaves to be controlled. What appears to the cognition is that this is "my body" and "my mind." [216] We are led to think that I am the owner of my mind, and I make efforts to reduce anger and desire and to increase love and compassion. I make these efforts because I am in charge of my mind. From another perspective, the mind is under the governance of the I. Likewise, the body is owned and cherished by the mind. For example, when my knees hurt, and I cannot tolerate the pain, my two hands massage the knees. This is like the I giving orders. This appears to our minds and when it does, this master-like I appears as self-sustaining, and existing with no dependence upon the servant-like body and mind.

The nonexistence of such a self or I is how no-self of persons is explained. The coarse no-self of persons is explained on that basis. The subtle no-self of persons is a little different.

There is not a self that is permanent, single, and independent. When the thought of I arises intrinsically within our mind, it does not appear characterized as permanent, single, and self-sustaining. The conception of a permanent, single, and independent self is one posited by a philosophical tenet. It does not arise intrinsically within our cognition. Adhering to a permanent, single, and independent self is a posited adherence.

So what is an intrinsic adherence? [217] The self is like a master and the aggregates are like servants. The master is in charge and is not reliant upon his servants. Similarly, there is a cognition that regards the self as self-sustaining and not reliant upon the aggregates. That cognition does not accord with reality and is one that perceives wrongly. This adherence is known as an adherence to a self, a misperceiving cognition, and an intrinsic adherence.

The most important understanding of no-self is not just the negation of a permanent, single, and independent self, but the determination that the self-sustaining I—which is like a master in charge of the aggregates—does not exist. That view of the nonexistence of the self-sustaining I is the view of no-self, and is the main object of contemplation, as expressed in the four seals commonly listed in Buddhist scriptures:

All composite phenomena are impermanent.
All afflicted phenomena are suffering.

All existences are empty and without self.

Nirvana is peace and pure virtue.[83]

According to the various assertions on how self and no-self are established, Buddhist philosophy can be divided into four main tenet systems. These are the Sautrāntika, Vaibhāṣika, Cittamātra, and Madhyamaka.[84] In terms of how a self is established, when self or I appears to the cognition, what is it that we are identifying as this I? The Madhyamaka school expresses the view that all phenomena are merely names and imputations and not established from the side of the phenomenon itself. However, the other tenet systems assert that everything must be established from the side of the phenomenon. Because they assert an existence and an establishment from the side of the phenomenon, that self, or I, must also be established from the side of the phenomenon. Therefore, they conclude that the self must be within the aggregates.

In that case, which of the aggregates is the self? [218] To posit the body as a self is difficult. The self moves from one physical basis to another, life after life, and so it is very evident that the I does not exist as the body. Therefore, it must move within the cognition or consciousness. Consciousness can be sensory or mental. Sensory consciousnesses depend upon the sense faculties, and the sense faculties in turn depend upon their physical supports. Therefore, there is no way of establishing a self within the sensory consciousnesses. For example, when we are in a deep sleep, the visual consciousness, audial consciousness, and so on are not operating, but at that time the I or self exists. It is not possible to say that when I am sleeping I do not exist. Therefore, I exist, but because the five sensory consciousnesses are not manifest during sleep, that I cannot be established on the five sensory consciousnesses.

Therefore, we need to look at the mental cognition. For that we should think about thoughts or cognition during the times of dreams, and so on. Self ought to be found upon this mental cognition and should be established upon it. We can consider this in terms of the types of mental cognition. There is a coarse mental cognition that is active while the five sensory consciousnesses are manifest. For example, when we see someone called Phuntsok, we see him by way of the visual consciousness. We see his form, complexion, and so on. At the same time, we hear what he has to say by way of the audial consciousness. Later, after our eyes have seen his form, thoughts about his face, the color of his clothes, the gestures he made while he was speaking, and so on arise within our mind. After listening to his voice, the comprehension of his words, and our thoughts about them arise in the mind. This is mental cognition.

[219] The totality of the form apprehended by the visual consciousness and the sounds apprehended by the audial consciousness is taken on by the mental cognition, which thinks "this is right" and "that is not right" and so on, contemplating the good and bad and so forth. All this is performed by mental cognition. When the eyes are closed, the visual consciousness does not operate, but mental cognition continues to think. Therefore, we have five sensory consciousnesses and a conceptual mental cognition. These two types of consciousness are very evident from our everyday experience.

During the time we are awake, there is conceptual mental cognition. That is a coarse thinking or mental cognition. During the dream state, there is mental cognition, which is a little subtler. During a deep and dreamless sleep, there is a mental cognition that is even subtler. When we faint and lose consciousness, the mental cognition becomes subtle, and when we come out of that faint and become conscious, the continuum of consciousness is there. In this way many coarse and subtle levels of mental cognition are explained. Finally, at death, the most subtle consciousness becomes manifest, known in the tantric texts as "clear light." This clear light can appear during sleep, but death clear light is the subtlest mental cognition. Therefore, with the thought that the I must be established upon mind, the illustration of the I is posited as being the primary mental consciousness.

This issue of the self can also be explained from the perspective of the Buddhist tenet system that asserts that there is nothing that can be established from the side of the object or phenomenon, and that all existence is merely established by name and convention, merely dependently imputed, merely imputed by way of name and convention, and merely imputed upon a basis of that imputation. [220] When searching for the I amid the aggregates it is not found, nor is it found on the various coarse and subtle levels of mind. Therefore, they explain "I" as something merely imputed upon body and mind, just a convention, and as something just dependently imputed. This is the subtlest and most profound view of the Madhyamaka school.

Moreover, they teach that this applies not only to the mere I, but to all existence, as categorized by the aggregates, and so on. Even the Buddha himself, when we attempt to identify him, cannot be found within his body. When we do not analyze, he appears. But if we analyze that appearance, nothing can be found.

Therefore, on this topic of the nature of I and how it can be identified, the assertion of an existing self that is permanent, single, and independent can be found in all non-Buddhist religious traditions. It is the Buddhists who say that the I is imputed upon the aggregates. Within the Buddhist tenet systems there are different assertions on the I existing or not existing among the aggregates, all of which are answers to the question "What is the I?" Dividing tenet systems in this way is the basis of the division of Buddhist and non-Buddhist traditions.

DOES SELF HAVE A BEGINNING?

If the answer to this question is that self has no beginning, it feels very uncomfortable. Even the external world has a beginning. It has so many evident changes and is subject to creation and destruction. Therefore, the thought that it must have a beginning will definitely arise in our mind. [221] On the basis of the thinking that all outer and inner phenomena must have a beginning, we think that I too must have a beginning.

The materialist Lokāyata school say there is no beginning. They do not claim that the world and its inhabitants just suddenly appeared like turning on a light. Instead, they say that the world and its inhabitants were formed by a gradual coming together of conditions, and therefore have no beginning. There is nothing we can point to and say this is the original cause. They just arise naturally. As for the self, they say that it is established from the union of our mother's egg and father's sperm and therefore has no beginning.[85] These phenomena do not arise from previous causes that create them, but spontaneously arise in dependence upon a particular circumstance, and have no beginning.

The Lokāyata, who deny causes, are an ancient Indian philosophy. Not only do they not accept past and future lives, they put forward reasoning to prove that. As for their reasoning, they say that if there were causes, that would result in these causes being infinite, and that would be unacceptable. Therefore, they talk about things naturally arising without causes, and that the self arises causelessly and without conditions.

The Samkhya school say that all outer and inner phenomena arise by design and sequence, and that there must be causes to create them. These causes arise through the creation and destruction processes of the world. They state that there is a universal principle that does not create and destroy and from which all expressions of samsara and nirvana arise and into which they subside. This universal principle emanates these expressions, but the self is unaware and ignorant of that fact, and instead, regards the expressions as real.

[222] Generally, these expressions are manifested by the universal

principle, and, ultimately, they all absorb into it. The universal principle also vanishes like a rainbow, and that is the liberation of the self.
Therefore, the self has no beginning and no end. This is similar to the
Buddhist position. However, that self is very different to the one that
undergoes change and is merely imputed on the aggregates. The self
that has no beginning, no end, and is permanent, single, and unchanging is the self asserted by the Samkhya.

The investigation on whether the self has a beginning and an end
from the Buddhist perspective is a little difficult. The self is something established in reliance upon the aggregates, and existing in
dependence upon the aggregates. Therefore, any examination must
proceed on the basis of whether the aggregates—as the basis or place
of dependence—have a beginning or not. To answer the question of
whether the self has a beginning we need to think about that.

This body came from our parents' sperm and egg, which came
from their parents' body. Their parents' body in turn came from the
sperm and egg of their parents, and so on back hundreds, thousands,
and millions of years ago, until we arrive at the time when the first
human-like creature who walked upright on two legs appeared. [223]
Going back even further, this body finds its origins in the four-legged
creatures who roamed the earth, in those legless snake-like creatures
before them, and even to those organisms who lived in water and later
emerged onto the land. According to science, it is from these organisms that our bodies evolved.

The Kālacakra texts talk about "space particles," and it seems that
these are related to the above. The way the world came about, according to the accepted explanation of creation, is that there was a huge
explosion. It is said that the countless stars we see these days are the
result of that single explosion. Whether this is true or not is hard to
verify, but that is the accepted explanation. The way the world was created was from the pressure exerted by a huge amount of energy. This
exertion of pressure must have also come from causes and conditions.

If the causes of subtle particles, which are devoid of life or consciousness, are traced back, eventually we will arrive at space particles, as discussed previously. Therefore, inanimate rocks, trees, and so on, as well as bodies—such as those of humans—that support consciousness, are brought into existence through these individual space particles. Both these types of phenomena are similar in that they arise from the causes and conditions by way of a process of cause and effect. However, from both being in the form of space particles, one becomes the support for consciousness, and one does not. We should think about whether that involves the intervention of any other cause and condition.

A universe that existed before this one was destroyed, resulting in an emptiness. That emptiness is not like the inner emptiness that results in the clear light mentioned previously, but rather, as described in Maitreya's *Uttaratantra*[86] treatise, coarse form became subtler, and earth, water, fire, wind, and space successively dissolved. When that dissolution reached its ultimate subtlety, it amassed a huge energy, and when that comes into contact with certain conditions, the creation of the universe occurred.

[224] In the reverse process—as described in the Kālacakra texts— from space came wind, fire, water, and earth, successively. Similarly, if we consider the subtle material cause of our body, it comes down to these subtle particles present when the world was created. With other conditions present it develops and declines. For example, this body was formed in dependence upon the tiny drop that is the union of egg and sperm at conception. When conditions accrue upon this small particle of matter, changes occur in its form, shape, complexion, and so on. Anything that is matter cannot possibly arise without a material cause that is itself matter or a material continuum. Therefore, if we focus on the subtle material particles of this physical body, it is very difficult to establish a beginning to its material continuum.

However, as I have just said, if we consider the material continuum of this sentient physical form, it arose from nonsentient matter. Nonsentient matter is by definition not the body of a living being. However, when it becomes a support for consciousness and is connected to consciousness, it becomes a sentient physical form, and the body of a person, or sentient being, is formed. It is not necessary for this body to have been a sentient material continuum since beginningless time. For example, the sperm and egg of our parents on their own are non-sentient matter. When consciousness gathers within them it becomes a sentient phenomenon. The origins of the continuum of the body, when traced back, is like that.

The five sensory consciousnesses, as mentioned before, are coarse consciousnesses. The mental cognition is subtler and itself has many degrees of subtlety. As long as it is a consciousness it needs conditions for it to be manifest. For example, any sensory consciousness needs three conditions: an objective condition, an empowering condition, and the immediate condition. [225] Candrakīrti's *Autocommentary on Entering the Middle Way* speaks of four conditions: a causal condition, an external objective condition, an empowering condition, and the immediate condition. The main condition of the first three is the immediate condition, through which the consciousness is created as an entity of clarity and knowing.

If there were no preceding stream of consciousness, even if the objective condition comes into contact with the empowering condition, a consciousness cannot be generated. For example, if there is a fault with the mental cognition, no consciousness will be produced even if the external objective condition and empowering condition combine. Therefore, the preceding consciousness is known as the immediate condition.

The production of an entity of clarity and knowing is explained as occurring by way of the immediate condition, and this has relevance for the existence of a past life. To say that a life is conceived in the womb means that consciousness combines with sperm and egg and a human life begins. The human form has not yet developed, and a human being has not actually been created. Therefore, we say it is in an embryonic stage. Teachings of what constitutes the act of killing talk about "a human being or embryo."[87] Therefore, the consciousness of an embryo that has just been conceived in the womb cannot have a wide range of cognition, but it is an entity of clarity and knowing. If something established as an entity of clarity and knowing has as its material cause something that is not an entity of clarity and knowing, then essential characteristics become confused. If mind can be created from nonsentient matter[88] in one instance, then it follows that mind can be created from nonsentient matter everywhere. Therefore, for its material cause, consciousness requires a similar-type continuum that is a consciousness of clarity and knowing.

Therefore, if we talk about whether or not there is a beginning to birth, we have to think about whether self has a beginning or not. For that we have to think about whether the basis for the labeling of self has a beginning or not. Generally, that basis is the aggregates and specifically it is the consciousness. Within consciousness there is mental cognition, which, according to tantric texts, has a very subtle form. [226] And if we have to posit a beginning to that, it becomes very difficult. We would have to accept that it has no cause or that it was produced by a creator. Both these positions do not withstand analysis. What is it that cannot withstand analysis? Consciousness must exist on the basis of a continuum of consciousness. If we posit a beginning to consciousness, then we must assert that it can be created from nonsentient matter. That leads to absurd consequences and so we cannot posit a beginning to consciousness. If that is so, the self or person, which is imputed upon the stream of consciousness—the most important of the aggregates—also cannot have a beginning.

Therefore, on the basis of the explanation in the Buddhist texts that the I has no beginning, it can be established that the I does not arise from no cause or from a cause that is permanent. It also does not arise from something nonsentient and was not created by a creator. It arises from its own similar-type cause, while consciousness is created from the continuum of its own preceding instances.

DOES SELF HAVE AN END?

In answer to this question, the materialist Lokāyata school asserts that the I has no beginning as such and just spontaneously arises. After death too, the body is the support of consciousness. They say "consciousness is an expression of the body" and that when consciousness no longer has the power to emerge, it too becomes nonexistent. The I or person also becomes nonexistent. This assertion that everything comes to an end seems to be a convenient explanation, but when examined, it is very troublesome. [227] How did this world come about? Does it have a beginning or not? What is the essence of a human life? What is the purpose of a human life? When such questions are raised, they would have to say that we are probably no different to animals, eating and drinking to sustain their lives and procreating to sustain their kind.

Those who assert the existence of God say that he created the self, and if we have been good, we will come to sit by his side. I do not know if there is anyone who clearly states whether this has an end or not. So, how do Buddhist texts answer this question? In terms of the coarse consciousness without any detailed presentations of the various coarse and subtle levels of consciousness, some who follow the tenets of the Vaibhāṣika school state that consciousness is a phenomenon that coexists with afflicted cognition. When the stage of an arhat is finally attained, all afflictions are eradicated, and for the time that their aggregates remain in this life, that arhat is known as "one with remainder." These aggregates are in the nature of suffering and were formed previously by karma and afflictions. When those aggregates are cast off, the four demons are destroyed. These are the demon of the aggregates that were precipitated by mental afflictions, the demon of mental afflictions, the demon of the lord of death, and the demon of the youthful god of distraction.[89] At that time nirvana is attained and because the demon of the lord of death and the demon of the aggregates have been destroyed, there are no remaining aggregates. Therefore, the self, which is labeled upon those aggregates, also disappears because the continuum of knowing has been cut like the extinguishing of a butter lamp flame. Thus, they say this is the end of self.

All other Buddhist tenet systems say that the self has no end. Why is that? [228] The ultimate basis for the labeling of self is consciousness, and that consciousness is an entity in the nature of clarity and knowing. As long as a consciousness remains, it remains in the nature of clarity and knowing. Afflicted states such as anger and desire do not enter the nature of consciousness. Therefore, in reliance upon the antidotes the strength of those mental afflictions will weaken and eventually be eradicated. That which exists as the fundamental state of mere clarity and knowing, and that which is a misperceiving cognition, exist distinctly and can therefore be separated. There is no powerful antidote or force that can oppose the entity of mere clarity and knowing.

When a misperceiving cognition comes into existence it wrongly perceives the reality of the situation. As long as that reality exists it remains as an existing phenomenon, regardless of whether or not an antidote to that misperceiving cognition has been applied in the mind. For example, there is a white flower and someone whose eyes are faulty sees it as yellow. According to common convention that flower is white. Therefore, at all times there exists an opposing force to that cognition perceiving the flower as yellow because of a fault with the eyes. Why is that? The cognition that sees the flower as yellow does so because of some temporary circumstance, but in reality the flower is not yellow. Therefore, the reality of the flower being white will remain until that flower is destroyed, and for that person who looks at the flower, as soon as the temporary fault with their eyes disappears, they will see it as white. The perception that sees the flower as white has a completely opposing mode of apprehension to the perception that sees it as yellow, because the perception that sees it as white abides in reality and the perception that sees it as yellow does not. [229] Therefore, if you ask someone with no fault in their eyes, "Is this flower yellow?" they will definitely say that it is not. When that person who sees the flower as yellow is cured of their eye ailment and they look again at the flower, they will see it as white. Seeing the flower as yellow is merely a mistaken perception brought on by a temporary aberration. It is not the reality and there is no valid cognition to support it. The perception of the flower as white, on the other hand, no matter how hard and how often you look, and however many times you ask others, the reality of it being white is firmly established. Therefore, it can be undeniably proven that there is a valid cognition to support that perception.

This is similar to the way that scientists investigate. Someone will discover something, and they will conduct investigations again to back up what they have discovered. Other people will also investigate this discovery, and if the results are similar, only then will it be accepted. They do not determine the definite existence of something on the basis of someone suddenly seeing something. Our procedure is similar. As described previously, it all depends on whether there is the support of a valid cognition or not. In the study of types of cognition, whether a cognition is a misperception or not is established by whether or not there is another cognition that opposes it. Even minds of anger and desire have opposing states of mind.

The psychiatrist Aaron T. Beck, who is in his nineties, has given very helpful advice for those with troubled minds. He has written many books, one of which he gave to me. In the introduction it says, "We are prisoners within the prison of anger." This is a wonderful sentence. In our discussions he said to me that when examining patients he found that many of them focus on one particular object that greatly disturbs their mind. [230] They become very angry and the person who is the object of their anger appears as very unpleasant. That appearance of unpleasantness, he continued, was ninety percent created by their own conceptualization. It had no existence in reality.

This is exactly what is taught in Buddhist texts. Ārya Nāgārjuna, in a Madhyamaka work, says, "Karma and afflictions come from conceptualization."[90] This conceptualization is described as "improper mental engagement."[91] When focusing on a particular object, that object will have good and bad aspects. Desire occurs when conceptualization improperly engages with that object by overstating its good aspects, and it appears as very attractive. Focused on that, strong attachment is born, in which there is a longing not to be separated from that object. This is desire.

There are great differences in the ways we regard these aspects. One woman in the eyes of another is a good person, a close relative, or a mother. Someone else will see her as their wife, thinking that sometimes we argue and sometimes we are loving. Someone else will look at her and think, "This is my daughter." Another will look at her and see an enemy, while another will look at her without any recognition and regard her as a stranger. Therefore, five or six people who look at one woman will have different ways of seeing her. This is a fact. When someone looks at her and says, "This is my mother," that is true. From his perspective she is a mother. But she is not the mother of all living beings. Someone else sees her as an enemy, because of some circumstance that gave rise to an unfriendly situation. But she is not the enemy of all sentient beings.

Therefore, there are these opposing views. [231] If her goodness was an actual reality, then she would be a hundred percent good, and that goodness would appear to everyone. But that does not happen. For each person who looks at her she has a different appearance. This clearly shows that one object can have many good and bad aspects. That is for sure. Moreover, these good and bad aspects are conditionally determined. They are not truly existing good and bad aspects.

Since these things are determined conditionally, then there are differences in the way things appear to particular cognitions and in the perspective of those cognitions. Therefore, if a particular object has a little good about it and we elevate that to a hundred percent good with improper mental engagement overstating the reality, the thought of not wanting to be separate from it will arise. If an object has something a little unpleasant about it, and we elevate it similarly by overstating the reality through improper mental engagement, then that object appears to the mind as undesirable and unattractive in every way. Aversion arises and we want to be far from it.

Concerning the individual ways that minds of anger and desire apprehend their objects, an object focused on with desire is seen as having hugely attractive qualities. We happily accept it and have no wish to be apart from it. Such attachment arises from a basis of conceptualized overstating. An object of aversion is regarded as very unpleasant and there is a strong desire to keep it at a distance and to be separate from it. This mind of aversion also arises from a basis of conceptualized overstating. A cognition that knows the reality of the situation becomes one that directly contradicts this overstating. If within the mind that sees only unattractive qualities, we can see that there are also attractive qualities, then the thought arises that this object is not so bad. There is a good side too. At that time, the previous cognition of that object as wholly undesirable, of being strongly averse to it and wanting to be far from it, starts to lose its strength. With minds of strong desire also, we can see the other side. Therefore, there are opposing minds to those of aversion and desire.

That which possesses an entity of mere clarity and knowing, and which knows its object, is the definition and the nature of consciousness. There can be nothing that contradicts the nature of consciousness. Physical form or inanimate matter and consciousness have different functions, but they are not mutually contradictory. Anything that is a consciousness will always be solely of the nature of clarity and knowing. Therefore, among consciousnesses there are none that have a contradicting mode of apprehending or a contradicting entity toward such a consciousness.

There is no consciousness that will contradict the nature of consciousness. There is no obstacle that can hinder its existence and thus it has no antidote. Anger, desire, and so on are misperceiving cognitions that contradict reality. Therefore, when a cognition is developed that knows the reality, it contradicts such cognitions. Therefore, there are consciousnesses that will contradict misperceiving cognitions. These misperceiving cognitions are in the nature of clarity and knowing, but they do not abide only in the nature of mere clarity and knowing. They misperceive reality by the force of other conditions, and therefore that misperceiving aspect can be contradicted and there is no way it can remain. The minds of anger and desire do not contaminate the entity of mere clarity and knowing, and therefore they can be separated from it and are temporary. They are called "temporary" from the standpoint of their being separable and subject to the force of antidotes, whereas the mere clarity and knowing aspect is known as "primordial." That never changes.

[233] Therefore, after the arhat has eradicated all mental afflictions and discarded the body formed by karma and afflictions, clarity and knowing will still remain. Moreover, even though there is no continuum of aggregates formed by karma and delusion, aggregates formed in dependence upon pure causes and conditions will arise. Therefore, in that way, the self has to be without an end. This is the answer to the question "Does self have an end?"

There are some disagreements on this topic of whether self has an end between Buddhists and non-Buddhists, and even between Buddhists. This is significant. The Buddhist position is based on there being no creator and that all things arise from causes and conditions.

CHAPTER 6

The Pāli and the Sanskrit Traditions

[241] TWO THOUSAND FIVE HUNDRED and fifty-nine years ago from this year of 2016, the Buddha first turned the wheel of Dharma in India. From this arose the sutras found in the Pāli and Sanskrit traditions of Buddhism. These two languages became the main media for the transmission of the great and lesser vehicles of Buddhism. The Buddha had fully absorbed the knowledge of the cultural traditions and religions of his own country but he was not content with them. On his own and with much hardship he completed the practices of insight and purification. This religious tradition is a wonderful legacy of that achievement.

According to the śrāvaka schools, when the Buddha was born in India he was a bodhisattva destined to become newly enlightened in that very life. When he became enlightened in Bodhgaya[92]—having previously undergone six years of extreme ascetic practice—he conquered the demon of mental afflictions and the demon of the youthful god of distraction. After enlightenment he remained in his body for over forty years. His life had been blessed and he had conquered the demon of the lord of death.[93] [242] Finally, in the town of Kushinagar at the time of his nirvana he conquered the demon of the aggregates. After attaining this "nirvana of no remaining aggregates" his continuum of consciousness was severed like the extinguishing of a flame.

On the basis of that explanation, firstly, if the result of the bodhisattva gathering vast merit for three countless eons[94] is to become enlightened and then to work for living beings for only forty years, this makes a mockery of the law of cause and effect. For example, a worldly task accomplished with great hardship should reap a result commensurate to the amount of effort put into it.

Secondly, our teacher, the Buddha, extensively taught both vehicles, as well as tantra, and to assert that this entire path arose in his mind during that one life of eighty-one years is very difficult. In particular, if the continuum of his consciousness was cut after the nirvana without remainder, then the blessings of the Buddha, various visions, and the mandalas of the tantras could not manifest later.[95]

Therefore, in the Great Vehicle tradition, although the Buddha was not enlightened from the beginning, he became enlightened many eons ago through a path of practice as a cause. Then in India, he performed the deeds of a buddha in the form of a supreme emanation. This emanation is known as the emanated body that arises from the enjoyment body of a buddha, which in turn arises from the sphere of the dharma body of enlightened qualities. This presentation on the three forms or bodies of a buddha is very important and is explained briefly later on.

[243] The twelve deeds of the Buddha, such as being born into the Śākya family in 626 BCE[96]—2,641 years ago from this year of 2016— are well described in the treatises. The deed of his words is the best of all the deeds of the Buddha. Consequently, through his enlightened speech, delivered skillfully and with great compassion, he completed the deed of delivering his teachings on the base, path, and resultant states of the three vehicles. Purely in historical terms, some Western scholars say that the Dharma was first taught by the Buddha in Pāli and then later it arose in Sanskrit. According to Buddhist thinking, the Buddha taught the eighty-four thousand categories of Dharma in languages suited to the minds of the disciples. As he said,

In the many languages of living beings,
I will teach the Dharma.[97]

Therefore, there is an explanation stating that no single language can be determined above any other. There also exists the alternative assertion that Sanskrit, which literally means the "well-constructed" language, is supreme among all others, and that the Buddha taught in Sanskrit.

The written words of the Buddha are found only in Pāli and Sanskrit, although a few sutras survive in local dialects. Apart from some corruption, Pāli and Sanskrit are quite similar in terms of grammatical rules, verbal expression, and linguistic family. Almost all of the great works found in Pāli and Sanskrit have been translated into Tibetan. [244] If Sanskrit and Tibetan are compared, apart from some differences in a few areas, they can be used similarly. There are about twenty prepositional prefixes in Sanskrit and their grammatical usage and characteristics are found only in Tibetan and not in other languages. The ability of Sanskrit syllables to be individually analyzed and the understanding of grammatical constructions all fit well in the Tibetan language. I believe that every work existing in Pāli and Sanskrit can be translated without loss and corruption into our Tibetan language. Therefore, as languages capable of expressing the presentations of Buddhist science, Pāli, Sanskrit, and Tibetan are equal.

Generally speaking, there are four Buddhist languages: Pāli, Sanskrit, Tibetan, and Chinese. Most of the scriptures found in the Tibetan Kangyur and Tengyur—the Tibetan Buddhist canon—were also translated into Chinese. However, early translators were at first unable to employ the more literal style of translation that was used for Tibetan translation and instead they followed a more general style focused on the meaning. This meant that the complete meaning was not always clearly expressed. Moreover, Chinese is far removed from Sanskrit and the linguistic construction of the two languages is quite distinct, making it difficult to compare them.

There are other issues too, but whatever the case, there are many Buddhist works translated into Chinese that just sit on library shelves, their archaic language making the textual meaning—right down to the individual words—difficult to understand. This means that religious groups in China, such as practitioners of the meditative absorptions and those of the Pure Land school have no profound interest in studying and training in the texts and the various philosophical views, meditative practices, and spiritual conduct. Instead, they focus on practicing single-pointed meditation or on reciting a specific sutra, explaining that this will result in birth in a pure land. Also, the tradition is said to have declined over time because of various circumstances and conditions.

[245] The complete teachings of the Buddha as found in the Pāli Canon are grouped into forty-six volumes comprising the three baskets.[98] The Great Vehicle sutras are not complete in the Pāli Canon and from the commonly accepted sutras there are four not present that are found in Tibetan. Most of the *dhāraṇī*[99] section is not there and there is no tantra at all.

The number of Buddhist works existing today in Sanskrit does not amount to even a hundred. In Tibetan there are over four thousand individual works in the Kangyur and Tengyur.

When translating back from Tibetan into Sanskrit, the words of the texts can mostly be replicated precisely. Not only this, but there are many instances where the Tibetan translation is better than the existing Sanskrit version. Although the source of the Tibetan Buddhist religious culture is Sanskrit and Pāli, if you want to look at the complete presentations of the three vehicles and the four classes of tantra, it is a fact that they are to be found in no language other than Tibetan.

At this present time the complete Great Vehicle collections found in the Tibetan language, and especially the collections of tantra, are incomplete in the other three languages. Because of this, there is no way to know those texts except to rely upon the Tibetan language. In the sense of being beneficial for the whole world, Tibetan is clearly an important language.

In particular, there is a living and widespread study tradition of the complete Buddhist treatises on Abhidharma, monastic discipline, Middle Way philosophy, the perfection of wisdom sutras, and epistemology in the Tibetan language. Many works on arts and craft, as well as works on all the major and minor sciences of grammar, medicine, and so on that have disappeared in India, are all found to this day in the Tibetan language. These include the forms and dimensions of mandalas and deity representations; [246] the choreography for religious dance; the ways to play musical instruments and to sing; diagrammatic notation of chants; Ayurveda traditional medicine— sometimes enhanced with indigenous Tibetan practice—preparation of consecrated diagrams and protection wheels; chemical processes involving powders, alchemy, the preparation of incense, and so on; the science of calculation including astronomical calculation; and prognostication methods such as those found in the *Arising Letters Tantra.*

The sources of all these scriptural traditions are the teachings of the Buddha, which were propagated in India at different times in different places. For example, to those disciples of sharp faculties and pure karma he taught the perfection of wisdom on Vulture's Peak,[100] and in the south at Dhānyakaṭaka[101] he taught the *Kālacakra Tantra* and others. After his doctrine had spread, monasteries and centers of learning such as Nālandā, Odantapurī, Vikramalaśīla, and Taxila appeared and flourished over the centuries.[102]

The most important of these was Nālandā Monastery. It has its origins during the time of the Buddha and flourished from around the fifth century up to the beginning of the thirteenth. In the seventh century the Chinese monk Xuanzang traveled to India and wrote in his diaries that there were about three thousand teachers and masters in philosophy and over ten thousand students in Nālandā. [247] He explained that the library had nine floors containing over nine million precious scriptures.

Most great Buddhist scholar-practitioners, exemplified by the glorious Ārya Nāgārjuna, studied at this monastery. Over time, it became a center for learning: not only for monks but for lay men and women also, and not only for the science of Buddhism but for sciences outside of Buddhism, including grammar, medicine, epistemology, arts and crafts, and so on. Moreover, it became an international center of learning for students from neighboring countries and was not just for Indians.

The religious traditions that spread from that monastery reportedly included those in the Pāli language, although the majority of the vast and profound philosophies as well as many wonderful commentaries were in Sanskrit. Scholars were able to study texts in both Pāli and Sanskrit. From the Pāli tradition they studied the paths of the thirty-seven facets of enlightenment, and so on. Of those in Sanskrit, they studied the perfection of wisdom sutras, and so on. In this way, they studied and practiced everything on the paths of method and wisdom founded on the two truths. When they composed treatises, they did so in the Sanskrit language. All the great works on the Middle Way and Cittamātra schools of the Great Vehicle were composed by Nalanda masters, and it is asserted that the source of these works were the sutras of the Buddha written in Sanskrit.

[248] In that way, two Buddhist traditions arose in the two religious languages of Pāli and Sanskrit. Through Pāli the Theravada doctrine gradually spread to Sri Lanka, Thailand, Myanmar, Cambodia, and other countries. From Sanskrit the teachings spread to China by way of Central Asia and then to Japan, Korea, Vietnam, and so on, as well as to Tibet.

If we rely upon the literal wording of teachings in Great Vehicle works that speak of the superiority of the Great Vehicle, a perception of the śrāvaka and pratyeka doctrines as being inferior automatically arises. However, such designation does not accord with reality. Moreover, it is important to establish those religious languages regarded as the main ones for the scriptures and by doing so make a division into a Pāli religious tradition and a Sanskrit religious tradition. This will have the worthwhile effect of avoiding such misunderstandings and be more in accord with reality.

These days those who follow the Theravada doctrine of the Pāli tradition in Thailand, Sri Lanka, Myanmar, and so on, and who work to preserve, protect and disseminate the teachings of the Buddha, are the very foundation of these teachings. Therefore, it is completely unfitting for such practitioners to be disparagingly and disrespectfully called "those of the Lower Vehicle." Many practices of theirs, while they may not be better than ours, are certainly not inferior.

If we look at the evolution of Buddhist literary tradition, many non-Buddhist scholars employed the medium of Sanskrit. They used new forms of reasoning to argue against the Buddhist scriptural positions. [249] As a result, Buddhist scholars had no choice but to respond with effective analysis and think of new forms of reasoning to oppose the non-Buddhist arguments. This all contributed to an excellent development of the Sanskrit literary tradition, and the placing of Buddhism into an academic framework meant that it became clearer than in the past. The language used by these Buddhist and non-Buddhist scholars alike was the rich language of Sanskrit. Therefore, classic works such as Dharmakīrti's *Treatise of Valid Cognition* had a topic of sound Buddhist philosophy and a medium—in keeping with Sanskrit's glowing reputation—of a perfect language. In this way, word and content complemented each other.

THE BUDDHISM OF TIBET AND NĀLANDĀ

The development of Buddhism in Tibet began during the reign of the Tibetan emperors. This occurred about four hundred years after Buddhism had spread in China. From the time of the first Tibetan king,

Nyatri Tsenpo, whose reign began around 127 BCE, the land that we now call Tibet has seen many kingdoms, and it was the thirty-third emperor, Songtsen Gampo (617–50), who had the noble intention to introduce and spread Buddhism in Tibet. In 633 the youth Thönmi Sambhota (seventh century) and others were sent to India to learn the art of translating. [250] Arriving at Nālandā they studied Buddhism and Sanskrit, and in 646 returned to Tibet bringing with them five volumes that were then translated into Tibetan. In this way, the tradition of transmission and teaching began.

In the eighth century, in particular, during the rule of the thirty-eighth emperor, Tri Songdetsen (742–97), the translator Bamang Jé Salnang[103] and others traveled to Nālandā. Tsang Lekdrup and Vairocana were enrolled at Nālandā and brought to Tibet many instructional teachings.[104] The emperor invited the Bodhisattva Abbot Śāntarakṣita, and the great Ācarya Padmasambhava, from India to Tibet. Because of the glorious activities of these two masters and the emperor, Buddhism gained a foothold in Tibet. The emperor invited many Nalanda scholars to Tibet, such as Ācarya Jinamitra, and twelve fully ordained monks of the Sarvāstivādin Buddhist tradition in order to begin a monastic tradition in Tibet.

During the reign of Tri Ralpachen (806–38) the Indian masters Surendra Bodhi, Śīlendra Bodhi, and Dānaśīla came to Tibet from Nālandā and they and others translated and disseminated many works.

Śāntarakṣita assumed the mantle of teaching and disseminating the three baskets of teachings, including works on Middle Way philosophy and epistemology, and the teachings of the Buddha in general. He constructed the first Tibetan monastery to preserve the teachings of the Buddha, known as Glorious Samyé, the Unchanging and Spontaneous Temple. On its upper eastern side was the Place of Pure Ethics where the first seven monks of Tibet were ordained.[105] On the middle eastern side was the Place of the Supremely Wise Mañjuśrī, where Buddhist philosophy was examined. On the lower east side was the House of

Linguistics, where grammar was studied. On the upper south side was the Place of the Tantric Subduing of Hindrances, where tantric ritual practices were performed. On the middle south side was the Place of Ārya Palo, where wrathful Hayagrīva practices were performed. On the lower south side was the Place of Indian Translation, where works that were in Sanskrit were translated into Tibetan. [251] On the upper west side was the Place of the Prophesized Vairocana, where the great translator Vairocana resided. On the middle west side was the temple of prophesies called Place of Ganden Maitreya. On the lower west side was the Place of Unwavering Concentration, where meditation was practiced. On the upper north side was Place of Various Gems, where gems were stored. On the middle north side was the Place of Bodhicitta. On the lower north side was a temple known as the Pehar Storehouse. Thus, departments for sutra, tantra, and the sciences, as well as individual temples, were constructed.

If the great abbot Śāntarakṣita had established a tradition of studying Buddhism in Sanskrit at that time, it would have been acceptable, but he recommended that it should done in the Tibetan language. The fact that up to today we are able to genuinely preserve, protect, and disseminate the entire canon of Buddhism solely in the Tibetan language, without having to depend upon Sanskrit, is due to the kindness of this great being. Some historians say that Śāntarakṣita himself studied Tibetan. There are claims that this great master lived a thousand years or nine hundred years, but some time ago at a conference in south India to celebrate this master, an Indian scholar called Madhur explained that Śāntarakṣita was seventy-five when he went to Tibet, where he stayed for about twenty years. Thus, he lived to be about a hundred.

The Indian scholar Professor Jagannath Upadhyay talks about how Tibetans like to add a zero to a hundred to make a thousand! By developing the power known as the Knowledge Immortality and reaching high levels of attainment, it is possible to have control over lifespan.

[252] However, even the Teacher and Master of the Doctrine, the Bhagavan—as the Buddha was known—did not live past eighty-one, and I think that those who came after him followed the ways of the world. Therefore, the assertions that Śāntarakṣita lived for a thousand years and that Nāgārjuna lived for six hundred years should be seriously examined. Such life spans may be possible, but it is also possible that with excessive pure perception[106] we are unintentionally turning lamas into frauds!

For example, in our reverential praise of Dharma King Songtsen Gampo we say that he actually had the head of Amitābha in a protrusion on the crown of his own head. I have my doubts about that. It is possible that in reality Songtsen Gampo was a manifestation of Avalokiteśvara and that he displayed a sign of Amitābha. A pure perception of that could arise. However, if the throat of Amitābha was planted within the brain of Songtsen Gampo—a man of flesh and blood—and another head resembling a flesh protrusion appeared on his own head, that naturally raises many questions. Could this head speak, for example? Therefore, foolish pure perception that goes to extremes is not good. It is important to proceed in accordance with reality.

Therefore, the statements that Songtsen Gampo lived to the age of thirty-five or to the age of eighty-five, as well as the assertions that at the end of his life he dissolved into the heart of the fivefold self-arisen statue[107] or that his body lies in the royal tombs, are, I think, different accounts according to pure perception and the generally accepted perception of ordinary believers.

The precious Ācarya Padmasambhava primarily took on the responsibility of dispelling the obstacles, human and otherwise, that were hindering the spread of the teachings of the Buddha in Tibet. [253] He also gave many tantric teachings such as Highest Yoga Tantra empowerments, teachings, and so on, to twenty-five very special and fortunate disciples, who included Emperor Tri Songdetsen, also known as

Dharma Emperor Lha'i Metok. This was the first appearance of tantric teachings in Tibet.

In short, the spread of the ten sciences[108] in Tibet was due to the kindness of these great scholars from India and Tibet. It was the legacy of those fresh-minded ancestors who traveled from Tibet to Nālandā Monastery and of those many scholars who later journeyed to the great learning centers of Vikramalaśīla and Taxila. According to the biography of Jowo Atiśa and the travel records of Naktsho Lotsawa (1011–64), so many Tibetans visited Vikramalaśīla that a special residence for Tibetans was established. Among those great translators who traveled to Nālandā Monastery, Tsami Lotsawa Sangye Drak (eleventh century) was made abbot of Nālandā.[109] Furthermore, many Tibetan scholars went to Nepal, Khotan, Kashmir, and so on, where they studied the local language and Buddhism.

In this way, during the seventh and eight centuries many Tibetan students were sent to east and west India, Nepal, and elsewhere. As a result, between the time of the translator Thönmi Sambhota and Chak Lotsāwa Chöjé Pal (1197–1264) about fourteen great translators studied at Nālandā. These details from Kyesar Ludrup's *Research on Nalanda* are worth knowing. [254] Also, beginning from Thönmi Sambhota up to Lotsāwa Ācarya Rinchen Chok in the middle of the fourteenth century about 243 translators appeared in Tibet. This and other interesting information can be found in Tsering Wangdu's *History of Translation in Tibet and Biographies of Translators*.

Furthermore, according to a short work entitled *Necklace of Precious Jewels: A List of Indian Pandits Who Visited Tibet and Tibetan Scholars Who Traveled to India between the Seventh and the Seventeenth Centuries, Their Dates and Brief Description of Their Activities*, among the scholars and pandits who were invited to Tibet, eight came from Nepal, and one hundred and twenty came from India and Kashmir, thereby spreading the lineage of Nalanda—the pure doctrine of the Buddha—in Tibet.

In Tibet we use the term *bandé* for these monks who preserved the religion of the Buddha.

KANGYUR AND TENGYUR

The Tibetan Buddhist canon, known as the Kangyur and Tengyur, preserves the Buddhist texts that were brought from India to Tibet. These were mainly translated directly from Sanskrit, but there are also texts that were translated from Pāli, Chinese, and Nepalese languages. In the eighth century, during the reign of Tri Songdetsen, the great translator Bandé Paltsek and others were the first to catalog the contents of the Kangyur and Tengyur that was housed in Phangthang Kamé Monastery. This became known as the Phangthangma Catalog. After that, in the same century, the translator Kawa Paltsek, Khönlü Wangpo Sung, and others edited and corrected the Kangyur and Tengyur in Tongthang Den Palace, to produce a catalog of listed contents known as Denkarma Catalog. [255] After that, the translator Kawa Paltsek and others again created the Chimphuma Catalog of the Kangyur and Tengyur that resided in Chimphu Palace. These were the first three catalogs of the Kangyur and Tengyur. Later, Chomden Rikpai Raldri (twelfth century) created an extensive catalog of the Kangyur and Tengyur as well as the Kangyur Sunray Catalog, while Losal Jangchup Yeshé from Central Tibet compiled an abbreviated catalog.

These two masters, together with others, from 1312 onward, gathered and compiled all available texts of the Kangyur and Tengyur into one complete edition. Together with an extensive, intermediate, and abbreviated catalog of contents, it was housed in Narthang Monastery. This was the first complete edition of the Kangyur and Tengyur in Tibet.

In 1323 Tsalpa Dorjé produced an edition of the complete Kangyur written in gold and silver and known as the Tsalpa Kangyur. Many other handwritten editions of the Kangyur and Tengyur, written in gold, silver, vermillion, or black ink, appeared around that time. Gradually fifteen different woodblock editions of the Kangyur and Tengyur appeared in various parts of Tibet, China, and Mongolia. The number of volumes within these editions varied a little, but in 1730 the woodblock Narthang Kangyur had one hundred volumes, while later, the corresponding Tengyur came to have two hundred and twenty-five volumes.

In 1609 the Kangyur edition housed in Chongyé Chingbar Taktsé Monastery was brought to Jang,[110] where for fifteen years it served as the source text for the first woodblock edition of Kangyur to be carved in Tibet. After this, in 1721, a second edition, known as the Choné Kangyur, was produced. [256] The third edition was the Dergé Kangyur produced in 1729. The fourth edition was the Narthang Kangyur printed in 1730. The fifth was the Zhöl edition produced in 1921, and the sixth edition was the Chamdo edition produced in the first half of the twentieth century.

As for the Tengyur, examples of the early handwritten editions were the Shalu Monastery Tengyur produced in 1334 and the Nedong Tengyur created in 1362. From early times in many parts of Tibet there existed the craftsmanship of carving deities, their name-mantras, and so on onto boulders and sides of cliffs. Consequently, the stone-carved Tengyur of Jangthang in Amdo was produced.[111]

The woodblock Dergé Tengyur produced in 1737, containing two hundred and eight volumes, was the first woodblock Tengyur produced in Tibet. After that came the Narthang Tengyur in 1741 and the Choné Tengyur in 1753.

To summarize, there were two woodblock editions of the Kangyur produced in China and six editions produced in Tibet. Of the Tengyur, forty-two woodblock volumes were produced in China, and two complete editions were produced in Tibet.

After 1959, the Kangyur and Tengyur have been reprinted and also produced digitally. Chinese publishing houses have produced comparative editions of the Kangyur and Tengyur, including book-format publications.

[257] For those who have never looked at the teachings in the Kangyur and Tengyur, the special terminology will be difficult to comprehend, but for well over a thousand years most people have been able to understand the words and meanings of this great literary tradition. Furthermore, the tradition of teaching and studying them has been maintained. Therefore, through this great achievement the teachings of the Buddha have spread throughout the three regions of Tibet, the Himalayan regions, Mongolia, and China. Through our proper and correct preserving of these teachings, it has not become a dead tradition but remains alive. This can be seen as the legacy of Tibetans bringing out the potential of their innate and excellent intellect to increase their knowledge.

The forty-first Tibetan emperor, Tri Ralpachen, undertook a revision of the Tibetan language with regard to translating Buddhist texts from Sanskrit. Rewarding translators and scholars was a great responsibility for him, whereas political discourse was a lesser one. In order to illustrate the offering of authority to the monastic community he laid his long hair on the ground as a carpet and invited the red-robed monks to sit on the right and white-clad lay practitioners to sit on the left, as objects of reverence. He performed an immeasurable service to the teachings of the Buddha, building many temples and statues and instituting almost a hundred meditation hermitages, colleges, seminaries, and so on. Such was his great legacy that Tri Ralpachen together with Songtsen Gampo and Tri Songdetsen are known as the three ancestral emperors.

[258] Since the time of those ancestral emperors, for well over a thousand years, we in the snowy land of Tibet have had a country, a race of people, and a culture all firmly established. We have our own separate script, which is considered to be among the world's oldest. Furthermore, ours is a language that has the capability to hold flawless translations of the vast and excellent texts of the Kangyur and Tengyur.

Most of the thousands of races in this world lack their own individual script. Our Tibetan culture, based on our own separate script, is long-lasting and stable. For any human society, wherever they are, if their culture is deep, then no matter how many changes occur over time, their customs and habits will not easily disappear. In Tibet various political changes may have occurred, but the inner spiritual attitudes linked to the Bön tradition and especially to the Buddhist tradition have remained firm even to the present day, and our people stand out in adhering to our excellent way of living. Moreover, our knowledge has been enriched with various fields of knowledge from India, China, Nepal, and so on. Therefore, this vast and deep treasury of knowledge that is a culture combined with Buddhism has arisen.

The source and transmission of this treasure house of religion and culture is solely down to the kindness of the great masters of the great monastic college of Nālandā Monastery, such as the seventeen pandits, who composed many works. [259] Therefore, to remember this, I wrote this praise of just a fraction and their main accomplishments and a brief illustration of what they composed.

A PRAYER TO THE SEVENTEEN PANDITS OF NALANDA

I bow my head to the mighty sage, the sun of all teachers,
who by gaining the supreme insight, the supreme abandonment,
and becoming the supreme protector, was a god among gods,
born from the great compassion of taking on the welfare of
     living beings,
guiding them with words of dependent origination.

1. I pray at the feet of Nāgārjuna, who by the profound means
of the reasoning of dependent origination
was skillful in clarifying the significance
of the perfection of wisdom sutras, mother of all the buddhas,

as an actuality free from the extremes,
and, as predicted by the Buddha, founder of the tradition
of the Middle Way of the Great Vehicle.

2. To his chief disciple, a supreme scholar and practitioner,
who journeyed across the great ocean of our and other tenets,
a crown jewel of all those who held the doctrine of Nāgārjuna,
I pray to the bodhisattva Āryadeva.

3. I pray at the feet of Buddhapālita, who elucidated the
        profound points
of mere names and imputed existence, the ultimate significance
of dependent arising, and the thinking of the Ārya,
and who traveled to the level of a great practitioner.

4. I pray to Ācarya Bhāvaviveka, a complete pandit who founded
the tenet system that refuted truly existing phenomena,
truly existing birth, and so on; who accepted external
        phenomena
as commonly appear to valid cognition.

5. [260] I pray to Candrakīrti, skillful in explaining the profound
        and the vast,
such as the Middle Way of emptiness and appearance,
in which the two extremes are dispelled
by dependent arising and mere condition alone,
and who expounded extensively the complete path of sutra
        and tantra.

6. I pray to the bodhisattva Śāntideva,
skillful in showing fortunate disciples,

through many profound and vast paths of reasoning,
the astonishing and wonderful path of compassion.

7. I pray to the great abbot Śāntarakṣita,
who, in keeping with dispositions of disciples,
founded the Middle Way path of nonduality,
who was skillful in bringing out ways of reasoning
within Middle Way philosophy and epistemology,
and who propagated the teachings of the Buddha in Tibet.

8. I pray at the feet of Kamalaśīla, who explained perfectly,
in accordance with sutra and tantra,
the stages of meditation of the Middle Way view,
free of extremes, the union of quiescence and insight,
and elucidated and freed from error the teachings of the
    Buddha.

9. I pray at the feet of Asaṅga, cared for by Maitreya,
who skillfully propagated all categories of the Great Vehicle,
who taught the path of the vast, and who, as prophesized by the
    Buddha,
founded the tradition of Cittamātra philosophy.

10. I pray at the feet of Ācarya Vasubandhu, who adhered to
the seven treatises of Abhidharma, and the tradition of
    nonduality,
while skillfully expounding the tenets
of the Vaibhāṣika, Sautrāntika, and Cittamātra,
a supreme scholar, renowned as the second Omniscient One.

11. I bow at the feet of Dignāga,
who opened a hundred gateways of reasoning

in order to reveal with phenomena-based reasoning
the scriptural tradition of the Buddha,
and was a dialectician who granted
disciples the eyes of discernment.

12. [261] I pray at the feet of Dharmakīrti, who reflected well
on all points of the presentations of valid cognition
as expressed by Buddhists and non-Buddhists,
and who, by the path of reasoning, provided conviction in
the vast and profound paths of Sautrāntika and Cittamātra,
skillfully explaining the wonderful ways of the Dharma.

13. I pray at the feet of Ārya Vimuktisena,
who commented on the meaning of
the perfection of wisdom coming from Asaṅga and his brother,
in accordance with the Middle Way
free of extremes of existence and nonexistence,
and lit the lamp that illuminated
the meaning of *Ornament of Realization*.

14. I pray to the master, Haribhadra,
prophesized by the conqueror Maitreya to elucidate
the meanings of the mother perfection of wisdom,
who clarified the works of the three mother sutras
in accordance with the core instructions of Maitreya.

15. I pray at the feet of Guṇaprabha, supreme scholar
    and elder
who synthesized the essential meanings
of the vast collection of monastic discipline teachings,
and explained without error the pratimokṣa,
in accordance with the Sarvāstivādin school.

16. I pray at the feet of Śākyaprabha, master of a treasury
housing the jewel-like qualities of the three trainings,
a supreme holder of the monastic discipline,
who commented excellently on the extensive literary tradition
of the doctrine of monastic discipline,
in order to preserve it flawlessly for future times.

17. I pray to Jowo Atiśa, who explained
all the vast and profound systems of the Buddha's teachings
as the paths of the three levels of living beings,
a hugely kind master who disseminated in Tibet
the doctrine of the Buddha.

Praying in this way, with unshakeable faith and clarity of mind,
to these adornments of the world, supreme scholars,
and great sources of wonderful teachings,
may my mind be blessed to become ripened and freed.

[262] Understanding the two truths as the base reality
to gain conviction in the ways of entering
and leaving samsara by way of the four truths,
and with firm faith in the three refuges induced by valid
    cognition,
may I be blessed to accumulate the sources of the path to
    freedom.

With a renunciation that seeks to end suffering and its causes,
and a foundation of compassion that reaches out in all
    directions,
wishing to protect living beings, may I be blessed
to perfect an uncontrived mind of enlightenment.

By studying, contemplating, and meditating
on the meanings within the compositions
of the great pioneering masters, may I be blessed to find,
without difficulty, conviction in all the paths of the profound
    points
of the perfection of wisdom Vehicle and Vajra Vehicle.

In life after life, may I soundly gain a form
endowed with the three trainings,
and in order to preserve and disseminate,
by way of explaining and practice,
the doctrine of scripture and insight,
may I engage myself in the teachings
in the manner of the great pioneering masters.

In all monastic communities may the time be spent
in study, contemplation, explanation, and practice,
and may great scholar-practitioners flourish there,
thoroughly abandoning all wrong forms of livelihood,
thereby constantly beautifying this vast world.

By the power of these words, may I travel all paths and levels
of sutra and tantra and soon attain the level of the Buddha,
the omniscience effortlessly fulfilling the needs of self and
    others,
and for as long as space lasts, may I work for the welfare of
    others.

Colophon

The wonderful and well-explained works on the vast and
profound Dharma excellently taught by the Bhagavan Bud-

dha, composed by the mighty scholars of India above, which are able to open the wisdom eyes of discerning individuals, still exist today undiminished as works to be studied, contemplated, and meditated upon, almost two thousand five hundred and fifty years after the Buddha's passing. Therefore, I composed this prayer in order to remember the kindness of these great masters in whose footsteps I yearn to practice.

[263] These days in this world, science, technology, and material progress is highly developed, and in these busy times of great distraction it is very important that we followers of the Buddha find a faith based on an understanding of the Buddha Dharma. Therefore, with doubt induced by an honest and unbiased mind we seek for reasons by examining and investigating in great detail, and seeing those reasons, we generate a faith that is accompanied by wisdom. For that to occur, the wonderful works on the vast and profound by the well-known Six Ornaments and Two Supreme Ones together with Buddhapālita, Ārya Vimuktisena, and others, are indispensable. Realizing that, I added nine other masters from the vast and profound lineages to the traditional painting arrangement depicting the Six Ornaments and Two Supreme Ones and commissioned a new painting of the seventeen Pandits of Nalanda.

In connection with this, I was inspired to compose this prayer of deep heartfelt respect to these great scholars, and other sincere Dharma friends had also urged me to do so. Therefore, this *Prayer to the Seventeen Pandits of Glorious Nalanda to Make Manifest the Three Kinds of Faith* was composed by the Buddhist monk Tenzin Gyatso, who has found an uncontrived faith and trust in the explanations of these great scholars, and who ranks as the lowest of those who study their wonderful works, on the first day of the eleventh month of the iron snake year in the seventeenth sixty-year cycle, corresponding to December 15, 2001, 2,545 years after the Buddha passed away according to the Theravada tradition, in Thekchen Chöling, Dharamsala, Kangra District, Himachal Pradesh, India. May it be auspicious.

Not all of the seventeen pandits named above were scholars who studied or lived at Nālandā, but they had a connection with it either directly or indirectly in their lives or as disciples of a lineage. Therefore, I think it is acceptable to refer to them as pandits of Nālandā.[112]

THE NALANDA TRADITION IS PRESERVED ONLY IN TIBET

[266] The first Buddhist tradition to spread to Tibet was the tantra tradition of the Nyingma, or "Old Translation school." This happened in the eighth century when "the Abbot, the Ācarya, and the Dharma King"[113] met in Tibet and it was transmitted through Śāntarakṣita from Nalanda and Padmasambhava, as described above. These two masters are the source of the Old Translation school. Therefore, the Nyingma tantra tradition is a Nalanda tradition.

Later, during the reign of the forty-second emperor, Lang Darma (815–46) a great disaster befell Buddhism. At the end of the tenth century, the great translator Ngari Rinchen Sangpo (958–1055) translated many new tantric works into Tibetan, and again the tantric tradition flourished. This was henceforth known as the new tantra tradition. Therefore, this determines the dividing line between the old and new tantra traditions, and later Buddhist traditions were included into the new tantra tradition, as will be explained.

The Kadampa School

[267] The first of these new tantra traditions was the Jowo Kadampa tradition, transmitted by Jowo Jé Palden Atiśa, also known as the Great Master Dīpaṃkara. In the early part of his life he studied at Nālandā and in later life assumed responsibility for Vikramalaśīla monastic college. After he came to Tibet, he taught by using the works of the Nalanda masters. He synthesized the instructions of the three baskets into the stages of the paths of the three types of person and primarily taught in accordance with Tibetan dispositions. His activities for the welfare of others such as reformation within the teachings were immense.

The Glorious Sakya School

The Sakya tradition is a very special system of instruction of the Nalanda tradition, beginning with the great siddha[114] Virūpa, also known as the Elder Śrī Dharmapāla, who became abbot of Nālandā. From him it was transmitted to Sachen Kunga Nyingpo (1092–1158), the first of the five Sakya Forefathers.[115] In his early life siddha Virūpa professed the view of the Cittamātra system of tenets. Therefore, his commentary on the *Four Hundred Verses* by Āryadeva is also written from the Cittamātra perspective. In later life he took to the tantric path and is renowned as having gained great insights and powers.

The Peerless Kagyu School

The Kagyu school began with Marpa Lotsāwa Chökyi Lodrö (1012–97), who relied mainly upon Maitripa as his source for cutting wrong conceptions regarding the view but received extensive instructions from Panchen Nāropa, the great pandit and northern gatekeeper of Nālandā. These were then transmitted by the great yogi Milarepa

Shepa Dorjé (1040–1123), revered unequivocally by all traditions within Tibet, and by the peerless Gampopa (1079–1153), and others. Therefore, the source of this profound tradition is also Nalanda.

The Riwo Gandenpa (Geluk) School

[268] The Geluk school began with Jé Tsongkhapa, Losang Drakpa. Mañjuśrī told him it would be better if he did not travel to India. Therefore, he did not actually meet any of the great scholars of India, but in all of his compositions, whether on sutra or tantra, he relied primarily upon the works of Nāgārjuna and his disciples, and in those extensive compositions on the stages of the path he relied upon the works of Asaṅga and Vasubandhu. It is still a pure transmission coming from a tradition whose source is solely the assertions of many genuine Nalanda scholars.

ONE INTENT

Alongside the Jonang, Bodong, Shalu, and Shijé schools, all major and minor Buddhist traditions of Tibet can trace their progenitors back to Nalanda masters. Therefore, even today, most Tibetan students will begin memorizing texts from the age of six or seven before moving on to the monastic manuals used for studying the root texts and commentaries of the classical Indian works, about eighty percent of which take the works of Nalanda scholars as their basis. This is the Buddhist tradition of Tibet. All the major and minor traditions that have arisen in Tibet, in terms of vehicle, are Great Vehicle traditions. Within that they practice sutra and tantra combined, and specifically are mainly practitioners of Highest Yoga Tantra. As for the view, they are probably all united in asserting that they follow the Madhyamaka school, and within that, the Prāsaṅgika Madhyamaka school that does not accept intrinsic existence even conventionally.

The great abbot Śāntarakṣita, foremost among the founders of the Buddhist tradition in Tibet, is reputed to have been an adherent of the Madhyamaka Svātantrika philosophical school. [269] It is said that he asserted intrinsic existence to exist conventionally and did not accept the existence of external phenomena. Therefore, it is taught that Rongzom Paṇḍita (1012–88) and some others of the old translation (Nyingma) school were adherents of the views of the Madhyamaka Svātantrika. However, they assert intrinsic existence to exist conventionally and do not accept the existence of external phenomena. However, in his writings, it is clear that Longchen Rabjampa (1308–63) does not accept intrinsic existence as existing conventionally and primarily professes the Prāsaṅgika system of Candrakīrti. Later, Künkhyen Jikmé Lingpa (1729–98) does the same. Therefore, there is no fault in ascribing the Prāsaṅgika Madhyamaka view to be the main view of the old translation (Nyingma) school.

In a Dzokchen work by Dodrup Jikmé Tenpai Nyima (1865–1926) he says that if someone knows through experience that all phenomena of samsara and nirvana are the play of the Samantabhadra awareness, then the Prāsaṅgika view of mere name and imputation naturally arises. This is probably similar to saying that the emptiness of existing by way of a nature that is not mere name and imputation will naturally be understood. He says, by way of an example, that if the obstructions to the eyes of a blind person are removed, it is by this mere removal that external form is naturally seen. There is no need to show the person some new form as a way to remove the obstructions. If the obstructions to the eyes are removed, the awareness of objects immediately arises. Therefore, when the primordial wisdom is realized, the understanding that the phenomena of samsara and nirvana are the play of this awareness will arise, and at that time the realization that all existence is mere name and imputation, and not established from the side of the object, will arise. I see this as expressing the same point made in the Geluk texts.

The texts of the glorious Sakya school speak of clarity as the essential characteristic of the mind and emptiness as the nature of the mind. The union of this clarity and emptiness becomes a union devoid of proliferation. [270] Therefore, there is the Cittamātra view and finally the Madhyamaka view of being beyond expression is ascertained. Ultimately this comes down to the Prāsaṅgika Madhyamaka view.[116]

For Marpa of the Kagyu school the authority for severing misconceptions concerning the view was Maitripa, and in one of his compositions, *Ten Verses on Reality*, Maitripa says, "Without the core instructions of the guru, even Madhyamaka will be mediocre." In a commentary to the above, "guru" is glossed as Candrakīrti, and that without his core instructions one's understanding of Madhyamaka will be mediocre. Therefore, he is clearly referring to the view of the Prāsaṅgika Madhyamaka.

The Sakya, Kagyu, Nyingma, Geluk, and other traditions of Tibet employ somewhat different terminology and the ways disciples are guided by instructions also differ a little. On the intent and significance of these differences, Panchen Losang Chögyen (1570–1662) says,

> When examined by those who are learned
> in reasoning and scripture on the definitive meaning,
> and by those yogis endowed with experience,
> they are seen to be of one intent.[117]

This citation is very significant. It is making the important point that if you become very learned and possess a vast understanding of the many Indian treatises of all levels that teach the definitive meaning of profound emptiness, and compare them with those works composed by great lamas from across all traditions until you gain familiarization with many works, and apply that knowledge to your experience—not just analyzing the words—then even if you lack any meditative realization and only rely on a part of your contemplation experience, you can see how they all come down to the same intent.

How do the instructions differ somewhat among the four schools? The old translation (Nyingma) school talks about the "Samantabhadra awareness" and the "unimpeded awareness." [271] The New Translation (Sarma) schools (Kagyu, Sakya, and Geluk) equate this with the clear light that will only arise after the coarse mind and wind have been forcibly negated. As long as the six coarse and temporary consciousnesses are manifest, the primordial mind cannot be directly experienced. However, Nyingma teachers say that all temporary consciousnesses proliferate from the clear light consciousness, and therefore all consciousnesses are pervaded by the awareness aspect of the clear light consciousness. This is very true and has great significance. Whatever consciousness comes into being, it arises from the clear light primordial mind, and any cognition of clarity and awareness[118] that rises from the clear light primordial mind is pervaded by its awareness aspect. Just as the whole of a sesame seed is permeated with oil, all consciousnesses are pervaded by the awareness aspect of the features of clarity and awareness.

Therefore, a lama endowed with experience will point this out experientially to a disciple endowed with single-pointed faith. Guided by the resulting unimpeded consciousness, which is not just nonconceptual cognition, when the blessings of a lama possessed of experience meet with the merit of the disciple endowed with devotion, the six coarse consciousnesses—especially at the time when mental afflictions are present—are seen to be pervaded by the awareness aspect. This consciousness is able to sustain itself without engaging any objects. The more that the clear light awareness is able to sustain itself, the more it becomes uncontaminated by its apprehending aspect, and when the meditation becomes strong, the coarse and temporary winds and mind become weaker.

When the Sakya tradition speaks of "mind of clarity," this is not to be understood as referring to all minds that are clear and knowing, but refers instead to the primordial clear light mind, I think. Alternatively, it could refer to the primordial clear light mind as a specific feature of general consciousness. [272] Khyentsé Wangchuk (1524–68), in his instruction manuals on the path and result teachings of the Sakya, says that from the vantage point of the two truths the primordial clear light is a conventional truth; from composite and noncomposite phenomena, it is composite; and from form, nonassociated phenomena, and consciousness, the primordial clear light is consciousness.

Mangthö Ludrup Gyatso (b. 1523) asserts a causal continuum foundation consciousness, or clear light, which he maintains is an ultimate truth. Künkhyen Śākya Chokden (1428–1507) and others claim that such an assertion is tainted by the "emptiness of other" view.

Whether this consciousness is described as a conventional or ultimate truth, they explain that its nature is recognized as being one of primordial clear light. Here, "ultimate truth" is not the ultimate truth asserted on a basis common to both sutra and tantra. According to Highest Yoga Tantra, "The ultimate is supreme clear light. The conventional is the supreme illusory body." When speaking of the illusory body appearance aspect and the illusory body clear light, the latter refers to the primordial clear light.

Therefore, each scholar has a different way of explaining. If we examine who had the greater intellect between Khyentsé Wangchuk and Mangthö Ludrup Gyatso, it seems that it was Mangthö Ludrup Gyatso. He was an exceptional scholar.

Concerning the referent of Sakya thinking, the impure world is viewed as possessing pure psycho-physical aggregates, spheres and sensory sources, and is in the nature of gods and goddesses. In this connection, the four physical supports of channels, winds, syllables, and drops within the body are viewed as being the entities of the four enlightened forms. Mangthö Ludrup Gyatso asserts that all phenomena and the primordial mind of innate clear light are of one taste with

the dharmadhātu. This is his view. Therefore, the referent of his thinking is the primordial mind. [273] With this understanding of the Sakya
texts these Sakya masters say that all animate and inanimate phenomena are pervaded by the clear light and that whatever arises appears
in the form of a deity. That which is described in the Dzokchen texts
seems to be particularly profound and reliable.

I think the Mahāmudrā practice of the Kagyu school is on the whole
similar to Dzokchen, specifically to the Dzokchen practices of Cutting
Through and Crossing Over. The Kagyu masters of the past talk about
single-pointedness, nonproliferation, one taste, and nonmeditation.[119]
Single-pointedness is quiescence (śamatha). Nonproliferation is meditation on insight (vipaśyanā). I think this has a generation stage aspect
and a completion stage aspect. Generally, nonproliferation—in which
all proliferation is absent—and "beyond expression" are both taught
in Hinduism. Therefore, Buddhists and non-Buddhists both accept
nonproliferation.

I think there are different ways of explaining the meaning of "one
taste." According to my understanding, many things being of one taste
should not be thought of as referring to the object but to the subject
consciousness. In that case, it should be researched as to whether or
not they are referring to the primordial clear light mind.

Regarding the view of the Geluk school, I think it is acceptable to
use the general term "Madhyamaka view" because the Geluk view
should be understood as being common to both sutra and tantra.
The Mahāmudrā view and the Dzokchen Cutting Through view is
explained as a way of meditating upon the view using a special subject
consciousness and is therefore the meditating mode for Highest Yoga
Tantra, and not that of the Madhyamaka view that is common to sutra
and tantra. It should be understood as a way of determining the view
using the subtle primordial mind. [274] Therefore, when we speak of
the view of innate mind of bliss and emptiness, or the innate inseparability of bliss and emptiness as found in the Geluk, this view is the

same as the Dzokchen Cutting Through view, the view of the union of clarity and emptiness in which samsara and nirvana are inseparable, as found in the Sakya school, and the Mahāmudrā view of the Kagyu.

When these meditations develop to higher levels, the coarse temporary minds and winds are gathered in and absorbed, after which the primordial clear light consciousness meditates upon emptiness. This is the same for all the above traditions. Therefore, I believe that ultimately they all come down to the same thing, although the ways of guiding will vary.

One cannot say that the Sakya and Geluk teach a path in which there is no penetrative focusing on or dependence upon the channels, winds, and drops. For the Geluk there can be no manifesting of the primordial clear light consciousness without a practice that relies upon the channels, winds, and drops. In the five stages of the Guhyasamāja completion stage, for example, there is the definite sequence of body isolation, speech isolation, and mind isolation.[120]

These days, those who follow the ascetic practices of the Jonang school and their doctrine of "empty of other" are well established in Golok Dzamthang district in Amdo, Tibet. One of their main meditations is the six-branch yoga of Kālacakra. Therefore, in terms of the six-branch yoga,[121] Jonang practice is very profound. Experiential guidance in the six yogas is very difficult to find in the Geluk and Kagyu schools.

The Jonang assert an empty-of-other Madhyamaka view. In the section on the four empty states[122] taught in the *Guhyasamāja Tantra* it speaks of the emptiness of all temporary phenomena. This is an emptiness of other. [275] Also, when the Kālacakra texts say, "From the sphere of emptiness," they are speaking of an emptiness of matter. Therefore, we can take an understanding of "empty-of-other" from the intent within particular contexts.

In the Dzokchen tradition also, the primordial and innate clear light consciousness, or Samantabhadra awareness, can be understood as empty-of-other, because it is empty of all temporary phenomena. Dodrup Jikmé Tenpai Nyima in his *Overview of Guhyagarbha Tantra* says this many times. He says that when the Madhyamaka view is ascertained, it is asserted to be a nonaffirming negation, and that is held to be prime. However, when meditating on the Madhyamaka view, it is asserted to be an affirming negation,[123] and that is prime. Therefore, he says that from such a perspective, it is similar to an empty-of-other state. Later, when I asked Dilgo Khyentsé Rinpoché (1910–91) about this topic, he said there was a black empty-of-other state and a white empty-of-other state.

These masters are of great insight, practitioners who hold aloft the great banner of accomplishment. They are inconceivable masters who preserve the doctrine of scripture and insight by way of teaching and practice, and when they write on a particular topic, their words represent their actual intent at that time, regardless of whether or not it is the actual thinking of the writer. In his Guhyagarbha overview, Dodrup literally says that dependent origination must only refer to that of composite phenomena, that the ultimate truth is permanent, unchanging, and everlasting, and asserts an independent affirmation empty of temporary phenomena. What the actual understanding of those statements might be is something to be considered.

Whatever the case, for the Sakya, Geluk, Kagyu, and Nyingma, in terms of the practice of the six-branch yoga there is no authority greater than the Jonang school.

Great masters of the past would debate with each other through reasoning and scripture in order to reform the teachings. [276] Among those who criticized the Nyingma teachings, the refutations of Drigung Palzin[124] are the most serious I have encountered. Not only did he attempt to completely refute the validity of Dzokchen, the Eight Sadhana Teachings,[125] and so forth, but it seems like he tried to refute the Nyingma school completely. I cannot be sure if Drigung Palzin had some political motive.

Khedrup Jé (1385–1438), in his *Dispelling the Darkness of Wrong Views,* says, "Some of those who adhere to the instructions of Dzokchen Aro...,"[126] thereby referring directly to the Nyingma tradition before refuting them. However, in one of Khedrup Jé's miscellaneous writings, a student asks seven questions, one of which is "Is Dzokchen a valid tradition?"

Khedrup Rinpoché replies, "Dzokchen is valid, and its practice is one performed on a very high tantric path. Therefore, those who belittle such a profound and peerless Great Vehicle teaching will certainly be born in hell."

Therefore, Geluk masters did not refute the Nyingma teachings in general but refuted the works of specific Nyingma masters.

Regarding the criticism of the Geluk by the Kagyu school, Karmapa Mikyö Dorjé (1507–54), for example, at first refuted the Geluk views with scholastic criticism but later praised the Sakya, Geluk, Kagyu, and Nyingma schools as sharing the same thinking. He especially singled out Tsongkhapa and the Geluk school through fifteen verses of praise, saying, for example,

> In this northern land, at a time when the conduct
> within the Buddha's teachings was solely at fault,
> I praise Tsongkhapa, the Riwo Gandenpa
> who reformed it without error.[127]

Many other masters from the Kagyu and other schools praised Tsongkhapa, and the tradition he founded, with great devotion.

[277] Tsongkhapa himself had great admiration for the Sakya school and praised it highly. After he had written about the meditational deities Guhyasamāja Akṣobhyavajra, Guhyasamāja Mañjuśrīvajra, and Cakrasaṃvara in his *Great Exposition on Tantra*, he stated, "I composed this *Great Exposition on Tantra* in order to lead others away from nonunderstanding and wrong understandings. The great Sakya mas-

ters of the past produced wonderful teachings and explanations on this Hevajra ritual, and therefore, there was no need to eliminate any nonunderstanding or wrong understandings about it."

Künkhyen Gorampa Sönam Sengé (1429–89) and Künkhyen Śākya Chokden of the Sakya school heavily criticized the Geluk followers. In response, Karmapa Mikyö Dorjé, replying to a letter sent to him by Jetsun Chökyi Gyaltsen (1464–1544) of Sera Monastery, said, "Your points of proof and rejection would be excellent answers for Künkhyen Gorampa and Künkhyen Śākya Chokden." Also, "I have a firm and sincere faith—not just for this world—in the great Tsongkhapa, through which I have no thoughts of this tradition being flawed, unlike that of Gorampa and Śākya Chokden."[128]

This illustrates the saying "The wise are beautiful among the wise." Therefore, its significance should be noted.

When it comes to the literature on the topic of epistemology, there are those who assert that the textbook literature of the Sakya school is much vaster than that of the Geluk. The epistemology textbook by Künkhyen Śākya Chokden is very extensive. Therefore, Geluk students should definitely study the Sakya texts. For example, on the topic of the phenomena of intrinsic characteristics and the phenomena of the characteristics of a universal, the understanding and explanation of the latter is primarily taken from Sakya literature. Therefore, their connection with the *Seven Works of Epistemology* [129] is a little stronger and the commentarial style in those texts seems simpler.

[278] Much of the terminology of the Geluk epistemological textbooks has come from the assertions of Chapa Chökyi Sengé (1182–1251).[130] He was also the first to set down the process of logical argument.

Whatever the case may be, in Central Tibet and Tsang the Geluk and Sakya ways of studying the classical texts through debate and explanation are excellent, while those of the Kagyu and Nyingma schools and colleges, such as those found in the Dzokchen monasteries in the eastern region of Kham, are truly excellent. It is just that these particular scriptural studies could not be that widespread in Central Tibet and Tsang.

Künkhyen Mipham Jamyang Gyatso (1846–1912) from the Nyingma tradition was a peerless scholar who composed commentaries on many classical works. Nevertheless, for explanations of subtle and difficult points Dodrup Jikmé Tenpai Nyima was an unbelievable master and hugely influential. When talking about the primordial mind, Künkhyen Mipham criticized some explanations by Tsongkhapa. This is criticism without understanding the totality of Tsongkhapa's position and seems to illustrate the saying "The sun of refutation rises before the dawn of the opponent has appeared." For example, Ācarya Bhāvaviveka was a great scholar and pandit, but seems a little imprecise.

Sometime ago, I was given a single volume from the collected works of the lama of Shechen Öntrul[131] by someone who was studying in South India. It was very useful for developing faith in and understanding the points of the Buddha's teachings as a whole.

In the past, works on history written in Tibet either took into consideration all major traditions with no sectarian bias or instead focused on their own tradition alone and paid no heed to others. This occurred in all traditions. [279] These days the nonsectarian approach is more in tune with reality. This is very important.

It is clear from looking at texts that, in the past, not only were there great masters from the Nyingma, Kagyu, Sakya, and Geluk schools, but there were many who practiced the teachings across the traditions without sectarian bias. In recent times also, the Geluk lama Amdo Jampal Rölpa Lodrö (1888–1936) was very well versed in Dzokchen. His students included Nyangön Sungrab Tulku Losang Dongak Chökyi Gyatso (1903–57), Drakar Tulku, and so on. The one who emphasized the doctrine of "one intent" across the traditions was Sungrab Tulku. Therefore, we should marvel at these great nonsectarian masters of the past, have great faith in them, and try to emulate them.

In this way, the Tibetan tradition, whether by meditation, view, or conduct, is a tradition that preserves, guards, and develops the pure Nalanda tradition, and, through practice and teaching, is one that disseminates the unblemished doctrine of the Buddha. There was once a time in which some Western scholars labeled Tibetan Buddhism as "Lamaism," claiming that it is mixed with the Bön religion and with Hinduism. Relying upon one or two spurious reasons they failed to comprehend the art of teaching by way of skillful means, or the practice of great lamas in accepting certain good points as part of the method to tame disciples, or the practice of making use of supplementary practices needed for ordinary people that cut across culture and religion.[132] Western scholars considered such acts as something quite separate from Buddhism. [280] But that misperception came from a lack of understanding about the profound way that we preserve, guard, and develop the doctrines of the Nalanda tradition by way of pure meditation, view, and conduct. The label of "Lamaism" is now universally recognized as baseless.

TIBET, MONGOLIA, AND CHINA

In the past, it was customary to regard Mongolia as being divided into Upper, Lower, and Middle Mongolia. These days that designation is not so clear. However, previously, Tibetans regarded Upper Hor, and those regions of Hor Mongolia known as Qinghai Mongol, as Upper Mongolia. The four Oirat tribes, the seven Khalkha races, Baatar Hor, Uriankhai, and so on were regarded as Middle Mongolia, and Barga, Buryat, Solon, and the forty-nine great Chahar tribes were regarded as Lower Mongolia.[133]

Generally, the term "Hor" has been understood differently throughout Tibetan history. It has been applied to Mongolia, to the northern nomadic regions of Tibet, and to Turkestan. However, here the tradition of regarding Hor and Mongolia as one and the same is adopted.

The Mongolian ruling dynasty is said to have begun with the youngest son of Drigum Tsenpo (fourth century?), the eighth Tibetan king, who was called Nyatri. He traveled from Kongpo in Tibet to Mongolia, where the people of a region called Peta or Pegal anointed him as their lord and master, and he became known as Borta Cheno. His twenty-sixth-generation descendant was said to be the emperor Genghis Khan (1162–1227), the first ruler of the Mongol empire.

Traditionally there was an early, middle, and late propagation of the Buddha's teachings in Mongolia. During the early propagation, the *Golden Light Sutra* was the first of the Buddha's teachings to arrive from India, from which the doctrine of the greater and lesser vehicles gradually spread. Most families kept a copy of this scripture as a household object of worship. The elders of the community said that by doing so, the needs of self and others would be fulfilled. Even today, this sutra continues to be held in great esteem in Mongolian society.

The middle propagation began from the time of Genghis Khan, who initiated the patron-priest system, although he himself never met any Sakya teachers. Although the propagation of the Buddha's teachings began at an earlier time, the propagation of scripture and meditative insight coming from the Tibetan tradition began in Mongolia from around this time. The later propagation will be discussed in more detail.

Mongolian Relations with the Sakya

In 1206, when Genghis Khan was forty-five, his army entered Tibet, but no large-scale or violent destruction ensued. This was at a time when the military might of Genghis Khan ruled most of that part of the world. About four hundred years had passed since the Tibetan empire had broken up into smaller kingdoms. Consequently, Tibet's army was no longer the force it once was, and lacked the ability and power to withstand the Mongolian invasion. Therefore, the chieftains of the various regions one after another submitted to the Mongols, and offered them the three regions of Ngari, the four districts of Ütsang, and the six districts of Kham. In 1234, Godan Khan (1206–51), the grandson of Genghis Khan, became ruler of the Mongol empire, and from 1239 onward, in tune with the changing times, the Sakya, together with the lay people under monastic control, submitted to Godan Khan. Drigung and Tsang Gurmo submitted to Möngke Khan (1209–59), [282] Tsalpa submitted to Kublai Khan (r. 1260–94), Phakmo Dru, Yalsang, and Thangpoché submitted to Hulagu Khan (1218–65), and Taklung submitted to Ariq Böke (1219–60).[134]

Therefore, from the perspective of military rule, Tibet was under Mongolian control from around 1209. However, the Mongolians had great respect for the Tibetan tradition of Buddhism and took the great Tibetan masters as teachers. Therefore, the Tibetan people were able to live normally with autonomy and self-governance. Moreover, in 1260, political control was given to the Sakya, and no Mongolian policies were implemented within the Sakya administrative rule. Sakya Pandita and his nephew Drogön Chögyal Phakpa[135] developed a new writing system for the Mongol language. With this and other deeds, it could be said that from the standpoint of the Dharma, Tibet controlled Mongolia.

In 1244 Godan Khan invited Sakya Pandita, Chögyal Phakpa, and others to Mongolia. There they taught extensively, worked on the new Mongolian script, and worked for living beings and the teachings of the Buddha.

In 1253 Drogön Chögyal Phakpa was again invited to Mongolia by Kublai Khan. Three times Chögyal Phakpa bestowed the Hevajra empowerment to twenty-five fortunate recipients, including the Khan. As offerings for the empowerments, Chögyal Phakpa was first given the thirteen administrative districts, in 1254; the three provinces of Tibet,[136] in 1260; and thirdly, in 1270, a six-column crystal seal and the "great weeding out of the Chinese population."[137]

As requested by the emperor, Chögyal Phakpa designed the new Mongolian "square script," and he instituted a system of teaching, study, meditation, and practice, and so on, thereby performing a great service for the people and the Buddha's doctrine.

[283] A succession of ten Sakya masters were appointed as royal tutors to the Mongolians and granted the title of "state preceptor."[138] The Sakya dynasty ruled the whole of Tibet from 1260 to 1353.

Invitation of the Karmapa Incarnations

In 1254 Möngke Khan invited the Second Karmapa, Karma Pakshi (1204–83), to Mongolia, where he remained for five years as the court lama. In 1332, the Yuan emperor Tugh Temür Jayaatu Khan—followed by the ninth emperor, Toghon Temür (r. 1332–68), in 1336—invited the Third Karmapa, Rangjung Dorjé (1284–1339), to Beijing. In 1358, the ninth emperor invited the Fourth Karmapa, Rölpai Dorjé (1340–83), to Beijing. In 1407, the third Ming emperor, Yongle (1360–1424), invited the Fifth Karmapa, Deshin Shekpa (1384–1414), to Nanjing. In this way these four Karmapa incarnations did much for the teachings and the people and received great praise and respect.

The activities of several Kadampa masters in disseminating the teachings can also be considered as belonging to the middle propagation in Mongolia and China.

The Later Propagation of Tibetan Buddhism in Mongolia and China

The explanations, compositions, and arguments of Jé Tsongkhapa on the sutras and tantras of the Buddha, as well as his practices of study, contemplations, and meditations, had spread far and wide and had come to the attention of Yongle, the Ming emperor, who invited Tsongkhapa to China. Tsongkhapa did not go but sent Jamchen Chöjé

Śākya Yeshé (1354–1435) in his place, who traveled to Nanjing in 1414 and on to Beijing 1429, where he was received with great honor and praise. [284] Jamchen constructed new temples and statues in each place he visited in China, restored those that had fallen into disrepair, and instituted monastic communities. His lineage of disciples was given the title of court lamas. In this way, the Geluk teachings spread far and wide in China.

In particular, in response to an invitation sent in 1577 by Altan Khan (1507–82)—the seventeenth descendent of Genghis Khan—the Third Dalai Lama, Sönam Gyatso (1543–88), journeyed from Tibet to Mongolia. There he turned the wheel of Dharma extensively and put an end to the barbaric practice of animal sacrifice. The kindness of these two beings in this patron and priest relationship meant that a law of virtuous behavior was firmly instituted in China, Tibet, and especially in Mongolia, where it was declared that the people had to follow the laws established in the Ütsang province of Tibet.

Altan Khan bestowed the title Dalai Lama Vajradhara on Sönam Gyatso, who in return bestowed the title Dharmarāja Devabrahma on Altan Khan.

The son of Altan Khan, Sengge Dürüreng, after he had been enthroned, again invited the Third Dalai Lama, and, in 1584, the Dalai Lama traveled once more to Mongolia, where he was afforded even greater honor than before. There he mediated in Mongolian disputes and brought peace to all. By giving many teachings requested by the people and by ordaining almost a thousand monks he accomplished much for the welfare of others. He passed away in Mongolia.

[285] The Fourth Dalai Lama, Yönten Gyatso (1589–1616), was a descendent of Altan Khan and was the son of Sūmirtai Chinghong Thaichi, the elder son of Sengge Dürüreng. Until the age of fourteen he remained to serve to the teachings and the people of Mongolia and then traveled to Tibet.

The kindness of the Third and Fourth Dalai Lamas ensured that the Mongolian emperors, their descendants, the rulers and people of Khalka, and the forty-nine tribes of Mongolia became very devoted to the Geluk tradition, thereby establishing a strong and deep patron-priest relationship.

During the time of Zheregethu Gushri Chöjé, the Pandit of Kharngön,[139] who was a direct disciple of the Third Dalai Lama, and later, during the life of Chahar Lekden Hothokthu, many scriptures, exemplified by the Kangyur, began to be translated into Mongolian.

During the time of Gushri Tenzin Chökyi Gyalpo (1582–1654) of Oirat in north Mongolia, Chahar Choghtu,[140] who controlled Kokonor (Qinghai Province), was hostile to Buddhism. Beri Dönyö, a follower of the Bön school from Barkham province in Kham, had seized control of about two thirds of Dokham. Phuntsok Namgyal (d. 1631), known as the Desi Tsangpa,[141] regarded the Karmapa as his main lama and object of devotion and controlled the large region of Ütsang, where he heavily persecuted followers of the Geluk tradition. These three rulers formed an alliance and waged military campaigns against other Buddhist traditions under their jurisdiction.

In 1637 Gushri Khan mobilized his army, conquered these three rulers, and released those lamas and officials of the Sakya, Geluk, Karma Kagyu, Drukpa Kagyu, Taklung Kagyu, and other schools who had been imprisoned.

[286] In 1642 Gushri Khan removed the rule of the Tsang ruler, offered dominion to the Great Fifth Dalai Lama (1617–82), and supported the institution of the government known as Gaden Phodrang.[142] Many Mongolians from all walks of life sought teachings from the Great Fifth. From his side, the Dalai Lama took on the great responsibility of spreading the teachings of Buddha in Mongolia, as can be known from the histories written on this topic.[143]

The first ruler of the Manchu Qing dynasty was Fulin, or the Shunzhi emperor (1638–61), the son of the second Manchu emperor and known as Dekyi Gyalpo in Tibetan. In order to extend his power over Mongolia he invited the Fifth Dalai Lama and Panchen Losang Chögyen to China. In 1652, accompanied by a large entourage, they set out for Beijing. On arrival they were accommodated in the palace of the Yellow Temple, which had been specially built by the emperor.[144] The Fifth Dalai Lama was enthroned as "Master of the Teachings" and conferred with the title of Vajradhara. He gave many teachings and, as a result, the Tibetans and Mongolians were able to have trust in the emperor and were brought into his fold.

The Kangxi emperor Shengzu (1654–1722), who was the son of the above emperor, founded many monastic centers. He invited Geluk masters such as the Ganden throneholder Ngawang Lodrö Gyatso (1635–88) and Changkya Ngawang Chöden (1642–1714) to China, where they were appointed court lamas. Editions of the Kangyur that had been translated into Mongolian were revised and printed.

The Yongzhen emperor (1678–1753) also invited Changkya Rölpa Dorjé (1717–86) and Ganden throneholder Losang Tenpai Nyima (b. 1725), where they further developed the patron-priest relationship.

[287] The Qianlong emperor, known in Tibetan as Chenlung Lhai Skyong (1711–99), followed the practices of his predecessors and in 1742 instituted the translation of the Tengyur into the Mongolian script. The publication was funded from his coffers and disseminated throughout Mongolia. In Beijing, he asked Changkya Rölpa Dorjé and Losang Tenpa Nyima that the Geluk tradition be preserved through teaching and practice and that new monastic colleges be instituted as centers of learning for the five sciences.[145] Consequently, in 1744, overseen by these two masters, a monastic assembly hall together with four colleges of philosophy, tantra, medicine, and the other sciences were constructed complete with all inner provisions. This center was called Ganden Jinchak Ling, or Yonghegong,[146] and can still be seen today.

In the same year, five hundred new monastics, all possessed of excellent intelligence, were assembled. They came from the forty-nine

Mongolian tribes and the seven Khalkha races, as well as from the Chinese and Tibetan communities. Three hundred entered the philosophy college, one hundred entered the tantric college, and fifty each entered the medicine and science colleges. Eighteen geshés as qualified teachers were invited from Tibet. A prayer festival was established and a tradition of geshé examination by debate was begun.

In 1779 the Qianlong emperor invited the Sixth Panchen Lama, Palden Yeshé (1738–80), to China. There he taught the emperor profound teachings that were translated into Mongolian by Changkya Rölpa Dorjé, and he worked for the benefit of the Chinese, Mongolian, and Manchu peoples. On the way to China, he traveled from Alashan to Ordos,[147] where he gave monastic ordination to 485 people. He also gave ordination in Chahar to 160 people and to 725 recipients in Tsodün (Dolonuur) at three different times.

[288] Many monastic centers sprang up in the lands of the seven Khalkha tribes, such as Riwogé Ganden Shedrup Ling (f. 1654) in Dākhural,[148] which had over twenty-seven thousand resident monks. There were also twenty-one monasteries that housed a thousand monks and thirty-eight that held over a hundred.

In the lands of the forty-nine tribes there were over seven hundred monasteries. Sixteen housed over a thousand monks and twelve had over a hundred monks.

There were forty-nine monasteries in the Buryat region, of which two held over a thousand monks and twenty-four had several hundred monks.

In the Kalmyk region of Russia there were two philosophy colleges that each had over five hundred monks, and about sixty other monasteries.

In the Turgut regions there were over twenty thousand monks studying at the philosophy, graduated path, tantric, and medicine colleges there.

In short, many monasteries appeared in regions throughout Outer and Inner Mongolia. The activities of the many lamas who were invited to Mongolia from all provinces of Tibet increased and flourished. Eventually many indigenous great masters from Mongolia performed great deeds for the teachings, as is evident from the many accounts in religious histories.

As described above, during the times of the Third, Fourth, and Fifth Dalai Lamas relations between Tibet and Mongolia were strong. Moreover, in a work on Mongolian history there are extraordinary accounts of the Sixth Dalai Lama, Tsangyang Gyatso (1683–1706), traveling to Ikhural[149] in Mongolia and spending a long time in Baldan[150] during the latter part of his life.[151]

[289] A nephew of the Eighth Dalai Lama, Jampal Gyatso (1758–1804), was recognized as the fourth incarnation of Khalkha Jetsun Dampa, thereby ensuring that the Tibet–Mongolia relationship remained strong.

During the time of the Eleventh Dalai Lama, Khedrup Gyatso (1838–55), there began a succession of Mongolian monks enrolling in Tibetan monasteries. As a result, many Mongolian scholars rose to become influential preservers and disseminators of the teachings.

In 1904, the Thirteenth Dalai Lama, Thupten Gyatso (1876–1933), traveled to Ikhural, where he stayed for about three years. Not only did he give extensive public teachings and confer vows and precepts to many novice and ordained monastics, but he also gave teachings on the classical Buddhist texts. This seems to be something that he did not even do in Central Tibet.

During the control of the Communists over many decades, religious faith in Mongolia was suppressed. Over a hundred thousand monks were killed and monasteries were completely destroyed. In 1979 I went to Mongolia for the first time, and since then I have been seven times in all. During those times I noticed clear signs that the oppression of the Communists had not been able to wipe out the people's faith. In particular, I often saw young children shedding tears of joy in expression of their natural and uncontrived religious faith. Therefore, in keeping with previous Dalai Lamas' special and strong relationship with Mongolia, I believe that in our generation too we should definitely do whatever we can to maintain this unbroken relationship, even though as refugees we cannot help much.

[290] In 1981 it was clear that discussions on how to further the relationship between Tibet and Mongolia would be held between the Tibetan Religious Affairs Department in exile and Ganden Thekchen Ling—or Ganden Monastery as it is known—the main monastery in Ulaan Baator. Having established a need for an exchange of scholars and students, I sent Yelo Tulku (b. 1943) from Drepung Gomang Monastery and Geshé Ngawang Lungtok to Mongolia. Since then, other teachers have been sent, and many hundreds of students from the regions of Mongolia have come to study at exiled Tibetan monasteries, schools, and other cultural centers.

Previously in Tibet, Gomang College of Drepung Monastery had sixteen monastic houses and twenty-two residential units. Some of these units were residences for monks from Mongolian regions. For example, Hardong House had nine residences, including Jurché residence, Hor residence, Turgut residence, and Tsenpo residence. Samlo House had ten residences, which included the Khalkha residence. In 1959 there were about sixty-five monks in these Mongolian residences. These days in Gomang in India there are about three hundred monks from Mongolia, seventy from Buryat, seven from Kalmykia, and fifteen from Tuva. In Tibet, Sera Jé Monastery had about sixty Mongolian monks. These days in India there are about a hundred.

[291] In Tibet there were many well-known learned Mongolian geshés. In Drepung Gomang Monastery these included Ngawang Dorjé, or Dorjé Yeb, who was an assistant tutor to the Thirteenth Dalai Lama; Samlo Geshé, Buryat Shiwalha; Samlo Geshé, Khalkha Losang Yeshé; the former and succeeding incarnations of Samlo Khalkha, Tailopa Hothokthu; Hardong Geshé Chödrak; Hardong Geshé Nga-

wang Losang, the sixty-ninth abbot of Gomang; Samlo Geshé Kalsang Lekden, the seventieth abbot of Gomang; Samlo Geshé Khalkha Ngawang Nyima, the seventy-second abbot of Gomang; and the Dulwa College abbot, Buryat Geshé Thupten Nyima. In Sera Jé Monastery, they included the assistant tutor Geshé Ngödrup Tsoknyi; the forty-first abbot Losang Tenpa; and the Lower Tantric College Lama Umzé, Hardong Geshé Yeshé.

Other influences on the strong relationship between Tibet and Mongolia are that I recognized and performed the official enthronement of the incarnation of the Mongolian grand lama, Khalkha Jetsun Dampa, an adherent of the Tibetan tradition of Buddhism. Also, many Mongolians from all walks of society continue to come to India for teachings and study. In this way the relationship between Tibet and Mongolia continues to flourish.

Jetsun Dampa

The spiritual and secular head of Mongolia in the past was Khalkha Jetsun Dampa Hothokthu. His first incarnation, Rabjung Yeshé Dorjé, or Losang Tenpa Gyaltsen (1635–1723), and the second incarnation were both born in Khalkha, Mongolia. However, the third was born in Lithang, Tibet. The fourth was born as the son of a brother of the Eighth Dalai Lama, Jampal Gyatso, in the Lhalu estate near Lhasa. [292] The fifth was born in Tsang, the sixth and seventh in Lhasa, and the eighth in Central Tibet; the ninth was born in Lhasa in 1933. Therefore, most incarnations were Tibetan. Moreover, their final recognition has been traditionally performed by the Dalai Lamas and Panchen Lamas, or by the regents and Ganden throneholders. Therefore, the cordial relationship between our two countries has been very influential at a fundamental level.

The Ninth Jetsun Dampa, Jampal Namdröl Chökyi Gyaltsen (1933–2012), sought exile in India because of the Russian Communist rule in

Mongolia. They had announced that the search for incarnations was forbidden.[152] Therefore there could be no actual enthronement and appointment. However, in 1991 when Kalsang Yeshé, the Tibetan minister of religious affairs in exile at that time, was visiting Mongolia, the prime minister, officials, and ordinary people asked for clarification on whether the widely accepted Jetsun Dampa incarnation had been accepted as the genuine incarnation, and particularly, whether he had been officially recognized by the Dalai Lama. Therefore, the Religious Affairs department submitted to me an official request, accompanied by a detailed account of the relevant events and the reasons. Consequently, on January 20, 1991, I officially recognized Rinpoché as the genuine Jetsun Dampa incarnation. This was followed by a suitably grand ceremony of official enthronement and honoring, as was the custom in the past. This fulfilled the wishes of the Mongolian government and people and therefore was instrumental in cementing the excellent religious relations that existed between Tibet and Mongolia.

Mongolian Visits to Dharamsala

[293] On December 10, 2006, a twenty-two-strong delegation of representatives from the Kalmyk government and its people participated in the ceremonies put on in Dharamsala to commemorate the anniversary of my receiving the Nobel Peace Prize. The delegation was led by Kirsan Ilyumzhinov, president of the Kalmyk Republic within the Russian Federation, along with the chairman of the parliament, and Buddhist spiritual leader, Telo Tulku Rinpoché, who were accompanied by members of a cultural performance troupe and twenty-eight Russian and Kalmyk journalists. They also commemorated the many hundreds of years of good relations between Tibet and Kalmykia. Furthermore, they presented me with the White Lotus, the highest award in Kalmykia. As the citation for this award they spoke of the benefit that had accrued to the people and the Buddha's doctrine by my three

visits to Kalmykia, how in recent times about thirty monasteries had been renovated, and that in India several Kalmyk students were being housed in Tibetan monastic and cultural centers. They expressed their gratitude for my kindness in sending many lamas, tulkus, geshés, and those learned in the sciences to Kalmykia to resurrect the Buddhist religion. I gave them teachings and discussions were held with the Tibetan ministers and members of parliament in exile to exchange ideas for fostering a strong and meaningful mutual relationship.

On November 5, 2007, a delegation from four different countries came to Dharamsala. They included over two hundred secular and religious representatives from the Republic of Mongolia and the Russian Republic of Kalmykia, headed by a parliamentary and peoples' delegation from Mongolia and the Kalmyk minister of development; [294] secular and religious representatives from Tuva headed by the director of the office of the president who was also a parliamentary representative; an ambassador of the prime minister of Buryatia; and various abbots and lamas. There was also an accompanying dance troupe, making a total of four hundred and fifty people. I granted their wishes by giving them teachings, and they offered me an extensive long-life ritual.

During the ceremonies the delegation honored me by saying that the Dalai Lama was not only the religious leader of Tibet but the main religious leader of Mongolia and all republics within the Russian Federation. They recalled that since 1974 I had visited the Mongolian Republic seven times, and in 1979 I visited Buryatia for the first time, describing the beneficial results of those visits. They also recalled that in 1991 and 1992 I went to Kalmykia, after which twenty-seven monasteries were built, thereby initiating a system of teaching and practice. They spoke about the beneficial effects of my first visit to Tuva in 1992, after which fifteen monasteries were built, and also mentioned the help we have provided from our side. They gave presentations about the hundreds of years of good relations between us, and showed us their culture with exhibitions, films, and performance. Many of us were visibly moved by this.

On December 22, 2007, a hundred and twenty selected monastics from monasteries within the twenty-seven states of the Mongolian Republic, including Ganden Thekchen Jinchak Ling, the main monastery in Mongolia, and the Dharma Centers of Jetsun Dampa, came to Dharamsala to receive teachings. [295] Fifty Mongolian monastics and fifty Mongolian lay people already living in India also came with that aim. I was able to fulfill their wishes with teachings they desired, and this became a further means to strengthen the bonds between Tibet and Mongolia.

On November 30, 2010, headed by three representatives of the Russian parliament, the Buddhist leader Telo Rinpoché, and the Kazakhstan finance minister, 1,127 people from Mongolia and the Russian Federations Kalmykia, Tuva, and Buryatia came to Dharamsala. For some days I gave teachings on sutra and tantra for which they were the main audience. The program of events on our firm religious and cultural relations were mutually beneficial. From then on, almost every year I give teachings either in Dharamsala or Delhi to Mongolian and Russian Buddhists.

THE SPREAD OF THE TIBETAN BUDDHIST TRADITION TO OTHER PARTS OF THE WORLD

From the nineteenth century up to 1959 the Tibetan tradition of Buddhism, its culture, customs, geography, politics, and economy, were described in published writings not only by Asian visitors but also by those who had traveled to Tibet from Western countries for research and studies. [296] By doing so, life and conditions in Tibet were revealed to a wide and unrestricted audience. These travelers included luminaries such as Alexander Csoma de Körös (1784–1842), Sven Hedrin (1865–1942), Alexandra David-Néel (1868–1969), Walter Evans-Wentz (1878–1965), Guiseppe Tucci (1894–1984), Peter Aufschnaiter (1899–1973), George Nicholas Roerich (1902–60), Edward Conze (1904–79), and Heinrich Harrer (1912–2006).

After 1959, various people from around the world with an interest in Buddhism continued to arrive in India and Nepal. They formed relationships with lamas from the various traditions and gradually established Dharma centers in various countries. These centers invited Buddhist masters and lecturers from Tibet and other parts of the world, who, together with resident teachers, disseminated and discussed Buddhism. Consequently, the numbers of people involved in study, contemplation, and meditation continue to increase and provide a firm basis for a growth in interest in Buddhism.

[297] In particular, in many universities around the world, Tibetology departments have attracted students, and the study of Buddhism and Tibetan culture has blossomed. Westerners have spent a considerable amount of time living among Tibetan communities studying Buddhism and Tibetan culture, where they have reached a high degree of knowledge and become proficient in Tibetan language. Some have taken the vows of monks and nuns, and by completing the study of the classical texts have earned the title of geshé. Some have gone to monastic colleges and meditation centers or to universities where they hold the position of teacher of Buddhism and Tibetology. Others have taken teaching positions at Tibetan Buddhist and cultural centers, and some hold the position of abbot at Tibetan monasteries. Their writings and compositions have also been widely published.

All this continues to be a catalyst for a surge of interest in the Buddhism of Tibet—its culture, history, politics, and so on—and since the twentieth century, and particularly in the twenty-first century, within these frenetic times of advanced scientific knowledge and technological progress, there has been a new interest in Buddhism. Moreover, the many numbers of people following Buddhism from most of the countries of the five continents of this world, each with their own history, different cultural backgrounds, and different customs, continue to grow. This represents a shift for the greater good.

[298] At the same time, with this particular spread of the entire Tibetan tradition of Buddhism, the essential meaning of the unified teachings of the Buddha, beginning with the four truths, is becoming progressively clearer by being transmitted into the many languages of this world.

Of the world's ancient literary languages, Latin, for example, is held in great esteem in the West, and Sanskrit is regarded with an equal reverence in the East. As far as the Tibetan language is concerned, Westerners interested in Buddhism noted its importance quite early. In 1959 one scholar and translator compared translations of Buddhist works into Tibetan and Chinese, and concluded that the Tibetan translations were highly compatible with the Sanskrit. These days university professors of Buddhism say that difficult points in Sanskrit Buddhist texts can be resolved when researched in Tibetan texts; because the Tibetan translators and editors of those times worked together, the complete meaning of a single Sanskrit term that carried a wide range of meanings was translated correctly, and Tibetan serves as an aid to understanding.

From 1977 the Central University of Tibetan Studies in Varanasi, India, has specialized in hosting Tibetan research scholars, and these days they are engaged in back-translating into Sanskrit those texts that are no longer extant in Sanskrit, but which were originally translated into Tibetan from Sanskrit in ancient times. These new translations have been praised by Indian scholars as being of a standard comparable to those ancient texts. Therefore, it can be shown that the richness of vocabulary in Tibetan works is comparable to that in Sanskrit works, and capable of carrying profound meaning.

[299] Similarly, Buddhist works composed by Tibetan scholars are said to be comparable with those works written by Indian scholars of the past, and this is something we can take pride in. The Tibetan language was not used for modern science, politics, and economics, and so we have not made progress in those fields. However, generally, the potential of Tibetan allows for the creation of appropriate terms found in these subjects. Therefore, from that perspective too, Tibetans can take pride. Through our religion and deep culture it can be established that we are an influential race possessed of a great legacy.

For over a thousand years the philosophy of Buddhism has been determined by the medium of the Tibetan language. These days the Tibetan tradition of Buddhism is gradually being translated and disseminated in the languages of the world, such as English. However, only a couple of generations have passed. Therefore, for discussing, studying, and thinking about the various presentations of Buddhist philosophy in great detail, there are no languages apart from Tibetan that can be relied upon and act as the final determiner. Consequently, if you have an interest in Buddhism it is important to hold the Tibetan language in great esteem.

THE NATIVE RELIGION OF BÖN

[300] The many religions that appeared in ancient societies over the last few thousand years have been centers and foundations of learning. The cultures and customs of individual countries, East and West, grew and developed in dependence upon those religions that had spread within those lands and had nourished and maintained them.

In common with the history of many other countries, it can be seen that religion also formed the backbone of Tibetan culture. Among Tibet's ancient generations the five elements[153] were revered, and gradually the beneficial powers of these elements were regarded as gods and their destructive power as demons and harmful forces. Thus, a primitive religion flourished, which followed practices of revering gods and expelling demons.

A Brief History of Bön

About six hundred years before the establishment of the Christian era, the Bön master Teacher Shenrab Miwoché appeared in the land of Shangshung Ölmo Lungring,[154] where he disseminated the teachings of Yungdrung Bön.[155] It is explained that these teachings are divided into outer, inner, and secret. The teachings disseminated before the appearance of Teacher Shenrab by the Bön form,[156] Kuntu Zangpo, on the Dzokchen path of freedom are those of the secret transmission. The tantric teachings taught by Shenlha Ökar, the enjoyment body, is the inner transmission. The teachings propagated in later times by Teacher Shenrab Miwoché, the emanated body, and which are primarily sutra, constitute the outer transmission.

The doctrine of the Bön outer transmission is made up of nine vehicles. These are the vehicles of prediction, visible world, magical rites, and existence that constitute the four causal vehicles; the vehicles of lay practitioners, sages,[157] white letter *a*, and the primordial, which make up the four resultant vehicles; and the supreme vehicle. These can also be classified as Four Gateways and a Treasury. [301] Moreover, divination, omen reading, rituals, astrology, medical diagnosis, and so on can be classified within the four gateways, and monastic discipline, sutra, and tantra can be classified in the Treasury.

It is explained that Bön had an early, middle, and late propagation, also known as new and old Bön. Some say that the Dzokchen philosophy of the Tantric Nyingma school is the philosophy of old Bön. Apart from these, other divisions such as black, white, and many-colored Bön, as well as revealed Bön, derived Bön, and transformed Bön, are described by some adherents to Buddhism in their histories of the Bön tradition, but they are not accepted by the Bönpo.

Shangshung

Shangshung was the land where the Bön teachings were propagated. According to old documents unearthed at Dunhuang, Shangshung was one kingdom during the time of the of the twelve minor kingdoms and forty principalities that existed before the reign of the Tibetan emperors.

According to Bön documents, there were eighteen renowned kings of Shangshung, such as Triwer Gulang Sergyi Juruchen.[158] The land of Shangshung itself is divided into regions called Gopa, Phuk, and Barpa.[159] It is explained that Gopa, or Dopa, is identified with the region of Tibet known as Domé. The Ütsang region is Bar, while Ngari and Ladakh is Phuk. Before the Tibetan empire took over Ütsang, and so on, the general name for Tibet was Land of Shang-shung. After the Tibetan empire controlled Shangshung, it was evident that the name Shangshung was restricted to wherever the king of Shangshung lived.

During the time of the Tibetan emperor Namri Songtsen (sixth century), who was the father of Songtsen Gampo, Shangshung rose up in revolt, and later Songtsen Gampo sent his sister Sema Kalalik[160] to be the bride of the Shangshung king Likmikya. [302] After this, history records that Shangshung was again subsumed into the Tibetan empire.

The doctrine of Yungdrung Bön remained widespread in Shang-shung and Tibet. Therefore, cultural aspects connected with Bön developed and flourished. There are also indigenous medical texts, diagnostic methods, and treatments that originate in Bön literary works of that time. It is very important to respect and give equal status to this religion of our forefathers and the fundamental culture of the Tibetan people, whose study and practice is well developed and continues to the present day.

Tibetan religious practitioners regard the three ancestral Dharma emperors as supreme in their achievement and kindness. Among them, Songtsen Gampo—the thirty-third emperor, who from the perspective of Buddhists is regarded as an emanation of Avalokiteśvara, the deity of compassion—was the first to propagate Buddhism in Tibet. At that time, he showed little interest in the Bön tradition, which was very widespread in Tibet, and had nothing to do with the Kushen—the Bönpo lamas that the Tibetan emperors traditionally took as their objects of reverence. He also persecuted Bönpo ministers and officials. In Bön historical accounts, therefore, Songtsen Gampo is not described as an honorable person. During the reigns of Tri Songdetsen and Tri Ralpachen, Buddhism was widespread and Bön histories record the many hardships that followed the criticism and resentment of the Bön doctrine by Buddhist monastics—such as imprisoning and killing Bönpo followers if they did not convert to Buddhism. This is not recorded in Buddhist historical accounts and, as in the works of many biased historical writers, seems to be a case of ignoring historical facts.

[303] After the Buddhism of Śākyamuni had become widespread in Tibet, Bön Madhyamaka, Bön perfection of wisdom studies, Bön epistemology, Bön monastic discipline, and so on came to exist in the Bön canon alongside the three original Bön baskets. These are very similar to those found in Buddhism. The Dzokchen teachings of the Nyingma and Bön are also for the most part similar in the way they are taught. The Bön practices of exorcism rituals; cross-thread rituals summoning prosperity, health, and so on; incense-burning ceremonies; and more have been adopted into Tibetan Buddhist culture. Likewise, various propitiations, and exhorting of protectors accompanied by musical instruments, use the Bön style of chanting. In some rituals much Bön terminology is used.

None of these are found in the Kangyur and Tengyur but we make use of them. Tibetans do not have the technology to make money and so we wave a piece of mutton about and summon prosperity, for example![161] Anyway, the principles of Buddhist and Bön philosophy, meditation, and conduct, and especially the elaborations within their ritual practices, seem to strongly echo each other. There are accounts of Bön masters of the past attaining the rainbow body, and so from the perspective of practice it is evidently difficult to say that Bön and Buddhism are fundamentally distinct.

It is said that in the activity of going for refuge, the Bön of Shenrab and the Buddhism of Śākyamuni Buddha are similar in accepting the Three Jewels as objects of refuge. However, in Bön the three refuges are the Buddha Jewel of Teacher Shenrab, and others; the Bön Jewel; and the Bodhisattva Jewel. Buddhists adhere to the religion of Śākyamuni, and the Buddha Jewel is Teacher Śākyamuni, and others, while the other two refuges are the Dharma Jewel and the Sangha Jewel. Therefore, there is a little difference in the names of the three refuges, but they are similar when identified. Also, in terms of that which differentiates Buddhists from non-Buddhists, such as going for refuge and accepting the four seals, Bön and Buddhism are also similar.[162]

Whatever the case may be, Yungdrung Bön, the religion of our forefathers, is to be respected and valued. These days we share all manner of rights, meaning that we have the right to follow the religion of our choice. This can be considered a credit to the human race. The ultimate goals of liberation and omniscience can be seen as existing similarly in the great religious traditions of Tibet and in Yungdrung Bön. However, in keeping with the dispositions of their followers, different assertions and positions by individual scholar-practitioners of the past arose. I see it as very important for the elder scholars still alive these days, who hold these tenets as treasures in their minds, to consider passing on to the younger generation, as best they can, the unbroken traditions of teaching, practice, and activities.

CHAPTER 7

The Paths of Sutra and Tantra

THE TEACHINGS OF THE BUDDHA are categorized into the three baskets of monastic discipline, sutra, and abhidharma. There are three reasons for this threefold categorization in terms of the mental afflictions to be eradicated, three reasons in terms of the trainings, and three in terms of objects of knowledge, making nine in total.

The basket of sutras is taught to be the antidote to the secondary mental affliction of doubt.[163] In this context, when the aggregates, the basic constituents, the sensory sources, dependent origination, the four truths, the levels, and the perfections—mainly grouped within the training in concentration[164]—have been ascertained and determined, doubts over the general and specific characteristics of their features will be dispelled.

The basket of monastic discipline is said to be the antidote to the secondary mental afflictions of partaking of the two extremes. By avoiding the faults proscribed by the monastic discipline, the extreme of indulgence is avoided. With pure ethics one should not engage in the difficulties of accumulating possessions, and so on. However, for those who possess the antidote of being able to shun desire and attachment, the use of nonharmful possessions is allowed within the monastic discipline, and the extreme of hardship is avoided.

[306] The basket of Abhidharma is said to be the antidote to the secondary mental affliction of holding one's views to be supreme. If we ascertain the particular and general features of phenomena and engage in study, contemplation, and meditation, then wrong views

concerning purity, happiness, permanence, and self[165] will naturally subside, as will holding as good practices the bad ethics and conduct induced by these views.

The basket of sutras can be categorized from the perspective of the three higher trainings of the upper and lower tenet systems, which are the topics of the sutras.

The basket of monastic discipline establishes pure ethics by mainly teaching practices to be adopted and those to be discarded. With pure ethics the mind is free from regret and torment, and the body becomes light and manageable. Inner joy increases and the mind remains focused. Therefore, a basket of monastic discipline is categorized in order to practice the training in ethics and the training in concentration.

Analyzing and determining phenomena means that any study of them will produce a wisdom that unerringly knows the characteristics of these phenomena. Therefore, the basket of Abhidharma is categorized in order to practice the training in wisdom.

The basket of sutras can be established by their extensive explanation of phenomena and their meanings. Names, words, and phrases are the phenomena, while aggregates, spheres, sensory sources, and so on are the meanings. Alternatively, the aggregates, spheres, and so on are the phenomena, while the eight kinds of explicit and inexplicit teachings[166] are the meanings. Again, the ten virtues as paths to higher realms are the phenomena, while the thirty-seven facets of enlightenment as paths to liberation are the meanings.

[307] By teaching the practice of pure ethics and the meditation on impurity, and so on, the mental afflictions are tamed. An understanding of these phenomena and their meanings is born in the mind. From that perspective the basket of monastic discipline is established by way of objects of knowledge.

The basket of Abhidharma was taught in order to become learned in discussions on the relationship between phenomena and their meanings.

THE THREE TRAININGS

The first of the three trainings is that of ethics. It is at the very essence of the practices of the Buddha's teachings. Beginning with the ethics of abandoning the ten nonvirtuous acts, it includes the many classifications found within monastic, bodhisattva, and tantric ethics.

The second training is that of concentration. Here, concentration means keeping the mind single-pointedly and unwavering on a particular virtuous object. First one trains to develop the state of quiescence, then insight, and then a state of concentration that is the union of quiescence and insight.

Training in concentration leads to the attainment of the mental states of the form and formless realms.[167] When single-pointed concentration is held by bodhicitta and the view of emptiness, it becomes the perfection of meditative absorption. There are worldly concentrations and nonworldly concentrations.

The third training is that of wisdom. Discerning and discriminating the types of phenomena by analysis and examination is wisdom. When perfected, it is called the perfection of wisdom. [308] It has three forms: (1) ultimate wisdom, which is knowledge focused on the way things exist, and which knows the reality of no-self, either by conceptual construct[168] or by direct perception; (2) conventional wisdom focused on the knowledge of the five sciences; and (3) wisdom that understands the way to serve the purposes of sentient beings.

Of these three trainings taught by the Buddha, the training in ethics is superior to the ascetic practices of non-Buddhists,[169] which torment the bodies of oneself and others through austere practices. Because the Buddhist training brings great benefit to oneself and others, it is a "higher training." Similarly, training in concentration becomes an antidote to mental affliction and wrong concepts, and in this and all future lives one moves from happiness to happiness, eventually bringing about the achievement of liberation and omniscience. It too, therefore, is higher than that of other traditions. Wisdom, with its power to directly and indirectly remove the obstacles of adhering to a self of persons and phenomena, is also "higher." In this way, they are known as "the precious higher trainings."

In terms of their practices, the three higher trainings will bring about the attainment of the state of an arhat for those of the Śrāvaka and Pratyeka Vehicles and the attainment of the state of buddhahood for those of the Great Vehicle. To achieve these goals, you first learn the doctrines of the Dharma from a qualified teacher. Then with regard to what you have leaned, you think that this is like this and that is like that, thereby developing new understandings and accumulating the wisdom of learning. Then you repeatedly contemplate those points you have learned, compare the relevant scriptures of various tenet systems, and by again analyzing thoroughly and profoundly what they teach, you will gain the conviction that the meaning of such and such a passage is this and no other. This is the wisdom of contemplation. [309] The meanings of those scriptures are again brought to mind and meditated upon to bring about the wisdom of meditation. In this way, you will traverse the paths and levels through learning, contemplation, and meditation.

THE FIVE PATHS

The śrāvaka paths are five in number: the path of accumulation, the path of preparation, the path of seeing, the path of meditation, and the path of no training. To give a brief explanation of how these five paths are traveled: samsara is explained as being the continuum of the impure psycho-physical aggregates wandering helplessly under the sway of karma and mental affliction. Understanding how we are persecuted by the three kinds of suffering[170] within this samsara, a sense of renunciation toward it is born, and an uncontrived mind intent on reaching the goal of liberation is produced. When this is experienced, you have entered the path of accumulation.

This path has three stages: lesser, intermediate, and higher. On these stages you engage in meditation on the unpleasant, the concentration of mindfulness of breathing, the four close contemplations, the four perfect abandonments, the four branches of magical powers, and so on. By the force of these meditations, the wrong apprehension of the truth of suffering—that it is pure, a state of happiness, permanent, and possessed of a self—and the afflictions of desire, anger, and so on are all suppressed. Consequently, there is no longing for the glories of samsara. Absorbed in the practices that lead to liberation, you are able at will to produce manifestations and to exhibit various qualities. You can also possess all or some of the five types of clairvoyance.

On the following path of preparation, the qualities achieved are much greater than those of the path of accumulation. This path has four stages: heat, peak, forbearance, and supreme attainment. Passing through these stages, a very special wisdom of meditation focused on the reality of the four truths is achieved, and very clear and special concepts of impermanence, suffering, emptiness, no self, and so on will arise. Unimaginable qualities such as those of the five powers, the five forces,[171] and so on will also be produced.

[310] After the supreme attainment stage of the path of preparation, you move to the path of seeing, where the power of the direct cognition of the reality of emptiness, as categorized by the sixteen aspects of the four truths,[172] will uproot a hundred and twelve mental afflictions, which are the eliminations of the path of seeing, together with the seeds of those afflictions. Such a person, in possession of superior characteristics, is now an ārya and becomes the ultimate Jewel of the Sangha.

After the attainment of the path of seeing, the direct cognition of reality previously achieved is now cultivated over a long period by way of the eightfold path of the āryas in order to destroy the seeds of the innate afflictions.[173]

Using the Pāli sutras as reference, the eightfold path of the āryas is classified within the three trainings and can be practiced now. Right livelihood, right speech, right action, right effort, right view, right thought, right mindfulness; these we can have right now. Right view and right thought are classified as the training in wisdom. Right mindfulness, right effort, and right concentration are classified as training in concentration. Right livelihood, right speech, and right action are applied to the training in ethics. This is the tradition that says the eightfold path can be practiced before becoming an ārya. Alternatively, they can be applied to the five paths.

Cultivating a previously achieved insight into reality will produce the direct antidote to the larger of the afflictions to be eliminated by the path of meditation. When that occurs, this is the attainment of the path of meditation. Of these afflictions to be eliminated there are those that are eliminated gradually and those that are eliminated simultaneously. The former begins with the gradual elimination of the nine—or three sets of three—coarse afflictions. These are classified as being at the level of the desire realm and are worldly eliminations of the path of meditation. [311] One continues up to the nine subtle afflictions that are peak of existence[174] eliminations of the path of meditation. This makes a total of eighty-one antidotes that are developed gradually. The last of the subtle antidotes is the path of meditation vajra-like concentration that leads onto the path of freedom. This is the śrāvaka path of no further training, equivalent to the state of becoming an arhat.

For those afflictions that are eliminated simultaneously, the nine coarser of the coarse path of meditation afflictions of the nine levels and three realms are eliminated simultaneously. This proceeds through to the simultaneous elimination of the nine subtler of the subtle afflictions. After these paths have been traveled, the state of becoming an arhat is reached.

Except for the way their goal is reached and the number of eons for which they have to gather merit, the way that the pratyeka travel the five paths is mostly similar to that of the śrāvaka.

The Great Vehicle path is divided into the causal perfection of wisdom Vehicle and the resultant Tantra Vehicle. The perfection of wisdom Vehicle also has five paths, each with their own subdivisions, as described above. You develop renunciation from contemplating how you are tormented by your own suffering, and on that basis you understand that others too are tormented by suffering and lacking happiness. You become motivated by love and compassion through which you take upon yourself the responsibility of achieving their happiness and well-being, and you train in developing bodhicitta, the mind of enlightenment. Through this training, you develop an uncontrived bodhicitta that strives to reach the state of complete enlightenment. At this point you have entered the path of accumulation.

As soon as you develop bodhicitta you gain a host of excellent qualities such as the purification of downfalls and previous bad karma, and the completion of a great store of merit. This precious bodhicitta of cherishing others more than oneself is a core instruction specifically developed from the Nalanda tradition. It is enhanced by practices common across the Great Vehicle such as those of the six perfections that ripen one's own mind and the four ways of gathering disciples[175] that ripen the minds of others. This is the Great Vehicle.

[312] Having produced the wisdom of contemplation concerning the meaning of emptiness, you familiarize yourself with it again and again in your mind in order to reach a genuine understanding or genuine conviction of emptiness. With the accompaniment of a state of meditative concentration or quiescence developed separately, you engage the union of quiescence and insight to focus upon—by way of conceptual construct—the emptiness that is the emptiness of the

true existence of all phenomena. This is the achievement of the path of preparation. Gradually, the coarse dualistic appearance of subject consciousness and object lessens, and a very special and clear appearance of the conceptual construct develops. In this way, the continuum of this present mind of ours transforms into the wisdom of the path of preparation.

We have developed a strong habituation with the mental afflictions of the three poisons since time without beginning, and it is not possible to destroy them by praying, "May all mental afflictions cease." However, by relying upon antidotes whose strength matches the strength of the habituation with the afflictions, gradually the power of the afflictions will weaken. To achieve this, we train in the four close contemplations and the four perfect abandonments. Then, by relying upon the four branches of magical powers and the power of meditative concentration, we train in the five powers, the five forces, the seven branches of enlightenment and the eightfold path of the āryas.[176]

It is taught that the five powers are developed on the heat and peak stages of the path of preparation and the five forces are developed on the two subsequent stages of forbearance and supreme attainment.

Training continually in this way, appearances within the heat, peak, forbearance, and supreme attainment stages of the path of preparation become subtler until finally even the subtlest dualistic appearance of emptiness subsides like water poured into water, and a direct knowing of the reality of emptiness occurs. [313] This is the first instance of the path of seeing, which at that time becomes the direct antidote to the three fetters[177] that are the eliminations of the path of seeing. The state of elimination of these three fetters is the attainment of the first truth of cessation. This is the wisdom of the path of seeing that directly perceives reality, and is also the wisdom of the first level from the ten ārya levels. With the advent of the uninterrupted path of the path of seeing[178] directly perceiving emptiness, the seeds of a hundred and twelve mentally constructed mental affliction obscurations of the three realms, as well as one hundred and eight mentally constructed obscurations to omniscience,[179] are eliminated simultaneously. Therefore, once the path of seeing is reached, birth, sickness, old age, and death under the sway of karma and mental affliction are no more.

With continued meditation, the ārya levels from the second to the tenth—which make up the path of meditation—the seeds of sixteen mental afflictions and one hundred and eight obscurations to omniscience—all of which are eliminations on the path of meditation—are eliminated in sequence. Therefore, the excellent qualities gained by eliminating these opposing factors increase throughout the levels.

The path of meditation is divided into great, intermediate, and small, each of which have three similar subdivisions, making nine divisions of this path.

Continuing to meditate on emptiness and to train in the six perfections will strengthen the collections of wisdom and merit, and one travels through the levels from the second to the seventh. The attainment of the eighth level coincides with all mental afflictions and their seeds being eliminated. Therefore, this continuum that is presently under the control of afflicted ignorance is cut and transformed into the wisdom of the pure levels.

On the eighth, ninth, and tenth levels, meditating on wisdom that perceives emptiness is for the purposes of eliminating the obscurations to omniscience. [314] Therefore those three levels are pure levels because they are already purified of mental affliction, whereas the seven previous levels are the seven impure levels.

By meditating on emptiness again and continuing to train in the paths of method and wisdom, the ten levels are completed. Finally, the direct antidote to the subtlest obscuration to omniscience at the completion of the training on the tenth level is attained. This is known as the path of vajra-like meditative concentration, and from the second instant of its continuum the continuation of obscurations to omniscience and their seeds is severed. Simultaneously, buddhahood is attained. That meditative state not only has the ability to fully know all existing phenomena but also, because the mental contamination that apprehended the two truths as being of different entities is completely gone, the meditative state and the postmeditative state are fused as one. Moreover, all activities are accomplished effortlessly and spontaneously. In short, our mental continuum develops through the wisdoms of the individual paths and levels to finally become the wisdom dharma body (dharmakāya) of omniscience.

With the wisdom dharma body as an entity, its suchness or emptiness is the entity body (svabhāvakāya). From the perspective of being suchness it is an entity body that has an aspect of being naturally pure. It also has an aspect of a temporal purity that is the state of elimination of the two obscurations or temporal afflictions. With the feature of this elimination of the temporal faults of the two obscurations, together with all imprints, the characteristic of the entity body is that it is the ultimate realm possessed of the two purities.

The wisdom dharma body—whose nature is the entity body—has been actualized for the sake of others. Therefore, merely by being actualized, a form body will arise. The type of form body that appears to the minds of pure disciples is the enjoyment body (sambhogakāya), and that which appears to the minds of impure disciples is the emanated body (nirmāṇakāya). This is how the four bodies of a buddha are explained.

[315] It is this present stream of consciousness of ours, by becoming purer and finally eliminating all faults and developing all excellent qualities, that will become that buddha of the four bodies. Therefore, the mind that becomes a buddha is a mind that has existed since time without beginning. The *Perfection of Wisdom Sutra in Eighteen Thousand Verses* says, "Such a mind is not mind. The nature of mind is clear light."[180]

I often say that this is the final destination of our mind, and in terms of the continuum of consciousness, it is the final achievement of the state of buddhahood whose nature is that of the four bodies.

THE FOUR CLASSES OF TANTRA

On the common Great Vehicle path, the difficult deeds of the bodhisattvas are to be carried out for three countless great eons, and so on. Merit and wisdom are accumulated and the state of buddhahood is achieved. During that time, with an overwhelming compassion that is unable to bear the suffering of sentient beings, you rely upon the practice of deity yoga, in which "the ascertainment of emptiness is induced and the objective aspect arises in the form of a deity."[181] This is an exclusive practice of the Great Vehicle whose methods are many and is of little hardship, and through which one quickly reaches the state of buddhahood. It is the Tantra Vehicle of Buddhism.

Tantra is included in the sutra basket of the three baskets. As one tantra says, "Listen and I will explain the tantra in the manner of sutras."

On the matter of when the tantras were taught, the *Kālacakra Root Tantra* says,

> In the way that the perfection of wisdom
> was taught upon the Vulture's Peak,
> the Teacher, in glorious Dhānyakaṭaka,
> taught all the tantras.[182]

It is the commonly accepted position that the classes of tantra were taught in accordance with worldly human perception and at a certain time. [316] However, more importantly, when the channels, winds, and elements of those disciples of pure karma became even purer, the Buddha taught the tantras by appearing as the mandala and its residents.[183] This is the uncommon way of teaching, and therefore, there is no certainty of the time they were taught.

As is clear from the *Kālacakra* citation, generally it is said that the perfection of wisdom sutras were taught on Vulture's Peak and the tantras were taught in glorious Dhānyakaṭaka. Similarly, there is one assertion that the tantric teachings mainly relating to Kālacakra were taught by the Buddha on the full moon of the *caitra*[184] month, the twelfth month after he became enlightened. Another position states that they were taught on the full moon of the caitra month that occurred in the year of his passing. However, the previous citation, "In the way that the perfection of wisdom was taught," with its comparison to the perfection of wisdom, suggests that the latter position is more plausible.

In some of the three lower classes of tantra the Buddha only taught in the form of a fully ordained monk. In others he arose in the form of the main deity of the particular mandala and taught solely in that form.

Within the Tantra Vehicle there are many ways to divide and categorize the classes of tantras. Of these, *Vajra Garland*, an explanatory tantra of the *Guhyasamāja Tantra*, says that the vehicle of tantra has four classes: Action Tantra, Performance Tantra, Yoga Tantra, and Highest Yoga Tantra. The first three are the lower classes. Their practices consist of a clear visualization of one's body as a deity, from which a wisdom that ascertains no-nature[185] is generated. These two combined are the yoga of the nonduality of the profound and the manifest. These constitute the path of characteristics and the path of no characteristics.

[317] During the meditation on the yoga of characteristics in Action Tantra, there are practices known as *the six deities*, which concern ways of generating yourself as a deity: (1) The emptiness deity. This is the meditation of yourself and the deity as empty of intrinsic existence. (2) The sound deity. Appearance in the nature of emptiness is regarded as an echo of the meditational deity's mantra appearing in space. (3) The syllable deity. The sounds of that mantra are visualized in the form of syllables around the edge of a moon disc. (4) The form deity. The moon disc and the syllables transform into the form of the deity. (5)

The mudra deity. The parts of the body of that deity are blessed with the mudras of each class of buddha. (6) The deity of characteristics. To illustrate the three vajras of the enlightened body, speech, and mind, you visualize a white *oṃ* at the crown, a red *āh* at the throat, and a blue *hūṃ* at the heart, and enter into a meditation upon the qualities of the deity or upon the form with all characteristics complete.

Through these techniques the practitioner moves through the five paths, and so on. The paths of training consist of the yoga of characteristics and the yoga of no characteristics. The first yoga has four branches: engaging with the basis of self, engaging with the basis of others,[186] engaging with the basis of the mind, and engaging with sound. These are known collectively as the absorption in reliance upon recitation.

By focusing on these practices, insights will develop within the mind, as described in the texts. Then, in order to strengthen meditative concentration, one trains in the absorption that is not in reliance upon recitation. This includes the absorption of abiding in fire and the absorption of abiding in sound. After these trainings comes the absorption granting liberation at the cessation of sound. This is the yoga of no characteristics and is a method to achieve the nonworldly insight (vipaśyanā) focused upon the entity of emptiness. [318] The main point is that while cultivating deity yoga, there is a focusing upon the ascertainment of the ultimate nature of phenomena.

In Action Tantra the yoga of characteristics is practiced on the path of accumulation. If the wisdom of meditation focused upon emptiness has been achieved, it becomes the yoga of no characteristics. It is taught that the yoga of no characteristics begins at the end of the path of accumulation and continues through the path of preparation and the remaining paths of practice.

The ways of traveling the paths of Performance Tantra are mostly the same as those of Action Tantra. However, a deity yoga that primarily meditates upon emptiness is yoga with no characteristics, and a deity yoga not primarily meditating upon emptiness is yoga with characteristics. Yoga with characteristics has stages of recitation within four external branches and recitation within four internal branches.

The Action and Performance tantras speak of the abilities to accomplish a host of tantric activities, to extend lifespan for eons, to have visions of the deities, and to be cared for by them, but they do not mention actually attaining the stage of union[187] in one life.

In the stages of the paths of Yoga Tantra, yoga with characteristics consists of a coarse yoga focused on the deity and a subtle yoga focused on a hand implement. Other paths are similar to the above. In this class of tantra, body, speech, mind, and activities are to be purified. The purifiers are the mudrā, or mahāmudrā, of the enlightened body, the dharmamudrā of enlightened speech, the samayamudrā of enlightened mind, and the karmamudrā of enlightened activities. The purification practices result in the creation of an enlightened being in which the perfect body, speech, mind, qualities, and activities are combined as one. Teaching this transformation process, the *Tattva-saṃgraha Tantra*, which is the root tantra of Yoga Tantra, is divided into four sections, and the structures of each path are divided into four sections.

[319] The Yoga Tantras teach a special method of achieving quiescence. This is a yoga that trains in the meditation of emanating and withdrawing, in which a tiny vajra, or other hand implement, is visualized and focused on at the tip of the nose. This gradually multiplies, filling the entire body and then pervading out in all directions; the process is then reversed.

Among Japanese tantric practitioners, *Vajradhātu Tantra*, *Vairocana Enlightenment Tantra*, and other tantras from the three lower classes, are widely practiced.

In Highest Yoga Tantra, the yoga of inseparable bliss and emptiness is cultivated through the practices of the generation and completion stages, and in order to purify ordinary death, intermediate state, and birth these three are taken as the path itself. In the resultant state these are transformed into the wisdom dharma body (dharma-kāya), the enjoyment body (sambhogakāya), and the emanated body (nirmāṇakāya).

The generation stage is divided into a coarse stage of single-thought yoga and a subtle stage of conceptual yoga. The first has a beginner stage and the attainment of "descent of a little wisdom." The subtle stage of conceptual yoga up to the body isolation, speech isolation, mind isolation, and impure illusory body practices of the completion stage constitute the attainment of "a little control over wisdom." The fourth stage[188] actual clear light and the practitioner stage of union of enlightened form and mind are the state of "complete control over wisdom." Finally, the nonpractitioner stage of union—the state of Vajradhara[189]— is attained.

As representations of the paths and stages of the Perfection of Wisdom Vehicle, the coarse and subtle stages of the generation stage are similar to the path of accumulation. [320] The attainment of the body isolation of the generation stage up to the impure illusory body is the path of preparation. The fourth stage actual clear light is the path of seeing. Reversing from the actual clear light into the "close to attainment" appearance, attaining the pure illusory body, achieving the elimination union, moving to the second bodhisattva level, and attaining the path of meditation are all simultaneous.

Fourth stage actual clear light occurs on the first bodhisattva level, while the elimination union up to actual clear light at the end of the path of practice make up the other nine levels. This manner of accommodating the stages into the levels is just representation and is not factual, as Tsongkhapa's *Lamp to Illuminate the Five Stages* makes clear. It is not necessary to match up exactly the qualities of these respective paths.

It seems as if tantra has a special method for attaining quiescence. As it is said, "By way of its meditative concentration, tantra is superior."

In the three lower tantras quiescence is achieved by placement meditation and, moreover, quiescence and insight are achieved in sequence. Highest Yoga Tantra has the separate practice of penetrating the vital points of the body, and so insight is achieved by placement meditation while quiescence and insight are achieved at the same time.

QUALITIES OF THE VAJRAYANA PATH

There are many areas in which the path of the great Vajra Vehicle is taught to be superior to the path of the Perfection of Wisdom Vehicle, and these should be known from the classical texts. However, I will explain a little.

In the Perfection of Wisdom Vehicle, bodhicitta is generated and the level to be reached is that of the two perfect bodies—the perfect form body and the perfect dharma body. These two bodies will not arise from no cause or from inappropriate causes, but arise from reliance upon appropriate and similar-type causes. [321] Therefore, practice is followed on the basis of concordant causes.

Even in the Perfection of Wisdom Vehicle the practitioner assumes a mental body from the first bodhisattva level onward. Especially in the three pure levels, a form possessed of the nature of mind and adorned with marks of enlightenment will arise from the imprints of ignorance level[190] and uncontaminated karma. That form is gradually perfected until finally it becomes the material cause for the enlightened form body. The texts of the two śrāvaka philosophical schools, which otherwise do not speak much about the methods to attain the omniscience of a buddha, do describe the particular type of body of a "bodhisattva dwelling in certainty" who accumulates the karma that will ripen as the physical features of enlightenment before the attainment of the enlightenment of a buddha.

Tantra speaks of exclusive material and similar-type causes for achieving the resultant form body and the dharma body. For achieving the dharma body, a wisdom comprehending emptiness that is a nonconceptual cognition of manifest pure suchness in which all elaborations of appearance have subsided, and which is grasped by bodhicitta and is similar in aspect to that dharma body, is generated many times and meditated upon. This is the exclusive cause of the dharma body and the cooperating cause for the form body.[191] This is the same for both tantra and sutra. However, removing the ordinary appearances and apprehensions we have in our minds right now, and meditating with a host of methods on the yoga of the deity form that resembles the enlightened form body as the ripening agent of the path to create the exclusive material cause of the form body, is the way of the Vajra Vehicle. Devoid of such a path and having to make efforts for very long periods of time solely in the six perfections, and so on, in the category of conduct, is the way of the Perfection Vehicle.

[322] In particular, in the tantric tradition, those two perfect bodies are not merely united. The enlightened body and mind are of a single entity. Therefore, when practicing on the path, it is taught that method and wisdom are practiced as an inseparable entity within deity yoga meditation as a way of achieving the dharma body and form body. This is not just a case of generating a vast mandala of deities and then meditating on the emptiness of them. First, conviction is brought to emptiness grasped by bodhicitta, and the objective aspect of that cognition of emptiness arises as the mandala and resident deities. Within that apprehension, the object is apprehended as being devoid of nature, and that is method and wisdom inseparable as a single entity.

Furthermore, the emptiness of oneself and the emptiness of the deity are identical in terms of their entities, but the view that comprehends emptiness—from the perspective of visualization—arises in the form of the deity. Therefore, the cognition of emptiness itself is imagined as the deity, and thus it is said, "Conviction is brought to emptiness and the objective aspect arises as the deity."[192]

At a basic level of practice it is not possible for the cognition comprehending emptiness to actually arise as a deity, but in the future it will be. Therefore, there is a need to imagine that happening now because of the significance of an apprehension of emptiness with its objective aspect in the form of a deity, both complete within one cognition. Ultimately, that emptiness will have to be apprehended by a subtle cognition that is the clear light that arises after the other three appearances have been purified. This has been stated by Nāgabodhi, a disciple of Nāgārjuna. The cognition that apprehends emptiness while the three appearances remain unpurified is of a lesser potential.

As we can see, the most profound features of tantra are mainly found in Highest Yoga Tantra. The clear light nature of mind spoken of in *Uttaratantra* is called the essence of the Sugata, the direct cause of the wisdom dharma body, and the uncontaminated wisdom. [323] The complete intent of this Sugata essence is taught in Highest Yoga Tantras, although individual masters have different ways of explaining it. The Sugata essence that is brought out and described in Highest Yoga Tantra is there in *Uttaratantra*, but to say that it is clearly expressed is a little difficult. However, the ultimate intent of the Sugata essence in *Uttaratantra* is found in the primordial and innate clear light mind taught in the Highest Yoga Tantras. This is very clear. When this primordial mind and innate wisdom is fully focused on and can be developed into the path, it has a potential unlike any other.

It is the generally accepted position in tantra that of the four classes of tantra taught in the explanatory tantra *Vajra Garland*, the three lower classes do not directly or clearly teach the primordial clear light mind. However, in these three classes there is type of exclusive path for ripening the primordial clear light mind, and this is the tantric path of the three lower tantras.

A special feature of Highest Yoga Tantra is that it is not only a coarse consciousness that creates the vast and profound paths and the various insights, but it is also a subtle consciousness that is transformed into the path to great effect. Simply put, when we practice on the paths with our present coarse cognition, there will be much uncontrolled mental wandering toward other thoughts. To eliminate such coarse conceptualization a strong mindfulness must be generated, and a lot of effort is required to hold the clarity of the object and not allow this mental wandering to occur. This is tiring. The significance of the method that generates the subtle consciousness into the entity of the path is that it does not deliberately make use of a coarse consciousness of mindfulness to prevent mental wandering, [324] but with the coarse consciousness itself dissolved into that subtle consciousness, those mental wanderings become powerless. At such a time all coarse consciousnesses have naturally ceased. Therefore, practice is easier, and it can be understood that this has a unique potential.

The general method in Highest Yoga Tantra of generating this very subtle mind into the entity of the path is that the coarse winds and consciousnesses are forcibly halted and the subtle primordial mind is applied to the path. There are different methods of halting the coarse winds and consciousnesses: penetrative focusing upon the channels, winds, and drops; wind yogas; penetrative focusing upon the four joys; and nonconceptual meditation alone. Mahāmudrā and Dzokchen are included within the category of nonconceptual meditations that do not employ penetrative focusing upon the channels, winds, and drops.

There is one thing about which we should be clear. Generally, something to be achieved is achieved by a number of methods, but in our minds, it appears as if it is achieved by one method alone. The reality is that it is achieved by many other conditions being complete. For example, a virtuous deed we have accomplished today is a cause for attaining enlightenment, but enlightenment will not be attained by this deed alone. Therefore, we should recognize the difference between achievement by something and achievement by something alone.

In the Perfection of Wisdom Vehicle, wisdom held by method is the wisdom cognizing emptiness held by bodhicitta, and method held by wisdom refers to the meditation on the nonapprehension of the agent, activity, and object[193] during the practices of giving, and so on. Thus, practice is carried out with method and wisdom combined. In tantra in general, and specifically in Highest Yoga Tantra, method and wisdom are produced inseparably within one cognition, and that inseparability of method and wisdom has to appear [325] to the primordial mind. Therefore, method and wisdom complete within a single primordial mind is the ultimate position of the Sakya, Kagyu, Nyingma, Geluk, and other Buddhist traditions of Tibet.

From the four bodies of an enlightened being, the wisdom dharma body, the enjoyment body, and the emanated body are composite phenomena and are dependent upon previous causes. The materials needed to produce these bodies are the winds and the minds. Therefore, in their reliance upon the primordial innate wisdom and clear light mind generated into an entity of yoga, the practices of deity yoga, Dzokchen, Mahāmudrā, union of clarity and emptiness, and of innate wisdom all come down to the same intent. As Panchen Losang Chögyen said,

> When examined by those who are learned
> in reasoning and scripture on the definitive meaning,
> and by those yogis endowed with experience,
> they are seen to be of one intent.[194]

This particular way of establishing tantra as the word of the Buddha has its origins in Highest Yoga Tantra.

In Highest Yoga Tantra, there is an entity body that is a composite phenomenon as well as an entity body that is a noncomposite phenomenon.

The empowerments in Highest Yoga Tantra are the vase empowerment that purifies the body, the secret empowerment that purifies speech, the knowledge-wisdom empowerment that purifies the mind, and the fourth empowerment that transforms the three secrets[195] into a single, inseparable entity. Therefore, on the basis of the three secrets being indistinguishable, enlightened activities will spontaneously and effortlessly arise. It cannot be anything other than that.

The causes for achieving the three indistinguishable secrets must also be accumulated on the paths of practice. Therefore, in order to achieve the resultant three secrets by the tantric path of inseparable method and wisdom, you practice deity yoga on a basis of the primordial clear light generated into the path. This deity yoga is of two types: that possessed of the ultimate aspect and that possessed of the conventional aspect. Meditating on one's body as the form of the deity, and developing that vivid appearance, is deity yoga possessed of the conventional aspect. [326] The cognition ascertaining emptiness, which is the mind as the wisdom of great bliss arising as the form of the deity and being held with divine pride, is deity yoga possessed of the ultimate aspect.

In the generation stage, meditation on deity form, and regarding whatever appears as the form of the deity, is not actual apprehension of deity form, but it serves a purpose. Therefore, it is said that this is a visualizing meditation, and that there is no mode of apprehension that is actually apprehending the body as a deity form.

When teachings on the three continuums of the Sakya path and result doctrine are given, the view of regarding samsara and nirvana as inseparable is taught first in order to bring about the total appearance of myriad purity. In his *Overview of Guhyagarbha Tantra*, the Nyingma teacher Dodrup Jikmé Tenpai Nyima, in the section on the practice of appearance as the deity, says that all pure and impure phenomena arise from awareness, that they are not beyond the realm of awareness, and that whatever appears is to be regarded as the play of the deity. This all comes down to the clear light mind, because all phenomena are the play of the clear light mind, are not beyond being an appearance of that clear light, and arise from the sphere of the clear light. In terms of how all phenomena appear as the play of the primordial and innate wisdom, appearance appearing as a deity can also be established. This and the previous assertion are fundamental to the Highest Yoga Tantra tradition. Nāgārjuna said,

> Dwelling in the illusion-like samādhi,
> everything is seen in this way.[196]

When those who propound the illusory body say that phenomena are seen as the play of the primordial and innate clear light, that has to mean that phenomena are seen as the expressed manifestation of that clear light. Although inanimate manifestations cannot be seen as being entities of primordial wisdom, this assertion is made in consideration of the ultimate basis of imputation of animate sentient beings.[197]

In the path of Highest Yoga Tantra, there are methods of focusing on and meditating on the channels, winds, and drops. For the channels, there are explanations based on physical channels [327] and explanations where the objects of meditation are merely visualized. The latter does not have to correspond with any kind of physical reality. The yogi directs concentration upon fluid, light, and syllables within the channels and cakras and meditates accordingly. The places in the body where this meditation occurs develop special force, which acts as an aid to the deity yoga practice of forcibly halting conceptualization. One reason why it is necessary to halt conceptualization is that the many levels of consciousness range from the coarse to the very subtle, and having halted the coarse levels, the subtle mind and the primordial mind will gradually be able to train in the path. Also, the insight that comprehends emptiness is achieved on the basis of concentrated placement meditation and enables the simultaneous arising of mental quiescence and insight.

Relying upon the yogas of Highest Yoga Tantra, the subtle consciousnesses are transformed into the wisdom on the path. For we ordinary beings, the coarse levels of consciousness are halted at the time of death, and the subtle levels become manifest until the subtlest consciousness—the death clear light mind—is manifest. However, at this time, for ordinary beings, there will be something like an unconscious state and nothing else. For the yogis, as long as the body has not deteriorated in its capacity as the support of the mind, the coarse consciousnesses will be dissolved through the force of meditation, and they will be able to practice with the ability to experience completely the subtle minds of clarity and awareness. With the coarse winds and minds dissolved the very subtle mind of clear light is made manifest, and if one is able to practice at that time, it will be swift and powerful.

[328] In his *Oral Teachings of Mañjuśrī* the Indian master Buddhaśrījñāna says that for beings possessed of the six elements,[198] when yawning, sneezing, during sex, sleep, and fainting, the coarse temporal minds are somewhat reduced and the clear light mind is manifest. During sleep especially, the coarse temporal minds are particularly reduced, and therefore the clear light of sleep has great significance for practice.

Similarly, the bliss that occurs during the melting elements will somewhat weaken the coarse minds. Therefore, in order to prolong that clear light–like experience, effort is exerted upon the bliss of the descending element, and, unlike that of an ordinary participant in sex, the "bodhicitta"[199] is held, prevented from being released, and returns upward. Therefore, using the desire of ordinary beings, that afflicted cognition itself is transformed into a cognition ascertaining emptiness, and that wisdom understanding emptiness can be used as an antidote to that mind of attachment. This is said to be like an insect born from wood that feeds on wood.[200]

Because of this, whenever the Buddha gave teachings involving the practice of such a path, he also arose in the form of the lord of the mandala in union with a consort. It is taught that practitioners too, when engaged in this kind of practice, must practice by way of such forms appearing to their minds. Therefore, it was on this basis of devoting oneself to the methods of halting the coarse mind and winds that the path of Highest Yoga Tantra arose.

Generally, mere meditation on channels, winds, and drops, as well as the practices of taking over a corpse, inner heat, consciousness transference, and so on, are found in Indian non-Buddhist practices. Therefore, tantra is common to Buddhist and non-Buddhist alike. However, for the Buddhist, bodhicitta and emptiness conjoined as a tantric practice is its most profound feature.

[329] In the practice of the Perfection Vehicle, there are no methods employed for the nonsuppression of the appearances of the phenomenal world. In the practice of tantra, nonsuppression of the appearances of the phenomenal world is deliberately cultivated. This too illustrates its profundity. In the practice of the Perfection Vehicle, generally, no allowance is made for mental afflictions in the pursuit of liberation. For the bodhisattva, if it can be an aid for the fulfillment of the welfare of others, sometimes afflictions are allowed. However, anger is never allowed.

In tantric practice, however, anger can be used by the beginner as a temporary aid for swiftly completing various feats. Therefore, it is taught that for the completion of feats involving wrathful means, and when all other fundamental conditions of method and wisdom are complete, there are occasions when anger is allowed for that time. However, the causal motivation at that time is not suffused with anger but influenced only by compassion. For the contemporaneous motivation,[201] you engage in the activity moved by the thought to carry out the wrathful feat. It is important to recognize the difference.

Generally, when practicing these profound features of tantra, emptiness as an object is no different to that of the Perfection Vehicle. However, the subject consciousness is not an ordinary consciousness but is held by great bliss, and this is superior. For the reality of the mind to be made manifest, the basis on which that manifesting depends must be a pure basis. "A temporal basis will not suffice," say the tantras.[202] Therefore, it is taught that the reality of emptiness must be ascertained on a basis uncontaminated by ordinary appearance and apprehension of that appearance. We can understand from this that reliance upon a pure basis is another difference from the Perfection Vehicle.

Generally, there is no difference in the emptiness found in all existence, and so it is explained that the lack of true existence perceived upon a sprout and the lack of true existence perceived upon a deity form are identical. [330] However, deity yoga must be practiced by entering meditation on emptiness dependent upon a pure basis.

Emptiness is the mere negation of that to be negated, but when *understanding* emptiness, it is very important that it is understood as existing within the realm of appearance. This is because it has to be understood as being the significance of arising by dependence[203] or being established by dependence. For the practice of tantra, the texts say that one has to have either the Madhyamaka view or the Cittamātra view. Therefore, at the very least you should have the Cittamātra view.

The word "empty" is understood differently by the separate tenet systems. The Kālacakra texts speak of an "emptiness of material particles," in which there is an apprehended emptiness and a nonapprehended emptiness. The *Guhyasamāja Tantra* speaks of the four empty states: the empty state, the very empty state, the great empty state, and the all empty state. These are applied to the occasions of the four appearances: appearance, increase, close to attainment, and clear light. Clear light is divided into object clear light and subject consciousness clear light.[204]

When Sakya Pandita and the Geluk masters say that between tantra and sutra there is no difference regarding the view, that statement is made on the basis of the object of the view. Also, when the Sakya tradition speaks of the four views of the four empowerments of Highest Yoga Tantra, that is on the basis of the view consciousness itself. There is a citation on this in *Extensive Work on Tenets* by Jamyang Shepa

(1648–1721). When the Nyingma and Kagyu traditions speak of differences in the views between sutra and tantra, they are based upon differences in the view consciousness. In Highest Yoga Tantra there are explanations of the view in terms of being viewed by this (subjective) and viewing this (objective). Related explanations concerning these assertions of the Sakya, Kagyu, Nyingma, and Geluk schools can be found in chapter 6.

[331] The main elimination pursued by those who practice tantra is that of ordinary perception and ordinary apprehending. Therefore, from the very day of receiving empowerment, the yogi should never be separate from deity yoga, whether in or out of meditation session, and should carry out all daily activities remaining within the pride of the deity. This is a very important method for the elimination of mental afflictions. Therefore, in reality, there can be no dwelling in the ordinary, as there was before entering tantra.

There are reasons why there are various forms of deities to be practiced in deity yoga. Those who have developed the bodhicitta mind aimed at the achievement of enlightenment aspire to fulfill the welfare of others. Therefore, at the time of attaining buddhahood, an enlightened form for the welfare of others will effortlessly and spontaneously appear. Here "appear" is within a place of appearance, just as the reflection of the moon appears in dependence upon a place of appearance. The size of the moon's reflection and its level of clarity and so on depend upon the receptacle that holds the water, and upon the place of appearance itself. It is the same with the appearance of an enlightened form for the welfare of disciples. In dependence upon the type, dispositions, and karmic propensities of individual disciples, the various qualities of the wisdom, compassion, and abilities of a buddha appear to the mind of the practitioner as the various faces, limbs, and bodily forms of a deity. The various forms of deities arise in this way.

However, these deities should not be seized upon as existing on their own like some intrinsically existing person, but should be understood as illustrative. Nevertheless, for those who have actual realization, various signs can appear, such as the whole of existence appearing as a myriad purity, and for some of pure karma, the hosts of meditational deities appear to them as if they were meeting real people.

The reality is that the meditational deities should be regarded as the Buddha Jewel, the Sangha Jewel who are like heroic beings that are beyond this world, [332] and the Dharma Jewel as exemplified by the excellent qualities of elimination and insight within the minds of the other two jewels. With this in mind, you regard the vajra master who initiates you into the mandala, the meditational deity, and your own mind as inseparably one, and without the fetters of expectations and anxiety, follow the excellent example of the Kadampa masters, who regarded "no signs as the king of signs,"[205] hiding your qualities like a flame unseen inside a pot, practicing year after year quietly and secretly, as the name "secret mantra"[206] indicates. You should understand how this is an essential point.

Without relying upon tantra, it is difficult to posit an exclusive material cause of the wisdom dharma body. A material cause of the form body is also very difficult to find. Therefore, with these two reasons it becomes necessary to ascertain the superiority of the tantric path. How is buddhahood attained by way of the tantric path? One method involves the penetrative focusing upon mind and winds and the union of illusory body and clear light to create a union of enlightened mind and form. Another method of achieving the state of union involves penetrative focusing upon the mind alone in which the empty form mahāmudrā of the Kālacakra tradition is united with supreme unchanging bliss. There is an exclusive tradition within the mother tantras of attaining the rainbow body, and in Dzokchen practice it is taught that the end of the four appearances is a special cause for attaining the "great transference into the rainbow body." A state of union can refer to the union that is the inseparability of bliss and emptiness and the union that is the inseparability of the two truths. The latter of these is so called because the former is taken as one part of the union and joined with something else.[207]

[333] It seems that in Highest Yoga Tantra the methods of achieving the inseparability of method and wisdom are unique. The very subtle wind and mind within this exclusive process are of one entity. There is one method of achieving the dharma body and form body of enlightenment in reliance upon the very subtle wind and mind, and one method in reliance upon the primordial mind alone. The *Guhyasamāja Tantra*, the *Cakrasaṃvara Tantra*, and others of the new translation traditions are systems that rely upon both wind and mind. Therefore, once four enlightened forms are asserted, these forms must be established on a basis of the very subtle wind and mind as found in Highest Yoga Tantra, and the way of attaining these four forms or bodies must be by way of primordial wisdom on the basis of an innate form.[208]

The method of attaining enlightenment in reliance upon the primordial and innate subtle mind alone is found in the Kālacakra tradition. I think that Mahāmudrā and Dzokchen are probably included here also.

TWO SCRIPTURAL CITATIONS ON TANTRA

On the above points, Lama Tsongkhapa, in his *Great Exposition of Secret Mantra*, says,

> If you understand well the nature of the empowerments, how their conferment empowers meditations on particular paths, and the particular results they produce, you will trust the praise given to empowerments that can be found many times in the tantras, and will come to hold empowerments themselves as the supreme core instruction.[209]

Also,

> After the third empowerment has been conferred, it is used as
> an example while the fourth empowerment is conferred. The
> master says to the disciple, "With your body as the enlight-
> ened enjoyment body of deity and consort in union, enter
> into meditative equipoise, and in dependence upon that,
> generate the innate wisdom concentrated into the reality of
> phenomena."

Here, the disciple's body is merely visualized as a body of
the deity. It has not become the enlightened body of a buddha. The mind engaged into the reality of phenomena also
lasts only for a short time and is a visualized mental engagement in which that reality is comprehended by conceptual
construct. [334] It is not engaging inseparably like water
mixed with water. Nor does it have the ability to engage in
such meditative equipoise continually.

However, it is a concordant cause, and therefore, if practiced together with the relevant methods, will finally no longer be mere visualization. The body becomes the enlightened
form of a buddha, and the mind engages inseparably with
reality, remaining constantly in that meditative equipoise.
This is known as the stage of the seven features, the goal
of tantric practice, but it is also called the fourth empowerment because it is an introduction to the enlightened stage of
union. This has been extensively explained.

The resultant stage of union, to which the above is an introduction, is the exclusive goal of Highest Yoga Tantra. This is
because, on the paths of practice, it is the power of bringing
into the path the innate bliss arising in dependence upon the
red and white bodhicitta meeting and joining from within

the practitioner's meditation in the aspect of the sought-for deity and consort.

The close cause of this stage of union is the body apprehended as the form of the deity simultaneously in union with the mind being of one taste with the ultimate truth, and not the alternating occurrence of the body being apprehended as the form of the deity when the mind is not of one taste with the ultimate truth, and, conversely, the mind being in such a one-taste union, when the body does not remain apprehended as the form of a deity. In dependence upon the special methods of making bliss into the path, such a union on the path of practice will be created. Although your body has not become the body of a buddha at that time, a special deity form, unlike that of the generation stage and the stages up to the illusory body, will be produced. This is explained in detail in the *Guhyasamāja Tantra*, but for fear of it taking too many words I will not write of it here.

For this union of the two truths to occur on the paths of practice, the individual meditative concentrations of the conventional truth illusory body and the ultimate truth clear light must have been developed previously because there can be no subsequent union of two without those two existing individually. The sequence of development is that the conventional truth is created first and the clear light subsequently. Therefore, the state of union must be produced after the manifestation of the meditative concentration of clear light and the mind as being of one taste. [335] To be able to meditate on that path, the third empowerment is necessary, and that empowerment must illustrate the clear light.[210]

Also, from the same work,

To be able to develop perfect insights from such a completion stage your mind stream must have been previously ripened by the first (generation) stage, which is the path of the vase empowerment. Therefore, by being conferred with the vase empowerment you become a fit vessel for the generation stage.

It is taught that by the vase empowerment you achieve the enlightened emanated body, by the secret empowerment you achieve the enlightened enjoyment body, and through the knowledge-wisdom empowerment you achieve the enlightened dharma body. The term "enjoyment body" is also used to describe the illusory body, and that is acceptable. However, generally in tantric language it is often explained as being the speech of the Tathāgata, and so for the time being, I will explain it that way.

The emanated body is the body of a buddha and will therefore be achieved by generation stage practice as a concordant cause and by the deity yoga of the completion stage that this generation stage practice symbolizes.

Here, "dharma body" refers to the mind of a buddha constantly absorbed into the nature of reality, and that will be achieved by the innate wisdom meditating on the nature of reality, which is its concordant cause.

Every aspect of the speech of the Tathāgata is achieved by the path of the secret empowerment, which gains power over the winds as the roots of speech.

Therefore, these three empowerments can be explained as the achievers of the three vajras of enlightened body, speech, and mind, while these three inseparably joined is the fourth empowerment. Furthermore, the two paths of the second and third empowerment achieve the fourth empowerment on the path, and the union on the path of practice will achieve the inseparability of enlightened body, speech, and mind on the path of no further practice. Therefore, all aspects of the two stages fit into the four empowerments.[211]

[336] The Seventh Dalai Lama, Kalsang Gyatso (1708–57), in his *Elucidating the Reality of the Empowerments*, states,

All those bodhisattvas, and others, categorically of the lineage of the Perfection Vehicle, will without doubt finally enter the path of tantra in order to become a buddha. The *Hevajra Tantra* says,

> Having manifested a mandala
> of a violent circle of flames,
> Tilottamā was summoned
> to confer vajra essence empowerment.[212]

Thus, the tenth-level bodhisattva, at the end of the path of the Perfection Vehicle, relies upon Tilottamā to receive the actual third empowerment, and so on, and enters the tantric path.

Also, in Nāgārjuna's *Five Stages*,

> As it is said in the *Great Play Sutra*,
> Śākyamuni, the Tathāgata,
> having vowed to attain enlightenment,
> intended that by the great emptiness
> he would become a buddha,
> and by the banks of the Nairañjanā River,
> he sat in unmoving samādhi.

Thus, the bodhisattva of the Perfection Vehicle, in his last life on the banks of the Nairañjanā River, wished to attain enlightenment by his path alone. There he was urged by all the buddhas.

At that time the conquerors in the vajra of space,
gathered like sesame in a sesame pod,
snapped their fingers at the son of the conquerors,
and called to him with a single voice:

"This meditative absorption is not pure.
Through it, you will not achieve the ultimate."

Thus, they revealed to him that by his own path he would
not attain the ultimate result of enlightenment. How will it
be attained?

"Focus on the clear light,
supreme like the sides of space."

It is attained by the actual clear light, the exclusive path of
Highest Yoga Tantra.

"Having reached the stage of clear light,
you will be born into the form of joy."

Thus, from the actual clear light the pure illusory body is
attained, and therefore it should be generated.

"At that time, the vajra form of joy
becomes the most powerful of all."

[337] Thus from the union of the path of practice comes the
union of no further practice, the stage of Vajradhara. This the
buddhas instruct. The bodhisattva, in accordance with these
instructions, practices the path of tantra,

On hearing these voices
he left the unmoving samādhi,
and in the middle of the night,
the bodhisattva focused on that.[213]

Also, in the same work,

> The wonderful all-empty state,
> a great wisdom bright and clear,
> by the kindness of the gurus,
> this he clearly sees.[214]

Also,

> By the vajra-like samādhi
> at the time that the dawn broke,
> like the moon in water, a mirage, and so on,
> he was adorned with illusion-like qualities.
>
> Abiding in the essence of enlightenment,
> he destroyed the hindering māras.
> The Śākya master, having gained
> the peerless and perfect wisdom,
> then taught it here
> to protect and benefit living beings.[215]

Sheaves of Instructions also says,

> "For the ultimate also, definitely rely on this method. I will explain. For example, having received the wisdom empowerment given by the perfect buddhas abiding in the skies above, the Śākya master relied upon it in order to attain enlightenment while sitting in front of the Bodhi tree. Also, the Bhagavan, by this alone, was initiated into the vajra essence by Tilottamā." This is extensively explained, which is excellent because those with knowledge of the instructions will clearly come to understand this point.[216]

Āryadeva, in his *Compendium of Practice*, says something very similar.

In the tradition of Highest Yoga Tantra our Teacher attained enlightenment countless eons ago and his attainment of enlightenment in this world was a mere show. Therefore, the explanations from *Five Stages*, and elsewhere, are given on the basis of this pretense. [338] However, for the Perfection Vehicle bodhisattva to newly attain enlightenment, such a process is actually necessary, and to complete the attainment the bodhisattva must rely upon the tantric path. It is to show this, that the above pretense was shown. The description in the *Vajra Peak Tantra* of the bodhisattva as an inhabitant of Akaniṣṭha[217] traveling as far as the tenth bodhisattva level of the Perfection Vehicle, then being entreated by the buddhas, receiving empowerment, entering the meditation on the meaning of the five enlightenments,[218] and becoming a buddha, is not given on the basis of the above pretense but is taught on the basis of a bodhisattva first becoming a buddha. Moreover, the *Hevajra Tantra* says,

> Purity is the nature of self-perception;
> freedom is not by another purity.[219]

There are many such references in the tantras that explain this point.

It could be argued, "The statements from the tantras that the tantric path is an addition to be placed onto the end of the Perfection Vehicle path is just to show the greatness of that path but is not a truth. This is because the Perfection Vehicle teaches enlightenment only by its own path and nowhere does it teach that another path has to be added to it."

This is nonascertaining reasoning. For example, the canons

of the lower vehicles do not declare that one has to enter the Great Vehicle path after having attained the goals of the śrāvaka and pratyeka, but such a declaration made in the Great Vehicle canon as a fact is not refuted by it not being mentioned in the lower vehicle canons.

ESTABLISHING BY REASON

Moreover, it can be proven by reasoning that the attainment of enlightenment must have been preceded by the tantric path: (1) within the mind stream of a buddha as described in the Perfection Vehicle is found the wisdom of great bliss and other types of qualities of elimination and insight that are exclusive to tantra, and (2) such qualities must have been created by the power of meditation on paths of similar types.

The first reason stands because if there were no types of qualities exclusive to tantra found within the mind stream of a buddha as described in the Perfection Vehicle, [339] then a buddha who became enlightened by the path of tantra and the buddha of the Perfection Vehicle would have different qualities of elimination and insight. That is not the case. The seventeenth chapter of the *Guhyasamāja Root Tantra* says,

> The bodhisattvas who strive for and seek enlightenment for the duration of as many eons as there are grains of sand in the Ganges, and yet do not achieve that enlightenment, are of the same number as those bodhisattvas who, by taking joy in the Guhyasamāja, achieve the enlightenment of the Tathāgatas in this very life.[220]

Śāntarakṣita says,

The great bliss Vajrasattva, which will be realized by
other paths over countless eons, is achieved in this
very life without hardship by those possessed of the
methods of the Vajra Vehicle.[221]

Ācarya Tripiṭakamala in his *Light of the Three Ways* says,

Same but without the hardship.[222]

Thus, sutra and tantra have differences in method but their
resultant attainments are the same.

The second reason stands because, in order to produce
the twenty-one categories of the uncontaminated wisdom
of the buddhas, and so on, the Perfection Vehicle teaches
the paths of practice of the yoga of the complete aspects of
the three wisdoms, which involve sequential meditation on
objects and aspects of the paths that are in the same class of
insight as those categories of enlightenment. These are peak
yoga, which gains mastery of those paths; sequential yoga,
which gains stability over the paths; and single moment
yoga, which in a single moment has the ability to meditate
on the aspects of the path without error and in sequence.
These yogas, in their correct order, are necessary meditations.
Therefore, eliminations and insights common to the Perfection Vehicle must be developed by paths of practice of similar
type, and there can be no reason why qualities common to
the tantric path should not be developed likewise. If meditation on paths of similar type to those tantric qualities are
necessary prerequisites, then there can be no alternative to
entering the tantric path because such paths are not taught
in the Perfection Vehicle.

[340] Furthermore, it would follow that the paths of the

Perfection Vehicle were more profound than the paths of Highest Yoga Tantra and that the disciples of the Perfection Vehicle were of sharper faculties than those disciples of the Tantra Vehicle because the resultant great bliss consciousness and the form body endowed with the seven features are to be similarly found in the resultant buddhahood of both vehicles, and the tantric practitioner must achieve these having meditated for one life, and so on, on the paths of representations of these attainments, while the Perfection Vehicle practitioner would be able to achieve these resultant states without meditating on such paths.

Also, if the enjoyment body of a buddha described by the Perfection Vehicle is not the ultimate form body endowed with the seven features, then it would be inferior to the Vajradhara of the tantric tradition. If it were the ultimate form body, then such a form body would be attained without conferring the ripening fourth empowerment and without practicing the fourth-empowerment liberating path of practice. Therefore, it would be a result without a cause.

Furthermore, did the Buddha with the enjoyment body as described in the Perfection Vehicle turn the wheel of Highest Yoga Tantra or not? If not, it would not have been possible to provide teachings for those unequivocal practitioners of the Great Vehicle who possess superior mental faculties. Moreover, it would follow that there would be an enjoyment body of the Buddha that would not make full use of Highest Yoga Tantra, the highest teachings of the Great Vehicle. If the Buddha in that enjoyment form did turn the wheel, did he turn it with the actual phenomena of the tantras manifest in his mind or not? If not, then the teachings would be no different to an ordinary being giving teachings. If the actual phenomena were manifest, then this is similar to the previous argument on whether similar-type causes should have preceded them.

In order to provide for the three types of practitioner,[223] bodhisattvas have to know and develop those paths comprised by the insights of the three vehicles. If that is so, then in order to provide for the exclusive tantric disciples, they have to know and develop all paths pertinent to those disciples. The reasoning is similar.

THE PERFECTION VEHICLE HAS NO EXCLUSIVE SIMILAR-TYPE CAUSE OF THE FORM BODY

[341] Also, it is not possible to become a buddha by relying upon the Perfection of Wisdom Vehicle alone because in order to attain the resultant form body and the wisdom dharma body, the complete material causes must have been developed as prerequisites. The Perfection Vehicle by itself cannot develop a material cause corresponding to the form body of a buddha nor can it develop a material cause corresponding to the wisdom dharma body of a buddha.

The first of these statements concerning the material cause of the form body can be established as follows. According to the tradition of the Perfection Vehicle, a body with the nature of mind, arising from the level of imprints of ignorance and uncontaminated karma, is created on the paths of practice. The continuation of that form is perfected until finally, in the last life of the bodhisattva, the very next instant of the similar-type continuum of that mental body becomes the form body of a buddha. This is the assertion of the Perfection Vehicle, but that mental body cannot function as the exclusive and similar-type cause for the form body of a buddha. This is because the form body of a buddha is of an inseparable nature with a wisdom of the same aggregation as that form body. In the Perfection Vehicle there is such a wisdom, but the mental body described above is not suitable to become part of an aggregation that is of an inseparable nature with a wisdom liberated from obscurations to omniscience. This is because this mental body arises from the level of imprints of ignorance, which are obscurations to omniscience, and is therefore created from an impure cause. There is no way to make this impure phenomenon into an entity inseparable from the wisdom of a buddha, which is liberated from all obscuration. For example, no matter how much you mix iron with gold, they can never be mixed to the extent of becoming an inseparable entity.

In this way, that mental body cannot function as a similar-type cause of the form body of a buddha because of being a distinct entity to that wisdom. Moreover, it is also right to differentiate between the wisdom of meditative equipoise found on the Perfection Vehicle's own paths and the wisdom of meditative equipoise found on the tantric path, in terms of there being or not being an exclusive similar-type cause of the form body that is one entity with that wisdom. [342] On the Perfection Vehicle path, during the wisdom of meditative equipoise on the eighth level, and so on, wisdom accumulation as a cause of the wisdom dharma body of a buddha is present, but that meditative equipoise alone cannot produce the form body of a buddha. Therefore, the yogi is urged to work on the accumulation of merit as a cause of the form body during the postmeditation sessions. This is stated in the Sutra of the Ten Levels and also by glorious Candrakīrti when he says, "The Buddhas arouse them from their cessation."[224]

Therefore, it can be established that there is no exclusive

similar-type cause of the form body that is of one entity with the wisdom of meditative equipoise.

On the tantric path, from the time the yogi has reached a high level of insight, only the meditative equipoise of bliss and emptiness combined is cultivated, and any deliberate accumulation of merit in the postmeditation sessions, such as arising in the form of the deity, prostrations, circumambulations, recitations, and so on, is negated. As is said,

> Physical activity such as that of mandala,
> do not undertake, even in dreams.[225]

Also, from the *Hevajra Tantra*,

> It is emptiness and compassion inseparable
> that is known as "bodhicitta."
> There is no recitation of mantras, no austerity,
> no fire offerings, no mandala inhabitants, and no mandala.
> That is mantra recitation, that is austerity,
> that is the fire offering, that is the mandala inhabitants,
> and that is the mandala. In brief, they are forms
> incorporated by that mind.[226]

The citation is stating that this innate wisdom protects the mind and is, therefore, the definitive mantra. Devoid of any wrongdoing and negating any wrong conduct, it is austerity. It burns away mental affliction, and, as the firewood of the aggregates, is therefore a fire offering. Being an entity incorporating every deity, it is every mandala inhabitant. By taking the essence of all phenomena it is also the mandala. In short, all paths by way of their functions are incorporated in that innate wisdom, and therefore external mantra recitation, and so on, is not necessary; that innate wisdom alone will suffice.

If an exclusive similar-type cause of the form body of a buddha did not exist within that meditative equipoise, [343] it would be no different than the Perfection Vehicle, and the practitioner would again have to engage in amassing an accumulation of merit. The citation is stating that this is negated and is replaced by the cultivation of this meditative equipoise alone. Therefore, it can be established within the tantric path that there exists an exclusive similar-type cause of the form body of a buddha, which is of one entity with the wisdom of that meditative equipoise.

THE PERFECTION VEHICLE HAS NO EXCLUSIVE SIMILAR-TYPE CAUSE OF THE WISDOM DHARMA BODY

The Perfection Vehicle on its own cannot produce an exclusive similar-type cause or material cause of the wisdom dharma body of a buddha, because on the paths of the Perfection Vehicle there is nothing that can function as that cause. This is because in Perfection Vehicle practice all uncontaminated meditative equipoises upon emptiness with duality subsided are only coarse mental consciousnesses, and such consciousnesses cannot become exclusive similar-type causes of the wisdom dharma body of a buddha.

In Perfection Vehicle practice there is also no subtle wisdom comprehending emptiness that arises from a mere coarse mental consciousness, because for a very subtle mental consciousness to comprehend emptiness, coarse consciousnesses up to the three appearances of appearance, increase, and close to attainment must have dissolved, and the primordial mind itself must have been generated in an aspect clearly capable of encountering the object. To produce that, the winds as mounts of the mind must enter, abide, and dissolve within the central channel,[227] by which all coarse winds will be halted. This is precipitated by the fact that wind and mind share the same engagement, and is a procedure accomplished by actually relying upon methods of penetrative focusing on places within the body or by training in that practice. In the Perfection Vehicle's own paths such methods are incomplete.

Apart from a very subtle mental consciousness possessing a one-taste engagement in emptiness, no other mind can function as an exclusive similar-type cause of the wisdom dharma body of a buddha. This is because any kind of coarse consciousness meditative equipoise will be a mental consciousness up to and including those consciousnesses of appearance, increase, and close to attainment. [344] The wisdom dharma body is a primordial innate mind, purified of all elaborations of duality, meditatively concentrated irreversibly upon emptiness. Therefore, the exclusive similar-type cause of that primordial mind cannot be a temporary, coarse mind.

The minds of the three appearances, and so on, must be irreversibly negated before the attainment of the actual clear light, which is the actual antidote to the obscurations to omniscience. Once they are negated, the primordial innate clear light mind becomes the wisdom dharma body. On this, *Analysis of Activity* says,

> For eons beyond measure,
> giving away head, wealth, and so on
> will not bring the fruit of enlightenment
> because the appearances are not purified.

> Likewise, for eons beyond measure,
> the practice of morality, patience, and so on

will not bring the fruit of enlightenment
because the appearances are not purified.

For eons beyond measure,
the samādhi of the mantra body
will not bring the fruit of enlightenment
because the appearances are not purified.

With the three appearances purified,
without doubt, omniscience is gained.[228]

Therefore, generally, from the two goals of omniscience and liberation, the Great Vehicle paths strive primarily for the attainment of omniscience. From the two kinds of obscuration, they hold the obscurations to the attainment of omniscience as the main obscuration to be eliminated. Therefore, in the practice of Perfection Vehicle, it is asserted that through the power of meditations on the paths of the accumulations of wisdom and merit, all aspects of obscurations to omniscience, which manifest to the coarse mental consciousness as a mistaken duality of truly existing appearance, can be purified. However, that path alone cannot purify those aspects of obscurations to omniscience within mistaken dualistic appearance found in appearance, increase, and close to attainment, which are subtler than that coarse mental consciousness.

Therefore, first of all, by the power of the meditation that is a method of penetrative focusing on places in the body, the winds enter, abide, and dissolve in the central channel. [345] With the coarse winds and consciousness dissolved, the subtle mind of clear light is developed into the entity of the path of bliss and emptiness. Finally, in correspondence with the death process, when all the pervading winds have also dissolved, the clear light becomes manifest. From that clear light the illusory body is formed. However, the subject consciousness, with regard to the object of emptiness, is still rendered impure by way of dualistic appearance, and emptiness is comprehended by way of mental construct. Nevertheless, at the end of this training, the actual clear light arises in which the subject consciousness directly perceives emptiness uncontaminated by dualistic appearance. From that is formed a pure illusory body, which is similar to the impure illusory body in terms of arising from just the mind and the winds, but because the mind as the basis of the impure illusory body possesses the obscurations of mental affliction and the karmic potential to take birth, there is a huge difference between the pure and the impure illusory body.

Once the pure illusory body has been produced, there can be no severing of its similar-type continuity. Therefore, it is called the vajra body. However, a meditative equipoise continuum that no longer arises from the actual clear light has not been attained, because the mind is still obstructed by the obscurations to omniscience in the form of the appearance of true existence. To purify that, the yogi trains in the path of the innate bliss and emptiness until finally all dualistic appearances are purified to never to be produced again. The resultant wisdom dharma body, never moving from clear light, is united with the form body as a single entity with that wisdom, and the final result is attained.

By way of the above reasons, this has been an explanation of the vast differences in status in terms of coarseness, subtlety, purity and impurity, between the coarse consciousness apprehending emptiness by way of nondualistic appearance as explained in the Perfection Vehicle, the illustrative clear light and the impure illusory body that is formed from it, the actual clear light and the pure illusory body that is formed from it, the ultimate actual clear light of the resultant state, and the enjoyment body of a buddha that is in union with that. These are to be compared, and the essential points of the paths of Highest Yoga Tantra definitely being necessary for the attainment of enlightenment should be understood.[229]

[346] The second heading from *Elucidating the Reality of the Empowerments*, called Points of Doubt, is not reproduced here. It should be known from the text itself.

WHO SHOULD PRACTICE TANTRA?

What type of person should practice tantra, and what is the sequence of practice? Someone with a genuine experience of renunciation, bodhicitta, and the view of emptiness—the three main elements of the path—or someone who has at least the beginnings of that experience, should add the profound tantric path to their foundation. Replete with these conditions, in the presence of a qualified lama they should enter the mandala of a particular class of tantra, take the empowerment properly, and guard the vows and pledges.

In order to attain the resultant form body of a buddha, they rely upon the wide range of peerless tantric methods not taught in the Perfection Vehicle, involving single-pointed focus upon a mandala of deities, in which conviction is brought to emptiness and the objective aspect arises as the deity, and they must practice a deity yoga whose aspects correspond to the four complete purities of place, body, utilities, and activities found with the resultant form body.

In order to attain the resultant wisdom dharma body, they should make efforts in the yoga of entering the clear light realm of a mind divorced from elaborations of true existence by relying upon the skillful practices of penetrative focusing on the inner channels, winds, and so on, as a practice for developing an antidote to the mental afflictions in their own continuum.

There are three kinds of empowerment: the ripening causal empowerment, the liberating empowerment of the paths, and the resultant empowerment of liberation. During the empowerments of the lower tantras, the water empowerment and the crown empowerment are conferred as ripening causal empowerments for the attainment of the wisdom dharma body and the form body.

[347] In the higher tantra empowerments, four empowerments are conferred to awaken, or ripen, the potential of those seeds that exist within the primordial mind and that will produce the four bodies of a buddha: the enlightened form of the emanated body, the enlightened speech enjoyment body, the enlightened mind dharma body, and the innate wisdom nature body, where the other three are located.

Therefore, at the time of becoming a buddha, the wisdom dharma body, whose entity is that of the nature body, is actualized for the sake of others. By that mere actualization the form body appears for the sake of others. To the minds of pure disciples it appears as the enjoyment body and to the minds of impure disciples it is the emanated body. In that way the four bodies are established.

The continuum of our consciousness at this present time will ultimately become a buddha possessed of the four bodies. Therefore, the "I" of this present ordinary existence will transform into the I of a buddha, and this is because of a mind that has existed since time without beginning. Therefore, it is said, "Such a mind is not mind. The nature of mind is clear light."[230] Not only will the continuum of mind finally become the wisdom dharma body—the mind of a buddha—it will also become the nature of the four bodies.

THE GREAT VEHICLE IS THE WORD
OF THE BUDDHA

There were those in the past who declared that the Great Vehicle teachings were not the words of the Buddha, and these days there are some who declare likewise. However, Venerable Maitreya in his *Ornament of the Sutras* established that the Great Vehicle was the word of the Buddha. [348] Ācarya Bhāvaviveka in his *Blaze of Logic* also taught extensively and profoundly on establishing the Great Vehicle as the word of the Buddha. In his *Sixty Verses of Reasonings*, Ārya Nāgārjuna determined that understanding the reality of dependent arising was not only necessary for the attainment of the state of omniscience, but was also indispensable even for the attainment of liberation.

In particular, in *A Compendium of Sutra* by Nāgārjuna, many Great Vehicle sutras are cited as authoritative references. It was by being convinced that these citations were the words of the Buddha that he identified them and held them as valid. It could never be that such a great guardian of monastic and ethical discipline would lie by saying that something assumed not to be the word of the Buddha was in fact the Buddha's word. Also, Nāgārjuna said that if there were no differences in the paths to be meditated on, such as those of the thirty-seven facets of enlightenment and others in common with the paths of the śrāvaka, there could not be any corresponding difference of superiority in the resultant attainments. Also, any difference in terms of superiority in the resultant attainment will reflect corresponding differences in the causes.

Generally, the practices of giving, ethics, patience, and so on are taught in Lesser Vehicle texts, but if in the Great Vehicle there were not extra paths for bringing out more profound and special features, those same features would not be found in the resultant attainment. This thinking of Nāgārjuna is a very forceful proof.

Ācarya Śāntideva, in his *Engaging in Bodhisattva Deeds,* also writes emphatically on the Great Vehicle being the word of the Buddha.

I always say that in the Great Vehicle sutras where the questioners and respondents were Maitreya, Avalokiteśvara, and so on, it is generally accepted that such beings were not visible to humans but only appeared to those beings of pure karma. Therefore, the compilers of the sutras also must have been similar concerning their ability to see speakers such as Maitreya, Samantabhadra, Mañjuśrī, and others.

[349] Therefore, in keeping with the maxim "Do not rely upon the words, rely upon the meaning," if you look at the meanings of the words of the Great Vehicle texts such as those on method—bodhicitta and the practice of the six perfections, and those on wisdom such as the detailed teachings on emptiness—it is very clear that what is taught in a very basic way in the śrāvaka and pratyeka canon is extensively determined and established in the Great Vehicle. Moreover, these texts declared by Nāgārjuna to be the words of the Buddha are not negated by direct valid cognition, inferential valid cognition, and so on, in their teaching of manifest and hidden phenomena. Therefore, I have every confidence that they are words coming from the valid speech of someone who can be considered a reliable and valid person.

If you claim that the Great Vehicle is not the word of the Buddha but was composed by learned followers of the Buddha such as Nāgārjuna, you are actually saying that they were more knowledgeable than the Buddha himself. Therefore, there may be Western scholars these days who say that the Great Vehicle teachings only began a hundred years or so after the Buddha, but to my mind, on top of those reasons given previously, there are others worth considering:

1. Those great Indian scholar-practitioners of the past, such as the master Nāgārjuna, were people of brilliant intellects, capable of separating out the definitive and provisional teachings of the Buddha, and in no way were they unable to distinguish

truth from lies and good from bad. The manner in which they determined phenomena with countless reasons in their compositions was well known and established by Tibetan and Indian scholars. Later unbiased scholars and those with the clear sight of wisdom have also been able to understand that. [350]

2. Glorious Ārya Nāgārjuna was a renowned historical figure who appeared in India about four hundred years after the Buddha. Present-day Western scholars live 2,500 years after the Buddha appeared. In terms of time, it is worth thinking about which of these two would be the more authoritative as a historian. It is very likely that Nāgārjuna—an Indian scholar living not long after the Buddha—would be well acquainted with the history of India and the life of the Buddha, and it is difficult to believe that the same could be true for later non-Indians. Therefore, Nāgārjuna must have had a greater knowledge of the actual life of the Buddha. This is a big difference. Also, the teachers of Nāgārjuna and their teachers before them would have provided an unbroken testimony stretching back to historical figures present at time of the Buddha.

3. In terms of the place, the Buddha appeared in India. Nāgārjuna was also a great scholar born in India. Therefore, we should ask ourselves whether a great scholar from India would be well acquainted with the events occurring in India, or would later Western scholars living far outside of India have a better knowledge of the history of India?

4. We should ask ourselves if Ārya Nāgārjuna was a sublime and reliable human being or some stupid person. [351] The fact is that he was an accomplished and learned master in all branches of knowledge—not only the inner world of the mind, but also of medicine, chemistry, arts and crafts, and many more. It is abundantly clear that he was an authoritative and trustworthy person

who analyzed everything deeply and categorized the provisional and definitive teachings of the Buddha by way of reasoning, in a way that cannot be refuted by scripture or logic.

If this great master was not someone who always spoke the truth, reasons for that should be put forward. However, if you evaluate his writings, it can be seen that he was an authoritative and trustworthy person who did not lie. Moreover, measured against those wise and brilliant pandits such as Ācarya Āryadeva, Buddhapālita, Bhāvaviveka, Candrakīrti, Śāntideva, and others, who were his direct and indirect disciples, how difficult is it to be convinced that this ācarya was a reliable master?

Therefore, by validating master Nāgārjuna through reasoning to be an authoritative person, we can increase our faith in him accordingly. This is the best way of proving that the Great Vehicle was the word of the Buddha, I think. Similarly, citing texts of the Great Vehicle as references in works that arose from the intellectual prowess of great scholars, knowledgeable in all religious traditions, is a recognition of these texts being the words of the Buddha. From this too we can conclude that the Great Vehicle is the word of the Buddha.

If the Great Vehicle was not the word of the Buddha, the Great Vehicle commentaries would also be unsound references. However, without relying upon Great Vehicle commentaries, not only is the attainment of omniscience impossible, even liberation would be difficult to attain. [352] This is because, although the *Sutra of the Four Truths* teaches the truth of suffering, the truth of the origin of suffering, the truth of cessation, and the truth of the path, without depending upon the Great Vehicle commentaries it is very difficult to establish the truth of cessation as something attainable. Without being able to establish a complete cessation it is not possible to establish the truth of the path. If it is not possible to establish path and cessation, the excellent qualities found in liberation and omniscience can certainly not be established.

Nevertheless, Great Vehicle sutras such as the perfection of wisdom sutras are spoken of as being taught on Vulture's Peak to a vast audience of gods and humans, whereas to our common perception there is only room on Vulture's Peak for tens of people. However, this clearly shows that the canon of teachings the Buddha gave for the ordinary disciples constitute the three baskets found in accepted historical accounts, whereas the Great Vehicle teachings were taught only to disciples of pure karma and not to everyone. Because of that, the Theravada tradition and present-day historians recognize that in the commonly accepted history there is no account of the Great Vehicle being taught by the Buddha, and without examining and contemplating its content they categorically declare that the Great Vehicle is not the word of the Buddha.

However, in the perfection of wisdom sutras, in exchanges between Śariputra and Subhūti, for example, both are in the form of human beings and so there is no basis for argument. When Śariputra and Avalokiteśvara are engaged in question and answer, the latter is a bodhisattva in the form of a deity, and there is no possibility for those of impure karma to see him. Either situation can occur. Therefore, it was not the case that there had to be a fixed time, place, and so on for Great Vehicle teachings. [353] Wherever disciples of pure karma were to be found, there the Buddha would appear to give teachings, and so on. This will be illustrated below.

Similarly, in the past there were those who wondered if the tantra canon was a Buddhist canon, and it seems there are those today with similar doubts. If it is accepted that the tantric teachings were not given by the Buddha but appeared much later, as maintained by present-day commentators, and that the present-day tantric lineage of the Great Vehicle passed down through Sanskrit cannot be accepted, then the presentation of the four bodies of a buddha, as given earlier, would not exist. If that is so, then the Buddha who appeared 2,600 years ago would have to be seen as an ordinary being.

Why is this? When the four truths are determined through reasoning in Dharmakīrti's *Commentary on Valid Cognition*,[231] and particularly when the four features of the truth of cessation[232] are similarly explained by way of valid cognition and Madhyamaka philosophy combined, it ultimately comes down to the Madhyamaka view, which in turn comes down to the view of dependent origination. Because of this, wherever the Great Vehicle tradition has spread, the name of Ārya Nāgārjuna, who was predicted by the Buddha, is well known. He and his lineage of disciples produced wonderful works that concentrated on the teachings on emptiness, the explicit topic of the Buddha's perfection of wisdom sutras. As these masters explicitly state, without the Great Vehicle it is very difficult to establish through reasoning the four truths in general, and in particular, it is difficult to explain the truth of cessation, even though it is possible to explain cause and effect of the two truths in the category of mental affliction.

Therefore, it is very difficult for the meaning of the truth of cessation that is the attainment of the four bodies to arise correctly in the mind, without contemplating the explanations found in the Great Vehicle texts [354] and especially those taught in Highest Yoga Tantra that describe winds and mind being of one entity, in connection with the presentation of the subtle primordial mind. Therefore, one cannot say that one can practice outwardly as a śrāvaka, inwardly as a bodhisattva, and secretly as a tantric practitioner on the same seat without any contradiction.

Therefore, having first built up an understanding of the entire doctrine, when you reach the point where you are able to have conviction and certainty in the presentations of the teachings through honest and discerning reasoning, that is a suitable position from which to refute and establish various positions.

To sum up, the Buddha, in his first turning of the wheel of Dharma, taught the four truths as the foundation of the common teachings, thereby establishing the framework of the Buddha Dharma. The middle turning concentrated on the truth of cessation, which is the essence of the four truths, and determined the object clear light, or emptiness—the ultimate focus of the truth of the path. The final turning taught the subject clear light, which refers to the cognition taking that emptiness as its object, and whose nature is the clear light. This turning also laid the foundation for tantra, and therefore is directly relevant to the non-dual profound and manifest taught in the tantras. They also teach the primordial and innate clear light, upon which the four bodies can be established. Therefore, Gunthang Jampai Yang (1762–1823) offered this metaphor: "Those who want to reach the mountain pass must start at the foot and climb to reach its peak."

Tantric teachings are given only to those of suitable karma. In *Compendium of Practice*—Āryadeva's commentary on the essential meaning of Nāgārjuna's *Five Stages*—he speaks of three types of practice: To those with liking for the inferior, the practice of nonattachment is given. [355] To those with a liking for the vast, the practice of the levels and the Perfection Vehicle is given. And to those with a liking for the profound, the practice of desire is given. Accordingly, the Buddha transformed his form of a monk and appeared as the lord of the mandala, where he taught tantra to a few fortunate disciples. This kind of teaching was not restricted to being given during the time the Buddha actually lived. To certain disciples of pure karma, the Buddha arose as the lord of the mandala and taught certain tantras. It is not possible to limit such teachings to a time and place by saying that they occurred over two thousand years ago in India but could not have occurred in Tibet, for example. When the inner mind stream of a person meets the necessary criteria, such teachings will appear. Therefore, even in later times, the Buddha and great teachers such as Nāgārjuna and his disciples, as well as meditational deities, have shown themselves, as though in face-to-face meetings, to many great beings within all Buddhist traditions, and particularly to those of all Tibetan Buddhist traditions. Such things still occur. Specifically, in teachings such as the mind treasure cycles of the Nyingma tradition, a special deity will appear and while teaching the practice cycle of the meditational deity will teach the tantra and relevant deity yogas. This is very widespread.

In this connection, I advised a fully ordained American nun to do research on the Śrāvaka and Pratyeka Vehicles. She traveled to Thailand to do this, and at that time in Thailand there was a Theravadin monk of impeccable monastic discipline who had been recognized as having reached the stage of an arhat. [356] She had an audience with him, and he told her that he had had a vision of the Buddha surrounded by an entourage of arhats. According to the actual tenets held by this Theravadin monk, he had to accept that after the Buddha had displayed his nirvana without remainder, his continuum of cognition was severed like the dying of a flame. However, such a sight had arisen to his pure mind and so he remarked, "The Buddha is still alive."

One time, a disciple of this Theravadin monk told of a pilgrimage to China. There, in the presence of a statue of Avalokiteśvara he bowed with great faith and reverence. From the statue a shaft of bright light, like a flash of lightning on a dark night, shot to the crown of his head. There is a photo of this, which I have seen.

Also, I met a fully ordained Korean nun. She also told me accounts of wonderful visions she had experienced.

Similarly, around the time of the Cultural Revolution, I saw a photograph of clouds that had amassed above Five Peaked Mountain (Wutaishan) in China, creating a stunningly clear form of Mañjuśrī. I also saw a photograph of a statue of the Buddha in China whose head was adorned with swirls of rainbow light.

Once when I was in Portugal, I went on a pilgrimage to a holy Christian site called Fatima. In the local church was a famous and venerated statue of the Virgin Mary. There, with my Christian brothers and sisters, I offered prayers. As I left, I turned and looked back, and as my eyes met Mary, she gave me a smile. Such amazing occurrences are possible.

[357] Those who claim that tantric teachings are not the words of the Buddha also doubt that tantric treatises composed by Nāgārjuna, Āryadeva, Candrakīrti, and others are works by the same great Buddhist scholars who composed the works on Madhyamaka philosophy, saying that it is just that the names are similar. However, toward the end of the twentieth century there was a Sanskrit scholar living in Varanasi called Ācarya Upadhyāya. He was a Brahmin by birth who later came to know of Buddhism, and having found great faith in it he became a Buddhist. Once he received from Nepal a fragment of the Sanskrit text *Cleansing the Obstacles of the Mind.*[233] It clearly described the Highest Yoga Tantra practice of taking mental afflictions as the path. Its verses were written in a style remarkably similar to the Sanskrit of (Āryadeva's) *Four Hundred Verses.* Comparing the compositional style of the two texts he was able to conclude that the tantric text was indeed written by Āryadeva.

Similarly, other Indian Sanskrit scholars have said that the writing styles of *Fundamental Wisdom of the Middle Way* and of the Guhyasamāja work, *Five Stages,* are the same and there can be no conclusion other than they were both composed by Nāgārjuna. Also, Candrakīrti's *Clear Words* on Madhyamaka philosophy contains a few special verbal roots not found in works by other authors. These roots can also be found in *Clear Lamp*—his commentary on Guhyasamāja—and therefore it can be concluded that the Candrakīrti listed as author of both is one and the same person. [358] On this basis, Nāgārjuna and Candrakīrti are asserting that Highest Yoga Tantra teachings, of which the most important is the *Guhyasamāja Tantra,* are the words of the Buddha and are teachings of the Great Vehicle.

In this connection the Sakya tradition, in its path and result teachings, speak of valid scripture, valid treatise, valid lama, and valid experience. On the basis of how these four arise within the doctrine of the Buddha, first comes valid scripture in the form of the words of the Buddha. Then comes valid treatises, composed by Nāgārjuna, and others, as commentaries to scripture. The meanings of the scriptures and commentaries are integrated into the mind, where insight is born and thus arises in valid lamas possessed of learning and attainments. Relying upon these valid lamas, valid insight and experience is produced in the minds of disciples.

However, on the basis of developing certainty and conviction within the mind, the sequence is reversed. First valid experience is developed within the mind, in dependence upon which we come to know that the lamas who give the instructions resulting in this valid experience are also valid. These lamas have become possessed of learning and attainments by studying, contemplating, and meditating on the treatises of Nāgārjuna, his disciples, and others. Therefore, we can know that the treatises are valid. Consequently, by developing valid conviction about the composers of these treatises, such as Nāgārjuna, we can come to see that the scriptures of the Buddha—for whom these composers had so much reverence—are also valid.

Contemplating this in great detail, the Great Vehicle as being solely the word of the Buddha can arise in the mind, whereas the biographies of ordinary beings and the lives of kings and queens, for example, which are based only on chronology, are not adequate to cover the entire activities, life, and so on of the Buddha.

SUPPLICATING GODS AND SPIRITS

[359] What is captivating when examining the sutra and tantra practices of our kind teacher, the Buddha, are the vast and deep meanings of the teachings on what is to be acquired and discarded within the doctrine of the four truths. In understanding the reasoning behind them we develop faith and find a firm conviction that the Buddha who taught this wonderful path is like no other. In short, it is love, compassion, bodhicitta, and the view of emptiness—the very essence of the Buddha's doctrine—that is captivating, not the splendor of some deity.

I am continually praising these unerring, wonderful, and profound instructions of the Buddha's doctrine that we Tibetans have in our country as the tradition of Nālandā Monastery. However, as the great Kadampa masters of the past would say, "Not being satisfied with stages of the path presented by Atiśa, they add a tantra and it all goes wrong." Many have no interest in even studying, contemplating, and meditating on the teachings of the bodhicitta of love and compassion and the view of emptiness, but engage instead in the widespread practice of supplicating gods and nāgas, or jump to tantric practice without the foundation of having trained in the common path. In terms of focusing on one thing to the detriment of something else, this is a great loss for the preservation and development of the stainless teachings of the Buddha.

These days there is a pressing need for the doctrine of the Buddha to be seen and heard as vast and profound and, in dependence upon that, as something that can bring about the wonderful qualities of peace and happiness in the mind. However, most monasteries, temples of all sizes, and even individual monastic quarters display in full view various representations of tantric deities with numerous faces, numerous hands and legs, [360] gaping mouths, protruding fangs, and embracing a consort. The air is filled with the clamor of drums, cymbals, and horns. As a result, even in photographic books on Buddhism, it is these kinds of things that are mainly displayed. Also, rituals such as lama dances are being used as means for introducing Buddhism. Consequently, these days, this particular aspect of Tibetan Buddhism has become well-known, and not even a part of the wonderful path of peace, with its depth and vastness that are the true qualities of Buddhism, is seen.

Therefore, to show that this doctrine of the Buddha is one that will grant the happiness of a peaceful mind, and to create wonder by portraying its wonderful profound and deep qualities, we should display representations of the lives of past buddhas and bodhisattvas, biographies of lineage lamas, and so on. Tantric representations should be recognized as such, so as not to bring about any wrong tantric behavior. In particular, representations of meditation deities and protectors connected with Highest Yoga Tantra are objects to be used by practitioners alone, and care should be taken to ensure that they do not become objects universally used by all manner of people.

I often mention that in the temples and shrine rooms of some of our monasteries a statue of our teacher, the Buddha, is not the main object, but rather one finds a statue of whoever is important for that tradition placed in the center and a smaller statue of the Buddha is placed next to them. Those who do such things lack the genuine faith of thinking, "The kind Buddha is our protector and support," and, "Whatever befalls us in this and future lives you will be aware of it." Instead, they merely mouth, "I go for refuge to the Buddha." This is an external sign that those who recite from the heart, "You are the lama. You are the deity," are very few.

[361] Moreover, in front of the Buddha there are just one or two lit butter lamps, with no inclination to set up grand offerings. However, inside the protector chapels and shrine rooms, with their unique dark atmosphere, people talk about Mahākāla, Palden Lhamo, and others, in various forms with bared fangs, blood-filled skull cups, and weapons such as arrows, swords, and spears in their hands. Walking inside, people are filled with awe and respect. Everywhere on the walls, inside and out, are terrifying depictions of rosaries made from human heads, entrails, flesh, blood, skin, bones, and so on, all from the bodies of wretched beings. There are weapons to threaten the lives of sentient beings, outer carcasses of animals, breath pouches, and so on. These gods, demons, and ghosts are as terrifying as possible, and made to look as if they are just about to leap into action.

The ordained and the lay people crowd together in lines and, with blind faith and fervent prayers for protection, entrust themselves to these deities. Even the miserly, if they have a little money, will make a hopeful offering for the deity libation. The temple caretaker, regardless of whether his mind has been embraced by training in the common and uncommon paths, calls out in a high voice the names of these deities with their gaping mouths and bared fangs and entrusts them to carry out tasks by offering a libation of alcohol. This has its origins in the Bön tradition, and its smell carries to the shrine room of the Buddha and to the courtyard of the ordained community. Moreover, male monastics and male laymen are allowed in the protector chapels, but women are not. Such discrimination and favoritism are still considered positive and important. This kind of behavior is in complete contradiction to the activities of the Buddha, which, like the sun, are equal for all beings. [362] They are wholly mistaken modes of conduct by many who claim to be Buddhists today, are completely outdated, and are an indication of having no understanding of the teachings.

Kalu Rinpoché (1905–89) once went on a pilgrimage to Sakya Monastery. He told me that in the various temples the caretakers would give guided explanations as usual, but when arriving at the door of one particular protector temple, the caretaker made three prostrations and gave his presentation holding sticks of incense and with exceptional reverence. Rinpoché told me that this was the temple of Dölgyal Shukden.[234]

To explain such behavior in psychological terms, this is an exploitation of the feelings of fear inherent in human beings and creates all kinds of tension. The buddhas and bodhisattvas will not cause harm. Bodhicitta and the view of emptiness, which are the heart of Buddhism, will never create fear in people. However, when seeing these frightening figures with their gaping mouths and bared fangs, we wonder if they are going to hurt us, while at the same time regarding them as very special. This way of thinking has no place in the conduct required of Buddhist practice, and is a mistaken attitude that lies outside of genuine practice.

The practice of identifying the beneficial and harmful effects of the natural elements with spiritual forces developed from the early religious traditions of Tibet. After that, the practice of supplicating gods, spirits, and nāgas was commonplace and rituals of offering blood, flesh, and bones became widespread practices. The Yungdrung Bön masters and the great upholders of the teachings of the Buddha corrected this through refutation and affirmation. They formed their positions on right view and proper conduct, ornamented that with various rituals, and in keeping with the wishes of the people they composed various supplications to gods, spirits, and nāgas. [363] These were adopted into the tradition and can be understood as aids to the taming of disciples. However, you will not find any accounts of Nāgārjuna and his disciples performing supplications to protectors with drums and cymbals. There is not a single page in the literary tradition of scripture dedicated to such practices.

The kind Buddha, who is the ultimate refuge and worthy of our trust, should be placed at the head of the rows.[235] With an understanding of dependent origination, we go for refuge focused on the Three Jewels. We practice the four immeasurable states[236] focused on sentient beings, the stages of training in bodhicitta, and the profound understanding of emptiness as the supreme protector. In connection with these, we practice guru yoga, the yoga of characteristics, the yoga of no characteristics, and the generation and completion stages. These practices will accumulate merit and purify obscuration, and in this era of degeneration will remove unwanted circumstances of outer, inner, and secret hindrances and accumulate all desired conducive circumstance.

However, instead of placing our trust in these peerless rituals—which will increase the insights of the paths and levels—we humans who have gained this wonderful, fortunate form of a high rebirth with all its leisure and endowments, place our trust in protectors of a low rebirth, suffering sentient beings belonging to the race of ghosts, who sit on the very lowest row, deities and spirits who at the slightest circumstance will petty-mindedly flaunt their pleasure or express displeasure. The torma[237] we offer them is in the nature of concepts produced by the three poisons, and the aspect that it assumes is the flesh, blood, and so on of our mother sentient beings. Its function is to create desire, anger, and fear with regard to the objects of the six senses. Such an offering is a widespread bad habit proclaimed as Dharma. It cannot produce even a seed of liberation.

Giving authority to an insignificant ritual with explanations of the profound illustrations of the provisional and definitive, and pretending to supplement it with emptiness and compassion, is to conceitedly assume it to be the essence of the genuine teaching of the Buddha of peace and nonviolence. Such practices proclaimed to be profound and exclusive instructions were not taught by the Buddha, the master of the teachings, [364] and they were not later ascertained by Maitreya, Mañjuśrī, Nāgārjuna and his disciples, Asaṅga and Vasubandhu, and so on.

The Three Jewels cannot grant refuge through these practices of offering to gods and expelling spirits. Not relying upon the profound practices of sutra and tantra and not regarding them as serving a useful purpose means that in reality we are placing our hopes in gods, spirits, and nāgas. This is a wasteful obsession that abandons the root and seizes the branch. It brings great obstruction to the essence of Dharma and travels down a very dangerous and wrong path. We should recognize this by all means.

Even in acceptable cases of entreating a nonworldly protector by supplication and propitiation, the person making the offerings should have a genuine foundation of renunciation and bodhicitta, on which is built the confidence of the view, an experience of meditation, and the skill of conduct. From a clear and firm visualization of themselves with the pride of being the meditation deity, the yogi visualizes the body of the protector of a height not extending beyond the knee level of themselves as the meditation deity, and orders the protector to provide such and such assistance. This is what is meant by urging the protector. Conversely, someone who maintains ordinary perception and apprehension, searching for some gain motivated by the eight worldly concerns,[238] may exert a lot of effort in supplicating and propitiating, but they will not fulfill their desires. Moreover, the god or demon becomes a laughingstock, which can become a cause of malice on its part. This can be known from the experience of many rituals that do not produce any effect.

Therefore, if you are able to tame your mind stream by the pure practice of mixing your mind with the Dharma, what greater joy is there for virtuous deities. I think that it is only natural for those deities bound by oath and instruction to be drawn to such people.

[365] Except for the accounts of the guardians of the four directions swearing an oath to protect the teachings in the presence of the Buddha, it is difficult to postulate if there are authentic accounts of other guardians being given orders and sworn under oath by the Buddha. Many works renowned as the tantras of particular guardians are open to question. Examining whether their little hand-sized volumes will lead to the pure practices of the three main elements of the path[239] or the two profound stages of tantra is to determine whether the practices of much tantric conduct these days is proper or not.

Therefore, in divination texts when the omens are bad you will usually find passages on the supplication of gods and spirits as a way to thwart them. However, if the Buddha were here and you could ask him for a divination, he would definitely say, "Meditate on cause and effect," "Meditate on bodhicitta," or, "Meditate on the view of emptiness." He probably would not say, "This is harm caused by a god. Perform the incense offering ceremony to the gods," or, "This is harm caused by a nāga. Perform the nāga torma ritual," or, "This is harm caused by a spirit or a demon. Make supplications to the spirits and demons."

Moreover, just before the Buddha showed the act of becoming enlightened, hordes of hindering demons looked for a way to distract him, and he defeated them with the power of love. There is no account of him using black mantras, sorcery, curses, or exorcism, and it is not possible that he did not know how to make use of wrathful activity, and therefore lacked the means.

Therefore, for those lamas who perform divination it would be better for them to say, "Meditate on methods of training the mind," or, "This is the result of karma," or, "Purify yourself of bad deeds done in the past." To look at the divination text and suggest supplicating the gods, the nāgas, or the spirits is of no use. To give advice that accords with the Buddha's thinking will be beneficial to all, I think.

[366] Furthermore, there seems to be a habit of threatening people by designating what is in reality some dreadful ripening experience of bad karma collected in the past to malice and punishment meted out by a protector. In the activities of the buddhas and bodhisattvas, deliberately causing harm to others is simply unknown. Therefore, an angry worldly god or demon can possibly bring about the immediate condition for the ripening of some bad karma, but nothing of great significance, I think. Fundamentally, how is it possible to play around with the law of cause and effect by saying that whatever happens could be the result of entreating a protector or the punishment of a protector?

It may be that, in keeping with the attitudes of the past, fear was often used to urge people into practicing Dharma. However, so that violence is not propounded as Dharma, in these days of increasing analytical ability through reliance upon discerning wisdom that examines phenomena, it is important not to cling to blind faith.

In particular, here in the twenty-first century we need good precepts to restrain improper verbal, mental, and physical behavior in keeping with time, place, and circumstance and all peoples and races of the world, whether Buddhist or not. This is only done through the practice of the four truths. The vast and wonderful, profound paths of sutra and tantra that explicitly teach these truths were spoken by the Buddha, ascertained by the explanations of the pandits and practitioners, and meditated upon by the great siddhas, thereby giving rise to insights in their minds. Returning to this genuine and stainless highway of the authentic teachings, we should practice to gain the states of liberation and omniscience.

CHAPTER 8

The Essence of Buddhism

[367] THE VIEW AND CONDUCT of the Dharma of Buddha Śākyamuni can be summed up as the view of dependent origination and the conduct of nonviolence. The essence of the view of Buddhism is that whatever exists does so by way of mutual dependence and arises by way of mutual connectedness. Having such a perspective we understand that if we harm others, it brings suffering to ourselves, whereas if we benefit others, we bring happiness to ourselves. Therefore, we see the reason why we should give up harming others.

The conduct of Buddhism is to not harm others. If we have love and affection for others, an attitude of not harming others naturally arises. This instruction applies not only to long-term cause and effect but even to the here and now. To the extent that we can broaden our mind and think of others, that much our mind will be relaxed and happy. If we only think of ourselves, however, eventually our mind becomes tense and unhappy. This we can all see. Modern science has also proven through investigation that a compassionate attitude brings happiness to the mind. [368] This reason for the necessity of love and affection basically comes down to the view of dependent origination. Therefore, the mutually connected relationship between view and conduct is of prime importance.

The view of dependent origination consists of cause-and-effect dependent origination and that of dependent imputation. These two should be clearly differentiated. Individual tenet systems in Buddhism will have different explanations of dependent origination, but as a whole it is understood as meaning that all composite phenomena depend upon causes. This dependence upon causes illustrates that there is no being who creates or organizes the world. Phenomena depend solely on their individual causes and conditions. Those causes too depend upon previous causes and so on, meaning that causes have no ultimate beginning. All phenomena undergo change due to these causes and circumstances. A new situation becomes the cause of a new event and that becomes a cause for creating a new phenomenon. This is what is meant by coming into existence through cause-and-effect dependent origination.

This understanding of dependent origination is accepted in all Buddhist tenet systems. However, the dependent origination presented by the Madhyamaka is one of dependence, in which all phenomena exist in dependence upon their parts. This is a higher level of understanding. For example, physical phenomena are established in dependence upon their spatially situated parts. Phenomena devoid of form, such as consciousness, are established in dependence upon the parts that make up their continuum. Likewise, space is established in dependence upon the obstructive nature of phenomena and the individual directions. Being phenomena with parts, they are all dependently arisen. In this way, this is a presentation of dependent origination not only of dependence upon causes and conditions but of dependence upon parts and directions.

[369] A subtler way of presenting dependent origination is that an object exists by the power of being conceptually imputed and established. When we take a specific object, such as a flower, and examine its reality and the particles that make up the flower, it is no longer the flower that appears to us. If we examine the particles more deeply, we can understand that phenomena are imputed by name and convention by the reason of atoms and molecules coming together to form a mass. Once the particles have amassed together, the function of being a phenomenon is complete, and we impute by way of names and convention.

There are three ways of understanding dependent origination:

1. The first understanding is that various aspects of happiness and sufferings arise in dependence upon causes and conditions alone. Through this, an understanding of the view of dependent origination is reached and is one professed by all Buddhists. Similarly, the "self" that is the experiencer of this happiness and suffering is a self that exists in dependence upon the psycho-physical aggregates, and there is no self that has an entity of being permanent and unitary, existing on its own, substantially separate from the impermanent aggregates.

2. More profound than the above, the second understanding is that of dependence upon parts. This not only encompasses phenomena produced in dependence upon causes and conditions but also those phenomena categorized as permanent by not depending upon causes and conditions.[240] Everything has parts. For example, matter has spatially situated parts. Consciousness has parts that constitute a continuum of former and later moments. There is no phenomenon that is without parts.

If something has parts, the part-holding phenomenon depends upon those parts and exists through dependence. Moreover, it is imputed in dependence upon those parts. [370] When a part-holding phenomenon appears to our cognition, an existing reality or self-instituting entity established by a collection of many parts appears to the cognition. For example, the single part-holding phenomenon of a sprout has individual parts such as the substance continuums of its shape, color, and so on. However, to our cognition a single, separate part-holding entity appears, which contains the phenomena of parts and part holder, aspects and aspect holder existing as possessor and possessed, feature basis and features, and so on.

If the way in which that appears to us is incontrovertible, then that mode of appearance must exist as a reality. If it does exist that way, part and part holder should be discovered as discrete entities, but that is not so. Therefore, the way in which it appears to us is not the way that it exists in reality. The mode of appearance and the mode of existence are in contradiction, and so appearance and reality must be separated. If a mode of existence contradicts a mode of appearance, that appearance is in keeping with being false and not in keeping with truth. If something is true, the way it exists should be the way it appears and the way it appears should be its reality. When the way something appears to us is one thing and the way it exists is something else, it has the nature of being false. Because of such reasons it is taught that all phenomena do not exist as truths.

3. The third understanding is even subtler than the above. Once any phenomenon exists, if you search for the actual reality of the phenomenon, on which a conventional designation is imputed, there is nothing that can be found. So, does it not exist? Because it has a direct connection with beneficial and harmful effects, it cannot be nonexistent. When you search for the thing that has this relationship, it cannot be found. Therefore, what is its essential reality? All phenomena exist through the force of imputation and are not established on the object itself.

[371] When explaining the second way of understanding dependent origination, it is recognized that all phenomena do not exist in reality and are of the nature of being false. However, in the Madhyamaka Svātantrika's way of asserting no true existence, their negation is of an object having a status of being established from its own side without depending upon being posited by way of appearing to a faultless cognition and conventional designation. However, this does not reach the understanding of the base or the phenomenon imputed by designation being negated as existing from the side of its basis of imputation. This is the way of understanding dependent origination for the Madhyamaka Svātantrika.

When explaining the third understanding of dependent origination, from the side of the basis of imputation no representation of the object exists at all. It is imputed solely by designation, or is wholly a designation, and conceptually imputed. It does not exist in any other way.

In that case, is it the case that there is only the name, and nothing with which the name engages? It is not being said that there is no object. The object exists, but when conventional designation or name posits the objects it engages with, it exists only by the force of name. There is no other way of positing it.

So, is it that whatever the cognition posits must exist? If it were the case that whatever the cognition posited had to exist, it would not be possible to separate a wrong and misperceiving cognition from a validly perceiving cognition. Also, when a misperceiving cognition misperceives something, whatever is imputed by that cognition would equally exist as designated by the force of that imputation. For example, with a conceptual consciousness that apprehends sound as permanent, it is the conceptualization itself that determines sound to be permanent. Therefore, there is a conceptualization determining sound to be permanent. If the meaning of existence was that whatever is posited by cognition had to exist, then permanent sound would also exist because there is a conceptualization of sound as permanent. Of the conceptualization apprehending sound as permanent and the inferential conceptualization of sound as impermanent, [372] one is a valid cognition and the other is a misperceiving cognition. Therefore, separating these two and determining whether sound is permanent or not is still something existing solely by the force of name, and solely by the force of convention, but it is not the case that whatever is posited by convention has to exist. This is a difficult point.

In this regard, if an object conventionally exists from its own side, this characteristic of conventional existence would exist objectively, upon the thing itself. If it did not exist conventionally, such a characteristic would also exist objectively. Therefore, any differentiation is made from the side of the object. If that is so, the object cannot be something existing merely by the force of imputation. If the dividing line between what is and what is not is to be posited from the thing itself, then a phenomenon is not something existing merely by the force of name. The potential to have an effect would exist from the side of the object and that effect would emerge from the side of the object. This is the meaning of the phrase "existing from its own side." If we were to search for the thing imputed, we would have to find it. Therefore, when articulating a division between existing and nonexisting from the side of the object itself, we must understand that nothing at all can be expressed from the side of the object.

So, how is the division made between that which is conventionally designated as existing and that which is conventionally designated as nonexisting? Generally, something existing does so by the force of cognition. Therefore, conventionally existing or not conventionally existing is determined by being consensually known to cognition or not, and whether that consensual knowledge can be challenged and refuted by the valid experience of another cognition. In this way we separate that conventionally designated as existing from that which is not. Not trusting merely in the appearance or the mode of appearance, but searching for how things exist, is a vital principle for Buddhists.

There are sutras that expound only the meanings of the first of these three understandings of dependent origination and there are tenet holders who adhere to these sutras. When considered from their point of view, the other two understandings of dependent origination, and especially the third, are regarded as being nihilistic. [373] There are also sutras that expound the meanings of the other two interpretations. From the perspective of those who only adhere to these two explanations, the first understanding of dependent origination falls to the extreme of permanence. In terms of scriptural citation, both sets of assertions have sound sutra references in which the adherents place their trust, and so nothing can be settled that way. We cannot ask the Buddha for an answer, and therefore a conclusion must be reached through reasoning. If what is taught in one sutra is refuted by reasoning, that sutra cannot be taken literally and must be posited as provisional. If what is taught in a sutra cannot be refuted by reasoning, it must be taken literally. Therefore, analytical reasoning is key. Because of this, types of reasonings, the presentation of logical statements, and consequences are taught in abundance in Buddhist epistemological texts.

THE THREE KINDS OF CONDITION

To summarize, happiness and suffering will not arise from no cause but must be produced by causes. Moreover, those causes must be conducive causes because they will not arise from inconducive causes. Sometimes things exist and sometimes they do not. What does this reveal? That things depend upon conditions in order to come into existence. Ācarya Asaṅga[241] designated such conditions as being without movement, impermanent, and possessing potential.

"Without movement" indicates that things are not produced by the movement of the mind of a world creator as a prerequisite condition for creation.[242] [374] Conditions are "impermanent" because if causes and conditions were permanent and did not depend upon other causes and conditions, they would not be able to produce results. If the cause were always there and unchanging, the result too would always be there, or, alternatively, it would never be there. However, the cause that creates a result is itself a result produced from a cause. Causes and conditions undergo processes of change.

"Possessing potential" means that it is not sufficient for a condition just to be impermanent; it must also possess the potential to produce specific results. A sutra on dependent origination says,

Because of this, that arises. Because this is produced, that will be produced. By the condition of ignorance, formative factors...[243]

Whatever aspect a result takes, it must have been created by a cause of similar aspect.

THE FOUR KINDS OF REASON

There are phenomena which come about naturally, and those which come about through the force of temporary conditions. When analyzing this, Buddhist texts talk about the four kinds of reason as the entrance into the analytic process. The first of these is the reason of nature. For example, through the changes brought about by previous particles, various shapes and forms arise. [375] In this category, one type of existence is produced naturally. Another type is produced by temporary conditions that produce feelings of happiness and suffering on the support of the first category. These are also conditions connected to the experiencer of that happiness and suffering. It is within the temporary conditions that are connected with the experiencer of that happiness and suffering that the doctrine of karma is explained.

Therefore, as an entrance to the process of analysis there are these four types of reason: nature, dependence, function, and validity. Here, the term "reason" should be understood as something like "natural law" rather than the "reason" of "scripture and reason."

1. *The Reason of Nature*

In the beginning, all phenomena, of whatever kind, were formed naturally. This we can know and accept. For example, if we ask the reason for the occurrence of subtle particles, space particles, and so on, the answer can only be "It is natural." Similarly, if we ask the reason for consciousness possessing the nature of experience and existing merely as an entity of experience, again we answer that it is natural. Any analysis is made on that basis alone and there is no need to seek any other. Therefore, the reason of nature is a natural or innate way of being, on which analysis is undertaken.

2. *The Reason of Dependence*

[376] When an external substance, or the inner substance of consciousness, meets with another substance, they come together and their form changes. By the condition of a thought or concept arising, a new thought is produced, for example, and the present consciousness undergoes change, such as becoming clear, or unclear, and so on. This is not necessarily a cause-and-effect process. It occurs through the arrival of some influence, which brings about an effect. Any change brought about through mutual dependence, or the presence of something that has the nature of dependence, is used as the basis for analysis and is the reason of dependence.

3. *The Reason of Function*

As described above, by way of a mutual dependence or by the condition of mutual influence, change occurs. Through this a new causal form emerges, which in turn creates a new resultant form. This process involving the relationship of cause and effect and the function of a cause creating an effect is taken as a basis on which analysis proceeds. This is reason of function.

4. *The Reason of Validity*

All the above comes down to nature. Therefore, when individual substances are brought together and a new force is created, that is the nature of substances. This is the natural process of creating different entities of cause and different forms of results. These are taken as a basis on which we analyze: "If it is this, it must be that. If this exists, that must exist." The basis of this way of analyzing is that the natural way of being is taken as a basis and analysis follows on from that. [377] In this modern cosmology, biology, subatomic physics, and modern psychology have a strong connection to the presentation of base reality explained in Buddhist texts. Because of this they are subjects to study and know. Buddhist psychology is far richer and deeper than Western psychology.

THE FOUR DEPENDENCES

Buddhist scripture instructs us to not depend upon the person but on their teachings. Of their teachings, do not depend upon the words but on their meanings. Concerning the meanings, do not depend on any provisional meaning but on the definitive meaning. With regard to the cognition of the definitive meaning, do not depend upon consciousness but on wisdom.

It is by examining the words of the Buddha that we should decide whether our Teacher is a supreme being or not. Generally, the most important teachings of the Buddha are pure by way of three types of analysis: (1) the evident and accessible aspects of the teachings are not refuted by direct valid cognition, (2) the slightly hidden aspects are not refuted by inferential cognition based on phenomena, and (3) the very hidden aspects are not refuted by inferential cognition based on trust. Moreover, they are not refuted by former words contradicting later words or by direct and indirect contradiction.

On the other hand, we might examine the teachings and find some contradiction. These are the words of the Buddha but if their intent and purpose of the writer are accepted as written, they will be refuted by these reasonings because of their contradiction to reality. Therefore, their explanation should not accord with the literal presentation. [378] For example, explanations in sutra or treatises on the size and height of the sun and moon are in disagreement with modern technology and mathematics, which are able to take direct measurements. Therefore, those specific points presented in specific sutras or treatises are refuted by direct valid cognition and are not to be accepted as written.

Therefore, on the basis of all phenomena being established by their own nature, the *Sutra Explaining the Intent*, for example, describes the three categories and explains the meaning of no-self. Of the three categories, the sutra teaches that mentally constructed characteristics have no intrinsic existence, while the characteristic of being dependent phenomena and the characteristic of an absolute reality do have intrinsic existence. Whether dependent phenomena and an absolute reality truly exist or not, and whether that which is mentally constructed has intrinsic existence or not, is difficult to ascertain through direct cognition, and is classified as slightly hidden. Therefore, it should be examined by using Madhyamaka reasoning. When doing so, contradictions surface. The slightly hidden points taught in this sutra on what does and what does not intrinsically exist in its presentations on the three categories are refuted by inferential cognition based on phenomena. Therefore, this sutra is not to be accepted literally, as written.

Similarly, with regard to the mind at death, Vasubandhu's *Treasury of Abhidharma*, from the lower of the two Abhidharma traditions, posits the possibility of a virtuous, nonvirtuous, and neutral mind at the time of death. Asaṅga's *Compendium of Abhidharma*, from the upper Abhidharma tradition, states that the mind at death is always a neutral mind.[244] Highest Yoga Tantra texts explain that the subtle mind at death has a virtuous state and that it can be developed into the path itself.

These matters are very hidden. When examining the words spoken by the Buddha for signs of internal contradiction, and even comparing them with those of other teachers, we see in Highest Yoga Tantra texts special provisions for practice by way of penetrative focusing on the channels, winds, and drops of the body—the supports of the mind—that are described in great detail. Therefore, we can have greater trust in the presentation of the coarse and subtle levels of mind taught in those Highest Yoga Tantra texts. Consequently, the teaching found in Highest Yoga Tantra that the primordial and innate clear light mind has a virtuous state is one that can be explained with great reliability. It is very difficult to prove it through reasoning. However, through the way it is taught, in terms of comparing former and later text, and direct and indirect meanings, as well as other ways, we must accept it as being literally true.

Therefore, the sutras that serve as authority for *Compendium of Abhidharma*, and the *Treasury of Abhidharma* from the lower Abhidharma tradition, can be explained as not being literally true.

Because we have to analyze by contemplating reasons, the presentation of logical reasoning and proof is considered to be very important. Therefore, from a Buddhist perspective and particularly from a Great Vehicle perspective, in the beginning we need to engage in some doubt about what something means, and over time by analyzing with perfect reasoning we will finally be able to sever all misinterpretation.

When Buddhists explain by way of dependent origination, what is being indirectly explained? From the changes brought solely by causes and conditions, things will arise without the need to posit a world creator or a universal principle. This is very special. When describing the formation of the inner and outer worlds, the classical Buddhist texts use phrases like "From this condition alone..." Therefore, from a Buddhist perspective, it is as if one is one's own creator.

BUDDHIST CONDUCT OF NOT HARMING

[380] The Buddhist conduct of not harming is not just a matter of not harming others, but is a practice of great compassion. Together with a heartfelt resolve to abandon harming others, we should help others as much as we can. If we are unable to do that, we should at least stop hurting others. This in essence is Buddhism.

The reason we should stop harming others is because everything exists in dependence on something else. Generally, not only does our future depend upon others but even our individual mental happiness comes about through dependence on many other factors. This is relevant to those who do not believe in religion also.

If we harm the lives of others in order to protect our lives, does that contradict Buddhist principles? In the canon of the monastic vows of liberation no allowance is made for the seven nonvirtuous acts of body and speech—namely, killing, stealing, sexual misconduct, lying, slander, harsh words, and idle gossip. This can be illustrated by accounts in ancient India when invaders regarded Buddhists as enemies, and when monks were being hacked with swords and knives, they made no attempt at retaliation. If someone is about to kill you, and you strike them on the head with a weapon to prevent them, it could kill them, but striking at their arms and legs might be acceptable, I think.

[381] The bodhisattva canon speaks of "Not suppressing according to circumstance."[245] This means that if those wicked persons who can only be suppressed by violent means are "not suppressed according to circumstance," that constitutes a breach in the precepts of the bodhisattva. There is a story of the Buddha in a previous life when he was known as "the compassionate navigator." Once, while on a voyage in pursuit of trade, among the five hundred merchants on the ship was "the wicked one armed with a spear," who was intending to kill his fellow merchants in order to steal their goods. The navigator was aware of this but no matter how much he told the man how wrong this was, he would not listen. If the man went ahead and killed his fellow merchants, he would accrue the evil of killing that many people. Moreover, the merchants would suffer greatly. The navigator could not bear this, and so with compassion he killed the would-be perpetrator. The navigator had accrued the nonvirtuous act of killing one person, but he had no regrets, and motivated by altruism he had practiced exchanging self for others. Therefore, it is said that the compassionate navigator amassed great merit.

The tantric canon describes all kinds of acts, categorized as pacifying, increasing, controlling, and wrathful. To prevent beings from carrying out heinous acts, wrathful means were taught to overcome those who cannot be controlled by peaceful means. However, a proper tantric practitioner will have bodhicitta and the view of emptiness, [382] and acts of bringing under control and wrathful activities are acceptable only when embraced by compassion and altruism. Such acts are not considered acts of harm.

To explain in a deeper way the difference between harming and not harming in accord with the scriptural traditions, it is not that easy to make the distinction on the basis of the act alone. For example, with the intent to cheat and deceive, someone is welcomed with pleasing words and smiles, seduced with gifts, and so on. Such acts by their characteristics are not harmful but by their intent they become acts of harm. Also, loving parents, for example, will, with affection, scold their children harshly in order to stop them from doing wrong. Outwardly such acts express harm but in reality they are methods to stop children from doing wrong and are not harmful acts. Therefore, it is important to separate harming from not harming by way of the inner intention.

THE FOUR TRUTHS AND THE TWO TRUTHS

The main topics of the Buddhist works transmitted by the Pāli tradition are the four truths, the three baskets, the three trainings, the twelve branches of dependent origination, the thirty-seven facets of enlightenment, and the practice of monastic discipline. It is very important to know and recognize that these form the foundation of the doctrines of all Buddhist vehicles.

In order to understand the reality of the truth of suffering, the truth of the origin of suffering, the truth of the cessation, and the truth of the path, first we should know the nature of the two truths. [383] Generally, the names of the two truths are mentioned in the works of ancient Indian non-Buddhist schools. However, these differ from the various assertions of the two truths found in the texts of the four Buddhist schools—that is, the Vaibhāṣika, the Sautrāntika, the Cittamātra, and the Madhyamaka schools.

To explain that briefly, ultimate truth is a presentation of the way things exist and conventional truth is a presentation of the way things appear. The way that the nature of the two truths is presented by the Cittamātra and Madhyamaka schools are not that different from each other, but illustrations of the two truths differ greatly. Both Cittamātra and Madhyamaka explain that the ultimate mode of existence is solely emptiness, but the Cittamātra posit an emptiness of external existence, or an emptiness of a dualistic apprehender and apprehended as the ultimate truth, while Madhyamaka state that there not being even an atom of true existence existing anywhere is the ultimate mode of existence.

The Madhyamaka texts speak of one object having two entities: the way an object exists in which it is comprehended merely through its appearance—with no analysis and no investigation—and an ultimate way of existing, comprehended through an analysis and investigation into that object's ultimate nature. These two entities are synonymous with the object's conventional truth and its ultimate truth. Conventional truth refers to phenomena that appear to us right now such as the world and its inhabitants, creation and destruction, growth and decline, cause and result, good and bad, and so on. For example, a pot that appears to us is a conventional truth. If we search for the pot in keeping with the way it appears, it is not found. Therefore, the reality is that it is empty by nature. While appearing it is empty, and while empty it appears. Therefore, the two truths are taught to be of one nature but separate isolates.[246]

There is good reason why we should be aware of the difference between the way something appears and the way it exists. [384] For example, when someone is brought before the law and the matter examined, the authorities do not put all their trust in the way things appear in cursory reports that are exaggerated in the telling, but will question those who actually witnessed what happened and conclude who is telling the truth by examining the facts. Similarly, we should by all means examine and see if there is any difference between the appearance and reality of phenomena. When we have minds of desire and anger, the object that generates our desire is very attractive and the object that generates our anger is very unattractive. These things appear to exist from the side of the object. In keeping with the appearances, we are fixated on the attractive object and desire arises. Fixating on the unattractive object, we see it as repulsive and a state of mind arises that wants to turn our backs on it and push it far away.

Misperceptions such as minds of desire and anger arise solely due to taking the mode of appearance as the basis of that perception. We can understand that these misperceiving cognitions are mistaken by using cognitions that do not misperceive. For that, we must investigate the basis of the appearing object. With this analysis we will come to understand that, in reality, the object does not exist as it appears. By training in such comprehension, the type of misperceiving cognition that fixates upon the way something appears will be uprooted. Any phenomenon that is posited without examination or analysis is a conventional truth, while its deeper and actual way of existing is its ultimate truth. Thus, there are two truths.

In the middle turning of the wheel of Dharma, the Buddha gives a more detailed presentation of the above. He describes the unanalyzed and unexamined phenomena of the base phenomena of the aggregates, sensory sources, spheres, and so on. He speaks about the six perfections and other qualities on the paths, and the qualities of Buddhahood, such as the ten powers, actualized at the resultant stage. [385] After these teachings he says that all of these are mere names, mere conventions, merely imputed by conception, and are not established as truly existing or by their own entity.

Therefore, all base, path, and resultant phenomena are said to possess these two natures: a nature that is just conventional appearance and a nature that is the ultimate reality of those phenomena. The reason for such a teaching, as said previously, is a variety of appearances existing and not existing as they appear. Therefore, it is emphatically taught that this should be investigated, and in order to know the contradiction between appearance and reality the characteristics of the two truths were taught. Through this, we will come to know the reality as it is, free from superimposition and deprecation.

In that sense, the truth of cessation must be established on the basis of the two truths. When doing that, we have to know the path to cessation and its branches, which are the causes of directly perceiving the truth of cessation. In the Buddhist texts we are introduced to the sequence that is the karma origin of suffering and the mental affliction origin of suffering—that is, the causes of suffering to be eliminated by the path and the sufferings created by these causes. Therefore, the Buddhist presentation of the four truths divides them into two sets of cause and effect, albeit in reverse order. The first set is made up of the first two truths: suffering and its causes, and the origins of suffering. The second set is the cessation of suffering and that which directly induces cessation, the path.

[386] These two sets of cause and effect illustrate how the four truths operate in a human life. We have a heartfelt wish to be happy and wish for nothing more than to fulfill our hopes of being free from suffering. Suffering is likened to an illness, and the origin of suffering is likened to the inner and outer causes and conditions that bring on that illness. The cessation of suffering and the causes of suffering is likened to the curing of the illness, and the truth of the path is likened to the medicine that treats the illness.

In the sequence of the four truths, the reason why the resultant truths of suffering and cessation come before the causal truths of the origin of suffering and the path is that first we should recognize the truth of suffering, the first of the four truths, as being like an illness. But merely recognizing illness is not enough. To know what kind of medicine and treatment to rely upon we need to investigate the cause of the illness. Therefore, the second truth taught is the origin of suffering. Moreover, it is not sufficient just to know the cause of the illness. We must look to see if there is a cure. Realizing that there is a cure is akin to knowing the third truth—the cessation of suffering and its causes. By first recognizing the possibilty of a cure, we can then pursue the means of that cure, which is akin to relying on the paths in order to reach freedom from suffering. Therefore, the fourth truth, or path, is taught.

THE THREE KINDS OF SUFFERING

There are a few ways of dividing the first truth into types of suffering, but in brief they can be subsumed into the suffering of suffering, the suffering of change, and the all-pervasive formative suffering. The first is that which we usually recognize as suffering, such as mental and physical feelings of suffering. The external and internal phenomena from which these sufferings arise are also said to be suffering, and the primary minds and mental factors concomitant with these phenomena are also labeled as suffering.

[387] The suffering of change refers to the happy feelings we usually regard as happiness. If this happiness were a genuine happiness, then no matter how much we were to increase its causes, it would increase proportionately and bring us satisfaction. However, it is not like that. Temporarily it takes on the appearance of happiness, but this only happens when we indulge in it at the beginning. Before long it no longer satisfies us and may even make us unhappy. Then, no matter how much we engage with it, it just causes trouble and brings unwanted results. Thus, it has changed into something whose nature is simply

suffering, and its suffering nature becomes clearer. Moreover, as long as we remain in samsara, our feelings of happiness and pleasure will be tainted with mental affliction and in the future will only bring more suffering.

The third type of suffering is the basis of the first two types. Illustrations of this suffering are the contaminated aggregates of our body and mind. Because it pervades or engages with samsara in all its forms, it is pervasive. It is the basis of our present suffering and will create and form suffering in the future. For this reason it is the "all-pervasive, formative suffering." This type of suffering is the truth of suffering from the four truths.

What is the origin of suffering? Karma and mental afflictions are the sources of all suffering. Karma refers to contaminated physical, verbal, and mental karmas. In terms of its nature, karma can be virtuous, non-virtuous, and neutral. Mental affliction refers to the prime afflictions of desire, anger, and ignorance, which in turn create many types of afflicted minds such as envy, resentment, and so on. [388]

To put an end to the types of nonvirtuous karma that are the causes of suffering, their causes in turn—mental afflictions—must be ended. Therefore, out of karma and mental affliction—the two creators of suffering—the latter is more important. This is the truth of the origin of suffering, the second truth of the four truths.

Suffering is something we have no wish for. Seeing that, we should investigate if that suffering is caused or not. If it is, we should investigate to see what the causes are and what circumstances it arises from. Having determined the causes, we should investigate if those causes can be eliminated or not. If they can be eliminated, there will be a method to accomplish that. If we were to determine that these causes cannot be eliminated, then this would mean that nothing could be done, in which case the suffering brought on by those causes could also not be dispelled and there would be no possibility of liberation. Therefore, we should examine this point.

Asking the question "Can suffering be eliminated" leads to an examination of the truth of cessation. If the mental afflictions abided within the very nature of mind, they could not be eradicated. For example, if anger abided as part of the nature of mind itself, then for as long as we possess consciousness, we would be angry. Clearly that is not the case. Similarly, love and anger cannot simultaneously develop in the mind of one focused on a single object at one time. If love is stronger, anger will become weaker. It is evident that whatever attitude we are more habituated with, its opposite will lose strength. It is the same with desire, and so on.

[389] Therefore, we can understand that the pollutants of the mind are temporary phenomena that can be divorced from the mind, and that the nature of mind is not contaminated by these pollutants. Because of this, it is established that karma and mental afflictions, as the origins of suffering, can be eradicated, and that if the origin of suffering is completely uprooted the truth of cessation will be obtained. This is the ultimate freedom and the permanent peace of liberation. This is cessation, the third of the four truths.

What paths and methods should we train in to reach this cessation? The faults of samsara arise mainly from the mind, and therefore, the antidotes also must be developed within the mind. For that, we need to know the ultimate reality of phenomena and specifically the ultimate reality of the mind. For the reality of the mind, we need to know it directly as a new realization and in a nondualistic manner. This is the attainment of the path of seeing. Dedicating oneself totally to the familiarization with that mode of cognitive apprehending is the path of meditation. Before the attainment of these stages on the path, a meditative concentration on the union of quiescence and insight in a dualistic manner has to be developed. This requires the attainment of a quiescence possessed of a stability of mind. These are the stages of the truth of the path, the fourth truth. This truth of the path is necessary for the attainment of the third truth of cessation, represented as the cessation of the first two truths.

To sum up, we all want happiness. So, is there an ultimate, solid, and unchanging goal of happiness that is attainable? There is, and the latter two truths of cessation and path were taught to show the paths and methods to achieve it. [390] What we want is happiness and what we do not want is suffering, and both only arise from their individual causes. Therefore, it was taught that we should investigate the causes and conditions of suffering and their results.

At the first turning of the wheel of Dharma, the Buddha spoke of the entities of the four truths: "This is suffering, the truth of the āryas. This is the origin of suffering, the truth of the āryas. This is cessation, the truth of the āryas This is the path, the truth of the āryas." He first introduced the four truths and taught the truth of suffering and the truth of the origin of suffering, both of which are included in the category of base existence.

Then he spoke of what is to be done with regard to the four truths, saying, "Suffering is to be known. The origin of suffering is to be eliminated. Cessation is to be actualized. The path is to be meditated upon." Thus, secondly, by teaching what is to be acquired and discarded within the four truths, he taught the truth of the path— the stages of the path to be traveled.

Then he spoke of what is to be done with regard to the four truths as well as the results: "The suffering to be known does not exist as that to be known. The origin of suffering to be eliminated does not exist as that to be eliminated. The cessation to be actualized does not exist as that to be actualized. The path to be meditated upon does not exist as that to be meditated upon." Thus, thirdly, by teaching the ultimate points of what is to be acquired and discarded within the four truths, he taught the process of actualizing the results—the truth of cessation. This is very clear. Whatever tenets and presentations of what is to be acquired and discarded that are described in the Buddhist scriptures are built upon reality. This is the fundamental process.

[391] Thus, in the scriptures known as the bodhisattva canon, or Great Vehicle canon, the two truths as the base, method and wisdom

as the path, and the two enlightened forms as the result also depend upon a presentation of fundamental reality. The ultimate reason that we are able to reach the final goal of the two enlightened forms—in particular buddhahood as the entity of the four forms—is that we possess right now the very subtle, primordial, and innate clear light mind, in which is found the intrinsic potential to create the four forms. Therefore, to sum up, it is very evident that all presentations in Buddhist texts rest upon a base reality.

This has been a brief teaching on the four truths. A more extensive presentation on these four truths, as well as teachings on the twelve branches of dependent origination that explain cause and effect in great detail, the three trainings, and other topics from the middling Lamrim, or stages of the path teachings, should be studied. These can be known from the perfection of wisdom texts, which teach the three baskets, the thirty-seven facets of enlightenment, and so on.

THE FOUR SEALS

All composite phenomena are impermanent.
All contaminated phenomena are suffering.
All phenomena are empty and without self.
Beyond sorrow is peace.

These four represent a synopsis of Buddhist doctrine. To adhere to these is to be a Buddhist; this view determines the division between Buddhist and non-Buddhist.

1. All Composite Phenomena Are Impermanent
[392] Anything that we look at will change, disintegrate, and finally be destroyed. For example, great mountains and mighty cliffs, said to have been formed a hundred or two hundred million years ago, also undergo change and will finally disintegrate. This very world

is something that has undergone evident changes over long periods of time. This process of change is not a case of something remaining without change for a fixed period, and then change begins. Something that will eventually disintegrate is undergoing change at all times. It is something that changes moment by moment, and it has to be that way.

Looking at the way Buddhist tenet systems approach this momentary change, the Vaibhāṣika position is a little different from the other schools when they say that phenomena of composite characteristics are first created, then remain, age, and finally disintegrate. The other tenets generally agree that from the moment something comes into being it already has the nature of disintegration, and the sequence of creation, abiding, aging, and disintegration is certain. There is no time when it is unchanging. Merely being created and merely existing means that it has the nature of disintegration, and therefore disintegration has already begun. Disintegration of a phenomenon does not depend upon some later cause; simply by virtue of the very causes that created it, it has the nature of disintegration. In the synopsis "All composite phenomena are impermanent," the impermanence is a subtle impermanence, and not a coarse impermanence. These days science speaks along the same lines.

"Composite" means phenomena created or existing in dependence upon the coming together of causes and circumstances. [393] Once something has been created from a collection of causes, it has the nature of momentary disintegration. Therefore, all composite phenomena are impermanent.

2. All Contaminated Phenomena Are Suffering

The contaminant of that which is "contaminated" is mental affliction, and something produced by the force of mental affliction is established as "suffering." There are differences in the way to posit mental affliction according to the higher and lower tenet systems.

3. All Phenomena Are Empty and without Self

I think it is acceptable to say that this refers to all phenomena being empty by nature. The way they are empty by nature includes being empty of a self that is permanent and independent, being empty of a self-sustaining substantial entity, the conceived object of a conceptual cognition being empty of existing from the side of the object, an object empty of existing by way of its own special status, without being posited by the fact of appearing to faultless cognition, and so on.

All Buddhist tenets accept the four seals. Therefore, being empty of intrinsic existence can be applied to the individual tenet systems. Nevertheless, it is said that the essential meaning of "All phenomena are empty and without self" reaches culmination in texts from the Madhyamaka tradition, which explain it to mean that all phenomena are empty of existing in reality. Here, "Madhyamaka tradition" refers to the thinking of the sublime guide, Ārya Nāgārjuna, as determined by glorious Candrakīrti and Ācarya Buddhapālita. From their position, all phenomena are empty by nature, and even conventionally all phenomena are empty of any intrinsic existence.

[394] On that basis, what is "All phenomena are empty and without self" teaching? In the second seal, "All contaminated phenomena are suffering," the ultimate contaminant is the mental affliction of ignorance that adheres to a self. The conceived object of this adherence does not exist even conventionally or as a reality, and yet such a cognition that apprehends in this way can be understood as being a misperceiving cognition. Except in the case of meditative, nonconceptual direct insights, whatever phenomenon appears to our cognition appears as being real. Therefore, when the cognition focuses strongly on such an object, it appears as if it is capable of sustaining itself. Such a cognition apprehending that object as real in the way that it appears, is a misperceiving cognition. Therefore, if we can develop a profound understanding of "All phenomena are empty and without self," we can understand

that the many types of cognition that arise to us right now, in terms of appearing as truly existing, are deceptive or mistaken cognitions.

Through this, we can understand that this mental affliction, under whose force all contaminated phenomena are explained as "suffering"—as in the synopsis "All contaminated phenomena are suffering"—is a wrong cognition and a misperceiving cognition. It is not supported by valid cognition. Not only is there is an antidote for this afflicted wrong cognition—the root contaminant on whose basis all contaminated phenomena are regarded as suffering—but it is a powerful antidote that has a directly opposing mode of apprehending. This powerful antidote has the support of valid cognition, whereas its opposite, the misperceiving cognition, has no valid cognition in support. Therefore, because this mental affliction has an antidote, it can be erased, and the ability of mental afflictions to cause suffering is finite. Therefore, it is taught that cessation and the end of suffering and its cause, the origin of suffering, does exist. What will that accomplish? As the Buddha said, "This is the cessation of suffering."

4. Beyond Sorrow[247] Is Peace

[395] "Sorrow" here probably refers to suffering, but primarily can be applied to ignorance, the ultimate root of suffering. I think it can refer also to true existence, the conceived object of ignorance. Whatever the case, sorrow refers to suffering and its cause, and that has to be completely and permanently pacified. Thus, it is said, "Beyond sorrow is peace." When the excellent quality of the cessation that is the elimination of ignorance has been developed by newly creating antidotes to ignorance and by increasing those already created, that realm of permanent peace in which all suffering and its cause is pacified is a permanent happiness. This exists as something to be attained. Such a realm can be achieved and is to be achieved. Thus, the Buddha said, "This is the truth of the path of the āryas."

THE MEANING OF "DHARMA"

Generally, the term "dharma" has ten meanings. In Vasubandhu's *Principles of Exposition*[248] it says,

> "Dharma" refers to phenomena, path, the state beyond sorrow,
> objects of mental consciousness, merit, life, and scripture,
> that to come, ascertainment, and religious tradition.[249]

However, here "dharma" is one half of the paired opposites "dharma and worldly" and "dharma and nondharma." In Sanskrit *dharma* means "hold." In that sense it can be understood as something that holds and protects from the fears of samsara and nirvana[250] or from suffering. The Tibetan term (*chos*) also means "to put right"[251] (*bcos*) and is also the imperative form of that verb. [396] In order to "put right" the untamed mind, which is the cause of suffering, we engage in "transformation" (*bsgyur bcos*), and to encourage transformation, the imperative form is used. Therefore, the English word "religion," which is used to refer to the Dharma of the Buddha, and which has the basic meaning of "a system of faith," is not enough. Moreover, this transformation cannot be carried out by force, threats, deception, and so on, but with a faith that is built on understanding the reasons and participating willingly from our own volition. We ourselves have to transform those mistaken and misperceiving mental attitudes.

In brief, in our daily life, holding as essential the commitment that our words, deeds, and thoughts should not harm and are helpful to others, integrated with the practices of acquiring and discarding in accordance with the law of cause and effect, is the very foundation of a Buddhist Dharma practice. On top of that, your study, contemplation, and meditation, as well as teaching, debating, and composition on the paths of sutra and tantra taught by the Buddha, the bodhisattvas, and their commentators, plus practices of offering, prayers, prostration, circumambulation, purification, and so on—whatever you immerse yourself in—should all be undertaken as much as possible as methods to tame the mind.

Deeds that are outwardly Dharma and devoid of the above are mere shadows of Dharma practices. An untamed mind can hurt other people and can bring great harm to ourselves. If we understand the mistakes of not transforming our mind, and also understand the great benefits of transforming the mind—such as the immediate and long-term benefit for ourselves and others—the joy we take in taming our mind will grow and we will make efforts with a firm resolve. Therefore, by knowing these benefits and faults we need to generate a natural desire to transform our mind. First, we need a thorough analysis, asking ourselves, "What is the nature of this unwanted suffering?" [397] "What are its causes?" "Do those causes have antidotes that directly oppose them?" and so on. When the force of the antidotes becomes stronger, the causes that create suffering become weaker. Knowing this and transforming our mind is Buddhism.

We recognize those cognitive states within us that have opposing modes of apprehending. Invalid cognition, noncomprehension, misconception, doubt, and so on—to use the language of the classical Buddhist texts—all cause suffering. The cognition that contradicts or opposes them is a valid cognition, of which there is direct valid cognition that generates experience as well as inferential cognition in which we first have to follow sound reasoning and make deductions. A cognition that has either of these as a support is a correct cognition induced by a valid cognition. Misconception and those cognitions induced by misconception are misperceiving cognitions. Knowing the differences between correct and incorrect cognitions, cognitions conducive to reality and misperceiving cognitions, valid cognition and wrong perception, if we create and develop the antidotes to these misperceiving cognitions, we will bring about change to our minds.

For example, the cognition that adheres to a self is a wrong perception. It will therefore produce pride, anger, desire, envy, and so on, which create trouble in society and unhappiness to ourselves. It creates great hardship here and now and in times to come. However, these states of mind have no valid cognition that will support and validate them. They can therefore be uprooted. To do that, we have to generate in our minds the wisdom comprehending no-self, which directly opposes that wrong cognition and is a perfect cognition possessing the validation and support of valid cognition. Other than that, prayers, prostrations, and offerings on their own cannot eliminate these misconceptions, as I have said many times before.

[398] Above, Dharma was described as that which protects from fear or suffering and that which "holds" us away from suffering. On that basis, in terms of the four truths, the buddhas taught how suffering arises in dependence upon a cause, and how the origin or cause of suffering produces suffering. Consequently, apart from eliminating the causes of suffering there is no other way of attaining liberation. Expressing this, a sutra states,

> The buddhas do not wash away the defilements with water.
> They do not wipe away the sufferings of others with their hands.
> They do not transmit their realizations to others,
> but by teaching the truth of reality, they liberate.[252]

The Buddha does not purify us through bathing ceremonies, nor is there any way that he can wipe away the sufferings of others with his hands. There is no way through the force of his great compassion that he can receive the sufferings of others and pass on his wonderful qualities in return. He taught that suffering occurs through ignorance of the reality of phenomena, and by teaching that reality exactly, we will be able develop in ourselves the recognition of that ignorance of reality, through which we can put an end to the cause of suffering and be liberated from samsara.

REASON IS MORE IMPORTANT THAN FAITH

We do not place our faith in Buddhism because it is our ancestors' tradition or because the Buddha is very special. First, in order to achieve benefit now and in the future for ourselves and others we need to identify the means and methods that are essential for us all. We should learn this by studying and thinking about causes and the reasons for gain and loss. [399] Through attitudes that help or harm us and others, the virtue and nonvirtue of physical and verbal deeds is amassed, whose results in turn bring experiences of happiness and suffering. We become convinced of this, and in order to transform our minds to a virtuous state, we are taught the common and exclusive precepts and the stages of practice together with reasons and in keeping with our ability. We should not be forced to follow these practices. If we have found trust in the reasons for essential Dharma practices, there is no way the mind will not be transformed.

Reasons for that trust will not be found in taking refuge in scripture alone, or by believing the word of some third party, but through analysis and examination by which we see reasons from our own side. For that to happen we first need the doubt that wonders and inquires. The objects to examine are the extensive phenomena found in the presentations of base reality, paths, and results. In particular, within the topics of base reality are found many explanations on the nature of cognition and the types of mental affliction. These presentations speak about states of mind that harm us, which are to be eliminated, and the antidotes to rely upon as methods to eliminate them. Through this, in our daily lives we will recognize precisely what will be beneficial and what will be harmful, paving the way for good prospects in the present and the future. If we are able to recognize the faults of mental afflictions, such as anger and desire, and the excellent qualities of virtuous minds that oppose them—the reasoning for which is clearly taught in Indian and Buddhist literary sources—we will generate conviction through the power of examining the reasons for happiness and suffering, and through our experience we will develop trust. If this happens, the application of antidotes to eliminate mental affliction will be powerful.

[400] The way to analyze causes is by way of the three kinds of analysis[253] on a path that follows the logic of valid cognition presented by the great scholars of India and Tibet. In this way we should develop conviction in their results. Just relying on the way things appear is of no help.

In this way, Buddhism explains with practical reasons how all sentient beings—but primarily humans—can achieve a level of happiness. In the manner explained above, it can definitely have a beneficial impact on the world at large. Therefore, if we can plant virtuous imprints within our attitudes and daily habits, our wisdom—defined as the ability to discern phenomena—will surely increase. We will come to understand many things, and by seeing the reasons, we will be able to engage in activities beneficial in the short and long term for everyone, whether they believe in religion or not.

Through these means, Dharma practitioners will find faith by seeing the reasons, and will finally achieve the wisdom of omniscience endowed with the ultimate qualities of knowing phenomena in their countless varieties and by way of their actual nature.

Buddhists place great importance on reasoning. In the past many scholars produced works that teach reasoning, such as Ārya Nāgārjuna in his *Compendium of Sutra*, Ārya Asaṅga in his *Compendium of Abhidharma* and *Summary of the Great Vehicle*, Dignāga in his *Compendium of Valid Cognition*. In such works we have a precious resource for developing the gateway of a discerning intellect. [401] Consequently, as a way of achieving happiness now and in the long term, we should place emphasis on a discerning wisdom without relying on faith alone. It is important to use discernment with reasoning as a basis. In his *Precious Garland*, Nāgārjuna says that in order to achieve our temporary and ultimate aims, faith and wisdom are important. Faith is the means for gaining a high rebirth, while wisdom will achieve liberation. Of the two, wisdom is the more important. Therefore, the scriptures speak of "the perfection of wisdom." They do not speak of the perfection of faith.

Also, in *Engaging in Bodhisattva Deeds*, Śāntideva says, "All these branches,²⁵⁴ the Buddha has said, were for the purpose of wisdom." He did not say they were for the purpose of faith. This principle was emphasized in Nālandā Monastery, and if you examine the works of its scholars, they mostly determine and ascertain their points for students of sharp faculties. Chapter 2 of the *Guhyasamāja Root Tantra* says, "Devoid of all phenomena . . ."²⁵⁵ and so on, in which high rebirth and liberation are established through reasoning, liberation and enlightenment are ascertained with valid cognition, and the intention to achieve these goals is generated.

In particular, in the works of Nāgārjuna, such as *Fundamental Wisdom of the Middle Way* and *Sixty Stanzas on Reasoning*, he determines emptiness by way of countless reasonings. This was the exclusive tradition of Nālandā Monastery, which was one of many profound philosophies in India during its heyday. Therefore, emphasis was given to explanations of Buddhist views clarified through reasoning. Thorough explanations of how to achieve a high rebirth and liberation were also given through reasoning.

Even today these great treatises can open our eyes to the practices of what is to be acquired and what is to be discarded. [402] For example, the valid cognition literature, Āryadeva's *Four Hundred Verses*, Nāgārjuna's *Dispelling Arguments* and *Detailed Disputation*, and the patience chapter of *Engaging in Bodhisattva Deeds* are generally works on practice, but they provide the opportunity and resources for studying the refutations of the assertions of non-Buddhists relevant to those times.

Recently we have discussed the creation of a compendium of science that would gather important topics from Buddhist science and non-Buddhist science, including modern science. Similarly, if there could be published works that did not include the philosophies of ancient India and religious topics, such as Buddhist presentations on paths and resultant states, but which compiled presentations of tenet systems as a whole on topics such as the two truths, universals and particulars, negation and affirmation, the four main philosophical schools, and so on, as well as on Western philosophies, old and new, I think it would be beneficial primarily for our schools and our society, and also for those who study the classical texts. If such books could be translated into Chinese, English, and other languages, it would be very beneficial in providing a new broadening of the mind for students from other Buddhist countries.

The responsibility now for such a task lies solely with Tibetan Buddhists. From the point of view of resources, no other Buddhist country could accomplish it. Many Tibetan scholars, such as Sakya Paṇḍita with his *Treasure of Reasoning,* have written works on the topic of valid cognition, for example. Chapa Chökyi Sengé and the lineage of scholars in that tradition studied the topic of valid cognition in great detail, and consequently a curriculum of topics such as the "science of knowing," "the science of reasoning," "collected topics," and so on spread extensively throughout Tibet. [403] Such subjects of study are not found in Pāli texts. The Chinese primarily adhere to the Sanskrit scriptural tradition, but apart from a few chapters of works by Dignāga and Dharmakīrti, works on valid cognition were not translated in their entirety. From works on Madhyamaka, some parts of Candrakīrti's *Clear Words* were later translated into Chinese, but there was no complete translation. Therefore, some years ago I said that *Clear Words* ought to be translated into Chinese, and that has now begun. These matters have become the responsibility of us Tibetans, although this is not something only for Tibetans. I see this as important for the service of the Buddha Dharma in general.

Whether the earth is round or flat, or whether Mount Meru exists or not, are not topics of prime importance here, but the two truths, and the four truths that depend upon the two truths, are realities we can directly experience. Therefore, it is important that someone who understands well the presentations on the four truths and the two truths finds conviction in the three refuges by way of valid cognition. If we know the main points of the five outer and five inner elements, and how the world is created from the five elements, we will generate certainty and a strong conviction in our minds, without any room for doubt. Jé Tsongkhapa, at the end of chapter 1 of his *Great Exposition of Secret Mantra*, says,

> Without separating out, with stainless reasoning,
> the good and bad explanations
> from ours and others scriptural traditions,
> and not differentiating precisely
> the main features common and exclusive to
> the Great and Lesser Vehicles, Sutra and Tantra,
>
> even claiming the teachings in general,
> the Great Vehicle, and particularly the Vajra Vehicle,
> to be the supreme gateway for the fortunate,
> is nothing but faith.
>
> Therefore, please, those with intelligence who aspire,
> train your eyes of wisdom with pure reasoning.
> Seek a firm conviction in the points of the teachings
> that cannot be moved by the arguments of opponents.[256]

This we need to do.

[404] This rather emphatic explanation that the practices of Buddhism are without question helpful for our happiness now and in the future is not given with any motivation of converting to Buddhism those who have faith in their own religion or those who have no

interest at all. Any means of bringing people to religion by force or deception is an unworthy practice. This is an important principle in Buddhism. Claiming that Buddhism is better than other religions, or looking down on and ignoring other paths, is even worse. With an honest appraisal this can be easily understood.

Not hurting others and working for the benefit of others is the foundation of all Buddhist vehicles. On that basis, with a mind of compassion that is equal for all, any victory for self and defeat for others is discarded, and we should train ourselves to have a pure perception of the tenets of all religions.

Helping appropriately those who have a natural interest and a curiosity to learn about Buddhist philosophy or any other religion is part of providing for the general welfare of others. Similarly, some people may not be satisfied with the religion of their own culture and turn away from it. Generally, they may have no faith in religion, but because of particular reasons such as the awakening of previously planted imprints, they develop a liking and an aspiration for Buddhism with genuine reasons, and desire to practice it. They should first engage in a period of study to assess just what Buddhism is, without thoughtlessly rushing in, and put its precepts into practice in order to test them. After this, if they develop a firm conviction and then enter its practice, they will have a sound and stable basis for the long term. [405] Such people should be introduced to and taught the foundation of Buddhism followed by the methods for striving for liberation in the correct order. These are the stages of progress for us Buddhists.

THE TWENTY-FIRST-CENTURY BUDDHIST

In this twenty-first century, great efforts are being made everywhere in the world to improve our general knowledge, and as a result the standard of knowledge is rising. Consequently, if we Tibetans lack an acceptable educational level, we will arrive at a time where we suffer the hardship of not being able to take our rightful place in humanity. Therefore, I often urge that Buddhists too should become twenty-first-century Buddhists.

What kind of Buddhist should that be? It should be one who is learned, ethical, and compassionate. In Buddhism we should not be random and unstructured by relying on blind faith, for example. We should be learned by being wise in the ways of developing faith through seeing and understanding the reasons, and possess a faith induced by a discerning wisdom that analyzes phenomena. Being ethical in conduct means to subdue the mind through Buddhist precepts. Being compassionate is to be a decent, good human being who primarily works for the sake of others. If we want to be Buddhists endowed with these three qualities, we should do so by "the wheel of reading that induces study and contemplation." This should not be regarded as knowledge that is solely the preserve of those who go to university. It is important to understand that this is knowledge for everyone.

Generally, Buddhism is not blind faith, but the way we practice it has become a kind of blind faith. Such practice is out of date, and we should move on from that. [406] In Tibet we have a profound and vast doctrine and yet in our Tibetan society practicing Dharma means doing prostrations, making offerings, reciting prayers, and repeating mantras for a set number of complete rosary recitations. If this is what Dharma practice is, that is nothing but blind faith. To think that such a form of practice is sufficient is simplistic. Just as we work to modernize our outdated economic system, we should modernize our outdated modes of practice. On the other hand, if we explain it by saying that this was the way of our ancestors, then it is like saying our ancestors were stupid so I will be stupid too. Or, my ancestors could not read or write, so I will be illiterate also, and my children will be illiterate. Such statements make no sense and are universally ridiculed. Whether you believe in Buddhism or not is up to you, but if you do, the Buddhism you believe in should be understood by investigation and by examining what it actually is.

Tibetans say, "I go for refuge to the Lama. I go for refuge to the Buddha." If this way of going for refuge is like saying, "All my suffering is in your hands," this completely contradicts Buddhism. If you are someone who accepts a creator of the world, everything is created by God, and it would be acceptable to say, "All my suffering is known by you." If we Tibetans do not understand the meaning of the statement "All happiness and suffering, all good and bad, is known by the Three Jewels," there is a danger of it becoming the same as that uttered by believers in a creator. In Buddhism it says, "I am my own protector." It does not say that the Buddha is the creator of the world. [407] Moreover, in Buddhist texts it says that if you posit a creator of the world, it can be refuted with many reasons.

In the past "learned, ethical, and compassionate" were among those qualities traditionally used to praise great lamas. However, times are changing, and in these times of a general improvement in education, all Buddhist practitioners of this world, whether they are monastics, laity, men or women, can become learned, ethical, and compassionate. It is not only applicable to lamas. Should that happen, the society where you live will benefit and it is therefore essential, as I always point out. It will automatically benefit you personally now and in the long run.

There is a big difference between educated and uneducated people practicing Buddhism. To be a Buddhist without education is outdated. Therefore, not only monks, nuns, and tantric practitioners—who bear the responsibility of being religious practitioners—but also society as a whole, whether young or old, should become good people of the twenty-first century with a decent standard of education.

My encouragement of the study of Buddhism is not pursued from some thought to increase the number of monks and nuns throughout the world, nor do I have hopes for the monks and nuns to become town ritualists.[257] I am not even saying that you have to become a Buddhist. So, what is it for? It is because I have a genuine belief that Buddhist education can accomplish great benefits for society. [408] The reason for this is that through Buddhist practices negative attitudes in the mind can be transformed and positive attitudes will increase. If we know this and make effort, whatever we do will naturally be for the benefit of others. Therefore, the greater the understanding of Buddhism is in society, the more that society will become convinced through experience of the potential that Buddhism possesses, and because of that, it is very evident that Buddhism can play a huge part in bringing happiness to the whole of society.

Wishing to bring happiness to society through Buddhism, we might extensively search the Kangyur and Tengyur for teachings on ways to establish and improve our standard of living, for example, but there are no practices in these scriptures that teach these things directly. Therefore, we must work to train ourselves in modern educational ways. However, important principles taught in the Kangyur and Tengyur are very beneficial as essential background supports. For example, primarily, the scriptures teach that all phenomena arise by way of dependence. That is directly relevant to the need to have a kind and loving mind that poses no harm to others. The scriptures also teach a fundamental love and compassion as the essence of all practices. With these firmly in our minds, even if we train in economics, the arts, science, technology, law, medicine, or anything else, and subsequently enter into practice, we will have a natural altruism with attitudes of honesty and a sense of responsibility, which will be able to accomplish something worthwhile in society, and our lives will become meaningful.

If, on the other hand, we are under the sway of the mental afflictions of desire, anger, and so forth, and we lack a motivation that has affection and kindness as its base, any expertise or high level of education in study simply becomes a condition for the detriment of happiness, as we can easily see.

[409] Modern science and nuclear technology are essential for the benefit of humanity. Yet these have been misused, killing people and destroying whole countries. Instead of being used in the service of humanity, these skills and knowledge have become tools for oppression and for creating suffering. As activities solely in pursuit of victory for self and defeat for others, even today they cause much harm to the well-being of communities, as I emphasized earlier.

Buddhism is a method to gain long-lasting happiness by using the potential of the discerning human intellect to a high degree. Therefore, it is not purely a religious pursuit but can be considered an educational one. Buddhist practice does not mean going for refuge to some faraway pure realm or to a supreme being, generating faith, performing the appropriate rituals, and making prayers, or following orders made by some religious authority or organization, saying you can do this, you cannot do that, and so on, without any direct connection to our own situation. Buddhist practices are those in which our innate discerning intellect is used properly and becomes beneficial and meaningful.

When studying and practicing Buddhism, we should do it from a place of joy, with effort motivated by enthusiasm. A joyful mind cannot arise from coercion and force. Therefore, by knowing the good points and benefits, a joyful feeling will arise naturally. In the past, there were practices such as instilling fear in others by talking about rebirth in hell in order to generate faith and belief, pointing out faults based on superstition, [410] resorting to scolding, beating, and other harsh methods of corrective discipline. These cause harm to others. As it is said,

> Striking with a single blade of grass
> does not constitute a beating,
> but striking, generally, is a type of harm.[258]

Therefore, cultivation should be practiced by explaining reasons with gentle words to create certainty and generate joy, accompanied by praise and encouragement. Also, in the instructions known as the "Four Ways of Gathering Disciples," it says, "Speak pleasantly." It does not say you should threaten people. Moreover, the four precepts of a religious practitioner are as follows: (1) having been criticized, not criticizing in return; (2) having been shown anger, not showing anger in return; (3) having being struck, not striking in return; and (4) having had one's faults pointed out, not pointing out faults in return. "Religious practitioner" is not only applicable to monks and nuns. All those who practice the Buddha's teachings, which are the very antithesis of those that are harmful, should follow the four precepts of a spiritual practitioner. Not hurting others is a practice of both higher and lower vehicles. On top of that, being altruistic toward others is a precept of the Great Vehicle.

We should think deeply about how we use our discerning intellect and transform for the good our basic attitudes and the behavior that arises from them. Buddhism means to study, apply it to the mind, put it into practice, and implement its precepts. It is not enough just to have faith and to simply follow customs and tradition. "Spreading the teachings" should be done by way of the mind. Amassing a great learning within our mind is to be rich in the qualities of scripture. Working to actualize the points of that learning and putting them into practice is to be rich in the qualities of insight. These are all qualities of the mind. To be possessed of them is the spread of the teachings.

[411] As for the expression "meeting the teachings," if you have been able to develop these two qualities of scripture and insight within your mind, you have met the teachings. Just by being born in a country where the teachings exist, assuming oneself to be a Buddhist, and by holding a rosary and reciting mantras endlessly, it is difficult to become a genuine Buddhist. Arranging representations of the enlightened body, speech, and mind on the altar and making offerings and prostrations to them, performing circumambulations, and so on, are activities in tune with Buddhism and therefore will accumulate merit.

However, these alone are not true practices of Buddhism. If you look at the works of the Nālandā masters, such as those of Nāgārjuna, they only speak of analyzing, investigating, thinking about the reasons. They do not say that prostrations and offerings by themselves are sufficient. Therefore, the genuine way to practice Buddhism should be understood through study. There is no easy way.

Even those who do not believe in Buddhism and have no faith in it, but who truly want to know how to benefit their own lives and those of the society they dwell in, should know about the deep practices of Buddhism, as I have occasionally mentioned before. For that, it is important to know Buddhist philosophy as well as modern science. The reason-based format of the Buddhist monastic curriculum subject known as *Collected Topics* may not have any immediate and direct benefit for practice, but it is helpful for gaining a detailed understanding of the nature of phenomena and is a pillar of inner development. External developments are completed within a set number of months and years, but inner development, from a Buddhist perspective, is not complete until the attainment of enlightenment.

[412] The foundation of inner development is good ethical behavior. This is not just the language of Buddhist practitioners. Generally, such behavior lies at the very root of human happiness. Therefore, whatever the situation is, we should not view it from a narrow or short-sighted state of mind. Whereas the basket of monastic discipline is mostly a subject of study for the ordained, the baskets of sutra and abhidharma are suitable to be studied by everyone. Therefore, everyone should try to put them into practice. This is my hope and the goal I am working toward.

When I say that it is important to study the classical works, there are some who say that to be a genuine Buddhist practitioner you need meditation and practice, and that being learned is not necessary. However, it is said, "For the teachings the general is the focus, for persons the specific is the focus." From the perspective of a general focus upon the teachings, study is certainly needed. Nothing will be accomplished through the superficiality of mere words or "dry faith." Moreover, study should not be understood as the posturing of becoming an expert in the scriptures. It is pursued in order to thoroughly understand and to develop conviction about the nature of happiness and suffering and their causes.

"For persons the specific is the focus" refers to the fact that there are those whose power of karma and prayer from previous lives is strong, and consequently they do not pursue a great study of the classical texts but attain liberation through practice alone. This is because of a special situation created by the awakening of imprints from their previous lives. Occasionally such people appear. Milarepa, for example, was one. However, looking at such practitioners, for we beginners to boast about attaining liberation without studying is to reach for the heights without the competence, like a fox leaping where a tiger has lept. Such a claim is a sign of not having understood the essential points made by the great masters of all traditions, who state that we should follow a graded system of training, in which we learn and determine through study, sever misconception through contemplation, and then practice by meditating on the points. [413]

There are those who slanderously claim that while the Nyingma and Kagyu traditions are genuine meditators and practitioners, the Sakya and Geluk tradition are completely caught up with explanations and discussions and do not practice. Such people have not seen the extensive writings by many great masters of all traditions on the classical literary corpus. They are not aware that many Nyingma and Kagyu masters, through their compositions, teachings, and arguments on the inner science of the Kangyur and Tengyur, have preserved, nourished, and developed the Buddha's teachings with practice and teaching combined. Nor have they understood that great accomplished practitioners who hold aloft the banner of practice shine vividly within the Geluk and Sakya like stars in the sky. Such people simply reveal their own faults, which have been produced by resentment and attachment.

If devotional meditation and faith were sufficient in Buddhism, many classical works in the Kangyur and Tengyur and the detailed commentaries would be irrelevant, and just a small collection of scriptures would suffice, as is the case in some world religions. However, faith alone is not enough. We need to make use of the complete power of the human intellect, and with a discerning wisdom come to understand the presentations of base reality, paths, and resultant states as taught in the texts. There is something to be known and something that can be known. Therefore, if we investigate how the seventeen pandits and other masters of ancient India explained these matters, we can see that they did not just sit upright and mainly teach how to meditate, but taught extensively countless kinds of knowledge, whose final significance is always to be found condensed within the practice of bodhicitta and the view of emptiness.

[414] When distinguishing classical text and core instruction, it is a big mistake to understand classical texts as being just for teaching and core instructions as being primarily for attaining the omniscient state of enlightenment. Otherwise, we would have to answer the question "Was it the case that the Buddha and Nāgārjuna did not give core instructions? Or were they not familiar with them? Was their knowledge not good enough?"

The mains methods for achieving the omniscient state of enlightenment are taught in the Kangyur and Tengyur compositions, such as Nāgārjuna's six works on Madhyamaka reasoning. Where are there any separate core instructions not mentioned in these works? Core instructions are for facilitating the comprehension of works such as *Fundamental Wisdom of the Middle Way*, *Ornament of Insight*, *Uttaratantra*, and so on. Going back earlier, if something lessens the difficulty in understanding sutras such as the *Avataṃsaka Sutra*, the perfection of wisdom sutras, or the *Sutra of the Ten Levels*, it is a core instruction. However, if you hold something that has no connection to these great works as a core instruction, that could result in being led along a mistaken path. That is not good.

To sum up, if you engage in transforming your mind by way of knowing the reasons, which becomes a practice with the potential to bring happiness and benefit to yourself and your community, that is what I call being a twenty-first-century Buddhist.

The Tibetan tradition of Buddhism is rich in philosophy, more profound than others, and hosts extensive commentaries. On that basis, the Tibetan language and culture has developed out of the creativity of the Tibetan intellect. Therefore, the profound religion and culture of Tibet, built on the intellect and legacy of our ancestors, is one we can rightly show off to the whole world. It is a heritage envied by others. [415] During the time it first spread in Tibet, throughout its duration and even now, when outer and inner hostile conditions are combined against us, it has been a combination of culture and religion that has stood out among other religious cultures. This is clearly a worthy attribute. It is a wonderful civilization intimately connected with Buddhist philosophy and has produced many good customs and habits. As a result, those who adhere to such values and qualities generally instinctively tend to be intelligent, peaceful, and well-behaved, holding kindness and compassion as fundamental values, and living their lives accordingly. This is an evident and valuable aspect or feature that stands out in the Tibetan people that others have seen and acknowledge.

Regardless of whether individual Tibetans have faith in Buddhism or not, the society we belong to has become a Buddhist society, and through its tradition of good customs and habits it will bring about the happiness and welfare of ourselves and others here and now and in the future. From that perspective and from the perspective of our history and our present situation, however you look at it, it is an important culture. We have a saying that if we have something of value, people will recognize that value. Therefore, this is a culture of which we can be rightly proud. Throughout the world a special interest in the Tibetan Buddhist tradition and its culture has developed, meaning that many Buddhist centers and cultural institutions have been created. For example, the greatest variety of food is found in Chinese cuisine, and as a result, Chinese restaurants are everywhere, but there are not that many Chinese Buddhist centers!

This religious culture is not just about outwardly expressing the intellect, but is a quality intimately linked to methods for taming the inner mind. In that sense, it is very special. [416] Moreover, this excellent quality, which stretches back to our ancient times, can be said to be the essence of the views and philosophies of this world, and it is a well-known fact that its complete subject matter can be accessed by way of the Tibetan language. This is something that up to now cannot be reciprocated in any other language. Thinking about such things and preserving our language with respect and esteem will be of great benefit to the whole of society.

For those reasons the Tibetan tradition of Buddhism can be seen not only as a hallmark of Tibet but also as a prominent and special feature of the Mongolian people, of the small populations of the Himalayan regions in and around Ladakh, Sikkim, and Bhutan. Therefore, it is important to treasure it. Whether you call it Bhoṭīya, Dzongkha, or something else, Tibetan is the common language of all Tibetan Buddhists. Therefore, we should have a fondness for it and hold it in high regard. When we have an interest in Buddhism and develop a competent understanding, we will see that Tibetan language is very special and indispensable, and we can take great confidence from that.

THE STUDY, PRACTICE, AND PRESERVATION OF BUDDHISM BY NONMONASTICS

In the past it was said that the preservation and continuance of the teachings of the Buddha depended upon the existence of a monastic community. However, that was something said at those times. [417] Those who can make prayers for and dedicate their practice for the preservation of the doctrine of scripture and insight are clearly not restricted to the monastic community alone. It is something that can be done by everyone.

The doctrine of the Buddha is one of scripture and insight, and is not a doctrine to be preserved solely by the venerable communities of the red-robed ordained monks and nuns and the white-robed, braided lay practitioners, but also by the lay community of men and women who have faith in the teachings. The majority of the public are not monastics or lay tantric practitioners and therefore, if the lay community put their energy toward the tasks of teaching and practice, it would be more prevalent. This would go a long way toward preserving, nourishing, and developing the priceless Buddhist teachings in general, and specifically the Tibetan Buddhist tradition, for generations to come.

For the doctrine of scripture and insight to spread in society, first there should be an understanding of the scripture. This produces a desire to practice, and practice leads to the qualities of insights being born in the mind. It is not sufficient, for example, for temples and monasteries, wherever they are, only to exist as places for making offerings and prostrations. They should be transformed into places of study, so that when someone says "temple" or "monastery" everyone understands them as places of study. The managers of such places should not be collectors of donations from devotees but should be given the responsibility of providing teachings for these devotees on the topics of going for refuge, the four truths as a prerequisite to that, and the two truths as a precursor to that.

From the nineteenth century onward people from various countries began taking an interest in Buddhism, and many of our young people continue to graduate within a modern educational system. [418] Therefore, it is the shared responsibility of we Tibetans to take on the task of providing the necessary and conducive conditions for people of all nations—monastic and laity, male and female—to have an equal opportunity to engage in an advanced study of Buddhism. For many years a topic that often comes up in discussions I have had is that when Tibetan students graduate from a modern educational system, they appear to have little interest in Buddhism. This is because up to now, within our community we have been unable to provide the perfect conditions for an interchange of Western and Tibetan education, and because these graduates have no knowledge of Buddhism, they have no interest in it. It is not that they first knew the principles of Buddhism and then lost interest in it. It is important to think carefully about a better way to give them the opportunity for an advanced study of Buddhism. These days the number of people from the West who have an interest and faith in Buddhism is growing. This is because they see something worthwhile in Buddhism and apply themselves to it. Therefore, on such a fundamental issue, we must make sure that we Tibetans do not waste what we already have.

If Buddhist study necessitates reliance upon the great Tibetan monasteries, then in keeping with the present system, a student will have to abide by monastic regulations. This means the necessary prerequisite of being ordained as a monk or nun. This is difficult. Therefore, these days it is really worthwhile for the present and the future to set up a system that affords an opportunity for the laity to study Buddhism. Consequently, the Central Institute of Higher Tibetan Studies in Sarnath and the Institute of Buddhist Dialectics in Dharamsala were set up to provide advanced Buddhist studies for the laity and monastics of all nations. Through such enterprises we are able to care for people with an in-depth and thorough Buddhist and Western education.

[419] Such an educational arrangement where both laity and monastics had equal opportunity for study in a single Buddhist institution existed in ancient India too. In his *Grains of Gold*, the great scholar Gendün Chöphel states,

> Nālandā was not only renowned for the learning of its scholars; in its ethics and altruistic behavior it was an example for the whole of India.[259]

Also,

> Not only monks resided here, but many lay students also.
> All non-Buddhist works—such as those of the Vedas, the
> Sāṃkhya, the Mīmāṃsa, and treatises of astronomy and
> grammar—as well as the canons of the eighteen Buddhist
> sects were studied here.[260]

This a worthwhile example to follow. In the past our great monastic institutions only admitted monks. Not only were the laity not admitted, but not even nuns could study there. This is outdated.

On the matter of awards of recognition presented to graduates, there were over twenty monastic institutions before the time of Jé Tsongkhapa that offered philosophical study, including Ratö, Narthang, Sakya, Shalu, Trophu, Nenying, and Kyormolung, who presented titles of recognition. Of the five great subjects of study, those who only graduated from the perfection of wisdom class were awarded the title of *parchin rabjampa*, while those who graduated from the monastic discipline, perfection of wisdom, Middle Way, and Abhidharma classes were given the title of *kashiwa*.

In the Geluk school it was the custom to award the title of *kachupa* to those who had completed the study of the five great topics. Later on, after the establishment of the three great monastic seats,[261] the degree of *geshé* was introduced, of which there are different levels. The *lingsé geshé* degree was awarded to those who were examined on the five great topics by way of debate with questioners from all monastic colleges. This followed the tradition of Sangphu Monastery. [420] Some monasteries presented degrees known as *tsokrampa, rikrampa, dorampa*,[262] and so on. During the time of the troubles between Central Tibet and Tsang, Panchen Losang Chögyen initiated the debate examination on the five great topics for the best geshés from the three great monastic seats. This took place during the Lhasa prayer festival and began the tradition of awarding the title of *lhaden rabjampa*, which became known as *lharampa geshé*.[263]

"Geshé" is a title awarded for graduation from institutions that study the classical texts. It is not reserved specially for monks. In reality there is no connection between being a geshé and being a monk. Therefore, without clinging to tradition, in the future we should initiate a system where monastics and laity have equal rights to receive the title of geshé.

Even in some Buddhist centers in the West arrangements are made for lay and monastic students to study the classical texts. It is only right to think deeply about providing the necessary conditions for such studies to continue and for other groups also to be able to pursue this kind of advanced study as an admirable provision and service for the highest benefit of the whole of society, regardless of creed or nationality.

For a long time, I have regarded raising the level of Buddhist education as important. Around 1960, immediately after Tibetans became refugees in India, Tibetan schools were set up and brief classes on general Buddhism and on the basics of advanced studies were established. Lamas, tulkus, and geshés were appointed as religious teachers. [421] Similarly, institutions for the elderly were built and in several settlements Buddhist centers were gradually established. Tibetan society as a whole can be said to be a Buddhist society, and with the hope that it would live up to that name and be a genuine Buddhist community, I implemented these as best I could.

Likewise, to those tantric monastic establishments who formerly specialized only in the practice of performing established rituals, I emphasized the importance of studying the classical texts. As a result, the *kyerimpa*[264] students of both the Upper and the Lower Tantric College initiated courses in the study of Buddhist philosophy. Similar classes were introduced in Namgyal Monastery also. Moreover, there is a movement in many monasteries of the Himalayan regions to institute the study of classical texts.

These days, in Tibet also, many monasteries of all traditions are showing an interest in setting up colleges for teaching, debating, and meditation. This is very hopeful. However, study programs should also be developed in nunneries and not only in monasteries. In the past, although teaching and meditation colleges were separate, it was the practice of great lamas to emphasize the importance of uniting them. Otherwise, if the monks and nuns only recite rituals and receive donations and communal tea offerings, it is very doubtful that this is beneficial for preserving, nourishing, and developing the doctrine or for giving hope to the living and the recently deceased.

In the past, it was the perception of the Tibetan people that listening, contemplation, and meditation on teachings received, for example, and in particular the course of study of Buddhism, were activities to be carried out by the monastic community, and not something that the lay community had to do. [422] Also, among the monastic community it was seen as the activity of the male monastics of the great monasteries, and not that of nuns. Such attitudes are wrong. On the other hand, some entertain the mistaken belief that memorizing recitation texts and performing rituals is sufficient. This is a result of there being hardly any practice of providing serious teachings for the general public, except for the occasional long-life empowerment. Even during long-life empowerments there was the feeling that congregating for an empowerment was incidental to having a good time and meeting friends.

To change all this and to raise the level of Buddhist knowledge among the general public, Buddhist study courses were set up in Dharamsala, resulting in a huge increase of interest in Buddhist teachings. In the settlements too, the movement to start courses in Buddhist studies is increasing. Accordingly, if some households could gradually acquire copies of classical texts such as *Fundamental Wisdom of the Middle Way* and get a taste of the vast philosophy of the Buddhist religion through their studies, regardless of whether they are practicing Buddhists or not, it would help them develop strength of mind and a sense of responsibility, and they would come into contact with a method for taming the mind. Firstly, this would be very helpful in living their lives, and secondly, it would clarify many aspects of Tibet's profound culture, making it possible to implement many worthwhile practices of benefit to society and the environment.

Therefore, the better the study, the better you will tame the mind. If you become a good and ethical person who controls your behavior, your outlook will not be one born from ignorance, attachment, pride, envy, and so on, but will be one of intelligence and excellent character. [423] You will develop confidence, and in the future Tibetan society will without doubt be happy and intelligent. When challenges are posed by science, if, instead of being a threat, they help in our advancement, that is a sign of a complete understanding of the meaning of study.

In Ladakh, around 1960, the people did not have a good view of their lamas and monasteries or hold them in high esteem. Later when I was visiting Ladakh, some local people who had received a modern education requested a meeting without these lamas present. They told me that for those who had received a modern education there was a great tendency to think and analyze, and they were not satisfied with the older generation's way of practice, such as merely saying, "I go for refuge." The monks from the monastery would run off to perform rituals in the towns and do their chanting, but they never saw anything more profound in them than this. This was dissatisfying to them, and consequently they had no faith or admiration for the monastic community.

For many years in the Himalayan regions from Ladakh in the west to Mön in the east I have stressed the importance of knowing the reality of Buddhism. Those possessed of a modern education took on this responsibility. They set up classes on Buddhism and embarked on a thorough investigation of the teachings. Previously, the monasteries of Ladakh and Khunu were mostly engaged in the recitation of prayers, the performance of rituals, and so on, but now they are taking great strides toward a deep study of the classical texts. Moreover, in the past, the people believed themselves to be faithful Buddhists because they merely recited mantras, but now a new and great tradition of regular introductions to Buddhism, discussions, provisions for study, and so on has been instituted for the general public. [424] In particular, among the educated young people and those of a good level of intelligence, the religion and culture of their ancestors and modern culture have joined together and a great wave of service for the progress of the region is steadily growing. As a result, several regions are witnessing the excellent results of a year-by-year advancement both inwardly and outwardly.

The number of those who have given up meat and are on a vegetarian diet continues to increase. One heartening development is that in many of the larger towns retail businesses not only from the Buddhist community but from Muslim and other communities also are following the wonderful practice of not selling butchered meat, cooked meat, and alcohol on the first, eighth, and fifteenth of each month.[265] This is a cause for rejoicing.

Similarly, among the people of our community the understanding and knowledge of Buddhism was very weak in the past. This was not blind faith from the side of those in whom the faith was placed, but from the side of those who have faith it was a case of merely carrying on the customs of faith and belief of our ancestors without any understanding of the realities of Buddhism. Society was following a tradition of faith, belief, and worship, and so it was probably something like blind faith.

Moreover, Tibetans lived in a vast land where there were no challenges or opposition by way of external influences. Therefore, Tibet remained unaffected by the desire to learn something new and conditions that would have promoted growth through new ideas—good and bad. [425] Therefore, the responsibility for raising the level of Buddhist knowledge in Tibetan society and among its people lies with institutions of the community and particularly with the monastic community of monks and nuns. Without resorting only to prayers for the teachings to prosper, and to actually implement the activities of preserving, nourishing, and developing the teachings in all quarters of society, the profound qualities of the Tibetan Buddhist tradition should not be restricted to preserving and developing teaching, practice, and study within the monastic environment, as it was done in the past. It is important to turn attention to increasing the understanding of Buddhism outside the confines of the monasteries for the people and wider society.

The way to benefit the community of countless living beings is to not just keep those beings as objects of prayer in the mind but to also look to the excellent examples set by Christianity and other religions, and to actually engage in activities that benefit others, and in the many precepts of the bodhisattvas, without leaving such things to remain as mere words in texts. We need to implement physical and verbal actions—even the very smallest—that will be of practical service to others. Tibetan monks and nuns in particular should shoulder this responsibility. These activities amass great swathes of merit. These activities are connected with the dictates of today's trends; therefore, a broad mind is required.

On the issue of preserving, nourishing, and developing the teachings, the practice of simply maintaining the tradition is not sufficient these days. The monasteries need to exchange experiences and, in a spirit of mutual cooperation, think about ways to bring about change, formulate plans, and, through the experience of implementation, travel along the road of progress.

[426] Sometimes, under the burden of narrow-mindedness, we cherish "the old ways" with ancient customs, superstition, and blind faith.

We regard things that are new as inferior and see them as bad omens. However, innovation can be good or bad. This is not a case of breaking down our good traditions and willingly accepting the proliferation of something inferior. Changing traditions and customs of the past that are outdated is a good innovation. The reality is that we need progress. The need for innovation is a fact.

From a Buddhist perspective, the attainment of liberation and enlightenment involves working to attain new and hitherto unseen qualities of extensive and profound insight by processes of taming the mind and investigating phenomena. Such development of insight is innovation.

Our Tibetan customs instinctively follow tradition and the protocol of the written word. I can recall that in Lhasa there were hardly any free-thinking and broad-minded discussions held by the ministerial committees, for example, on the importance of the common good. Instead, there was a lot of talk about annual ceremonies and rituals, which were given so much significance. Looking back from today's viewpoint, we held meaningless and unessential activities to be of great importance. Not realizing what was meaningful and essential we just ignored them and let them go. The result of this failing is the situation we are in now. There is much that is good in Tibetan tradition but there is much that has become outdated and a product of neglect.

Therefore, those who wished to change and improve this poor situation faced the difficulty of not being confident enough to speak out and implement these changes. [427] Those few who dared to do so were like white crows,[266] and under the threat of being attacked, the long line of improvements they had originally planned could not happen. For example, in the past, except to the monks of the great seats of learning, we were not able institute the practice of extending our unique and precious education to most monastics from the smaller monasteries, and especially to the general public, such as craftsmen, farmers, and nomads. More than that, we were not even able to establish schools throughout Tibet. This was wrong. Such practices are now outdated and were the prime obstacles to progress.

Such a state of affairs was not brought about by a lack of aspiration or resolve, but by an inability to comprehend the reality of the situation because of narrow-mindedness, by being uninformed, and by shortsightedness. In this way we held on to that pretense. This was a great waste.

In the past, before the great changes, there was reluctance on the part of Tibet to have relations and dealings with other countries in the world at that time. As a result, we neglected to develop interest in any outside education systems. This was wrong and is outdated thinking. Being able to maintain one's country while keeping in step with the changes in the world is something we have not done, and because of this we have lost out. We have not suffered from having too few monasteries or too few Buddhist practitioners, but Buddhism alone cannot protect our country. Rituals cannot protect it; magic powers cannot protect it. These are facts. Therefore, if we do not cast off the hat of confusion, embrace modern education, and understand the changes that are taking place in the world, we will be left behind as equal partners in the communities of the five continents of this world. [428] That would be a tragedy. Therefore, I stress that we should take these past experiences as a lesson, and Tibetan youth everywhere, even in nomadic encampments, as well as future generations, should develop interest and enthusiasm in such learning.

There are many young Tibetans who have their lives in front of them. From the perspective of the world community or from the perspective of Tibetan society, if they wish to become people who are of benefit to the world, it is important to have an interest in studying and becoming educated. If you are an educated person, you will be well prepared for your own life, your family, your community, and any aspect of worldly life. Wherever you look in the world, in those places where the level of education is good, there is great progress. This is clear. Therefore, everyone should be focused and see it as being very important to apply themselves to their education. There are two kinds of education: education developed through a reliance upon the external world and phenomena, and one developed in reliance upon the inner world of thought. We need to be enriched by both.

To spend the time of youth in distractions—gambling with dice and mahjong, drinking without restraint, disreputable behavior, taking drugs, and so on—is the main cause for a waste of a life, and to live a life this way brings great detriment and loss to any society. Knowing this, such activities should be avoided, as should those who set bad examples.

There is no one who can look down upon our language, our good customs, and our fortitude. [429] But when we have no modern education others can and will look down upon us. In the past, countries like Tibet had their own customs, through which they were able to sustain their everyday happiness. However, these days the world population has grown greatly. Travel is much easier and close relationships have developed everywhere. Interdependence is very real and there is no way not to rely upon new fields of knowledge and new methodologies. Therefore, the reality of having to rely upon each other is widespread and a great change. It is as if we are all a part of each other. Therefore, if we do harm in our own neighborhood, in reality we are destroying ourselves.

We Tibetans also belong to this reality, and if we rely only on the traditions of our ancestors, there is no way to live in this world. Therefore, you should see working to live a life that is in accord with modern ways as being similar to the responsibility I am supposed to have for the world as a whole.

The movement to expand Buddhist knowledge among the general populace is not because there is a lack of provision preventing such a development. It is primarily because of our inability to initiate new traditions. Therefore, we also need to broaden our minds on this point.

For example, most Tibetan exile settlements will have a temple for general use, in which various prayers and devotions take place, such as the *mani* recitation accumulation. In addition to such practices, these days it is important to increase provision for Buddhist discussions. As for someone to explain Buddhism, there is no need to seek out a lama, seat him on a throne, and ask him to teach. It is perfectly acceptable to sit together in a circle to explain and discuss Buddhism. [430] Even if it is not possible to establish ongoing classes, something could be set up and held from time to time. It is time for everyone to think about these things.

As a provision for the above it is my hope that individuals and institutions with the resources will be able to publish certain texts that are hard to come across. In the Tengyur there are twenty-one Indian perfection of wisdom commentaries and many commentaries on Madhyamaka. Having the Tengyur does not mean having all the volumes and not having the Tengyur does not mean not having all the volumes. If relevant chapters from some of the great classical texts could be published it would definitely help the monks and nuns, and the general public. In particular, those engaged in study should use the monastic textbooks of the individual traditions and colleges like keys, and having comprehensively studied primarily the Indian commentaries, they should expand their reasoning, as I have stressed many times before.

Similarly, if the lamas, tulkus, and geshés and others wish to make a contribution to the monasteries and colleges, the classical texts are essential and therefore it is very worthwhile to publish them. I am not talking just about the monastic textbooks, but also about the important classical works such as the six works on Madhyamaka reasoning, *Entering the Middle Way, Ornament of Realization, Four Hundred Verses, Stages of Meditation,* and so on, and—if the list is expanded—the five works of Maitreya,[267] and so on, could be published in bulk. Doing so and distributing them, not only to monasteries but to the households of the general public, would benefit the movement to boost the fundamental knowledge of Buddhism in our society. Therefore, I always say that for the public to keep copies of these texts and to begin a tradition of study is very worthwhile.

[431] Otherwise, the many elaborate buildings in the exile monastic communities of our major traditions in India and Nepal, with their extravagant offerings, only increases the sense of competitiveness and envy among the monasteries. If you compare these places with living standards of the poor Indians and Nepalese of the region, and even with Tibetan settlements, there is a huge discrepancy in prosperity, and this is not in keeping with the practice of those that bear the name of Buddhist practitioners, who should cherish others over self. Moreover, these days, in the eyes of many non-Tibetans, and even Tibetans, such practices are uncomfortable and generate a bad reputation. All the profits go to the sellers of the material, the laborers, tailors, and so on. They do not benefit anyone else. There is a need for representations of the Buddha's body, speech, and mind as objects of faith, but wanting to construct excessively elaborate statues motivated by the eight worldly concerns, as if you were flaunting your wealth, is to discard the trunk and seize the branch. This is very sad. The statues do not even speak. Those who speak are the great texts.

Furthermore, those candidates who wish to make extensive donations as part of their expenses for sitting the geshé examination will seek out many sponsors, and the larger the donations are, the greater the number of monks who are pleased, and thus these candidates become renowned. This is a meaningless activity. The fruits of studying the classical texts should be the renown gained from witnessing the qualities of their responses during the examination debate. Gaining renown from making extensive, ill-gotten donations is nothing wonderful.

Therefore, we need to think about reforming our attitudes toward elaborate constructions, exam donations, and so on. I have expressed this many times before, but I do not know if most people think it advice worth paying attention to.

[432] When patrons of the monasteries meet with me, I tell them that it is good to appropriately help the historic monasteries. At the same time, I say that it is good not to help individual lamas and geshés. For these people to build big houses within the monastery is of no use. The doctrine of the Buddha is one of scripture and of insight. The scripture is studied and the insights are developed in the mind. Then, through teaching and practice, the doctrine is preserved, nourished, and developed. Constructing elaborate temples and representation of the Buddha's body, speech, and mind is of no use in preserving the doctrine.

Therefore, first you develop your learning and knowledge through reading, learning, and contemplation and then pursue activities that engage with the Kangyur and Tengyur. Regarding activities unconnected with that pursuit as being the Dharma of the Buddha is to run the risk of the Tibetan tradition of Buddhism becoming "Lamaism," as some people used to call it.

Similarly, these days some students rush through their geshé exams, and with their eyes fixed on dollars, and the like, they try to go to a Western Buddhist center. They build elaborate homes in the settlements and become involved in the multifaceted life of the settlement. There is nothing wonderful about that. Having few desires and few activities, thereby living up to the name of being a follower of the Buddha and a monastic who has gone "from home to homelessness," having self-respect because of what is expected from yourself and a conscience because of what others expect from you, are necessary qualities. It is important for everyone concerned to develop a regard for these, to practice restraint and live within the four contentments of an ārya.[268] [433] Therefore, we should take as our examples and as inspiration those monastics of the various Pāli tradition countries and Christian monks and nuns we see these days and whose contentment and lack of desire is inspiring. Following the ways of a proper Buddhist practitioner, we should build a legacy by preserving, nourishing, and developing the doctrine through teaching and practice. Building houses and setting bad examples is not the way to build a legacy. There is the risk that such things can be conditions for accumulating bad karma through attachment and arguments at the time of death, thereby giving a bad name not only to individual monastics but also to their monasteries, disgracing the name of Buddhist practitioners, and bringing ruin to our society. Therefore, administrators, teachers, and students must understand the commitment of proper behavior.

GENDER INEQUALITY AND LOOKING DOWN ON WOMEN CONTRAVENES BUDDHIST TENETS[269]

In ancient societies there was no inequality between men and women. Tasks were undertaken together and there are accounts that even as hunters, women were equal to men. However, gradually, as societies developed, factors such as sexual misconduct led to communities being ruled by chieftains. In the past few thousand years of human history, power and might were seen as especially important, and without paying any heed to mental strength, physical strength was considered to be of prime importance. Thus, men became important and were regarded as being possessed of power. This led to the male sex occupying the front row both in society and in the home. Because men had more power to confront enemies—were braver, more heroic, had more anger—they were leaders in warfare. In the past there were no female soldiers, butchers were men, and so on. This too is because of the above reasons, it seems.

[434] In ancient times local Indian tradition paid considerable attention to caste divisions and their relative purity. In particular, it was a society in which men traditionally held the power. This concept of

men and women possessing a different social status was absorbed into Tibetan society. This was true not only in the religious world but could be seen even in some established secular traditions, where men were regarded as powerful, while blacksmiths, butchers, and so on were held to be of low caste. Such attitudes of the past are completely outdated. In many countries, even in China, India, and Africa where women were traditionally bound into servitude and there was no recognition of gender equality, campaigns and effective protests are working to override these outdated customs and to bring about improvements. These are excellent. Therefore, I always take the position of sincerely supporting the struggle for women's rights.

Modern generations have been taking an interest in the progress of human society and in education, and there has been a gradual recognition of the importance of the power of the intellect, through which it has become abundantly clear that the capabilities of females are on a par with those of males however you look. Therefore, discussions on the need for gender equality are right and sensible. In this new generation, in keeping with the increase in population, I think it is important that caring and nurturing be accomplished with intelligence, discernment, kindness, and compassion. [435] That involves connections on both the physical and mental level, I feel. For example, men are not that effective in caring for children with great love and compassion, whereas in women this is a natural aptitude. Similarly, women have a greater tolerance for facing up to hardships; they easily express their feelings, are kinder, more affectionate, have a greater sense of concern, are humbler than men, their physical expression of emotion is better, and so on. With such qualities they have greater capabilities of caring for others. These days most nurses are women. The "eight nannies"[270] described in Buddhist texts are probably so-called because of the above qualities.

Generally, in human nature both anger and love exist, but there clearly seems to be this difference in the strength of these two between men and women. Therefore, we need to create an education system based on compassion, which can transform the mind. On that point, from the perspective of possessing a greater natural affection, women should take on greater responsibilities. Therefore, I think that if there were more intelligent women elected as influential world leaders, the world would be safer and less troubled.

From a Buddhist perspective, in the final thinking of the Buddha there is no view that discriminates between men and women. He taught that all living beings are capable of, or have the same opportunity of, attaining enlightenment, and he did not make a distinction by stating that women had less opportunity. [436] All human beings enjoy equal rights when it comes to happiness and suffering. This is a value shared by all those who possess a human form. When explaining whether the eighteen freedoms and endowments[271] are complete among those who possess a human form, no distinction is made on the basis of gender. All the practices taught from the gaining of a human form, with its hard-to-achieve freedoms and endowments up to the final practices of bodhisattva training, are there to be practiced by male or female, monastic or laity equally.

Even the manner of entering the monastic life and taking vows is same for men and women, and no differentiation is made on the basis of gender. This is a feature of Buddhism. During the time of the Buddha, the monastic discipline sutras speak of male and female lay practitioners. Therefore, the highest set of vows—those of full ordination—were available for both male and female. The entourage of the Buddha consisted of fully ordained monks and nuns and male and female lay practitioners. Wherever these four sections of the ordained and lay entourage were assembled, that place was said to be a "central region." Anywhere else was regarded as a peripheral region.

However, reflecting the gender inequality of ancient India, fully ordained monks and nuns and novice monks and nuns were subjected to unequal status, and the Buddha was said to have required fully ordained monks and novice monks to always go first and sit in front at any assembly. However, fundamentally he himself afforded them equal status.

With the bodhisattva vows and the tantric vows there is no division on the basis of gender and no difference in the number of vows to be taken. In the tantric vows especially, as well as there being no inequality in terms of gender, in the higher class of tantra, it is not only improper to look down on women, but to do so constitutes a breach of a root tantric vow. The same is not taught for looking down on a man. [437] Moreover, not physically circumambulating or not prostrating to a woman, or not visualizing oneself as doing so, is taught as a fault that contravenes the Vajra Vehicle discipline.

The deity Tara, from the time she generated bodhicitta until she became enlightened, remained in female form. She is the personification of the actions of every buddha and the most renowned of all the important goddesses. In deity assemblies and as the sources of instructions there are many of female form. Because of this, it is said that if a practitioner of tantra dreams of a woman, she is to be regarded as a dakini, and there are accounts and biographies where the words she speaks are recognized as prophecies. Most pure vision lineages are transmitted through dakinis and the custodians of teachings are mostly dakinis. There is also a tradition of referring to female practitioners as "dakinis." Offerings are made by offering goddesses; there are no "offering gods." The deities who actually confer empowerments are the four goddesses, and so on, as is clear in the empowerment manuals.

There are praises of women in *Life Stories of a Myriad Dakinis*, and in the prayers *Treasure House of the Four Joys* and *Magic Vajra Key*, all by the Fifth Lelung Jedrung (1697–1740), AKA Pema Zhepai Dorjé. Also, Ju Mipham composed (1) *Pleasing Smile of Sarasvati: A Brief Description of the Yoga of the Mudra of Bliss and Emptiness*, (2) *Hook to Attract the Heart*

Essence of the Host of Dakinis, (3) *Courier of the Four Joys: A Song to Recall the Queen of Passion,* [438] and (4) *A Dance to Move the Hearts of the Dakinis: A Great Bliss Whorl of Joy.*[272] In all of these he praises and venerates the qualities of women.

Therefore, it is not just that womankind holds an important position because of being placed in the category of wisdom,[273] even the common high regard of just the word "mother" is something that we do not see fit to expunge from our traditions and customs. For example, the person we recognize as our closest companion or relative is our mother, and that importance is represented in the phrase "all mother sentient beings." It is also used in common expressions such as "mother monastery" to refer to the central monastery, "the mother house" to refer to the main house, "mother department," "mother meaning," "mother base" (foundation), "mother money" (capital fund), "mother cost" (wholesale price), "mother scripture" (original manuscript), and so on. The custom of adding the word "mother" to words in order to emphasize their importance is evident everywhere.

Nevertheless, it is in dependence upon male and female together as equal partners that we have the external world and its inhabitants, and especially our human societies with their family networks, political systems, economies, religions, cultures, and so on. Everywhere we have to live in the reality of mutual dependence. Therefore, equality between men and women is fundamental. This is illustrated with examples such as man and woman, brother and sister, elder brother and elder sister, younger brother and younger sister, son and daughter, maternal and paternal aunts and uncles, husband and wife, male and female, king and queen, master and mistress, hero and heroine, warrior and warrioress, nobleman and noblewoman, layman and laywoman, novice monk and novice nun, fully ordained monk and fully ordained nun, and so on.

[439] However, some Buddhist scriptures seem to teach a difference

of status between men and women. The Buddha preached *The Sutra of Women Becoming Men*,[274] for example. In the Vinaya sutras, when explaining the eight faults to his disciple Ananda, the Buddha says,

> Do not request for women to be ordained and to become full monastics.

And further on,

> Although an entourage of women has not been accepted, you have interceded for Prajāpati[275] to become ordained. As a result, where the doctrine of the Buddha was to have lasted for five thousand and five hundred years, with women ordained, it will last for five hundred years fewer.[276]

Furthermore, the *Sutra Requested by the Householder Ugra* describes about sixty faults of women.[277] In the sutra tradition, *The Treasury of Abhidharma* states a definitive bodhisattva has to accumulate for a hundred eons the karma that will ripen into the major features of an enlightened being, and that the body required for such an accumulation, and the body of the enlightened being itself, has to be a male body. When enumerating the eight fruitions[278] it says, "Being a male," and "The focus of the prayer is to take the body of a male."

As mentioned above, in the monastic discipline sutras the Buddha did not differentiate between male and female on the issue of ordination. Therefore, the above statement that if men were ordained and thereby plant the roots of liberation it would benefit the duration of the doctrine, whereas if women, such as Prajāpati, were to be ordained and thereby plant the roots of liberation it would shorten the duration of the doctrine, is clearly contradictory if held as true. Moreover, the buddhas who show the deeds of the supreme incarnation would not have all four components of their entourage, and Śariputra and

Maudgalyāyana would not have been prophesized.[279] Moreover, the Buddha said that until his mother and father were placed into the realm of the truth, he would not reveal the deed of passing into nirvana. [440] Therefore, regardless of whether he was requested to do so by Ananda, the Buddha definitely ordained women over time. Furthermore, if the above were true, we would have to say that the Buddha working for the benefit of others and treating all equally like the sun would also shorten the life of the doctrine.

Therefore, it is not impossible that the above scriptural texts were tainted assertions influenced by the attitudes of society in those times. Without examination and analysis, merely on the basis of that scriptural text existing, it is not right to hold it as being literally true and to accept it.

Generally, in his discourses Buddha always says, "Son or daughter of the noble family..." thus addressing both male and female disciples. This also shows that our compassionate teacher does not discriminate between men and women. The habit of holding men to be superior and those partisan statements that express the same are completely at odds with the fundamental philosophy tenets of all Buddhist vehicles. Attachment and resentment may well produce a division of men as superior and women as inferior in the world of the householder, but in the Buddhist world, which strives to suppress attachment and resentment, holding men as superior to women is an internal contradiction.

Here I would like to say something on the related matter of the lineage of the vows of the fully ordained nun not being transmitted previously within the Tibetan tradition of Buddhism. In the eighth century the fully ordained Indian monk Śāntarakṣita ignored the hardships of old age and traveled to Tibet. According to Tibetan calculation he was ninety years old, and according to an Indian scholar he was seventy-five. In Tibet he disseminated the Sarvāstivādin Buddhist tradition of the vows of a fully ordained monk. [441] To receive the vows of a fully ordained nun in that tradition, both ordained monks and fully ordained nuns have to be present in the ceremonial rows, and at that time, only fully ordained monks were available. Therefore, a necessary prerequisite was absent, and the vows of a fully ordained nun could not be given.

Later on, there were some Tibetan lamas who bestowed the vows of a fully ordained nun. However, this gave rise to an argument on whether bestowing vows without the presence of fully ordained monks and fully ordained nuns was in accord with the strict practice of monastic discipline law. Therefore, in order to disseminate the vows that a fully ordained nun has to follow, a monastic discipline association would need to be formed, consisting of upholders of monastic law who follow the Pāli monastic tradition, such as Sri Lanka, Myanmar, Thailand, and Cambodia, and of those who follow the Sanskrit monastic tradition, such as China, Japan, Vietnam, Korea, and Tibet. This association should discuss and determine how to disseminate the lineage of the vows of a fully ordained nun in those countries where such a lineage is lacking. This is important.

As mentioned above, the tradition of vows that spread throughout Tibet was that of the Sarvāstivādin, although the Dharmaguptaka[280] tradition of vows was also present. After we arrived in India in 1959, gradually I had the opportunity to have discussions with other Buddhist traditions and especially those from China where the lineage of the vows of a fully ordained nun were still extant. I also consulted Buddhists from Vietnam and Korea, and it has now been more than thirty years since research began on the corpus of monastic discipline. I have heard that there are those in Sri Lanka who wish to disseminate the vows of a fully ordained nun, and through those I have met from Thailand, I have heard that the same wish exists there too.

[442] Therefore, I think this is a very important issue, and I would be overjoyed if there were a movement to implement the dissemination of the vows of a fully ordained nun within the Tibetan Buddhist

tradition. Still there is much research to do. In the eighth century Śān-taraksita and Kamalaśīla strove to ensure the sun of the dissemination of the vows rose when they initiated the bestowal of the vows of a fully ordained monk, and in this century we should search to see if there is a method of disseminating the vows of a fully ordained nun.

There are some who say that the Dalai Lama has the authority in this matter of disseminating the lineage of the vows. However, the monastic discipline code states that the monastic community should decide, not a single person. The authority I have is to urge and encourage research into this matter. Other than that, I have no power. It is the business of those upholders of the monastic law, I mentioned earlier, to discuss and decide.

A few Tibetan nuns have taken full ordination by way of the Chinese tradition. This has become a separate tradition, and so no one can find fault with it. I see this as something to be wished for.

In addition to the above, another cause for regarding men as superior to women is that when Buddhism spread to Tibet from India, Indian vocabulary came too. In its terminology men are termed "victorious by birth" and "elevated by birth," whereas terms used for women were degrading. These include "inferior by birth," "defeated by birth," "inconspicuous," "drawn downward," and so on. Many such words spread into our culture, and through this contamination the term "of beneficial birth" (skyes sman), which was used for women, was changed to "of inferior birth" (skye dman). Also, the word for young girl meaning "the flowering of benefit" (sman shar) was written as "inferior flowering" (dman shar).[281]

[443] In a similar fashion, our culture also came to be tainted by the caste system that divided people into a ruling caste, a Brahmin caste, a merchant caste, and a laboring or low caste, which reflected the attitudes of Indian non-Buddhists. This led to the practice of those who were considered to be low caste not being allowed in our temples that were regarded as sacred places of refuge. As a result, our women

were also regarded as inferior and not allowed in temples. There was this great pretense that they were not allowed to touch revered objects or statues of important protectors with their hands. If they did touch a protector statue, it was claimed, with great exaggeration, that this would cause a great hindrance that would somehow weaken the protector. This practice still exists today.

Referring to the wife whose husband has died by way of the derogatory term for widow (*yug sa ma*)[282] is pure superstition. There is no special terminology for a husband whose wife has died, nor is he looked down upon. How can that be right?

Having to sit in the back row because of being a woman, and so on, are bad traditions that have been allowed to become customs.

Since the advent of Buddhism in Tibet, nunneries have spread far and wide. Those existing today have the ability and the right to set up teaching and practice colleges, as monasteries do. However, there are some that only engage in chanting practices of offering and ritual, and do not set up proper teaching and practice colleges. Most nunneries do not have an abbess but appoint a monk as abbot and teacher. Such things are a result of not being given a proper education, and also of the nuns themselves having the habit of being too timid and not being confident. [444] However, that is not the only reason. It is also the attitude that it should be monks in charge of such matters, and the pressure, evident or not, of wanting to be in charge.

Furthermore, since the time of the spread of the old and new Kadampa traditions,[283] there has been a strong tradition of protecting the purity of the monastic code. As a result, connections with nuns and especially laywomen have naturally become distant. In practice, anthropologists have noticed that this has resulted in those women being held in low regard.

There have been a few eminent women from various Buddhist traditions who have been elevated to the ranks of pioneers of certain instruction lineages. These include Gelongma Palmo, Machik Drup-gyal, Machik Lapdrön, and Niguma. However, in other lineages, the names of preservers of the Buddha's doctrine are those of men, and for the most part, women do not appear at all. The fact that women possessed of learning and practice, perfectly capable of preserving the doctrine of teaching and practice, do not appear is suspicious. Is this not a distortion of the facts of history and the machinations of a society dominated by men?

The practice in the nunneries of nuns sometimes not wearing the attire of an ordained monastic is not just a local custom. It seems to stem from the instinctive belief that nuns cannot wear the upper and lower robes as worn by monks. The inferiority of the food, clothing, and general provisions found in nunneries to that of the monasteries can be understood by the number of devotees making donations and the number of estates offered. [445] This is also illustrated by the pathetic saying "If a boy becomes a monk, he will be a master. If a girl becomes a nun, she will be a servant."

Generally, Tibetan women, unlike some other societies, have never had to live totally under the domination of men or have been prevented from studying, and thus enjoy the rights and status of not suffering those hardships. However, about ninety percent of women have not received an education, and so very few are learned in Buddhism and the sciences. Moreover, in keeping with the cultural characteristics of ancient times, many writings on the history of Tibet fail to record the achievements of women. In compositions such as Nāgārjuna's *Letter to a Friend* there are many degrading verses about women, and *Engaging in Bodhisattva Deeds* says, "May all women be reborn as men." Many such prayers exist. Following these, the *Maṇikabüm*[284] lists twenty-seven faults of women. Also, the Bön work *Stainless Wonder*,[285] and works such as *The Chronicle of Queens*,[286] *The Blue Volume*,[287] *The Biography of Marpa*, *The Biography of Thangtong Gyalpo*, *The Songs of Trulshik Padma Düdul*, various confession rituals, and others all speak of the five faults of women.[288] Many works in the Kangyur and Tengyur list the faults of women, stating that they have no good qualities. Despite the fact that men and women are equal in possessing a wonderful human form, such quotes that proclaim the faults of women can produce bad imprints of thinking that women are inferior to men.

In order to reduce desire and attachment, monks and nuns have to think about various unclean features of each other's bodies. [446] Because of this, it is taught that men and women are equally composed of the thirty-six unclean substances of blood, bones, skin, and so on. Therefore, having expressed the faults of women it is only right that the faults of men should follow. However, this is not the case, as citations below will attest.

Those passages that express only the faults of women, with men seemingly faultless, are clearly the result of the proliferation of tainted customs and non-Buddhist religious practices that were widespread outside of Tibet. The Amdo scholar Gendün Chöphel says,

> Similarly, "Widows are unclean and therefore,
> even food they make, you should not eat,"
> thus, some sacred commitments do explain,
> but these are the words of heartless Brahmins.
>
> In olden times, in India, when their husband died,
> the wife would throw herself onto the pyre.
> If she could not, she would live, but be considered a corpse.
> A widow was just a source of uncleanliness.
>
> Common to all, the body inside is unclean,
> while outside is the covering of skin.
> Dividing humans into clean and unclean
> is ultimately the Hindu religion.[289]

Also, in *Grains of Gold*, he says,

Likewise, the all-knowing Butön was the greatest treasury of tantras, but when one looks at his *Wheel of Abuse to the Demoness*, it seems as if he was not concerned about the root infractions of the tantric vows. I don't know if an exception is made for being abusive in verse. Many vajra holders endowed with the three vows uttered very abusive words about women.[290]

In the codes listed in *Mirror Illuminating the Royal Genealogies*[291] it states, "In discussion, do not listen to the words of women, and stand your ground."[292] It goes on to say that women are without shame and conscience, and therefore cannot be relied upon to swear an oath.

[447] In the *Thirteen Laws*,[293] in the section on resolving separation in families, it states,

When husband and wife separate, even though she is in the right, the wife must bear the greater fault. Moreover, though the woman is more in the right, because the husband bears the name of being in the right, it should not be given to the woman.[294]

From a legal document unearthed at Dunhuang[295] on the rights of women, it is clear that women enjoyed rights, unlike the picture portrayed in legal documents of the later propagation of Buddhism. Therefore, as evidenced in many documents, there are reasons to believe that these were later altered.

In the biography of Yeshé Tsogyal[296] written by Taksham Nuden Dorjé, Yeshé Tsogyal says,

Women, such as I, are weak and of little power.
Of lower birth, we are despised by all.

When we go begging, we are attacked by dogs.
If we have food and drink, thieves are a threat.

If we are beautiful, the lecherous come for us.
When busy, the people despise us.
When we do nothing, we are slandered by gossip.
When we do something wrong, everyone despises us.
Whatever we do, it is not easy.

For a woman abiding in this form,
how can they sustain themselves within the Dharma?
We cannot even sustain ourselves in life.[297]

These verses illustrate the status of women. Also, there are many sad folk operas that do the same, such as that of Nangsa Öbüm,[298] who was helplessly beaten to death in her husband's house, and of Drukmo,[299] who was kidnapped against her will.

There are also folk sayings: "If a boy grinds his teeth when asleep, he is attended by the warrior spirits. If a girl grinds her teeth when asleep, she is a demoness." "If a boy has a mole on his face, he is a conqueror of enemies. If a girl has a mole on his face, she is a cannibal." "Among a hundred men, one will be a demon. Among a hundred women, one will be a dakini." "If a woman is made head of the household, it is a bad omen." "Before the man utters a word, the woman speaks." "A woman does not have a profound mind." "Do not trust dogs and women." [448] "Roads and women are of common ownership." "There is no reliability with women and clouds." "Women and drums are to be beaten." These and others can be found in the written and oral tradition.[300]

These attitudes of wrongly conceiving women generally to be of lower form of birth and of lesser merit have been prevalent for a long time. This has to be rectified. In recent times the study of the classical texts was introduced into nunneries in exile, and now we have been able to establish the worthy practice of awarding the title of geshé-ma[301] to those who have completed their studies.

In this way, through a practical altruism that does not discriminate against anyone, it is important to be of benefit to the world at large and to be in accord with Buddhism. Understanding how to be a good example for all people of today's world is the responsibility of all monks and nuns, laymen and laywomen.

Also, Tibetan men lack the sensitivity of understanding the hardships and position of women, and thus have little interest in their situation, and in daily life these things are ignored. There is no reflection on whether such attitudes are acceptable or not and they just adhere to the idea of the situation being what it is. Moreover, they ridicule and pay little attention to the arguments for women's rights and status. Also, women themselves do not stand up to these things. Therefore, it is possible that this matter can appear as unimportant. However, the reality is that this is something significant that has been created by the instincts of having a negative attitude toward women, and that the happiness and welfare of men and women are not treated equally. In that sense, this is a problem created by both men and women. [449] Therefore, both sides should confront it and "men should work for women, and women should work for men," as the saying goes.

Therefore, through education, both men and women should understand the equal value of all human beings and recognize the hardships of women as being hardships. We need to create an environment where whenever there is a hardship there is a place for it to be discussed and listeners to hear it.

This position is not coming from an attitude that thinks women are helpless and need support. It is an acceptance that women have capabilities on a par with men, and in order to bring that to the fore, the situation of women should be discussed. This should not be seen as arguing the rights of individual women. The loss born by one woman is to the detriment of all women. Therefore, it should be recognized as a struggle of society. We need to raise our level of thinking to be able to carry the responsibility of confronting it and see it as a service to our society.

Instances of inequality in terms of enjoyments and benefits between men and women should not be hidden away but be brought into discussions within our society as a way of bringing out the truth, so that we reach an understanding that can change our society for the better. Without living in our society with a narrow frog-like perception, we should look for examples in countries far and wide.

Take the crime of rape for example. In old Tibet and in some Tibetan settlements in India these days it is only regarded as a disgrace, shame, and degradation of the woman. Beset by the worry of finding her future husband, the parents will seek a way to give her away as a bride quietly and hurriedly, while the rapist can freely hold his head up high and go his own way. [450] This must change and be rectified.

For women too they should never meekly accept putting up with the wretched attitude of taking the blame unfairly on themselves and carrying the ingrained habit of seeing themselves as inferior, thereby breaking their own backs.

GREAT WOMEN OF TIBETAN HISTORY AND LITERATURE

In our and many other countries the attitude and practice of holding men to be superior has prevailed for a long time with the result that in society there has been a lack of gender equality in varying degrees. However, as everyone knows, in Yungdrung Bön and the noble religion of Śākyamuni Buddha the importance of practicing love and compassion equally toward all sentient beings without discrimination is particularly emphasized. Therefore, in these religious practices the notion that men and women have equal rights in wanting happiness and not wanting suffering is a basic tenet, while malign states of mind that arise from societal concepts that discriminate into superior, inferior, and middling and into friend, enemy, stranger are to be disciplined and tamed. This is the fundamental practice of these religions.

However, in practice, the Tibetan religious and cultural historical writings contain many biographies of great men, whereas those of great women are rare. [451] Today's generation are discussing this and are wondering if there were any female scholars and practitioners in Tibet's past who can be said to have accomplished great things for the teachings. There were indeed renowned Tibetan women whose legacy was one of preserving, protecting, and disseminating the teachings of the Buddha by teaching and practice. They came from all walks of life and included nuns, yoginis, tulkus, consorts, queens, and princesses, as well as wealthy and poor householders. There were so many women who, by cultivating their innate capabilities, made contributions for the sake of the conservation and development of Tibet's people, of its politics, economy, culture, and religion, and demonstrated genuine human values that were on a par with the great men of their time.

However, these days most of their stories are like water that has soaked into the sand, and to find them we have to rely upon incidental mentions occurring in religious histories, biographies, royal genealogies, lineages, family genealogies, past-life narratives, stories, and so on. This is a weakness and a fault in the chronicling of our history.

The book *Stories of Tibetan Women* by Drigung Resa Könchok Gyatso, a teacher also known as Dawa Döndrup, documents the stories of one hundred and twenty-five remarkable women, from the time of the early Tibetan emperors up to the twentieth century, who preserved, protected, and disseminated the Bön and Buddhist traditions through their teaching and practice. The book also includes mentions of many other women, all set out according to the period in which they were born, together with brief biographies. Also described are the great

Tibetan female incarnations. These include the twelve incarnations of Samding Dorjé Pakmo and the six incarnations of Gungri Khandroma.

[452] There must be other yoginis who remain unknown and great women who were not written about. However, it is my hope that for the time being, the examples of those great Tibetan women whose achievements for the teachings and living beings have actually been recorded, and recollecting their wonderful deeds, will enlighten those who doubt that there were any renowned Tibetan women in the past and will go some way to restoring the faulty presentation of our history.

Today there are great women to be found among all the religious traditions of Buddhist and Bön Tibet. Also, many women from across the world have developed faith in the teachings of the Buddha, engaged in practice, and by teaching and accomplishment are working hard to preserve, protect, and disseminate the teachings. These too are great women worthy of praise.

Excerpts from *Stories of Tibetan Women*

The period before the advent of the first Tibetan king, Nyatri Tsenpo (127 BCE), and long after the advent of primitive societies, is known as the time of the twelve rulers or the time of the twelve independent kingdoms. Many people believed that these twelve rulers were not human beings but types of spirits, but we might say that such belief is a religious imputation. The reality is that, like the thirteen gods of the emperors' songs [302] and the twenty-one laymen, they were simply renowned human beings of those times. Also, those beings who were later on regarded as being guardian spirits—such as local protectors, Dharma protectors, and so on—were in all likelihood our ancient ancestors. [453] By identifying them as powerful protectors they were imputed as nonhuman and were regarded as regional spirit lords, earth spirit lords, and so on. Thus, a tradition of worship began. For example, in the province of Amdo are found Amnye Machen,

Amnye Dungring, Amnye Bayan, Amnye Shawo, Amnye Lumo, and Ama Zorgu.[303] Being called "Amnye" (grandfather) and Ama (mother) we can understand as ancestral reverence.

Likewise, Dargyal Mangpo Jé in Gengya, Amdo, was a minister of Emperor Songtsen Gampo and passed away in that place. Lonpo Serchen Ri is so called because Minister (Lonpo) Gar passed away there.[304] Similarly, Lingjé Gesar, Gyatsa, Gadé, Nyibüm, Denma, and Trothüng,[305] who arose in later times, are revered as deities. Furthermore, the class of spirits known as "died human, reborn as powerful spirits," who were tamed and bound by oath to become worldly protectors, with the localities they inhabited becoming places of worship, is religious contamination, of which there are many examples.

WOMEN IN EARLY TIMES

The history of primitive societies up to the present time is researched by modern generations primarily by way of inference. The same applies to the history of Tibet. Tai Situ Jangchup Gyaltsen's *The Single Volume of Lang*[306] states,

> Generally, if human beings are unaware of their ancestry, they are like monkeys in the forest. If they are unaware of their family line, they are like the deceitful dragon.[307]

"Family line" refers to relatives from the maternal line. This shows that in Tibet, the maternal line was originally regarded as the more important. Also, the family names of the seven kings,[308] who appeared later, were derived from their mothers' names. When the eighth king, Drigum Tsenpo, was born, it was the tradition to request the grandmother for a name.

[454] As time progressed the power of women was vanquished and men began to dominate, so that by the time of the thirty-third king,

Songtsen Gampo, all female power had vanished. A decree states, "Queens are not to be included in discussions." *The Chronicle of Queens* states,

> From the time of Nyatri Tsenpo
> to the "three Dé of the lower regions"[309]
> there were seventy-five queens.

However, no records of these queens or their names are to be seen. They are far less visible than previous queens that appeared in written records.

In *How the Gods Were Divided*,[310] which is one the earliest Tibetan documents, as well as in *The Single Volume of Lang* and Ngawang Kunga Sonam's *The Sakya Lineage*, the names of many women are listed, but they are described as being the daughters of gods or nāgas. However, the reality is that these women belonged to clans and family lines of those times. They had elegant names and were found in good households in their communities. Therefore, in all probability they were renowned women of their time. However, they are not listed in the histories predating Nyatri Tsenpo, and not even in those up to the time of Songtsen Gampo. Therefore, this is something to be examined through ancient materials.

THE PURGYAL PERIOD[311]

From the time of the seven heavenly kings up to the period of the emperors, the names and details of many queens appear in old documents. During those times there appeared a group of twelve renowned women who were later identified as the Twelve Earth Goddesses.[312] The status of their race, their family line, their measure of power, and so on, as well as their domains, are briefly described. Also described is, for example, Jomo Tashi Tseringma, who was a famous woman of the Tö region of Tibet. Her father was Pholha Thenpo and her mother was Drangyul Men. They had seven sons and five daughters. [455] The other four daughters were Miyo Lang Sangma, Tekar Dro Sangma, Thingi Shal Sangma, and Chöpen Dring Sangma.[313] It is clear that these names are not their original names but were given later by religious traditions.

The above women are described in different ways, and their body colors and hand implements also vary. This has arisen from the ways religious traditions view them. They can also be understood as being renowned Tibetan women of that time from the way later generations revere them as deities. The twelve grandmothers, the twelve female protectors, and so on that have become local deities and earth goddesses throughout Tibet may have started out as renowned women in various locations who came to be regarded as deities in order to recall their great achievements. This can also be understood if you examine the names of mountains, rivers, and so forth, such as Jomo Langma, Namtso Chukmo, Trishor Gyalmo, Jomo Kharak, Jomo Gyalsang, Phakri Jomo, Jomo Nang, Jomo Gangkar, Repgong Tsenmo Ri, Gyalmo Mudo, Ama Druktso, and Jomo Dzong.

THE PERIOD OF THE EMPERORS

Tshepong Sadrima Thökarma was the mother of Songtsen Gampo. Together with the five queens of Songtsen Gampo; his sister, Tsenmo Sema Kar; and thirty-one other women, she did much for the unity of Tibet, helping to consolidate the rule, initiate the union of state and religion, and disseminate Buddhism.

Drosa Trima Lö[314] was the queen of Emperor Mangsong Mangtsen (653–76) and the mother of Emperor Dusong Mangpo Jé. When her husband died, their son was too young to rule and so she took up the reins of the kingdom, not once but twice.[315] [456] In the royal dynasty of Tibet she is the only recognized empress and is famed for being wise, brave, powerful, and open-minded. As her power grew, the might of Tibet threatened the eastern plains of China. Consequently, the minor kingdoms of Serab, and so on, rose up in revolt, but she waged war against them, brought them under the rule of law, and captured their kings. With this and other deeds she consolidated the strength of the kingdom and contributed greatly to the security of Tibet.

Drosa Trigyalmo Tsen was one of the five wives of Emperor Tri Songdetsen. Her achievements include constructing the Gegye Jema Temple at Samyé Monastery—one of the three queen temples. Also, at Samyé she took on the responsibility of translating Buddhist works, and engaged in study and meditation. With her great wisdom in the administration of the kingdom she initiated a set of laws known as the "Son of Drosa."

Having no children, she was among the hundred women, such as Dru Tsunmo Gyal, who became novice nuns under the preceptor Barana.[316] Her ordained name was Jangchup Jé. She was the first woman in Tibet to be ordained as a nun. She introduced religious laws, and a prayer she composed can be found in the Tengyur.

Chimsa Lhamo Tsen was a queen of Tri Songdetsen. She was offered as a wife to Ācarya Padmasambhava and thus it seems she left no legacy of accomplishments in the secular field.

Kharchensa Tsogyal was also one of Tri Songdetsen's queens offered as a wife to Ācarya Padmasambhava. She applied herself to practice and became known as Khandro Yeshé Tsogyal, one of the most famous women of Tibet. She is the source of the Jomo tradition of Vajrakilaya practice, and having listened to treasure teachings from the Ācarya, she wrote them down and hid them in various places. Her birthplace and parents' names have been variously described.

[457] It is clear from various documents that in addition to the above Chimsa Lhamo Tsen and Tsogyal, the Ācarya had other wives, such as Shelkar Dorjé Tsho the secret queen, Drosa Tipangma, Rungyongsa Mathingma, Chim Rinchen Salé Ö, Marmé Gongsa Rinchen Tsuk, Mönmo Tashi Khyedren, and so on.[317] Although it is uncertain how many more are indicated by the phrase "and so on," it is clear from later entries that Chokrosa Palkyi Chönéma and Dro Jomosa Salé are also included in the list of wives.[318]

According to *Guru Tashi's Religious History*, Drosa Tipangma was among the main consorts of Ācarya Padmasambhava, while Mergongsa[319] and others were included in a list of seventeen yoginis. So there might be some doubt as to whether they were actually wives of the Ācarya. Nevertheless, they are all definitely Tibetan women with great accomplishments in the religious field. The Vajrakilaya teachings arose from Chokrosa Palkyi Chönéma, Dro Jomosa Salé, and Yeshé Tsogyal, and this tradition is known as the Jomo tradition and Cham (or "Wife") tradition.

Bönmo Takber Leber was the mistress of Shendrenpa Namkha, and the wonderful qualities, such as clairvoyance and magical powers, found in Bön were among her capabilities. This is described in Sharza Tashi Gyaltsen's *The History of Bön: A Treasury of Explanation.*

Chokrosa Palkyi Ngangtsulma was one of the five queens of Emperor Trisuk Detsen (otherwise known as Ralpachen). Documents record the others as Chimsa Khyung Karma, Nanamsa Ajé Pholak, Tshepongsa Lhungyibumo or Tshepongsa Yumjé Tsenmo Phen, and Lhalungsa Metokma.

This queen constructed the Tsanthang Yu Temple near the region of Yarlung Sheldrak. [458] She had great respect for Buddhism, and she was of great service in her support for the emperor in his rule of the kingdom. As a result, the power of the emperor was turned to

Buddhism and the numbers of practitioners increased like the rising sun. Religious provisions were made available from the storehouses and each monk was offered seven servant households. The military might of the country waned and lands previously seized from China were lost. The people became impoverished, and when the emperor's ministers were unable to destroy his religious rule it became inevitable that with the border regions lost, the country would collapse in the center.[320] The emperor's enemies saw that sullying the excellent qualities of this great queen and of Minister Denka would overcome the emperor and so reverse his adoption of Buddhism. They therefore slandered the queen and Denka by spreading the rumor that they had a sexual affair. When they were sentenced to death, the queen committed suicide, the emperor was murdered, and Langdarma (r. 836–42) seized control.

THE PERIOD OF DISSOLUTION[321]

Drigung Achi Chödrön (b. 1020) was born in Drigung Shotö to father Jowo Pal of Nanam and mother Darjam of Dri. She was given the name Chökyi Drönma (in some sources her name is Drölma). Because she was the ancestor of Drigung Kyobpa Jikten Gönpo (1143–1217) she was later called Achi ("grandmother"). At the age of twenty she traveled to Kham with traders from Lapa. When they reached Denyul she said to the traders, "This is my place."

She went to the home of brothers Tsultrim Gyatso and Yungdrung Gyatso of the Kyura family and became their mutual wife. At the wedding feast she magically showered the guests with whatever food and drink they desired, and the local people said that Tsultrim Gyatso was keeping a dakini as a wife.

She made a home at Tara Rock in Upper Den and had four sons: Namkha Wangchuk, Peka Wangyal, Sönam Pal, and Kathung Drupshi. [459] Chökyi Drönma liked to use the corpses in the cemetery for ritual feasts[322] and could travel through cliffs without obstruction. Such feats brought her great fame. Mother and the four sons all meditated, and the sons gained great realizations. She bound by oath the eight malicious classes of spirits and led her followers inside a deep cave by Pamé River where she performed a feast ritual using corpses. It is said that various powers arose in those who partook. Even today, this cave is known as Achi's Cave.

Finally, in her testament she wrote, "This body of mine has done its work. To my sons is bequeathed a special teaching. Therefore, I will become its protector. If it is important, summon me!"

It is said that without abandoning her body she left for the land of the dakinis. Later she was revered as a protector by the Drigung Kagyu sect and the Kyura clan. She is said to be a wisdom dakini.

Majo Könchok Kyab was born in Tö and was a disciple of Drokmi Lotsāwa (993–1064). She came to Jonang and her achievement was of devoting her whole life to practice. This is recorded in Ngawang Lodrö Drakpa's *Jonang Religious History.*

Dakméma was born in Lhodrak and was the main consort of Jé Marpa, who had nine other wives, including Selkyi, Jomo Chebu, Lungzé Horé, Nyemo Sangmo, and Chakthungma. She gave birth to a son, Darma Dodé, and also gave teachings to Jetsun Milarepa.

Marpa's other wives were also endowed with great religious accomplishments. [460] Together they bore seven sons: Darma Dodé, Darma Pal, Samten, Bachen Sangé, Ngen, Gendun, and Jathri Khorlo. Other sources list nine sons: Darma Dodé, Gendun, Chöpel, Marlep, Palkyi Ö, Draksö, Sönam Pal, Namkha Pal, and Nyima Pal. This is stated in Tsewang Gyal's *Lhorong Religious History.*

Nyima Palmo (1012–95) was born in Phenyul. She devoted herself to Marpa Lotsāwa, receiving all his teachings and putting them into practice. As a result, her biography states, "Nyima Palmo of Phenyul was one of the four fortunate female disciples who attained powers."

Peta Gönkyi was the younger sister by three years of Jetsun Milarepa. When she met Milarepa in Drindrak Mar, years after he had gone to the mountains to meditate, he encouraged her to practice the Dharma. With great faith she entered the religious life and received the complete teachings of the Kagyu tradition. She engaged in practice with great austerity and attained the rainbow body before Jetsun Milarepa passed away. This is described in *Lhorong Religious History*.

Dzesema, or **Leksé Büm**, was born in Gungthang in Upper Ngari. Among the human and nonhuman consorts of Jetsun Milarepa, she was a human who was betrothed to Milarepa in childhood. Later, when the Jetsun was residing in Drin, she received teachings from him and entered a retreat hermitage where she attained the rainbow body. This is described in *Drigung Treasury Biography of Milarepa*. In Tsangnyön Heruka's *Biography of Milarepa*, Dzesema and Leksé Büm are described as different women.

Salé Ö was born in Drin in Tö. She met Milarepa when he came to Nya. Developing great faith in him she requested teachings. She became proficient in producing spontaneous Dharma songs. Her poetry and composition were not only outwardly remarkable, but with respect to its meaning she seems to be someone of great learning.

[461] Having received complete instructions she entered practice and developed qualities of realization such as signs of the blazing of the inner heat. She remained constantly by the side of the Jetsun, being the keeper of his texts and serving as his consort. She was given the name Ngakyé Lhenkyé Drönma, which means "Mantra Born Innate Lamp." She was prophesized to become a great tamer of nonhuman spirits, and ultimately attained the rainbow body.

Rechungma was born in Chokro on the Dri border and met Jetsun Milarepa while he was staying there. At first, she tested him by singing to him a somewhat teasing song. From his reply she developed faith. She offered him all her jewelry and followed him as a servant. At Lotö Monastery in Drin he gave her instructions on inner heat practice. After three days inner heat arose and she only needed a thin cloth for her clothing, after which she became known as Rechungma.

After seven months she had received all teachings on the six yogas of Naropa and developed special realizations. Later she met Rechungpa on Yarlung cliffs. She offered him details of her insights and he saw that she was a suitable vessel. He gave her the oral transmission instructions and she became his wife. She was one of the realized consorts of Rechungpa, alongside Lhachik Yarlungma Dembu and Jomo Yangmo.

For eight years she ceased speaking, meditating continuously like the current of a river and attained the ten signs of practice and the eight qualities. She too attained the rainbow body.

Naro Böncham was born in Ngari Shangshung. She entered the Bön faith and taught its tenets to her brother, Naro Bönchung. Later, Bönchung and Milarepa had a contest of magical powers. Milarepa defeated Bönchung and Tisé, as Mount Kailash is known, fell to the Kagyu sect. At that time Naro Böncham was many times greater in magic and power than her brother, and Jetsun Milarepa realized it would be difficult to beat her in a contest of powers. Therefore, he appealed to her by gentle means and was able to convert her. [462] Because she did not help Bönchung, Tisé was given over to the Buddhists.

Jomo Jocham Yulkyi was born in Nya in Tö. Jetsun Milarepa and Jomo were lama and disciple to each other. *The Biography of Mila: A Lamp of Sunlight and Moonlight*, composed by Shijé Ripa, states:

Incarnations that Mila received teachings from: Jomo Jocham Yulkyi of Phadruk, Jomo Dronmé of Drik, Yonchukma Lekyé, Yonchukma Khujuk, Yonchukma Ormo, Goma Gyatso Dren,

Machik Shama Lhajé, Shemo Gyacham Rema, Gakmo Rema, Sormo Lekyé, Lhacham Ödé Rema, Dzangmo Kyidren Rema, Gemo Chamtsun Rema, and Jomo Yangchung Rema. These were pure vision Dharma sisters.

Nangsa Öbüm (eleventh century) was born in Pé Valley in Nenying, which was in Nyangtö in the region of Tsang. She became the bride of the Rinang governor and gave birth to a son. However, the governor's sister, Ané Nyimo, feared that she would lose her authority to Nangsa and made false accusations against her. Not realizing this, the governor beat Nangsa until she died. However, she returned to life, and I think she was the first "death returner"[323] recorded in Tibetan history.

She fled to Sedrak Yalung, where she received Dzokchen and other teachings from Lama Śākya Gyaltsen and retreated into meditation. The source of water she used in practice and imprints of her body in the cave rocks can still be seen today. She ultimately attained the rainbow body.

The story of her returning from death spread throughout Tibet and later was included in the repertoire of Tibetan folk operas.[324]

Ané Nyimo was not a nun but was called "Ané" because of being part of the governor's family.[325]

[463] **Tömo Dorjé Tso, Dregom Sangmo Köné, Shapamo Chamchik,** and **Changmo Namkhama** were four great yoginis mentioned in Gö Lotsāwa's *Blue Annals* (p. 208) and *Biography of Lama Phak Ö.*

Jomo Jemo was born in Gungthang in Mangyul. She entered the religious life and practiced constantly, becoming renowned for her attainment of powers. She renounced this life and lived in a mountain hermitage where she lived to the age of one hundred and one. This is recounted in the *Blue Annals.*

Machik Shama, or **Shama Lhajé**, (1062–1149) trained in the tantras and many tantric practice texts received from Ma Lotsāwa, to whom she became consort. In accordance with his instructions, she went into retreat for four years, where she overcame all hindrances. When she was residing in Upper and Lower Dzong for four months at a time, she was able to hold down the red and white elements within her body. She attained qualities such as knowing how to manifest her body wherever she wished and could bring the inner winds to wherever she desired.

At the age of twenty-eight Ma Lotsāwa passed away and she performed extensive funeral rituals for him. Then, for three years, she was afflicted by seven kinds of hindrance and nothing she did could dispel them. Therefore, she went to Dingri to meet Phadampa Sangyé (d. 1117) and by following his instructions was able to rid herself of the hindrances.[326]

Because of her attainment of powers, she visited the twenty-four regions and many frightening places in Tibet, where she dwelt and meditated. Many astonishing events occurred around her, such as dakinis coming to wait upon her. Consequently, her fame spread far and wide.

In some texts she is called Shama Lhajé ("doctor"). Therefore it seems she must have been learned in medicine.

Her many students include Jé Pakmo Drupa (1110–70). She passed away at the age of eighty-eight. A full biography of her exists.

[464] **Machik Labdrön** (1149–1201)[327] was born in Drongmoché in Elab in Lhokha to mother Bümcham and father Chökyi Dawa. At the age of eight not only would she recite the *Perfection of Wisdom Sutra in Eight Thousand Verses* twice every day, but she also comprehended its meaning, and thus she became known as one of great wisdom. She was learned in the extensive, middling, and abridged perfection of

wisdom sutras and in all their commentaries. Therefore, at the age of sixteen Drapa Ngonshé (1012–90) appointed her for four years as his officiating assistant.[328] She also became his consort.

Although she had not taken monastic vows, she was included in the ranks of the nuns and everyone had had great faith and respect for her.

She devoted herself to many scholar-practitioners, such as Kyotön Sönam Lama, the Shamarpa, Betön, Yarthingwa, and Phadampa Sangyé, from whom she received teachings on Shijé, Dzokchen, Mahāmudrā, and so on. Through practice and meditation on these teachings she became a great yogini.

At the age of twenty-three she was betrothed to Thöpa Bhadra and went to live in Kongpo and Central Tibet. She gave birth to two sons, Drupa and Drupchen, and to a daughter, Labdü Dorjé. After Thöpa Bhadra passed away, she encountered many hardships such as having to support herself and children by reciting scriptures.

From the age of thirty-four it is not clear where she lived and practiced, but eventually she practiced in Sangri Khangmar and elsewhere. She gathered many students to whom she taught Mahāmudrā Chö, whose essential meaning is that of the perfection of wisdom sutras. She also taught the practice of "transforming the body into food," which gave rise to the well-known tradition of "scattering the body for the birds," popularly known as "sky burial."[329]

There are two traditions of Chö[330] in Tibet, known as male Chö and female Chö. The latter is the tradition of Machik Labdrön. This tradition has become the largest to have pervaded all the philosophical sects in Tibet and has achieved the worthy result of raising the status of women in Tibetan society.

[465] Her ten Chö compositions include *The Great Exposition*, *The Further Exposition*, *The Essential Exposition*, *Supplements*, *Stages of Crucial Points*, *Refutation of Opponents*, *Secret Signs*, *Three Collections on Recitation*, *Taking the Basis as the Path*, and *Special Core Instructions*.

There are different assertions concerning the date of her passing.

Chukmosa Gendun Kyi was born in Latö. She met Phadampa Sangyé and, having received blessing from him, she became a self-liberated yogini. She expressed her insights in song:

> There is the wish-fulfilling jewel of one's own mind
> and the wish-fulfilling jewel of the ocean
> to accomplish the needs of this and future lives.
> This beggar woman chooses the jewel of the mind itself.

> As provisions for death, the harvest of the two accumulations.
> As provisions for life, the harvest of wealth and possessions.
> The wise woman attends to her wealth.
> This beggar woman makes ready the provisions for death.

> Death is the enemy of the body,
> the five poisons, the enemy of the mind.
> There is inner and outer bravery;
> this beggar woman subdues the enemies of the five poisons.

> There is the fortress, stronghold of the proud and famous,
> and unmoving concentration, stronghold of the mind.
> Both will guard the turret of fearlessness.
> This beggar woman guards the turret of concentration.[331]

Majo Dargom, Jomo Kyurmo Jangchup Drön, Jomo Dütsi Kyi, Jomo Rongchungma, Goma Jangchup Ö, and others were close disciples of Phadampa Sangyé, who attained nonhuman powers. This is related in Khachö Gyepa Dorjé's *Biography of Dampa Sangyé: A Sun that Blazes with the Rays of a Thousand Siddhis*. Kongtrul Yonten Gyatso's *Treasury of Knowledge* lists four disciples of Dampa Sangyé: **Goktsa Gyen, Palden Gyen, Sönam Gyen,** and **Rinchen Gyen**. [466] There are various ways of explaining the term "Jomo." In the uplands of Tibet, it refers to a lama or the wife of a high-ranking official. In the lowlands it refers to monastic nuns. Moreover, in the past "Jowo" was the honorific term for a son and "Jomo" for a daughter. "The twenty-four Majo,"[332] who were realized disciples of Phadampa Sangyé, are often mentioned in texts. They are as follows:[333]

1. **Majo Sangyéma** was born in Śrī Chusang in Latö Gyal. In 1100 she came to Langkhor in Dingri, where she met Phadampa Sangyé and received instructions in Shijé practice. She meditated for nine years in her own native place[334] and developed realization. When she passed away, the cremation area was filled with rainbow light. She was the first of the twenty-four nuns to be cared for by Phadampa and his foremost disciple, Kunga (1062–1124).

2. **Majo Sertsunma** was born in Latö Phadruk. She learned Shijé practice from Phadampa and lived to be a hundred.

3. **Jomo Lenchungma** was born in Latö Takdé and learned Shijé practice from Phadampa. After the master passed away, she devoted herself to his disciple Kunga, from whom she received a one-to-one transmission. She meditated, gained powers, and lived to be eighty-one.

4. **Jomo Barma** was born in Nyangtö in Tsang. She was the wife of the Lama Dampa Chuk, a disciple of Phadampa Sangyé. She traveled with him to Dingri where she met Phadampa. Having received Shijé teachings from him she lived for three years in the mountains like a deer, immersing herself in meditation.

5. **Jomo Rima** was born in Tsangrong. She learned Shijé practice from Phadampa for seven years and put her efforts into meditation. When she passed away, Phadampa made many circumambulations of the cremation site, much to the amazement of his disciples.

6. **Jomo Yeshé Cham** was born in Gungtang in Mangyul and became attendant to the siddha Jomo Jemo, described above. She was very skilled in making offerings to the Guru. As soon as she heard the name of Phadampa Sangyé, great faith arose in her. She met him and received teachings on Shijé. Meditating on them, insights were born in her.

7. **Jomo Chödrön** was born in Dokpa in Latö. In her youth she married Phadampa's disciple, the bodhisattva Kunga. [467] She received Shijé teachings from Phadampa and put them into practice.

8. **Jomo Chema** was born in Manga in Latö. She met Phadampa when she was young. She received Shijé teachings from him, meditated on them, and developed realizations. After Phadampa passed away, she attended upon the bodhisattva Kunga. She received many core instructions from him and developed siddhis. Later she became a wife of Kunga.

9. **Jomo Chökyab** was born in Khulé in Nyangtö. Although she was of a wealthy family, she was not attached to wealth, and traveled to Dingri Langkhor to meet Phadampa and his disciple Kunga. She received teachings on the Shijé cycle. She practiced for twelve years, subsisting only on the bare necessities, and gained realizations.

10. **Jomo Chökyi** was born in Khowalé in Yardrok. From an early age she was a housewife, and although she had children and wealth, she reversed any attachment to this life and went to Latö Dingri. She met Phadampa and his disciple and developed unshakeable faith in them. Having received all Shijé teachings and core instructions, she devoted herself to practice.

11. **Jomo Gurmo** was born in Śrī Chusang in Latö. From an early age she had great religious faith. Devoting herself to Phadampa and his

disciple she received many teachings on Shijé. For ten years she practiced in Langkhor.

12. **Jomo Lhamo** was born in Rima in Tölung. When she was young, she
traveled to Dingri and attended upon Phadampa. She devoted herself
to receiving and practicing the Shijé teachings and stayed in Langkhor
for six years. In 1117 she returned to Tölung and devoted herself to
practice for three years. She returned to Dingri, where she attended
upon the bodhisattva Kunga. Having received many teachings on Shijé
from him, she concentrated solely on practice and remained there for
a long time.

13. **Jomo Nyangmo** was born in Tsarong in Nyangmé Shab. She had
great faith from an early age, and through merely hearing the name
of Phadampa and his disciple she felt great devotion and traveled to
Dingri. [468] Having met Phadampa and his disciple she requested
teachings on the Shijé cycle. She remained in Langkhor, practicing for
ten years and developing realizations.

14. **Jomo Wangchuk Cham** was born in Tökhung in Tölung. From an
early age she had a pure perception of the Dharma and traveled to
pilgrimage places in Nepal and elsewhere. On the way home she went
to Dingri and attended upon Phadampa and his disciple. She studied
Shijé and philosophical views. She practiced for eleven years, remaining in Langkhor, where she passed away.

15. **Jomo Dorjé Gyen** was born in Dongwa in Dingri. She came to
Langkhor where she received Shijé teachings and instructions from
Phadampa and his disciple. She practiced for fifteen years and became
"one who has destroyed all mistaken perception."

16. **Jomo Khasel** was born in Ölkha in Central Tibet. When she was
young, she traveled to Dingri. Devoting herself to the lotus feet of Phadampa and his disciple, she received teachings on the Shijé cycle and

practiced them for six years in Langkhor. Even after Phadampa passed away, she stayed there, practicing for another four years. Then she returned to Central Tibet where she spread the transmission of Shijé. She passed away at eighty-four.

17. Jomo Dröné was born in Tsang. From an early age she had great religious faith and took great pleasure in giving. On hearing about the reputation of Phadampa and his disciple, she left behind her servants and possessions and traveled to Dingri. Devoting herself to Phadampa and his disciple, she received all teachings on the Shijé cycle and put them into practice.

18. Jomo Phenmo was born in the town of Rikpa Jung in Phenyul. At an early age she traveled with an attendant to Dingri. She attended upon Phadampa and his disciple. Having received teachings on Shijé she put them into practice and attained siddhi. When she died all the surrounding valleys were permeated with a medicinal aroma and many signs of her accomplishment were seen.

19. Jomo Je'u Ma was born in the district of Ongpo. [469] From an early age she had a clear and intelligent mind, and whatever activity she pursued, she became learned in it. She traveled to Dingri and received Shijé teachings from Phadampa and his disciple. She spent many years meditating in Langkhor and attained siddhi. She then spent many years in Gungthang working for the teaching and sentient beings.

20. Jomo Shang Chungma was born in Shangpu. At an early age she turned away from this life and developed renunciation. She went on pilgrimage and met Phadampa and his disciple when she arrived in Dingri. She received teachings on Shijé and practiced for six years in Langkhor, where she attained siddhi. In 1118 she returned to Shangphu and meditated.

21. **Jomo Rosenma** was born in Gungthang. From an early age she had a sharp and clear intelligence. She became the consort of Lama Gyagompa and traveled to Dingri with him. There she became a student of Phadampa and his disciple and received teachings on the Shijé cycle. She practiced constantly and developed realization.

22. **Jomo Shangmo Gyathingma** was born in Tsang. She entered the religious life and immersed herself in practice. Later she became the consort of Phadampa Sangyé and is one of the four renowned dakinis. Majo Jangchub of Nyaltö and Shelmo Gyajam are also two disciples of Phadampa who are included in the four dakinis.[335]

23. **Jomo Shönuma** was born in Maryul of Upper Uru. In her early life she traveled with her father, who was a trader. She arrived in Śrī Chusang in Latö Gyal, where she became a student of Phadampa and his disciple and received teachings on the Shijé cycle. Having adopted the behavior of being incapable of speech, she meditated and quickly gained realization.

24. **Jomo Nyama Khyimpa Mo** was born in Nyama Do. From a young age she had great faith, determination, and wisdom, and was of a generous and compassionate spirit. Having become a householder, she had children and wealth, but with no attachment to them she left for Dingri. She became a student of Phadampa and his disciple and received teachings on the Shijé cycle. Practicing constantly, she attained siddhi.

[470] To sum up, the twenty-four Majo made their lives inseparably one with practice. When they passed away many wondrous sights were observed. At their cremations, extraordinary signs occurred, relics were produced, and so on.

Brief accounts of their lives can be found in *Blue Annals* (pp. 915–20).

Jomo Rachikma was born in Phenyul. She was the sister of Kadampa Geshé Sharawa Yonten Drak (1070–1141). Having entered the religious life, she became a remarkable yogini. She was famous for producing an extraordinary miracle. Although she only possessed one goat (*rachik*), its milk was able to provide a yogurt offering for eight thousand monks.

Her cremation was at Shara Monastery. Although I[336] have not found a detailed biography, Kathok Situ in his *Guide to Central Tibet and Tsang* states,

> On the left is yogurt and the relics of Rachik, the sister of Sharawa, whose single goat was able to provide a yoghurt offering to eight thousand monks. To its east are the relics of Khandro Namkha Büm and Büm.[337]

It can be understood that the other two women mentioned were also renowned at that time.

Majo Mangchungma was born in Tsang. She attended upon Sachen Kunga Nyingpo (1092–1158) and is one of "the seven disciples who attained forbearance." She had many students, including Phakmo Drupa. Therefore, it is certain she a was a great scholar-practitioner.

Machik Shachungma,[338] or **Shangmo**, was the disciple and consort of Khön Könchok Gyalpo (1034–1102), the founder of the Sakya dynasty. She was the mother of Sachen Kunga Nyingpo. [471] She was a renowned woman who gathered many disciples, including Phakmo Drupa.

Majo Göchungma was one of the "thirteen Majo" who were teachers of Phakmo Drupa, as mentioned in his biography. She was obviously a great woman, but I am unable to provide definitive details.

Jocham Phurmo was the wife of Kunga Barma,[339] who was the son of Sachen Kunga Nyingpo, and was a well-known disciple of Sachen. Ngawang Kunga Sonam's *Sakya Lineage* states, "...Mangchungma from Mangkhar, Jocham Phurmo, and Yalung Jomo A U Ma. These were the eleven disciples that he cared for, consisting of eight men and three women."

Lhachik Yarlungma Dembu was the daughter of the Lhokha Yarlung ruler and was born in the Demkyo Palace. Jé Rechungpa came to the palace in search of alms. She was milking the cows and his arrival startled her. She became angry and went to throw dust at him, but on seeing his face was captivated and invited him inside the palace. Her father appointed him as his ritual officiator and Rechungpa took Lachik as his bride.

For some time, circumstances between them were unfavorable but when Rechungpa was staying in Loró, Lachik came and repented. She trained herself in practice and became an unrivaled yogini. This is told in Gö Tsangpa's *Biography of Rechungpa*.

Jomo Yangmo was born in Nyal. She met Rechungpa when he was staying in Loro. He accepted her as his disciple, and she became his consort. She received the entire oral transmission, put it into practice and gained powers.

[472] **"The Leper of Ölkha."** I cannot find the name of this woman, but she was born in Ölkha. She had been afflicted with leprosy for a long time. Her limbs were eaten away, and she was in a wretched state. The unparalleled Gampopa Dakpo Lhajé was renowned as having a powerful blessing, and that merely meeting him would bring great benefit. She was not able to approach him, but while looking in the direction of where he was staying, she saw a protruding white snow mountain. Gazing at it she experienced great joy and devotion and became cured

of her leprosy. She also experienced signs of Mahāmudrā realization, and blissful heat automatically rose within her. In a state of limitless joy she went to meet her lama. He also saw her as a suitable recipient and gave her meditation instructions, and in a short time in the locality of Peu Chung she became a remarkable nun. This is told in Karma Chakmé's *Biography of Dakpo Lhajé*.

Machik Onjo. I cannot find her birthplace.[340] She attended upon Khungtsang, the foremost disciple of Rechungpa. She received the wish-fulfilling oral lineage cycle of teachings and put them into practice.

She became a great yogini who sang many songs of realization.[341] For example, on having no attachment to possessions and offering them all to her guru:

> With all material goods the nature of an illusion,
> where can there be miserliness?

On endowing her mind with the three sets of vows:

> With this precious human birth of opportunity and leisure
> given over to the Dharma supreme,
> the three vows are produced in the mind.

On severing her mind from misconception:

> Through the wish-fulfilling oral-lineage transmission,
> misconception was severed.

On her experience through effort in existing and nonexisting:

> With a generation stage never apart from the four sessions,

my body, speech, and mind I know as enlightened.

On mind becoming flexible:

> Through the channels and winds of undistracted meditation,
> a natural uncontaminated great bliss is experienced.
> Meditative concentration held in the session
> now moves like the stream of a river.

[473] On understanding the no-nature of all phenomena:

> Effortless great bliss, the nature of phenomena
> seen as empty by valid cognition,
> beyond names and words,
> the unborn dharma body, devoid of fabrication,
> by the kindness of the guru, is understood.

Majo Nyangmo was the fourth generation of the family of Aro Yeshé Jungné and was known locally as Jomo Nyangmo. She became a Dharma master of the Aro tradition. Chetön Gyanak (1094–1134) requested teachings on the Aro tradition from her. Jé Phakmo Drupa also received teachings from her, and she is included in the thirteen kind female gurus, or Majo, of Phakmo Drupa. It is said that she was a nun.

Ngulmo Gyalé Cham. Her birthplace is not recorded. She received many teachings on sutra and tantra from Dzeng Dharmabodhi, or Chökyi Jangchup. He taught her the four syllables tradition and gave her instructions on Dzokchen. She became "one who has destroyed all mistaken perception." Finally, she entered the rainbow body.

Surmo Gendun Büm was born in Lower Tsang, in the area of Sur.

From an early age she realized the faults of samsara and became a nun. She was a natural yogini who developed many gateways of meditative concentration—such as that of understanding reality—and actualized the two stages of the tantric path. She was a great scholar-practitioner, and while living a meditation hut in Lower Nyang she accomplished much for the teachings and living beings.

She bestowed empowerments, such as the Sutra empowerment,[342] on Surtön Śākya Shenyen of Ben Sangak Ling. She is among the lineage lamas of the Kham tradition of the Sutra empowerment and is renowned in the Kama Nyingma tradition.

[474] **Machik Jobüm.** Chökyi Wangchuk, the son of great siddha Yumo Mikyö Dorjé, had three offspring. Machik Jobüm was one of the two who were of great benefit to the teachings. She thoroughly integrated into her mind the Dharma in general and specifically Puṇḍarīka's *Kālacakra Great Commentary*. From her father she received teachings on the six-branch yoga of the Kālacakra completion stage. When she meditated on them, the ten signs of accomplishment appeared in one day. After seven days her winds dissolved into the central channel and a flawless view of "the emptiness of other" was born in her. She became a great siddha who nurtured her disciples and produced great accomplishments within the Jonang tradition. Khenpo Sherab Ösal of Nyak also was her disciple.

Gangpa Muyan was born in Lhokha. She was a disciple of Thönyön Samdrup, the son of Machik Labdrön, and received Chö instructions from him. She undertook retreats in remote places, snow-mountains and in wild and dangerous places. She severed the root of the dualistic view and became an unparalleled "destroyer of mistaken perception." *Instructions on Chö* states, "Thönyön had eight female siddha disciples, of which the foremost was the unparalleled Ganga Muyan."[343]

Khandro Sönam Drenma was the youngest sister of three in a large estate in Phakmo Dru in Ngamshö. When her spiritual yearnings awoke, she entered the path of Dharma as a disciple of Phakmo Drupa Dorjé Gyalpo. Seeing that Taklung Thangpa, an attendant of Phakmo Drupa, was practicing tantra, she asked her lama, "Give me a blessing too."

Phakmo Drupa said to Khandro, "Daughter, if you serve as a consort, you will enter the rainbow body. Therefore, seek it and practice."

This she did, but doubts caused her to abandon her practice a few times. Her lama said, "The night of the tenth you must spend inside a cave. Whatever happens, you will receive blessing."

[475] On that evening in the cave she heard the frightening sounds of wild boar surrounded by blazing fire. Becoming afraid, she could not ask for blessing. Sometime later, she left her body and passed away. Ling Repa (1128–88), a disciple of Phakmo Drupa, took her skull and placed it upon Mount Tsari as instructed by Phakmo Drupa. It is said that Taklung looked for her remains at the cremation, but they had disappeared.

The *Blue Annals* says that Phakmo Drupa Dorjé Gyalpo and Khandro Sönam Drenma were actually the deity Cakrasaṃvara and his consort Dorjé Phakmo. Others say that she was not the consort of Phakmo Drupa.

About this time, places of monastic study for monks and nuns began to be separate. Before that, monastic study had been well established in Sangphu Monastic College, and monks and nuns were equally afforded the opportunity to study. The practice of debate was also established but the monks could not compete with the reasoning of the nuns and were constantly defeated. Therefore, Geshé Chapa Chökyi Sengé in his *Collected Topics*[344] established a new science of reasoning known as "opposing logic."[345] After this, it is said that the monks would regularly defeat the nuns. Whatever the case, the above proves that the intellect of a woman is not inferior to that of a man.

Chapa Chökyi Sengé saw that it would be wrong for monks and nuns to study together and so he separated them. This also improved monastic discipline.

From about this time onward, the excellent tradition of observing and cherishing monastic discipline increased considerably, and thus became a wonderful way of maintaining the purity of the Buddha's teachings. From this we can infer that more attention was paid to the development of the male monastic community, while interest in the situation of the female monastics waned.

[476] **Jomo Chugoma** was a disciple of the First Karmapa, Düsum Khyenpa (1110–53). She evidently became a renowned yogini and siddha because Karma Chakmé, in his *Instructions Given to Jomo,* says, "Düsum Khyenpa had many female disciples who achieved powers, such as Jomo Chugoma."

Söpa Ringmo was the sister of Sakya Pandita. She studied at Sakya Monastery. When Sakya Pandita went to Mongolia, Söpa Ringmo followed him as a renunciate. When they met in Landru (Liangzhou), Sakya Pandita said to her,

> Is this Söpa Ringmo who has arrived? Is the earth covered with her footprints? Has she broken the jaw of an old dog?[346]

She replied,

> Is this Sakya Pandita who has arrived? Has he bestowed the Vajra Garland? Is the earth now covered with vow-violators? Has the rope of hell been made?[347]

She lived in a hermitage for a long time. When she heard that Sakya Pandita was unwell, she looked toward Landru again and again.

Whenever she saw someone, she would ask for news. When she heard he had passed away, she immediately said,

> Generations of Tibetans will lie down and die.
> I, Söpa Ringmo, will rise and die.

So saying, she rose and passed away. A funeral reliquary was built for her in Landru, which apparently can still be seen today.

Machik Repma Jangchup Darma devoted herself to Jé Kunden Repa (1148–1218). She received the complete teachings and instructions of the Trophu Kagyu tradition.[348] She practiced single-pointedly and said, "My realizations have become a worn-away knife and a worn-away stone."[349]

All scholars praised her by agreeing that she was a great yogini who had perceived emptiness directly and perfectly.

Because of her unimpeded perception, she realized that an incarnation of a Phadampa Sangyé would be born to a fisherman called Lukyé in a valley in the district of Je. [477] On the morning of the child's birth she brought butter for his palate and raised him as her own. When he was an adult, he became Sherab Dorjé of Chegom Dzong, a great siddha and founder of Khakyong Monastery in Tanak, who achieved much for living beings. It is said that Machik gave him teachings and removed obstacles for him.

Drowa Sangmo was a contemporary of Gyalwa Götsangpa (1189–1258), preserver of the teachings of the Drukpa Kagyu school. Her birthplace is unrecorded. She was known as "an Orgyen yogini" because the great Drukpa Kagyu siddha Orgyenpa (1230–1309) saw that she would travel to the land of Orgyen[350] and sit in the rows of the ritual feast ceremonies.

In *Heavenly Raiment*, the autobiography of the Fifth Dalai Lama, it speaks of "the long-life practice in the tradition of Drowa Sangmo, the consort of Götsangpa." Therefore, there existed a Drowa Sangmo tradition longevity ritual.

The *Lhorong Religious History* states,

> She came to complete the enlightened activities of Gyalwa Götsangpa and his disciples. A year after the master passed away, not being requested by Orgyenpa to remain, she passed away.[351]

This is all I can find of her biography. Therefore, whether this Drowa Sangmo is the same as that found in our folk opera tradition is something to be investigated.

Drupamo Kalsang was one of Götsangpa Gönpo Dorjé's disciples who was endowed with magical powers. Khandroma Drowa Sangmo, Drupamo Kalsang, Jangkyong, and other disciples of Götsangpa, who were female "meditators who wore yak-hair blankets" of Dechen Teng Hermitage, were probably Orgyen yoginis, because in the daytime they would sit and listen to teachings from the Dharma Master, and in the evening it could be clearly seen that they would be sitting in the rows of the ceremonial feasts in Orgyen. This is told in Sönam Öser's *Biography of Siddha Orgyen*.

Therefore, at those times there were certainly many renowned women who preserved the teachings either by way of magical powers or by practice and teaching.

THE PERIOD OF SAKYA RULE (1260–1353)

[478] **'A ma Kalsangma** was a siddha who resided at Butra Monastery. Yangönpa Gyaltsen Pal (1213–58), in his *Mountain Dharma Miscellaneous Writings*, says,

As a young monk I went before 'A Ma Kalsang in Butra. It was said she was a great siddha. I asked her, "For thirteen years I have meditated but have made no progress or have any qualities. Please give me instructions on how to make progress."

"Son," she replied, "Meditate for a long time without any hopes or expectations."[352]

Three times she repeated this. Through this and her other words, it is clear that she was a great woman who upheld the banner of practice.

Jomo Tsultrim Drön was a siddha and disciple of Götsangpa. In the chapter on the joining of the upper winds in *Mountain Dharma*, Yangönpa writes,

During the time of the precious Dharma Master[353] there were many cotton-clad female practitioners. During the time of Jomo Tsultrim Drön, when I was very young, I was afraid to go close to her. She would raise the red drop by uttering the long and short sounds of the vowel *i*. Because of my fear, people would quickly appear in front of me and I was pushed further back. I cried a lot! These kinds of things happened.[354]

Rema Zhikmo Kunden Yeshé lived in a market town in Tsang. From an early age she contemplated impermanence and developed a distaste for worldly life and was determined not to become a housewife. At the age of thirteen she learned reading, writing, and chanting.

She had a desire to wander off into retreat in the mountains. Her father said, "You are young, and retreat is not possible. It would be of more benefit to be in a community of disciples. Therefore, go and study."

Studying the *Golden Light Sutra* and the *Perfection of Wisdom in Eight*

Thousand Verses, she understood the reality of the two truths. This gave her great joy, which she expressed in many songs. [479] In keeping with her father's instructions, she received complete teachings on the old and new tantras, various sadhanas, Mahāmudrā, and especially on the wish-fulfilling oral-lineage transmission. She received instructions from Trophu, Karmapa. Dzamling Gyen, Druptop Gönpo Yeshé, Tharpa Lotsāwa, and Khedrup Chöjé.[355]

She traveled to Shang in Tsang and in Phunglung practiced the water austerity.[356] Although she experienced much obstruction in body and mind, such as hindrances caused by nonhuman forces, and so on, she brought them all into her practice. When she went alms collecting, she would bless sick people and cattle and bring them relief. Many came to her for teachings. In places such as Menkhar Cliffs in Zhalu, in front of the Jowo Statue in Lhasa Jokhang, at Gyeri Cliff in Shangs, and at Mishik Cliff, she exhibited many magical signs of accomplishment.

To Lama Delek, when asked for signs of accomplishment, she replied,

> From the age of eighteen to now at the age of seventy-five,
> I have dwelt in mountain retreats and practiced. Under the
> uncanopied skies I have wandered like the unbridled snow-
> lion. Is that not a sign of accomplishment?

She had many visions and was able to subdue nonhuman spirits. Orgyenpa said that she was a rebirth of Machik Drowa Sangmo and that she would be of great benefit for living beings. Having spread the oral teaching lineage of Rechungpa, she probably passed away in her eighties, because the monk Drimé Siji wrote that she told her life story when she was in her eighties.

Machik Palkyi Dorjé was one of the four great Tsang scholars of Tibetan geomancy. These four scholars came to Lake Manasarovar, where they studied and contemplated *Geomancy: A Precious Garland of the Earth Spread Out and Amassed.* Ridding themselves of misconceptions they became scholars in the field. The manner in which they propagated the science of geomancy is found in *The Sand Spread Out and Amassed: A Presentation of the Correct Practices of Geomancy.*[357]

[480] **Jomo Menmo** (1248–83) was born near Sarmo Valley in the district of É to father Dorjé Gyalpo, a tantric practitioner of the Dak clan, and mother Pema Palzom. Once when she was tending the cattle in Sarmo, she came across the title of a treasure text. On the tenth of the month, from a cave where Padmasambhava had meditated, she obtained a treasure text cycle called *Sacred Dharma: The Heart Drop of the Dakinis* and used it for her practice.

She traveled to Layak in Lhodrak, where she met Guru Chökyi Wangchuk (1212–70). By receiving teachings from him and becoming his consort, the innate bliss of exalted wisdom was born effortlessly within her. Together they completed their tantric meditation and worked for the welfare of others by secret means.

Finally, at the age of thirty-six, on the tenth day of the first of the three autumn months in the water sheep year of the fifth sixty-year cycle, she arrived on Lhari Mountain with two local companions. There they performed a ceremonial feast, and it is said that all three, without abandoning their bodies, soared into the sky like birds and went to the dakini lands.

Dujom's History[358] and other sources state that Jomo Menmo met Ling Repa and taught him the symbol methodology of opening the channels of wisdom. However, Ling Repa was born in the earth monkey year of the third sixty-year cycle whereas Menmo was born sixty years later in the earth monkey year of the fourth sixty-year cycle.[359] Also, the Jomo Menmo who was the wife of Ling Repa was born in Nyangtö in Tsang, whereas this Menmo was born in É in Lhokha. Therefore, this is a case of a similar name but a different person.

Shangtsunma Yonten Tso was a siddha and disciple of Jonang Kunpang (1243–1312). In his *Places of the Jonang*, Tāranātha says,

> In the hills around Jonang in a valley known as Dza Khyi'u
> lived the Dharma master Jé Kunpang and his great bodhi-
> sattva disciple, the siddha Shangtsunma Yonten Tso. [481]
> She had perfected all realizations held in her mind. She had
> developed manifest qualities. For example, she could walk
> unimpeded through walls. If she did not eat, she was never
> hungry, and whatever she ate, she digested. By retaining the
> downward winds she experienced great bliss. It was reported
> that she flew back and forth between the east and west
> higher reaches of the valley. Letöpa Wangyal also praised
> her greatly.[360]

Khandro Sönam Paldren was born in Jangdam Shung. Guru Tashi's *Religious History* says she was born in Powo. Other documents record her birth as being in Gyashö Benga. She is traditionally included in the past incarnations of Samding Dorjé Phakmo. It is said she possessed extraordinary signs of a dakini, such as exhibiting magical powers.

She came as a bride for governor Rinchen Pal in Gyashö. Together with her son Döndrup they founded Jada Khachö Ling nunnery, where she propagated the Kagyu teachings. It was in this place that she passed away. Kathok Situ in his *Guide to Central Tibet and Tsang* says,

> At Yangdo in Gyashö Benga, at a crossroads, at the spur of
> a mountain is the reliquary of Khandroma Sönam Paldren.
> There you can find a self-arisen skull, her brain and blood
> blended in the stones, and containers of relics.[361]

There are extensive biographies of Khandro Sönam Paldren.[362]

Machik Gönchungma Yeshé Büm was from the Nyak clan. Her father was Kunga Gyaltsen. Her elder brother was the spiritual master Dorjé Nyingpo, and she became the spiritual master known as Yeshé Büm.

She was a disciple of her father, her brother, Khenchen José, Khenchen Sherab Öser, Khenchen Shākya Gön, and others. She developed a comprehension of all existence and achieved stability in the generation and completion stages. As a result, the female protector deity Dhūmāvatī said to her, "Spiritual master, whatever deeds you entrust to me, I will carry them out exactly in accord with your wishes."

[482] Gyaltsen Palsang,[363] with his clairvoyance, foresaw her birth. He wrote a message and sent it to Trophu together with two gold earrings. It arrived to coincide with her birth and read, "This child will become a great guide and refuge for all beings of this degenerate age. Name her Bümsang."

Because she lived in Gönchung, she was known as Gönchungma. She meditated in a large wooden box while immersed in meditative concentration. It is said that this box was later used in the religious dances at Gönchung Monastery. From her early life until she passed away, many extraordinary signs were seen around her. This is recorded in the *Nyak Chronicles*.

Drupmo Yeshé Gyen was a disciple of Jonang Kunkhyen, Dölpopa Sherab Gyaltsen (1292–1361). She concentrated on the six-branch yoga of Kālacakra, and so forth, and realization was born within her. She developed great clairvoyance was able to unimpededly know all immediate and long-term occurrences, external, inner, or between. This is described in Tāranātha's *Places of the Jonang*.

Zhangtsun Chötso was a disciple of Jonang Kunkhyen, Dölpopa. Because of the great power of her bodhicitta and her practice of exchange of self for others, she was able to say to the monk Tashi

Sangpo, who was on the brink of death, "The remaining seven years of my life, I offer to you. I will pass away in your place."

With these words she passed away in perfect health. The monk Tashi Sangpo was restored to health immediately and lived for another seven years. Tāranātha's *Places of the Jonang* says that this Jonang place where she passed away was a habitat for beings with such extraordinary accomplishments.

[483] **Drupchenma Ösel Kyi** was a disciple of Jonang Kunkhyen, Dölpopa. There was also a disciple of Kunkhyen called Drupchenma Palmo Tso, but her biography is not recorded. Tāranātha states,

> The meditation place of Drupchenma Ösel Kyi, a disciple of the great Kunkhyen, and the meditation place of Drupchenma Palmo Tso are these days widely known all around Dza.[364]

As exemplified by the above, there were without doubt several great women in this period who preserved the teachings and exhibited the experiences and realizations of accomplishment.

The Period of Phakmo Drupa Rule (1354–1435)[365]

Khandro Kunga Büm was born in Ön Tashi Dokha. At the age of six at Densatil Monastery she offered the hair from the crown of her head to Tseshi Nyingma Drakpa Gyaltsen (1293–1360). She relied upon many other lamas and received sutra and tantra teachings, as well as empowerments and guidance, primarily from the Kagyu school. Devoting herself solely to practice, her meditation insights suddenly burst forth.

One evening, at the third watch, she heard a voice: "Oh, fortunate woman! In Clear Light Cave at Drak Yangdzong, meditate for seven years, seven months, and seven days. With the prophecy of the dakinis you will travel to the dakini lands."

Accordingly, she immersed herself in meditation. She received the prophecy of Dorjé Phakmo and from that cave she revealed the treasure cycle *Mother Tantra of Bringing the Secrets into the Path* and its supplements. She transmitted it widely over Central Tibet and brought many fortunate disciples to maturation and liberation. In keeping with the treasure text instructions, she gave the cycle to Chödak Dungtso Repa, which continues to this day. She also retrieved treasure texts from Drak Yangdzong, thereby "opening it up as a sacred place."[366]

In places such as Ön, Dokhar, Samyé, and Surkhar and others,[367] auspicious signs were seen. [484] She gathered about her many disciples, including lamas, monks, geshés, officials, and lay men and women, and taught them extensively. She made Ön Tashi Yangön and Jemo Chöten her main places of residence. She had many visions, and many of her students attained the rainbow body.

Finally, at the age of seventy-five, she went into retreat at Jemo Chöten hermitage. Accompanied by inconceivable auspicious omens of sounds, lights, and rains of flowers she entered into the rainbow vajra body, without abandoning her own body. The treasure texts she revealed can be found in volume *ti* of Kongtrul's *Precious Collection of Treasures*.[368]

Madrup Tri'i Gyalmo Sönam Dzom was born in Yardrok district. She dedicated herself to Bodong Panchen Chöklé Namgyal (1375–1451). She received many teachings and spent her whole life in practice. Future generations include her in the four Bodong disciples who hold aloft the banner of accomplishment.

Lhasumsa Jangchup Palmo was born in Rong of Sok District. She received teachings from many lamas and immersed herself in practice with the result that special insights were born within her. She spent a long time in Nakshö and Sokshö working for the welfare of others.

In later life she lived in Kongpo, and it seems she also lived in Powo because Tertön Taksham writes about her meditation caves in that region. She was very skilled in performing wrathful tantric deeds. In particular, she had powerful accomplishments in the cycle of Shinjé Trochu.[369] Consequently, there are many accounts of those who witnessed her wrathful tantric abilities, such as (1) capturing, burning, and expelling; (2) powers, curses, and hail; and (3) summoning, casting spells, and averting. She is probably the only woman who mastered these wrathful activities. She had a son called Yeshé Rinchen. She is very well known and is in the Shinjé Trochu lineage of the Drigung Kagyu.

[485] **Machik Chödron** was born in Latö. She is included in the list of abbots of Phadruk Monastery, which was founded by Phuriwa Könchok Gyaltsen, a disciple of Gyalwa Yangön whose ascetic practices were equal to those of Yangön himself. She held the post prior to Phakmo Drupa Sönam Gyaltsen and did much to develop the monastery. This is told in documents. She was clearly a great woman and a true scholar and practitioner.

Around this time many of the centers of the male monastic tradition of the unparalleled Kadampa tradition, which in the past was widespread in Tibet, had fallen into disrepair and were being restored as nunneries. The reason for that is that in the past the Kadampa monks strictly avoided women. Therefore, once when a manifestation of a dakini entered a monastery she was forcibly expelled by the monks, causing her to utter a curse, "You shun my kind. In the future, may the ruined monasteries be taken over by women."

Many nunneries were established in old Kadampa monasteries. This is related by Thuken Chökyi Nyima in his *Philosophical Systems*.

Pönmo Kalsang was an aristocrat of Nezong in Kyishö. She held Drupthop Thangtong Gyalpo[370] as her venerated lama. In 1430, when the bridge over the river Tsangpo in Lhasa was being constructed, she appealed to her circle for donations and was able to provide gold and silver for the project on many occasions. Fulfilling the hopes of her lama, she summoned her own craftsmen and commissioned the construction of jeweled shrines. Through her philanthropy, this aristocratic woman was responsible for untold accomplishments.

This is told in Kathok Situ's *Guide to Central Tibet and Tsang*. The shrines she commissioned were not completely destroyed by the Cultural Revolution and can be found in Chakpori in Lhasa.

[486] **Drupamo Sangmo Büm** was a disciple of Chengawa Sönam Gyaltsen of Phakdro. For thirteen years she practiced in a single meditation session. This is described in *Songs of Lhasik Repa* but there is not much other detail.

Jetsun Khachö Wangmo was a disciple of Jé Tsongkhapa and Gungru Gyaltsen Sangpo (1383–1450). She was born a boy but early on became a girl.[371] She entered a retreat center in Sera Monastery, established by Rabjam Chöjé, who was a disciple of Zhang Yudrakpa (1123–1193). She engaged in study based on the works of Jé Tsongkhapa and his disciples. Gungru appointed her as instructor of the nuns. She separated the nuns from the monks and moved the nuns to Khyung Hill, and left a great legacy through her acts of preserving, nourishing, and developing the teachings.

Jetsunma Kunga Sangmo was born below Tsodrak in Nechen Sang. She relied upon Trulshik Dāki Repa from whom she received general teachings and the Rechungpa oral transmission in its entirety. Through practice, realizations were born within her.

The secret mantra Vajra Vehicle practices of cakras, winds, and drops were taught for both yogis and yoginis, and in Tibet the custom of women entering the Tantra Vehicle was widespread in the old and new tantra schools. However, apart from the Rechung oral transmission, the tradition of giving instructions to women was very rare elsewhere. The white instruction[372] teachings on methods for women to engage in cakra and wind practices, dispel hindrances, and enhance experiences, as well as the medicinal practices to avoid karmic retribution, exist because of the kindness of Jetsunma Kunga Sangmo.

[487] She became so well known that Taklung Ngawang Drakpa, Shamarpa, Pawo Chöwang Lhundrup, and other well-known figures relied upon her. Her extensive deeds and activities are found in Pawo Tsukla Trengwa's *Religious History of Lhodrak*.

Tashö Bumo Pema Tso. Kathok Situ's *Guide to Central Tibet and Tsang* says, "Near Drakar Lhachu, in Upper Kongpo, is the ruin of the birthplace of Tashö Bumo Pema Tso." It can still be seen today. She had clairvoyance and magic powers and performed countless deeds for those afflicted by illness and demons, madness, and spirits. Even now many popular stories about her destroying nonhuman malicious spirits are retold by the local people. I have not found any written accounts of her life and that remains a topic of research.

Various religious objects related to this great woman can be found in new Nedo Monastery in Ngom, Riwoché Monastery, Showa Do, and elsewhere. In Tshurphu Monastery her skull is embossed with self-arisen figures of the five classes of dākinis. Therefore, it is clear she was a renowned woman.

Semo Ödé was born in Upper Tsang. Her father was the treasure revealer Guru Rinseng. Her father's treasure teachings revealed from Traduntsé Temple were entrusted to her by Nepo Dawa Drakpa. They consisted of *General Compilation of Treasure and Tantra*, practice texts, a small work on Namchak Urmo,[373] and *Protecting Oneself: Taming the Seven Planets*.

When her karmic link had awoken, Semo applied herself assiduously to the practice of the treasure texts and finally gained siddhi. It is said that her propagation of her father's treasure texts is described in documents listing the teachings received by the Great Fifth Dalai Lama.

[488] **Nemo Gayakmo** was born in Dakpo Gar. While she was the housewife of a mute, she met Drukpa Kunlek (1455–1529) and was his wife for a year. She requested teachings from him and put them into practice.

She went to Mount Tsari to live in retreat in a mud hut. While she was there, an avalanche occurred and blocked all paths up and down the mountain. Everyone concluded she had died. However, although she only had three measures of tsampa[374] and no other provisions, she was able to remain for one year within a single meditation session by the power of her meditative concentration.

Drukpa Kunlek is said to have had five thousand consorts, of which it is said that many, like Nemo, had achieved tantric qualities. They include Kongmo Sumchok, Yarlung Jatsön Pönmo, Aché Lugu, Jayul Pönsa, Buga the wife from Tsethang, Gadra Pönsa Tsewang, Semo Samdrup Pemo, Shaltama Butri, Tsezom Butri, Gyaltsen Sangmo who perfected the meditative concentrations of a three-year retreat, Aché Namkha Dzom, Palzom the trader of Shelkar, Semsangma of Nekartsé, Yangchen Aché Palha, Ani Kunzang Dzin of Sharlü Phak Lake in Mön, Gakyi Palmo of Wachen, Khyaknang Kyizom Alhé, Gyalchok Palzom Butri, Bömo Kyi of Wachen, Wamsa Norzom Chökar, and Palsang Lhamo.

Lolek Butri was born in Sakya. She was beautiful woman and Drukpa Kunlek intended to rely upon her as a consort, but she would not agree to it. Therefore, he magically left a footprint in a bar in Sakya, and when word of this achievement got around of, she felt remorse, brought him some tasty beer, and declared her remorse. "Please care for me," she asked. She entered the teachings and received the name Lhachö Drölma.

[489] Having received instructions she left to meditate on Mount Jomo Lhari. Once there was an avalanche and for three years the trails were cut off. However, to the astonishment of everyone she survived on the "food" of meditative concentration, and her fame was widespread. This is told in her *Autobiography of Drukpa Kunlek*.

Dölpa Drupchenma was born in Döl in Ngari. According to Guru Tashi's *Religious History*, Lama Dorjé Senge of Kyidrong relied upon her and received the cycle of Chö, *Compilation of the Guru's Intent*, and other revealed treasures of Sangyé Lingpa, as well as the treasure texts of Samten Lingpa. She was a woman possessed of great learning and insights.

Jetsunma Dorjé Karmo and **Drupmamo Ösel** were two of the treasure revealer Pema Lingpa's six main disciples who manifested signs of tantric achievement. Therefore, they were without question great women practitioners.

Jetsunma Dorjé Karmo left handprints in rocks and could fly through the sky like a bird. Drupmamo Ösel could magically produce blessed water. These and other qualities are described in Guru Tashi's *Religious History*, but I have not found any other details on their lives.

Yumchen Kunga Sangmo[375] was a daughter of the Takla family in Nyanang. At an early age she was given the name Gönmo Kyi. She was brought up by an elderly female relative. She was a beautiful woman, had a great liking for the Dharma, and was sent against her will to become the bride of a Nyingma lama in Tashi Khar. Consequently, she prayed that within three years she would become a widow. After a few months the lama passed away, and so she left for Palmo Chöding and became a novice nun. There she began receiving and studying teachings such as those on the Chö practices of Machik Labdrön.

The Takla family of her birthplace and the Tashi Khar family of her husband were involved in a lawsuit, and she stood to gain a lot of money. [490] However, from her compassion she put an end to the lawsuit—thereby provoking the wrath of her relatives, who stopped sending food and provisions to her.

Around that time there were many reports that Tsangnyön Heruka had compiled the songs of Jetsun Milarepa in Shelphuk in South Latö. She traveled to meet him and became his disciple. She received many oral transmissions and with great determination put them into practice. She gained siddhi and became the consort of Tsangnyön.

She brought many beings to liberation and maturation. Her magical abilities were known everywhere, and she nurtured many disciples. These and other details are found in Lhatsün Rinchen Namgyal's (1473–1557) *Meaningful to Behold the Extraordinary: A Roughly Complied Biography of Tsangnyön Heruka.*

Ötso Gyalmo was one of the female disciples of Tsangnyön Heruka who had attained siddhi. Götsangpa's *The Heart of the Sun Illuminating the Vajrayana: A Biography of Tsangnyön Heruka* (p. 134) states, "The four fortunate yoginis were Ötso Gyalmo, Gurpa Chö Dzema, Jñāna Sadakara, and Buddhai Minchen."[376]

Lhatsün Rinchen Namgyal's biography (p. 56) says, "Furthermore, the consort siddhas were Khenmo Namkha Drölma, Ngari Dorjé Palmo, Armo Sangyé Sangmo, Drupchen Sangthalma, Drupchen Tsasenma, Drupchenma Kunga Sangmo, and sixteen other yoginis."

These were truly women practitioners renowned for their control over meditative concentration.

Choté Drupchen Chözé was from the Dra clan. She relied upon Pawo Chöwang Lhundrup (1440/55–1503) and was renowned as a great practitioner and his foremost disciple. Around the age of sixty she was in retreat in Phara lay hermitage in Dra Samdrup Chözong when it was struck by a lightning bolt. [491] Everybody thought she had been killed. However, Drupchen was sitting in the "binding posture of the six stoves."[377] The bolt of lightning had landed between her knees and forehead. Although her seat coverings, the ceiling beams, and so on had been burned, she had not felt the lightning and her posture was not destroyed. For a few days her mind was a little unclear but gradually she recovered.

Pawo Tsukla Trengwa remarked that he had met her when he was ten years old.

Goma Rinchen Palmo was born the daughter of Taktsé administrator Samdrup. She was taken as a wife of the Drigung Dharma master, Rinchen Chökyi Gyaltsen. Later she gave birth to the Drigung Dharma master Kunkhyen Kunga Rinchen (1475–1528).

When her husband died, she assumed the responsibility of being the administrator, or *goma*, of the Drigung myriararchy.[378]

At this time, Drigung was experiencing some trouble in the form of military incursions from Kyiyor and elsewhere. However, as administrator, Gönpo Gyaltsen skillfully quelled the troubles and maintained her rule without loss.

When she grew old, Gönpo Gyaltsen was appointed Gopa, and Rinchen Palmo retired. She was the only woman in the line of Drigung administrators.

THE PERIOD OF RINPUNG (1435–1565) AND TSANGPA (1565–1642) RULE

Pönsa Serkhangma was the daughter of governor Garpa and a natural yogini. She was married off to Rinchen Tsé of Nyemo. [492] Without reliance upon religious or secular resources she boasted a natural intelligence, and her fame grew.

She devoted herself to Rinchen Phuntsok of the Drigung Kagyu school and became his patron. In order to promote the Drigung Kagyu tradition in Nyemo she offered the land for Shakram Drupdé Monastery and provided sponsorship for its construction. She also became administrator. The account of her extraordinary meditation practice is described in the works of Jé Rinchen Phuntsok.

Chökyi Palzin was born in Lhokha Jayul, the daughter of Chögyal Jawa. She devoted herself to the Drukpa Kunkhyen Pema Karpo (1527–91) and received many oral transmission lineages, especially the Dzokchen instructions on the channels and winds. She requested him to compose instructions on the channels and winds for female practitioners, in which the methods for males and females were separated out. This is described in the Collected Works of Pema Karpo (vol. *zha*). She was definitely a great female practitioner.

Jetsunma Kunga Trinlé Wangmo (1585–1668)[379] was born in Ngamring in Tsang. She was a disciple of the Jonang Kunkhyen, Tāranātha. She received, contemplated, and put into practice sutra and tantra in general, and specifically the practices of the glorious Jonang tradition, and became a top disciple.

After Kunkhyen Tāranātha passed away, she turned the wheel of Dharma many times in Jonang Hermitage, Takten Monastery, and elsewhere. When Sarawa Kunga Gyaltsen of Gyalmo Tsarong came to receive teaching, Kunkhyen Tāranātha had already passed away, and so Sarawa Kunga received teachings from Jetsunma. While he was receiving the Cakrasaṃvara empowerment, he thought, "I was not able to meet Kunkhyen and now I have to receive teachings from this woman."

Jetsunma read his thoughts with her clairvoyance, and said, "Son, no need to be sad. Cast your eyes upward." In the space above him he saw the complete mandala of Cakrasaṃvara with all its celestial residents, and great faith was born within him. [493] He received many instructions from Jetsunma.

Drogé Kunga Palsang came to Central Tibet and also received many instructions from her. When he was receiving instructions from her on training in the physical postures of the profound vajra yoga, Jetsunma, with her legs in the crossed vajra position, exhibited the extraordinary spectacle of rising up and remaining in the air for a long time. He asked her for a prediction concerning the establishment in Kham of a base for the definitive teachings. She replied by describing the geography of land where the monastery would be and the wonderful features in the area, all of which was exactly as she described it.

It is through Jetsunma's kindness that the Jonang tradition is still alive in Ngawa,[380] and she is included in the lineage lamas.

Rikden Orgyen Butri was the consort of Rikzin Düjom Dorjé (1615–75). Guru Tashi's *Religious History* says,

> Rikden Orgyen Butri was an incarnation of the practitioner Sönam Paldren of Powo and Pema Tso of Tashö. Encouraged by Rikzin Düjom Dorjé, she opened up Droklung and Gawalung in Powo as sacred places. Her rebirth was Dechen Trinlé Tsomo, who was the consort of Chöjé Lingpa.[381]

Gyalmo Tashi Palzom of Tsangtö was the daughter of the Tsangtö governor Phuntsok Namgyal (d. 1632). She was taken as a bride by Kunkhyen Chökyi Drakpa, the family lineage holder of the Drigung Kyura clan. From him she received many teachings on sutra and tantra and by putting them into practice she became a yogini.

After she passed away her mummified body was placed into a reliquary. During the Cultural Revolution the reliquary was broken into pieces and it was seen that her body had not decomposed at all and her hair had grown to cover her back. [494] When her hand was cut off in order to remove her conch shell bracelet, blood emerged from her wrist. This was witnessed by many people.

Chöden Tsomo was a practitioner born in Döl. She was among the foremost disciples of the Drigung Rikzin Chökyi Drakpa. This can be known by the question-and-answer advice found in his Collected Works.

Lhacham Tsering Butri was the aristocratic daughter of (father) Sakya Ngawang Kunga Rinchen Tashi Drakpa Gyaltsen and (mother) Sönam Palzom. She took lay vows at an early age. She entered tantric practice and her tantric powers became great indeed. This Dharma master became famous for treating those tormented by illness and demonic forces, and especially those suffering from difficult-to-cure diseases, such as epidemics, and so on. Merely by giving them a form of protection they would be completely cured.

When Amnyé Zhab (1597–1659) began his chronology of the Sakya dynasty in 1621, he mentions that Tsering Butri was living in Rinchen Gang Labrang.

The Period of the Gaden Phodrang Rule

Minling Jetsunma Mingyur Paldrön (1699–1761) was born in Mindröling in Lhokha. Her father was Terdak Lingpa (1646–1714) and her mother was Phuntsok Palzom. At the age of twelve she performed the ceremony of offering a lock of hair to her father and was given the name Mingyur Paldrön.

At thirteen she began to receive from her father all the profound core instructions of his treasure teachings. Putting them into practice she achieved realizations. Also, from Lochen Dharma Śrī, Trakthung Jikmé Dorjé, Kathok Rikzin, Shabdrung Gyurmé Shenphen Wangpo, Shenyen Orgyen Khyenrab, and others she received many teachings on the old and new tantras.

[495] When she was twenty and the Dzungar Mongols arrived in Central Tibet, bringing about great harm to the Nyingma tradition, she

fled to Dzokchen Monastery in Sikkim, where she turned the wheel of Dharma. At twenty-two she returned to Central Tibet and with her brother, Rinchen Namgyal, restored Mindröling.

She performed the ceremony of offering a lock of hair to the Seventh Dalai Lama, Kalsang Gyatso, and received the name Jetsun Sherab Drölma.

At the age of thirty-six, in Mindröling Monastery, to an assembly of over 270, she gave the entire transmission of her father's thirteen volumes of teachings, together with empowerments and explanations. She constructed many representations of the enlightened body, speech, and mind, and though teaching and practice, she greatly enhanced the tantric doctrine. She passed away at the age of seventy-one.

With the great benefit she brought to the oral and revealed treasure teachings of the Nyingma tantric tradition in general, and specifically to Mindröling tradition, this great being has been of immense kindness, and sits among the dynasty of lamas. She gave many compositions to her successor, and produced many disciples, such as Khyungré Ösel Long Yang, who would preserve the teachings.

Pönsa Palsang Kyi was the daughter in the Shigatsé Pelkyang family. Miwang Pholha Sönam Topgyal[382] (1689–1747) through his military might, took her as his bride and foremost queen. She had great faith in the Dharma and in politics was of great assistance to her husband. She passed away sitting in the lotus position and after the cremation her heart, tongue, and eyes were left untouched by the fire. The figure of the deity Amitābha appeared on her skull and a silver reliquary was constructed for her. This is related in Dokharwa's *Biography of Miwang*.

[496] **Nyangpo Drupchenma** was born in Nyang in upper Kongpo. From the Drigung spiritual head Kyabgön Döndrup Chögyal (1704–54) she received extensive teachings. She meditated in Nyang and Terdrom and became known as "the practitioner of Nyang" (Nyangpo

Drupchenma). Later in Terdrom she developed a meditation center. This is told in the biography of Kyabgön Döndrup Chögyal.

Daö Wangmo was born in lower Kongpo. She became the consort of Treasure Revealer Daö Dorjé, or Dorjé Thokmé (1749–97), who was born in Draksum. Entering the religious life, she received many initiations and explanations. After Daö Dorjé passed away she constructed shrines and so forth. In keeping with the instructions of Chöjé Lingpa and Gampowa Orgyen Drodul Lingpa (b. 1757) she lived in Rinchen Pung temple in Pemakö,[383] where she propagated treasure teachings.

When she passed away many extraordinary signs were seen, and she probably achieved something resembling the rainbow body. This is related in the first volume of Khenpo Kunphel's *Biography of Patrul Rinpoché* and in Rikzin Kunsang Ngé Dön Longyang's *A Jewel Necklace of Biographies*.

Jetsun Yangchen Drölma was the daughter of the Degé ruler Tenpa Tsering (1678–1738). At an early age she entered the religious life by the Sakya tradition of Ngor Ewam Chöden Monastery. There she received teachings of the old and new schools alike from Ngor Palden Chökyong, Sharchen Dorjé Chang, Shuchen Tsultrim Rinchen, Situ Tenpai Nyinjé, Dzokchen Gyurmé Thekchok, Kathok Shingkyong Drimé, Nyidrak Tulku, and more. She also studied medicine, and thus became a great scholar.

With a vast understanding of secular and religious ways, and a nonpartisan attitude, she engaged profoundly and skillfully in nurturing her own domain and outshining those of others.

[497] She founded the monastery of Thupten Norbu Ling, and constructed temples with sacred artifacts in Dratho, Dzongsar, Khorlo Do, and elsewhere. At Changra she initiated the great pot consecration ceremony. With this and much more she carried out many religious deeds. After the Degé ruler Kunga Trinlé Gyatso passed away, she

administered the Degé kingdom in the customary manner until the prince Sawang Sangpo, came of age.

Shukchung Jestun Khandroma Kunsang Chökyi Drölma was a yogini who appeared in Ngajong in Domé at the time that Jonangpa Ngawang Kunga Phuntsok, the Sé incarnation of Dzamthang, was alive. When he came and met Khandroma, she was very pleased and burst into spontaneous song. She also gave him prophecies and descriptions of many of his future incarnations. This is told in Ngawang Lodrö Drakpa's *Jonang Religious History*.

Minling Jetsun Trinlé Chödrön was born into the Mindröling monastic family, and as custom dictated, she became a nun. With her great study, contemplation, and meditation she became known as the Minling Jetsunma. She gathered many disciples, such as Dzarong Phu Ngawang Tenzin Norbu (1867–1940). The Kathok Situ's *Guide to Central Tibet and Tsang* speaks about "the three-foot silver reliquary of Jetsun Trinlé Chödrön" and "the good quality life-size statue with throne." Therefore, she was an object of great reverence.

Pema Trinlé Düdul Wangmo was born into the Sakya dynasty. In keeping with tradition, she became a nun. She applied herself thoroughly and assiduously to study and meditation and became very well known. She gathered many disciples and became the head lama of many scholar-practitioners, such as Sakya Simok Tulku Kunga Tenzin, Jamyang Loter Wangpo, and Ngor Khenchen. [498] Her deeds of preserving the teachings, alongside Ju Mipham, Jamgön Kongtrul, and others, are described in her biography.[384]

Shuksep Jetsunma Rikzin Chöying Sangmo (1853–1951) was more commonly known as Shuksep Jetsun Kushab and Shuksep Mani Lochen. She was born in Tso Pema[385] in India. At birth she was given the name Chonga Lhamo. The family made a living from begging. Her father, Döndrup Namgyal, had a great liking for alcohol, because of which life was hard for Chonga Lhamo and her Nepalese mother, Sapenpa Drölma. Therefore, Chonga Lhamo was sent to be a helper to the yogini Tsering Butri.

From the age of sixteen she became a Lama Manipa.[386] From Lama Tashi Namgyal she learned reading and writing. Her father would sing while she danced as they begged their way through Nepal visiting various pilgrimage sites.

From Trinlé Namgyal from Bhutan she learned the Kagyu preliminary practices and the fivefold Mahāmudrā.[387] For thirteen years she performed rituals to produce a son for the king of Zahor. When a son was born, she was appointed head lama. She received complete instructions from the (Tibetan) Kyirong lama, Pema Gyatso, and for three years she meditated in the hidden valley of Hé. She trained in the wind-pot practice. Traveling to Nepal she offered coats of white paint to the three main stupas, and printed a list of the deeds involved.

Returning to Tibet, she visited nearly all the sacred sites and shrines. At the age of thirty-six she was given the name Rikzin Chöying Sangmo by Shabkar Tulku. She received teachings from Yangti Lama, and from Khenchen Ngawang Tenpai Nyima she took ordination. It is said she did not shave her head and she dressed in aché (laywoman) robes.

[499] She practiced on White Skull Mountain and on Five Peak Mountain (Wutaishan) and showed signs of having mastered the winds and cakras by immediately appearing in Lhasa, and elsewhere.

From the age of fifty-four she lived and meditated in Shuksep, south of Lhasa, and as "Shuksep Jetsunma" she was taken as an object of reverence by high and low alike. She primarily practiced Chö and there were those who proclaimed her as an incarnation of Machik Labdrön. As a result, she became very well-known.

At the age of eighty-three she received many Nyingma teachings from the Menying practitioner Dawa Dorjé. She gathered many yogini disciples. Finally, at the age of ninety-eight, on the thirteenth day of the third month of the iron rabbit year in the sixteenth sixty-year cycle (April 19, 1951), she passed away. Her autobiography and its supplement are extant.[388] Her incarnation has been discovered and recognized.

Khandro Dechen Wangmo (b. 1868) entered the practices of the Bön religion and through her meditation practice became renowned as a dakini. Her footprint was left in Shen Tenzin Rinchen Ling, a Bön monastery in Yetha Lungkar in Drachen County. Therefore, it seems that she spent some time there, but not much else is known about her.

Rikzin Chöden Sangmo (1871–1958) was born in Druphö Dogang in Drigung to a family descended from Jikmé Lingpa's daughter. At home she herded cattle. One day Rechen Rinpoché arrived and told her she should become a nun. Soon after, she traveled to Drigung Terdrom and joined the community of nuns there. They lived by seeking alms because they had no property as a source of revenue, meaning that in the autumn months she too often had to go out seeking alms.

[500] From Drigung throneholders Zhiwai Lodrö (1886–1943) and Kyabgön Chökyi Jungné (1909–40), as well as Drupchen Rechenpa, Drupwang Trinlé Öser, Drupwang Tseten, and others, she received many of the main teachings of the Drigung tradition. In a place called Gyangdrak in Terdrom she entered single-pointedly into practice. When she returned to her home, she was fearful of meeting men and would spend her time wandering in the mountain valleys, living a simple and humble life. "Néné (nun) Chöden Sangmo," as she was known, was highly regarded among the community of nuns, and was regarded with reverence by all. Whatever she predicted by way of divination would unfailingly come to pass. She would give away pills that she had consecrated by mantra recitation and that would be beneficial in times of epidemics.

Not only from Drigung but from everywhere people would come to seek her audience. Many came to ask for prayers for deceased loved ones and for divination. The treasure revealer Ösel Dorjé, Tulku Dongak Tenpai Nyima, and many other great practitioners praise and revered her. Her hair was tied into a bun. She was small and her body was slight. She was someone who treated everyone she met with respect. She gathered many yogini disciples.

Finally, at the age of eighty-seven, she passed away on the twenty-third day of the tenth month of the earth dog year in the sixteenth sixty-year cycle (December 3, 1958).

Üsa Khandro Kunsang Chönyi Dekyong Wangmo (1880–1929)[389] was born to father, Jampa Gönpo, governor of Ragashar in Lhasa, and mother, Tsering Chözom from Nup. From an early age she exhibited qualities more advanced than in other children and extraordinary signs that were difficult to comprehend. She would speak and sing spontaneous verses that were difficult to understand and seemed to come from nowhere. She was always bringing in strange substances that she said she had found, even though they did not exist in that land.

[501] She had no liking for household work and when she was about ten, she said again and again that the great Dharma of Dzokchen exists in Dokham, and in this life that is what she had to do. At sixteen, in Lhasa, she met members of a caravan from the household of Gyalsé Rinpoché Tulku Drimé Öser of Tergar in Serta County. She secretly followed them and in the following year arrived in Dokham.

For a while, in order to live, she had to work as a servant for a wealthy nomad family in Golok. Gradually the family began to care for her, but she had no desire to do household work and so in order to follow the Dharma, she became homeless. Wherever she went, no matter how she tried to hide her extraordinary intellect, her intelligence, and her natural qualities that far exceeded those of others, they were clearly visible and captivated the minds of everyone. Also, because she was very beautiful there were those who falsely slandered her, and some hindrance came her way.

However, over time she received profound and exclusive instructions from many indisputable and accepted treasure revealers and great practitioners, such as Trakthung Düjom Lingpa, Riksé Drimé Öser, the Garwa treasure revealer Düdul Wangchuk Lingpa, and Palyul Gotrul Rinpoché. Consequently, she exhibited the profound qualities of the paths and levels. Her former altruistic aspirations and prayers had come to pass, and her activities of body, speech, and mind were peerless. As a result, effortlessly and without obstruction, she was of great benefit for the teachings and living beings. She had mastered benefiting others through the profound treasure teachings and opened wide the gateways of teaching, composition, and the giving of Dharma. Such wonderful deeds spread throughout Golok and Serta primarily and the whole of Dokham.

[502] There existed many compositions by Khandroma but in the troubled times of the Cultural Revolution their number declined. Those that remain total six volumes, but extant texts are rare. They include special commentaries such as *Notes on the Great Vehicle Dzokchen Work, Buddhahood without Meditation*,[390] and profound core instructions on methods of practicing the deep and secret nonduality. Her exclusive profound treasure teachings of the close lineage include mainly many sadhanas on meditational deities, generation and completion stage practices, and rituals for destruction. Also included are methods for pacifying epidemics, dispelling hindrances, rituals for preventing loss of cattle and poor harvests, protecting the environment, restoring goodness to the earth, and so on.

There is a single volume of her extraordinary autobiography, as well as songs of experience, songs of expression, spontaneous compositions, and many more. Like the autobiography, these latter compositions are clear and easy to read. Without contravening the basic rules of Tibetan grammar, they are expressed with a strong flavor of the way people in that region naturally speak. Therefore, they come across as down-to-earth compositions that are pleasant and appealing. Just the way they are expressed they exude a feeling of trustworthiness and an air of truth, as opposed to something made up.

Her songs of experience and of expression are endowed with the good qualities of the Tibetan skills of composition in general, and in particular, because of the special and intelligent feelings innate in womankind, the way she experiences her surroundings, life, affection, and so forth are perfectly expressed. As such, she manages to express vividly special features not found elsewhere. In this sense, in the garden of the art of Tibetan composition hers are rows of a new profusion of flowers rarely seen before.[391]

[503] She nurtured countless disciples from all walks of life, as can be known from her autobiography.

To sum up, although it is not possible to describe her life story in all its exclusive detail, even for the eyes of ordinary beings her extraordinary autobiography of wisdom, perseverance, and beauty undifferentiated, has been created in this world,

Under the past cultural conditions that afforded scarce opportunity to Tibetan women to receive an education, she secretly climbed to the exalted terrace of learning, ethics, and compassion. Finally, around the age of forty-nine, at Riwoché, in Kham, her body withdrew into the dharmadhātu realm.[392]

Tenzin Chönyi Wangmo entered religious practice in Taklung. Through her learning, contemplation, and meditation she developed great qualities. She was a death-returner who showed signs of tantric achievement and possessed clairvoyance. Merely by meeting her those afflicted by illness and demonic forces were cured, it is said. She lived mainly in Drilung Hermitage in Taklung, working for the teachings and living beings, and was consequently renowned everywhere as the Taklung dakini.

Around this time, Tenzin Chönyi Wangmo, Shuksep Jetsunma, and Drigung Rikzin (Néné) Chöden Sangmo, described above, were three women of great religious renown, and were called "the three Jetsunma." [504] The incarnation of Tenzin Chönyi Wangmo has been discovered and identified.

Tsunma Yulha (1901–80) was born in the town of Khethong in Drakyab Oda. She studied under Dzokchen Khenpo Ngakchung, Adzom, Gyalsé Mingyur Dorjé, and others and trained in sutra and tantra, and especially medicine. Her view, meditation, and conduct were proper, and she carried out her bodhisattva commitments as she had vowed to do. In particular, she handed out medicine to those who needed it and paid great attention to working for others. She was revered by everyone as Ashé Yulha (Turquoise Deity Householder). She passed away at the age of eighty.

Néné Metok was born in Drigung Terdrom. She became a nun and studied under many lamas. Focusing totally on practice she developed profound tantric powers. She was very effective at destroying demonic forces, and healing wounds, swellings, and inflammations.

In 1956 she traveled to Mount Tsari. The pilgrimage party was attacked by the Lopa[393] tribe and many injuries were caused. Using her tantric powers, Néné Metok was able to heal them. She did not eat ordinary food but relied only upon various elixirs, such as stone, grain, flower, and space elixirs, thereby cutting any attachment to food. Through this practice, her senses grew very acute, and she could detect the aroma of a person from far off. Her body became youthful, and so forth. She wore her matted hair tied up on her head. She passed away toward the end of the Communist Cultural Revolution.

Doctor Yangchen Lhamo, or **Khandro Yang Ga** (b. 1907[394]), was born in Pemakö to her father, Jampa Jungné, the Jédrung[395] of Riwoché in

Kham, and her mother, Bumo Tsultrim, the daughter of the Ngom governor. Her father encouraged her to study the medical texts, and in a very short time she was able to recite fifteen pages.

[505] When she was eleven, and her father was living in Taklung, two doctors arrived from the Medical College in Lhasa. While they were receiving transmissions and teachings on medical practice from her father, he expressed to them his wish that his daughter learn the surgical techniques of correcting eyesight[396] at the Medical College. Consequently, by the age of thirteen, she was working in medical practice and traveled to the Medical College, where the director, in keeping with her father's wishes, urged her to learn these techniques. When she had mastered them, she restored the sight of many poor people in Lhasa, Chamdo, and elsewhere. Not only did she not take any money for her work, but for the treatment of wind ailments, and so on, she even gave away her own provisions.[397] In this way she was of huge benefit to the sick and ailing who came to her from all over Tibet. As a result, the people gave her the affectionate name Khandro Yang Ga (Dakini of Pleasing Voice) and she was revered everywhere.

In 1948 she traveled to Bhutan, where she treated the king, Jikmé Wangchuk, for eye problems. She also treated other Bhutanese for eye complaints and became very well-known there.

Under the auspices of the Medical College, she performed eye surgery and dispensed medicine in eighteen Tibetan districts, and over three years she restored sight to about three hundred patients. Because her treatments were so effective, she became very famous, and in 1958 she joined the Medical Center organization. There had never been such a renowned female doctor and as a result those who were able apply the effective treatments for women's and children's diseases described in the medical texts to the illness itself were almost nonexistent. It was Yangchen Lhamo who completely restored these treatments.

Later she was inducted as a worker for the state and was appointed the first director of the gynecology and pediatric department. In 1964 she wrote a paper on gynecological treatments and presented it to a conference, and her fame and reputation grew even more.

[506] Yangchen Lhamo was the first female doctor of the Lhasa Medical College. Gradually the number of female medical students grew, and in this way her great legacy has been the emergence and nurturing of Tibetan female doctors.

Tsultrim Wangmo appeared in Khyungpo Tengchen and is renowned as a dakini who entered the religious path of Yungdrung Bön. In 1928 she founded Khapung nunnery in the Gangé region of Tengchen County, where she spread the teachings. I cannot find more about her.

Khandro Tamdrin Lhamo (1923–79) was born in Gojo Nyakla Gar as the daughter of (father) Nyakla Jangchup Dorjé and (mother) Drimé Wangmo. She received the complete empowerments, transmissions, and core instructions of her father's revealed treasure texts, such as *Ocean of Collected Teachings*. In particular she constantly practiced "guiding the winds" from the Phakmo tradition and could sit subsisting on elixir pills for twenty-one weeks and on space elixir for a week. Moreover, her main practice was her father's revealed treasure text *The Black Golden Seal Profoundest Essence*. Her father declared that she was a "consort whose touch brought liberation." With a single strand of her hair she could remove cataracts from eyes. With no anger or desire she did not recognize any division into friend and enemy. She nurtured many faithful monks and nuns as disciples.

On the twenty-seventh day of the second month of earth sheep year (1979), when she was fifty-seven years old, she called her disciples together and said,

> Now, do not be sad. Death is the inevitable end to birth. My allotted lifespan was fifty-two years, but by the kindness of my lama and because of my little daughter I have been able to

live a little longer. I have had visions of Phakmo a few times. I must go for a while to the Realm of Turquoise Leaves. Do not hold on to my body out of attachment.

That evening she passed away. [507] Her body was left for seven days, after which it dissolved into light, leaving a corpse of only about twenty-six centimeters in height. This was witnessed by thousands of the local community. Those who had slandered her in the past were remorseful and made their confessions.

The ways in which these great women listened to and studied sutra and tantra teachings, the manner in which they passed away accompanied by extraordinary signs, their attainment of the rainbow body (or of their bodies shrinking to a height of about two feet), and the rainbow lights and other sights that were clearly observed at their cremations have been described by recourse to the main source texts only and lengthy presentations have been avoided.

There are many other women born into or married into great dynasties, queens and administrators of minor Tibetan kingdoms, female officials, and so on who studied the Dharma and whose legacy of service in the twin rule of religion and politics has undoubtedly been significant. However, because it is not clear whether they actually engaged in teaching and meditation, they have for the most part been omitted here. Moreover, it is clear that throughout Tibet there have only been about seven women who had an active role in political administration.

FEMALE INCARNATIONS (TULKUS)

In Tibetan history there have been two incarnation lines in female form: Samding Dorjé Phakmo and Gungri Khandroma.

Samding Dorjé Phakmo[398]

[508] The Samding Dorjé Phakmo incarnations hail from the Ütsang area of Tibet and follow the Bodong tradition.[399] Up to the time of writing there have been twelve incarnations.

1. Jetsun Chökyi Drönmé (1454–88/1422–55).[400] King Kyidé Nyima Gön, a descendant of the Tibetan emperors, settled in Ngari. His descendants included King Sönam Gyaltsen, or King Gyal Sönam Dé (1371–1404), in Gungthang and King Lhawang Gyaltsen (1404–1502). The latter and his queen, Dodé Gyalmo, had three children: sons Tri Namgyal Dé and Namkha Norbu, and daughter Adröl Chökyi Drönmé, who became the first incarnation.

The *Biography of Yeshé Tsogyal* says,

The incarnation of her activities and speech will appear in Ngari.[401]

Also, in the homage it says,

To be born, as prophesized by Padmasambhava,
into the Gunthang race as Chökyi Drönmé,
cared for by Jikdral Shab[402] and Drupchen Thangtong Gyal,
I pray to the supreme adept.[403]

In keeping with the prophecy, she was ordained by Bodong Chöklé Namgyal and given the name Könchok Gyalmo. Like filling a pot to the brim, he gave her countless teachings from the three baskets, explanations designed to ripen and liberate, core instructions, and transmissions. She traveled with him as an attendant all over Tsang and Central Tibet.

In her travels she met the great siddha Thangtong Gyalpo and received tantric teachings of the old and new translation schools. As instructed by the great siddha, she meditated at Tsari Chikchar for a long time. On the way back she was ceremonially escorted by the ruler Drakpa Gyaltsen (1374–1432), who offered her from his treasury the hair, turquoise earrings, and other ornaments belonging to Yeshé Tsogyal, and requested her to keep them as a glorious and perfect field of merit for the teachings and living beings.

She received a vision of Lion Face Dakini, who uttered a prophecy concerning the construction of a monastery and then dissolved into the very place where the monastery now stands. Therefore, Könchok Gyalmo traveled to Yardrok, where in 1440, assisted by funds from the local ruler, she built a small meditation center consisting of one lama and six monks. [509] Later, that number increased to about seventy monks. They followed the Bodong tradition, which meant practicing the teachings of the Sakya, Geluk, Kagyu, and Nyingma in a nonsectarian manner.

She was the disciple of Bodong Chöklé Namgyal and Thangtong Gyalpo, and because she was primarily engaged in practice, she became the Dharma holder of the Bodong tradition and was the consort of Chöklé Namgyal. She shared the responsibility of managing the religious and secular affairs of the Bodong monasteries. At that time, she was not known as Dorjé Phakmo, but as Khandro Thöpa Mukchung.

It is also written that she founded Samding Monastery in Yardrok Yutso in 1429, and that the monastery's full name is Samdrup Chökyi Dé, also known as Khachö Ding Samten Chökhor Ling.

There are two different dates recorded for the founding of the monastery: 1440 and 1429. *A Suckling Dowry: The Religious History of Lhokha*[404] clearly says 1440, so either there is a mistake in the dates, or these are two different monasteries.

2. **Kunga Sangmo** (1490–1533/1459–1502) was recognized by Thangtong Gyalpo and was installed in Samding as her monastic seat. Through her practice and teaching she spread the Collected Works of

Bodong Chöklé Namgyal and printed its hundred and twelve volumes in gold and silver ink.

She traveled to Ngari and other places, and the rulers at Yargyab, Yartö, Yardrok, and so on became her patrons. She developed the temple and assembly hall at Samding and commissioned the construction of their sacred objects. She passed away at the age of forty-three. [510]

3. **Nyandrak Sangmo** (1534–74/1503–42) was born in Damshung Nyandrung to (father) Pawo Lhudrup and (mother) Tashi Palbar. She was recognized by Chimé Palsang of the Jora Bodong Monastery. Under the Fourth Bodong Loten, Kachu Namkha Palsang, and others, she studied the sutra and tantra traditions. She maintained the monastic center with wisdom, ethics, and compassion, and passed away at the age of forty.

4. **Orgyen Tsomo** (b. 1586/1543) was born in Orgyen Sowashi to (father) Pawo Chuden and (mother) Khandro Thok. She was recognized by Jamyang Tenzin Drakpa and others and installed as the throneholder. She passed away at the age of ten.

5. **Khachö Palmo** (1589–1640/seventeenth century)[405] was born in Karma Drongsar in Chamdo. She was installed as the monastery throneholder by Drogön Trinlé Namgyal and others. With a great breadth of vision she studied, contemplated, and meditated, and was possessed of learning, ethics, and compassion. As a result, she propagated the Bodong tradition from all its aspects. She encouraged practice, instituted ritual dance, cross-thread,[406] and torma rituals, and constructed many sacred objects. She passed away at the age of fifty-four.

6. **Tenzin Dechen Trinlé Tsomo** (1641–1707) was born in Bönsim in Yardrok Taklung. She was installed as the throneholder by Jora Trinlé Gyatso. She took novice monastic vows. From Drogön Dorjé Nyingpo

and others she studied and trained in Dharma generally and specifically in the Bodong practices. Having overseen the teachings and their propagation, she passed away at sixty-six. [511]

7. **Chödrön Wangmo** (1708–52/46) was born in Samdrup Thongmön in Nyemo. She studied under several mentors and received many teachings.

One time the Dzungar Mongols, under the leadership of Tsewang Rabten, arrived at the monastery and posed a great threat. When they entered the monastery, she had transformed herself into a fearful wild pig surrounded by loud crackling, shooting flames. This quelled their evil intentions, and they offered their armor, helmets, and weapons to her, promising not to attack the monastery.

She passed away at the age of forty-four.

8. **Kalsang Chokden Dechen Wangmo** (1753–1802/1746–74) was born in Shang Tashi Tsé in Namling. She was the sister of the Sixth Panchen Palden Yeshé (1738–80), who installed her as the Samding throneholder. The Seventh Dalai Lama, Kalsang Gyatso, awarded her the title of *hothokthu*,[407] and her power and religious estates grew. The Manchu Qianlong emperor invited her to China, where he offered her many gifts. She passed away at the age of forty-nine.

9. **Chöying Dechen Tsomo** (1805–55/43) was born in Lhalu Estate in Lhasa, and was a niece of the Eighth Dalai Lama, Jampal Gyatso, and of Panchen Tenpai Nyima (1782–1853). It is said that after the eighth incarnation passed away, there was no hint of the new incarnation for a few years.

She was taken care of by the Panchen Lama and others, and is reputed to have had a wide knowledge in religious and secular affairs. Jamyang Khyentsé (1820–92) and many others took her as their teacher. She lived to be about fifty.

10. Ngawang Rinchen Kunga Wangmo (1857–97). Her place of birth is not determined. In *Guide to Lhasa and Centra Tibet* it says, "According to the Indian Tāsi, she had long hair, was of good character, very elegant and graceful, like a princess."

[512] She was enthroned as custodian of the Dharma teachings of Chokgyur Lingpa (1829–70) and consequently propagated revealed treasure teachings. She lived for forty years.

11. Thupten Chöying Palmo (1898–1937) was born in Mönkyi Khangsar in Yabda, Tölung County, the daughter of (father) Namgyal Dorjé and (mother) Jangchup Drönma. She received teachings in the Bodong tradition from Gelek Dorjé and Pawo Wangchuk, and was ordained by the Thirteenth Dalai Lama, Thupten Gyatso. He also conferred on her the title of *hothokthu*, meaning that her existing authority to exercise legal jurisdiction was strengthened.

When an order came from the government to thwart an advancing army, she performed rituals, such as the torma of expelling, and the army retreated. With this and other deeds her fame soared. She passed away at the age of thirty-nine.

12. Dechen Chökyi Drönme (b. 1938) is the present incarnation and was born in Nyemo Shikyé to (father) Rikden Gyalpo and (mother) Sönam Drönma. She became ordained as a nun in Lhasa Tsamkhung Nunnery. She was recognized as the incarnation at the age of six and installed as the Samding throneholder. She studied under many masters, such as Jora Rinpoché, and trained in her own Bodong tradition. From Kyabjé Yongzin Trijang Dorjé Chang (1901–81) and others, she received many empowerments and teachings.

In 1959 she fled to India but returned soon after. Currently she is a member of the Chinese People's Political Consultative Conference and of the People's Congress of the Tibet Autonomous Region.

Gungri Khandroma

The Gungri Khandroma incarnations are a line of renowned female incarnations who appeared in Domé.

1. **Losang Chödrön** (seventeenth century)[408] moved to Domé out of necessity and because she was unable to carry out her work for others in Central Tibet. [513] She provided great assistance to many monasteries there, such as Jakhyung and Kubüm monasteries. She was a disciple of Depa Tsang Chöjé.

In 1623 Depa Tsang Chöjé and Gungri Khandroma were instrumental in instituting a new philosophical college in Jakhyung Monastery and worked to develop its curriculum. *Jakhyung Incarnations* says,

> The ninth throneholder of Jakhyung Monastery, Tsang Chöjé Tenpa Rinchen, in the fifty-seventh year of the twelfth sixty-year cycle (1623) instituted a new philosophical college.

And also,

> When he was twenty-six, Depa Kyishö Tenzin Losang Gyatso (1593–1638)[409] left Central Tibet and traveled to Amdo. In the following earth sheep year of the tenth cycle (1619) he came to Jakhyung. To a large assembly that included the ninth throneholder, Chöjé Tenpa Rinchen, he gave profound teachings on whatever he was requested.
>
> In his thirty-fifth year, the fire rabbit year of the eleventh cycle (1627), he bestowed the Cakrasaṃvara empowerment upon a large assembly that included the former Chöjé, Tenpa Rinchen; the incumbent, Jampa Dargyé; Ko'u Chö Gyatso (1571–1635); and many others. At that time Gungri Khandroma Losang Chödron also received many teachings. Jhakyung had instituted philosophical studies, [514] and

Depa Chöjé and Khandroma Losang Chödron had been instrumental in providing for the establishment of a college.

Shar Kalden Gyatso (1607–77) declares that Khandroma was a genuine siddha. Working tirelessly for others and becoming very well-known, she settled in Gungri and passed away peacefully.

2. **Losang Drönma** could remember her previous life and made her way to Gungri, the residence of her former incarnation. Once there, she said, "I am going to the protector temple."

"Since the passing of the previous Khandroma, the door to the temple has not been opened. No one knows where her key is," came the reply.

"Her key is here," Losang Drönma said, and taking the key from among an assortment of earrings, she opened the door. With this and other signs, she was recognized as the incarnation of Khandroma.

A decree from the government offering her great praise meant that she was able to accomplish much more for the welfare of others than the previous incarnation did. Also, works on the history of arts and crafts state that Losang Drönma is counted among the foremost masters who had perfected arts and crafts. She also left behind many accomplishments.

3. **Könchok Chödrön** was born in Shikor Be'u Tshang in Gengya. From Jamyang Shepa Könchok Jikmé Wangpo (1728–91) she received many teachings, including those of the Indian master Mitra Yogi.[410] She worked extensively for the welfare of living beings.

4. **Rikzin Drolma/Rikzin Palmo** (1814–91) was born in Shikor Be'u Tshang in Gengya, the home of her predecessor. She was ordained by Gungthang Jampai Yang (1762–1823). She received teachings from Jamyang Shepa Thupten Jikmé Gyatso (1792–1855), Detri Rinpoché

Jamyang Thupten Nyima (1779–1862), and others. The well-known Akhu Thabkhé Tenpa Gyatso (1825–97) received many teachings from her. [515]

5. **Könchok Tenpai Wangmo** (b. 1895) was identified by Akhu Thabkhé. She was given her title and installed a throneholder. Nothing more of her has come to hand.

6. **Könchok Damchö Drölma**. In 1990 she was over fifty years old.[411] More than that I have not been able to find.

THE EXCEPTIONAL FEATURES OF THE TIBETAN TRADITION

There are a hundred or so volumes of the Kangyur—the teachings of the Buddha—consisting of texts that extensively teach the view of dependent origination and the conduct of not harming others. There are commentaries on these teachings of the Buddha, as well as commentaries of commentaries. This constitutes the Tengyur with its more than 220 volumes, composed by masters who include the six ornaments and two supreme ones—such as the renowned Nāgārjuna and his disciples, the two brothers Asaṅga and Vasubandhu, and so on[412]—Ācarya Padmasambhava; the great master Śāntarakṣita; his disciple Kamalaśīla; Neten Chökyong, or Drupchen Virūpa; Nāropa, the northern gatekeeper of Nālandā; the great and kind seventeen pandits directly and indirectly connected with the glorious Nālandā Monastery or University, such the glorious Jowo Atiśa and others; and many more.

Beginning in the seventh century these were gradually translated into the Tibetan language. Consequently, many Tibetan scholars of all philosophical traditions composed many excellent commentaries and syntheses of the vast number of works in the Kangyur and Tengyur, resulting in a Dharma tradition that has been transmitted flawlessly from Nālandā.

[516] The first to propagate the Dharma of the Buddha in Tibet was the great master Śāntarakṣita, who with his profound analysis was a renowned philosopher. In Tibet the systems of many such pandits and adepts were established as a foundation, and a tradition of following the Dharma by way of an intellect that concentrated on reasoning took hold and proliferated across all philosophical traditions and all systems of study, contemplation, and meditation. The work *Essence of the Reality of Valid Cognition* by Śāntarakṣita, for example, is still held in great esteem by all Indian philosophers, Buddhist or not.

For determining the reality of all base existence, the Madhyamaka view of Nāgārjuna on the ultimate nature of reality is primarily relied upon. The stages of progressing along the paths are determined from the stages of insight that constitute the hidden teachings within the perfection of wisdom sutras from the works of the Great Vehicle. These are accessed from the two brothers Asaṅga and Vasubandhu, and so on, with the core instructions of the works of Maitreya as their foundation.

Presentations on cognition and the validity of cognition are taken from the assertions determined by Ācarya Dignāga, the master of reasoning, and the glorious Dharmakīrti and his followers. For an understanding of the aggregates, spheres, and sensory sources; mind and its factors; karma and afflictions, the upper and lower Abhidharma traditions of Ārya Asaṅga and Ācarya Vasubandhu are relied upon.

The practice of monastic discipline began in the eighth century when Śāntarakṣita ordained the first seven monks in order to propagate the Dharma in Tibet. The monastic discipline tradition followed that of the Indian Sarvāstivādin school, which is explained by Ācarya Guṇaprabha's *Vinaya Sutra*, and so on.

The traditions that focus upon the teachings and meditation practices of the four classes of tantra of the profound Vajra Vehicle, and the Highest Yoga Tantra within that classification, have been transmitted as wonderful explanations from pandits and adepts of India who include the glorious Ārya Nāgārjuna and his followers, Ācarya Padmasambhava, Siddha Lūipa, Siddha Lālita, Pandit Nāropa, and others.

[517] These teachings and practices remain unblemished to this day in the form of the Tibetan tradition of Buddhism, in which interest is increasing from millions of people from various countries around the world. Moreover, discussions are being held with modern science on the nature of phenomena in general and particularly on the nature of mind. These are reasons to be proud and pleased.

To sum up, our Dharma is built on a foundation of faith that follows reason, compassion, and wisdom, and a code of ethics that depends upon these. Their source is glorious Nālandā Monastery, whose very name raises the hairs on our bodies and brings tears of joy to our eyes. Such things do not arise from any outer cause such as the great monastery building itself, but from the works of its great scholars that captivate the mind.

Therefore, who can preserve and disseminate this vital and stainless glorious Nalanda tradition? In terms of the world situation these days, generally the people of Tibet, China, and Mongolia; the monastic community in particular; and especially the several thousand monks engaged in study have been its proprietors. In recent times the teachings suffered a serious decline in China and Mongolia. However, among Mongolian communities in various countries, the teachings of the Buddha are enjoying a fundamental restoration. Even among the Chinese people interest in Buddhism is increasing once again.

We Tibetans have suffered the calamitous misfortune of the Cultural Revolution and of being forced into exile. However, relatively speaking, the situation is now a little better. [518] Therefore, right now it is probably only the Tibetan people who can preserve the Nalanda tradition. Among the Tibetans many are refugees in India, and during our time in exile monastic establishments for monks and nuns from all traditions have been newly constructed. Monastic students from the Himalayan regions, and those from other countries, such as Mongolia, have also enrolled in these institutions. This has ensured the broad establishment of a teaching and debate environment for the study of the classic texts. Learning and contemplation have increased and in those areas in which these have declined, great efforts are being made to restore them. In this way, they have become prime centers of cultural and religious education, worthy of admiration, and possessing an unrivaled curriculum of teaching and practice of the scriptural and insight doctrine, capable of continuing its preservation, development, and dissemination to the highest degree. In these days of the twenty-first century, with the close connections between the people and countries of the world, the religion and culture of Tibet have become great objects of praise and interest and have become known around the globe.

The history of nunneries within the Tibetan tradition of Buddhism is not that revealing, and over the past few hundred years the opportunities for nuns to study the classic texts have been inadequate. However, here in India, during the past thirty years or so, the study of the classical texts in nunneries has been initiated. As a result, many have now graduated and, without any of the stubborn small-mindedness of wondering whether or not it was a custom in the past, a new tradition of awarding the title of geshé-ma is being instituted. This will be an excellent institution, of service to our religion and culture and of benefit to the teachings and living beings.

Although initially the abbots had to come from one of the great monasteries of male monastics, [519] fully trained abbesses have already emerged from the female monastic community, and by all means Tibetan nunneries should find ways to become independent like the nunneries of other religions in the world.

In this way, nuns who have graduated from their studies should have the confidence and courage to strive in the activities of study, contemplation, and practice in order to be able to carry out the duties of a Dharma teacher. These responsibilities include preserving, developing, and disseminating Buddhism in schools, in monasteries, nunneries, Dharma centers, and so on. This is not just to implement the gender equality of geshé-mas, abbesses, and female Dharma teachers, but should be seen as a way to further the activity of working for the welfare of others.

The preservation, development, and dissemination of the scriptural and insight teachings by those who maintained the transmission of the Tibetan tradition of Buddhism through a combination of teaching and practice is the main reason for the teachings of the Buddha becoming so widespread in Tibet. In China, for example, the preservation, development, and dissemination were less than it was in Tibet. As a result, many texts written in Chinese are in an old language, difficult to understand, and apart from reciting the sutras not much extensive and deep study is undertaken. In other countries to where the teachings spread from China, such as Korea, Japan, Vietnam, and so on, the unification of study, contemplation, and meditation by way of teaching and practice, as it is done in Tibet, is scarce.

Therefore, within the Tibetan tradition of Buddhism lies a rich philosophy, more profound than that of others, and hosting an ocean of commentaries. This is a very special and exclusive quality.

Appendix 1: Selected Compositions of the Seventeen Nalanda Pandits as Chosen by Dagyab Rinpoché

1. Nāgārjuna

The six works on Madhyamaka reasoning:

1. *The Fundamental Wisdom (Verses) of the Middle Way* (AKA *Fundamental Wisdom: Treatise on the Middle Way*). *Mūlamadhyamakakārikā. Dbu ma rtsa ba'i shes rab tshig le'ur byas pa (Rtsa ba'i shes rab).* Toh 3824, dbu ma, *tsa*. Translated into English by Mark Siderits and Shoryu Katsura as *Nagarjuna's Middle Way: The Mulamadhyamakakarika*. Boston: Wisdom Publications, 2013.

2. *Sixty Stanzas on Reasoning. Yuktiṣaṣṭikākārikā. Rigs pa drug cu pa.* Toh 3825, dbu ma, *tsa*.

3. *Seventy Stanzas on Emptiness. Śūnyatāsaptatikārikā. Stong nyid bdun cu pa.* Toh 3827, dbu ma, *tsa*.

4. *Dispelling Arguments. Vigrahavyāvartanī. Brtsod pa zlog pa.* Toh 3828, dbu ma, *tsa*.

5. *Detailed Disputation. Vaidalyaprakaraṇa. Zhib mo rnam 'thag.* Toh 3826, dbu ma, *tsa*.

6. *The Precious Garland. Ratnāvalī. Dbu ma rin chen 'phreng ba.* Toh 4158, springs yig, *ge*.

Compendium of Sutra. Sūtrasamuccaya. Mdo kun las btus pa. Toh 3934, dbu ma, *ki*.

Condensed Sadhana. Piṇḍīkṛtasādhana. Sgrub pa'i thabs mdor byas pa. Toh 1796, rgyud, *ngi*.

Generation Stage of Glorious Guhyasamāja Related to the Sutra. Śrīguhya-samājamahāyogatantrotpādakramasādhanasūtramelāpaka. Rnal 'byor chen po'i rgyud dpal gsang ba 'dus pa'i skyed pa'i rim pa bsgom pa'i thabs mdo dang bsres pa. Toh 1796, rgyud, *ngi.*

Commentary on the Bodhicitta. Bodhicittavivaraṇa. Byang chub sems kyi 'grel pa. Toh 1801, rgyud 'grel, *ngi.*

Friendly Letter. Suhṛllekha. Bshes pa'i springs yig. Toh 4182, springs yig, *nge.*

Praise to the Transcendent. Lokātītastava. 'Jig rten las 'das par bstod pa. Toh 1120, bstod tshogs, *ka.*

Praise to the Peerless One. Nirupamastava. Dpe med par bstod pa. Toh 1119, bstod tshogs, *ka.*

Praise to the Ultimate Sphere. Dharmadhātustava. Chos kyi dbyings la bstod pa. Toh 1118, bstod tshogs, *ka.*

2. Aryadeva

Four Hundred Verses. Catuḥśatakaśāstrakārika. Dbu ma bzhi brgya pa. Toh 3846, dbu ma, *tsha.* Translated into English by Karen Lang as *Arya deva's Catuhsataka: On the Bodhisattva's Cultivation of Merit and Knowledge.* Copenhagen: Narayana Press, 1986.

The Measure of the Hand. Hastavālaprakaraṇakārika. Rab tu byed pa lag pa'i tshad kyi tshig le'ur byas pa. Toh 3848, dbu ma, *tsha.* Translated into English by Fernando Tola and Carmen Dragonetti as *On Voidness: A Study on Buddhist Nihilism.* Delhi: Motilal Banarsidass, 2002.

Reasoning Refuting Error and Establishing Proof. Skhalitapramardanayuktihetusiddhi. 'Khrul pa bzlogs pa'i rigs pa gtan tshig grub pa. Toh 3847, dbu ma, *tsha.*

Compendium of Gnosis. Jñānasārasamuccaya. Ye shes snying po kun las btus pa. Toh 3851, dbu ma, *tsha.*

Lamp of the Compendium of Practice. Caryāmelāpakapradīpa. Spyod pa bsdus pa'i sgron ma. Toh 1803, rgyud, *ngi.* Translated into English by Christian K. Wedemeyer as *Aryadeva's Lamp that Integrates the Practices: The Gradual Path of Vajrayana Buddhism according to the Esoteric Community Noble Tradition.* New York: AIBS/Columbia University Press, 2007.

Chapters on Removing the Veils of the Mind. Cittāvaraṇaviśodhaprakaraṇa. Sems kyi sgrib pa rnam par sbyong ba'i rab tu byed pa. Toh 1804, rgyud, *ngi.*

3. Buddhapalita

Buddhapālitamūlamadhyamakavṛtti. Dbu ma rtsa ba'i 'grel pa buddha pā li ta. Toh 3842, dbu ma, *tsa.*

4. Bhāvaviveka

Lamp of Wisdom. Prajñāpradīpa. Shes rab sgron ma. Toh 3853, dbu ma, *tsha.*

Blaze of Reasoning: An Autocommentary on the Madhyamakahṛdaya. Tarkajvālā. Rtog ge 'bar ba. Toh 3856, dbu ma, *dza.*

Essence of the Middle Way. Madhyamakahṛdaya. Dbu ma snying po. Toh 3855, dbu ma, *dza.*

Explanation of the Difficult Points of the Illuminating Lamp. Pradīpoddyotanaviṣamapadapañjikā. Sgron ma gsal bar byed pa'i dka' ba btus pa'i 'grel pa. Toh 1792, rgyud, *a.*

5. Candrakīrti

Clear Words: A Commentary on the Fundamental Wisdom of the Middle Way. Prasannapadā. Dbu ma rtsa ba'i 'grel pa tshig gsal. Toh 3860, dbu ma, *'a.*

Entering the Middle Way. Madhyamakāvatāra. Dbu ma la 'jug pa. Toh 3861, dbu ma, *'a.*

Illuminating Lamp. Pradīpoddyotana. Sgron ma gsal bar byed pa zhes bya ba'i rgya cher bshad pa. Toh 1785, rgyud, *ha.*

*Autocommentary on Entering the Middle Way. Madhyamakāvatārabhāṣya.
Dbu ma la 'jug pa'i bshad pa.* Toh 3862, dbu ma, *'a.*

*Entering Middle Way Wisdom. Madhyamakaprajñāvatara. Dbu ma shes rab
la 'jug pa.* Toh 3860, dbu ma, *'a.*

*Commentary on Four Hundred Stanzas. Catuḥśatakaṭīkā. Bzhi brgya pa'i
'grel pa.* Toh 3865, dbu ma, *ya.*

*Commentary on Seventy Stanzas on Emptiness. Śūnyatāsaptativṛtti. Stong
nyid bdun cu pa'i 'grel pa.* Toh 3867, dbu ma, *ya.*

*Commentary on Sixty Stanzas of Reasoning. Yuktiṣaṣṭikāvṛtti. Rigs pa drug
cu pa'i 'grel pa.* Toh 3864, dbu ma, *ya.*

*Explanation of the Five Aggregates. Pañcaskandhaprakaraṇa. Dbu ma phung
po lnga yi rab tu byed pa.* Toh 3866, dbu ma, *ya.*

*Six-Branch Yoga Guhyasamāja Commentary. Gsang 'dus sbyor ba yan lag
drug pa'i 'grel pa.* Toh 1786, rgyud, *ha.*

6. Śāntideva

*Guide to the Bodhisattva's Way of Life. Bodhicaryāvatāra. Byang chub sems
pa'i spyod pa la 'jug pa.* Toh 3871, dbu ma, *la.* Translations include
the following:

Bodhisattvacharyavatara. Vol. 1, *Engaging in the Conduct of the Bodhisattvas, by Shantideva.* Vol. 2, *A Commentary on Shantideva's Engaging in the Conduct of the Bodhisattvas, by Sazang Mati Panchen.*
Translated by Kalsang Gyaltsen and Ani Kunga Chodron. New
York: Tsechen Kunchab Ling, 2006.

*Drops of Nectar: Khenpo Kunpal's Commentary on Shantideva's Enter-
ing the Conduct of the Bodhisattvas.* Translated by Andreas Kretsch-
mar. http://www.kunpal.com/ (chapters 1–5 only).

*The Nectar of Manjushri's Speech: A Detailed Commentary on Shan-
tideva's Way of the Bodhisattva,* by Kunzang Pelden. Translated by
Padmakara Translation Group. Boston: Shambhala Publications,
2010.

Bodhicaryāvatāra with Commentary, by Sonam Tsemo. Translated by Adrian O'Sullivan. N.p.: Dechen Foundation, 2019.

The Way of Awakening: A Commentary on Shantideva's Bodhicharyavatara, by Geshe Yeshe Topden. Translated by Manu Bazzano and Sarita Doveton. Boston: Wisdom Publications, 2005.

Entering the Way of the Bodhisattva: A New Translation and Contemporary Guide. Translated by Khenpo David Karma Choephel. Boulder, CO: Shambhala Publications, 2021.

A Guide to the Bodhisattva's Way of Life. Translated by Stephen Batchelor. Dharamsala: Library of Tibetan Works and Archives, 1979.

A Guide to the Bodhisattva's Way of Life. Translated by Vesna Wallace and Alan Wallace. Ithaca, NY: Snow Lion Publications, 1997.

Compendium of Training. Śikṣāsamuccaya. Bslab pa kun las btus pa. Toh 3940, dbu ma, *khi.*

7. Śāntarakṣita

Ornament of the Middle Way. Madhyamakālaṃkāra. Dbu ma'i rgyan. Toh 3884, dbu ma, *sa.*

Commentary on Ornament of the Middle Way. Madhyamakālaṃkāravṛtti. Dbu ma rgyan gyi 'grel pa. Toh 3885, dbu ma, *sa.*

Discussion on the Establishment of Reality. Tattvasiddhaprakaraṇa. Tshad ma'i de kho na nyid sgrub pa. Toh 3708, rgyud, *tsu.*

Establishment of Reality. Tattvasaṃgrahakārikā. De kho na nyid bsdus pa'i tshig le'ur byas pa. Toh 4266, tshad ma, *ze.*

8. Kamalaśīla

Stages of Meditation. Bhāvanākrama. Sgom pa'i rim pa. Toh 3915, dbu ma, *ki.*

Commentary on the Seven Hundred Perfection of Wisdom Sutra. Ārya Saptaśatikaprajñāpāramitāṭīkā. Sher phyin bdun brgya pa'i rgya cher bshad pa. Toh 3815, shes phyin, *ma.*

*Commentary on the Vajra Cutter Perfection of Wisdom Sutra. Ārya Pra-
jñāpāramitāvajracchedikāṭīkā. Sher phyin rdo rje bcod pà dbu ma'i tshul
du 'grel pa.* Toh 3817, shes phyin, *ma.*

Commentary on Ornament of the Middle Way. Dbu ma'i rgyan gyi bka' 'grel,
Toh 3885, dbu ma, *sa.*

Light of the Middle Way. Madhyamakāloka. Dbu ma snang ba. Toh 3887,
dbu ma, *sa.*

*Commentary on the Compendium of Views on Reality. Tattvasaṃgraha-
pañjikā. De kho na nyid bsdus pa'i dka' 'grel.* Toh 4267, tshad ma, *ze.*

9. Asaṅga

Bodhisattva Grounds. Bodhisattvabhūmi. Byang chub sems dpa'i sa. Toh
4037, sems tsam, *wi.*

*Commentary on Uttara Tantra. Uttaratantravyākhyā. Rgyud bla ma'i 'grel
pa.* Toh 4025, sems tsam, *phi.*

*Compendium of Abhidharma. Abhidharmasamuccaya. Mngon pa kun las
btus pa.* Toh 4049, sems tsam, *ri.*

Summary of Synonyms. Paryāyayasaṃgraha. Rnam grangs bsdu ba. Toh
4041, sems tsam, *zhi.*

*Summary of the Great Vehicle. Mahāyānasaṃgraha. Theg pa chen po bsdus
pa.* Toh 4048, sems tsam, *ri.*

Summary of the Base Realities. Vastusaṃgraha. Gshi bsdu ba Toh 4042,
sems tsam, *zhi.*

Summary of Explanations. Vivaraṇasaṃgraha. Rnam par bshad pa'i bsdu ba.
Toh 4039, sems tsam, *i.*

10. Vasubandhu

Treasury of Abhidharma. Abhidharmakośa. Chos mngon pa mdzod. Toh
4089, mngon pa, *ku.*

*Commentary on the Treasury of Abhidharma. Abhidharmakośabhāṣya. Chos
mngon pa mdzod kyi bshad pa.* Toh 4090, mngon pa, *ku.*

Explanation of the Ṣaṇmukha Dhāraṇī. Ārya Ṣaṇmukhadhāraṇīvyākhyāna. 'Phags pa sgo drug pa'i gzungs kyi rnam par bshad pa. Toh 2694, rgyud, *nu.*

Explanation of the Gayā Śīrṣa Sutra. Ārya-gayāśīrṣa-nāma-sūtravyākhyāna. Ga ya mgo'i ri'i mdo'i rnam par bshad pa. Toh 3991, mdo 'grel, *ngi.*

Commentary on the Ten Grounds Sutra. Daśabhūmivyākhyāna. Sa bcu pa'i rnam par bshad pa. Toh 3993, mdo 'grel, *ngi.*

Commentary on the Akṣayamati Sutra. Akṣayamatinirdeśaṭīkā. Blo gros mi zad pa'i mdo'i rgya cher 'grel pa. Toh 3994, mdo 'grel, *ci.*

Commentary on the Samantabhadra Prayer. Ārya-bhadracaryāpraṇidhānaṭīkā. Bzang spyod smon lam gyi mdo'i 'grel pa. Toh 4015, mdo 'grel, *ngi.*

Explanation of Ornament of Sutra. Sūtrālaṁkāravyākhyā. Mdo sde rgyan gyi bshad pa. Toh 4026, sems tsam, *phi.*

Commentary on the Differentiation of the Middle and Extremes. Madhyānta-vibhāṅgabhāṣya. Dbus mtha' rnam 'byed kyi 'grel pa. Toh 4027, sems tsam, *bi.*

Commentary on the Differentiation of Dharma and Dharmatā. Dharma-dharmatā vibhāṅgavṛtti. Chos dang chos nyid rnam 'byed kyi 'brel ba. Toh 4028, sems tsam, *bi.*

Twenty Verses. Viṁśatikā. Nyi shu pa. Toh 4056, sems tsam, *shi.*

Commentary on Twenty Verses. Viṁśatikāvṛtti. Nyi shu pa'i 'grel pa. Toh 4057, sems tsam, *shi.*

Discussion on the Five Aggregates. Pañcaskandhaprakaraṇa. Phung po lnga'i rab tu byed pa. Toh 4059, sems tsam, *shi.*

Rational System of Explanation. Vyākhyÿukti. Rnam par bshad pa'i rigs pa. Toh 4061, sems tsam, *shi.*

Discussion on the Establishment of Karma. Karmasiddhiprakaraṇa. Las grub pa'i rab tu byed pa. Toh 4062, sems tsam, *shi.*

Treatise on a Hundred Dharmas of the Mahayana. Dacheng baifa mingmen lun 大乘百法明門論. *Theg pa chen po'i chos brgya gsal ba'i sgo'i bstan bcos.* Toh 4063, sems tsam, *shi.* (Translated from Chinese.)

11. Dignāga

Compendium of Valid Cognition. Pramāṇasamuccaya-nāma-prakaraṇa. Tshad ma kun las gtus pa zhes bya ba'i rab tu byed pa. Toh 4203, tshad ma, *ce.*

Compendium of Valid Cognition Autocommentary. Pramaṇasamuccayavṛtti. Tshad ma kun las gtus pa'i 'grel pa. Toh 4204, tshad ma, *ce.*

Examination of Objects. Ālambanaparīkṣā. Dmigs pa brtag pa. Toh 4205, tshad ma, *ce.*

Commentary on Examination of Objects. Ālambanaparīkṣāvṛtti. Dmigs pa brtag pa'i 'grel pa. Toh 4206, tshad ma, *ce.*

Examination of the Three Times. Trikālaparīkṣā. Dus gsum brtags pa. Toh 4207, tshad ma, *ce.*

Valid Cognition: Entrance to Reasoning. Nyāyapraveśa nāma pramāṇaśāstra. Tshad ma'i bstan bcos rigs pa la 'jug pa. Toh 4208, tshad ma, *ce.*

The Essential Lamp: Commentary on Abhidharmakośa Abhidharmakośavṛtti-marmaddīpa. Chos mngon pa mdzod kyi 'grel pa gnad kyi sgron me. Toh 4095, mngon pa, *nyu.*

Commentary to Praise of Limitless Qualities. Guṇapuryantastotra-ṭīkā. Yon tan mtha' yas par bstod pa'i 'grel ba. Toh 1156, bstod tshogs, *ka.*

Ascertaining the Wheel of Reasoning. Hetucakraḍamaru. Gtan tshig gi 'khor lo gtan la dbab pa. Toh 4209, tshad ma, *ce.*

12. Dharmakīrti

Treatise of Valid Cognition. Pramāṇavārttika. Tshad ma rnam 'grel gyi tshig le'ur byas pa. Toh 4210, tshad ma, *ce.*

Drops of Reasoning. Nyāyabinduprakaraṇa. Rigs pa'i thigs pa. Toh 4212, tshad ma, *ce.*

Drops of Proof. Hetubindunāmaprakaraṇa. Gtan tshig thigs pa. Toh 4213, tshad ma, *ce.*

Analysis of Connection. Sambandhaparikṣāvṛtti. 'Brel ba brtag pa. Toh 4214, tshad ma, *ce.*

Establishing the Mental Continuums of Others. Saṃtānāntarasiddhināmaprakaraṇa. Rgyud gzhan sgrub pa. Toh 4219, tshad ma, *che.*

Ascertainment of Valid Cognition. Pramāṇaviniścaya. Tshad ma rnam nges.
Toh 4211, tshad ma, *ce.*

The Rational of Argument Vādanyāyanāmaprakaraṇa. Rtsod pa'i rigs pa.
Toh 4218, tshad ma, *che.*

Autocommentary on *Commentary on Valid Cognition. Pramāṇavārttika-
vṛtti. Tshad ma rnam 'grel gyi 'grel pa.* Toh 4216, tshad ma, *ce.*

13. Vimuktisena

*Light on Perfection of Wisdom in Twenty-Five Thousand Lines. Pañcaviṃśati-
sāhasrikāvṛtti. Nyi khri snang ba.* Toh 3787, shes phyin, *ka.*

14. Haribhadra

*Clarification of the Meaning of the Ornament of Realization. Abhi-
samayālaṃkāravṛtti. Shes rab kyi pha rol tu phyin pa'i man ngag gi bstan
bcos mngon par togs pa'i rgyan zhes bya ba'i 'grel pa. 'Grel pa don gsal.*
Toh 3793, shes phyin, *ja.*

*Explanation of the Eight Thousand Perfection of Wisdom Sutra. Light of
the Abhisamayālaṃkāra. Aṣṭasāhasrikāprajñāparamitāvyākhyābhi-
samayālaṃkārāloka. Brgyad stong pa'i bshad pa mngon par rtogs pa'i
rgyan gyi snang ba.* Toh 3791, shes phyin, *cha.*

*Summary of the Twenty(-Five) Thousand Perfection of Wisdom Sutra in
Eight Chapters. Pañcaviṃśatisāhasrikāprajñāpāramitā. Nyi khri'i bsdus
don le'u brgyad pa.* Toh 3790, shes phyin, *ga.*

*Commentary on Condensation of the Bhagavan's Precious Qualities.
Bhagavadratnaguṇasañcayagātha. Bcom ldan 'das yon tan rin po che sdud
pa'i 'grel pa.* Toh 3792, shes phyin, *ja.*

15. Guṇaprabha

Vinaya Sutra. Vinayasūtra. 'Dul ba'i mdo. Toh 4117, 'dul ba, *wu.*

*Autocommentary to Vinaya Sutra. Vinayasūtravṛtti. 'Dul ba'i mdo rtsa ba'i
rang 'grel.* Toh 4119, 'dul ba, *zhu.*

*One Hundred and One Activities. Ekottarakarmaśataka. 'Dul ba'i las brgya
rtsa gcig pa.* Toh 4118, 'dul ba, *wu.*

16. Śākyaprabha

Verses on the Novice Monk of the Mūlasarvāstivādin. Āryamūlasarvāsti-vādiśrāmaṇerakārikā. 'Dul ba sum brgya/'Phags pa gzhi thams cad yod par smra ba'i dge tshul gyi tshig le'ur byas pa. Toh 4124, 'dul ba, *shu.*

Radiant Commentary on Verses on the Novice Monk of the Mūlasarvāsti-vādin. Āryamūlasarvāstivādiśrāmaṇerakārikā-vṛttiprabhāvatī. 'Dul ba sum brgya'i rang 'grel 'od ldan/'Phags pa gzhi thams cad yod par smra ba'i dge tshul gyi tshig le'ur byas pa'i 'grel ba 'od ldan. Toh 4125, 'dul ba, *shu.*

17. Atiśa

Lamp on the Path to Enlightenment. Bodhipathapradīpa. Byang chub lam gyi sgron ma. Toh 3948, dbu ma, *khi.*

Jewel Garland of the Bodhisattvas. Bodhisattvamaṇyāvali. Byang chub sems dpa'i bslab bya nor bu'i phreng ba. Toh 3951, dbu ma, *khi.*

Sadhana of Glorious Guhyasamāja, Lord of the World. Śrīguhyasamāja-lokeśvarasādhana. Gsang 'dus 'jig rten dbang phyug gi sgrub thabs rgyas bsdus gnyis. Toh 1892, rgyud, *pi.*

Appendix 2: Essence of Thought: A Summary of *The Fourteenth Dalai Lama's Stages of the Path, Volume 1*

Compiled by H. E. Dagyab Kyabgön Rinpoché
Translated by Chandra Chiara Ehm
Edited by Ven. Konchog Norbu and Sophie McGrath

INTRODUCTION

His Holiness introduces this two-volume series by illustrating how fundamentally important it is to develop and strengthen our basic goodness through cultivating virtuous qualities such as mindfulness, conscientiousness, patience, and contentment, as well as how to completely abandon the negative actions of body, speech, and mind, such as what are known in the Buddhist teachings as the ten non-virtues.

Guidelines as to what conduct one should adopt and abandon were not an invention of the Buddha. The Dalai Lama addresses this in his introduction, stating that the concept of abandoning non-virtuous actions also exists in non-Buddhist traditions, and was originally introduced as a method for creating a harmonious society.

This understanding that virtuous or non-virtuous states of mind and actions have to be respectively adopted or abandoned was gradually integrated into the different religious traditions and their teachings to foster a contented way of life. This process of integration was surely of benefit. However, it is important to be aware that when someone intends to engage in an ethical way of life, they need not feel compelled to rely on religious explanations on virtue and non-virtue such as the Buddha's word, or the word of God.

Not everybody in the world adheres to a religion. As such, it would be of more benefit to investigate whether adopting secular ethics is worth doing, and if so, to observe such ethics from the standpoint of what is beneficial and what is harmful with regard to our own well-being and the well-being of others. This is illustrated with examples from everyday life.

CHAPTER ONE

The Dalai Lama formulated three commitments to address the problems in this world. The first of these commitments is the active promotion of basic human values, otherwise known as secular ethics. Secular ethics are comparable to water, and religion to tea, in that life without religion is possible, but a life without basic values is not.

CHAPTER TWO

The second commitment is to promote harmony and understanding among the world's religions. This commitment underscores that whether we are religious or not, or even if we reject religion altogether, we all have the wish to achieve happiness. It also emphasizes that we should actively take responsibility for preventing any kind of religious persecution or violence related to religion.

CHAPTER THREE

This chapter offers detailed insight into the similarities between Buddhism and modern science, employing logical reasoning aimed at bringing about an understanding of the nature of phenomena, and explaining how these different approaches are of mutual benefit.

CHAPTER FOUR

Chapter four sheds light on how cosmology is presented in both classical Buddhism and modern literature, raising the question as to which approaches are relevant to the quest for understanding the nature of reality and which are not.

CHAPTER FIVE

Further discussed in this chapter are the views and principles that the world's religions hold in common, as well as the aspects that make each unique, in the context of bringing about interfaith dialogue.

CHAPTER SIX

This chapter outlines the way in which the Buddhist canon has been transmitted through different lineages and traditions in Pāli, Sanskrit, and Tibetan. Furthermore, it explains how the latter transmission was sustained by erudite scholars and translators, the translation into Tibetan of the Kangyur and Tengyur, the first block prints, and the supplication prayers to the seventeen Indian pandits and their work.

Moreover, this chapter relates how Tibetan Buddhism spread to China and Mongolia and how even today Mongolian pilgrims travel to India to receive Buddhist teachings and extend their knowledge of Buddhist philosophy. Beyond these regional affiliations, it also discusses how interest in Tibetan Buddhism and the academic branch of Tibetology unfolded throughout the five continents.

Finally, this chapter provides a comprehensive introduction to Tibet's native Bön religion and the Buddhist tradition founded by the historical Buddha Śākyamuni that was established much later in Tibet. It explains how today Tibetan Buddhism is the only Buddhist tradition that preserves in their entirety the sutra and tantra lineages that derive from India's Nālandā Monastery, and how the core teachings are the same in all its sub-schools and traditions.

CHAPTER SEVEN

What is authentic Great Vehicle dharma? This question is answered here with reference to the "grounds and paths" in both the sutra and tantra traditions, and a detailed exposition of the "four bodies."

This chapter also takes a critical stand on how the tantric traditions have developed up to the present day. Unfortunately, worldly deities and spirits are frequently worshipped and there is too much focus on the veneration of dharma protectors, to the point where practitioners actually pray to these protectors. Furthermore entire walls in Tibetan temples are decorated with images of meditation deities of Highest Yoga Tantra and wrathful dharma protectors openly on public display—representations that should be kept secret. Henceforth it is extremely important to identify and make clear how the tantric tradition has been corrupted by such approaches and practices.

In everyday life, many Tibetan Buddhists attribute their negative experiences to dharma protectors, feeling that they are in a position to intimidate or punish them. To blame negative experiences on dharma protectors is nothing other than superstitious belief, and a misguided attempt to justify the ripening of negative karma. If dharma protectors really are emanations of buddhas or bodhisattvas, then under no circumstances would they harm sentient beings.

If the dharma protectors could simply be commanded to dispel obstacles and punish others according to our wishes, then the karmic law of cause and effect would be fundamentally corrupt. This kind of unfounded belief is so ingrained that even negative actions such as ritual animal sacrifice are excused as religiously motivated. Consequently, it is of upmost importance to completely dispel these misunderstandings and to return to the roots of Buddhist teaching.

CHAPTER EIGHT

The Buddhist way of life is commonly known to be a peaceful one—peaceful in terms of its conduct but most importantly in terms of its motivation. A complementary and vital aspect to this is the freedom to scrutinize the Buddhist teachings and not follow them blindly. In this spirit, core teachings such as those on the two truths, the four noble truths, and the four seals should be investigated on the basis of logical reasoning, and not accepted by faith alone. Such an approach leads to a solid understanding of the essence of the Buddhist doctrine.

The Buddhist view is that all phenomena arise through dependent arising, which should be verified through logical analysis. In illustrating the three levels of understanding dependent origination using the four kinds of reasons, the three kinds of conditions, and the four dependences, we gain helpful tools to deepen our understanding of dependent origination. The eighth chapter touches upon all of these points in detail.

Exploring these points leads to the following questions: What qualifies one to be a Buddhist in the twenty-first century? How should she or he be knowledgeable?

When we take refuge in the Three Jewels without relying on knowledge acquired through in-depth study, there is the danger that we will ascribe all of our life's happiness and suffering to the Three Jewels alone. It seems as if the Three Jewels must then take responsibility for everything good or bad that we encounter in life. Misunderstanding the meaning of taking refuge in this way, our refuge closely resembles a belief in a creator god. This would not just contradict the logical modus operandi we cherish in Buddhism, but also the approach of being our own master and living our life in a responsible way.

Without a foundational knowledge of Buddhism, we might come to incorrect conclusions such as asserting that harm and punishment in the name of the dharma is a reality. The most effective antidote to such misinterpretations is the cultivation of wisdom, and a reorientation toward the essence of the Buddha's teaching.

Traditionally in Tibet, authentic Buddhist teachers were supposed to be endowed with the qualities of scholarly erudition, ethical personal conduct, and altruism. In this age of broader education these qualities are by no means exclusively reserved for monks and nuns but are also to be cultivated by lay practitioners. If any practitioner embodies the qualities of erudition, morality, and good character there is benefit for society as a whole, regardless whether they are lay or monastic.

How should we consider the path of practice leading to those qualities? Study and practice should be characterized by a vivid sense of joy that flows from one's own motivation. Practicing with such delight will never occur in a state of mind derived through suppression or force; it has to originate from a strong conviction in the benefit of the dharma. It is detrimental when Buddhist teachers intimidate their students with punishments or tales of torture in hell if the students accumulate bad karma. Instead, they should inspire their students through the four ways of gathering disciples. Each of these four represents a positive approach, not intimidation. Therefore, the four precepts of a religious practitioner are applicable to every Buddhist and are taught equally in the Theravada and Great Vehicle traditions.

The statement that the preservation of the Buddhist doctrine depends solely on the ordained sangha is rather outdated. The principal causes for the preservation of authoritative Buddhist scriptures and their heritage of practices are dedications and the power of aspirational prayers, which are not only performed by the monastic community but also by all lay practitioners. In the same way, the preservation of the Buddhist doctrine should not only be the responsibility of the twofold ordained community. Since the majority of people in our society do not belong to the community of ordained practitioners, it would be too narrow to only posit the "ordained community who wear saffron-colored robes and the ordained lay community in their white robes adorned with plaited hair" as the only worthy objects of refuge. If all lay practitioners take responsibility this sets a good example and ensures the long-term preservation of the Buddhist teaching on a broad level.

This is also reflected in today's Tibetan youth, who with the completion of their modern secular schooling have developed a keen interest in Buddhism. With this kindled interest, it would also be important to revive the studies of the great classical treatises in the tradition of Nālandā Monastery. In the same way that Nālandā did not discriminate in favor of monastics over lay students, or males over females, these classical studies should be opened up to everybody. The geshé title should be reformed and updated accordingly. In the first place the geshé title marks the completion of a course of studies and should be conferred independently of whether the student is monastic or not, or where they studied was a monastic university or not. For these reasons, it is a real necessity to make the geshé title available to ordained and non-ordained students, and to women and men alike.

Against this backdrop, the question might be asked as to how far the framework of Buddhist study and practice should be adjusted or improved. In order to give a simple introduction to Buddhism there could be discussion groups, for instance, instead of someone on a high throne who must be accepted as a teacher right away. Also continuing to make the publication of rare Indian commentaries widely available would be an important step in the transmission of the BuddhaDharma.

The Dalai Lama also clearly indicates time and again the institutional challenges Tibetan Buddhism is facing. He condemns the immoderate attention that monasteries devote to luxurious building projects, the disproportionate amounts that single monks have to pay upon their geshé graduation, and the priority certain foreign benefactors give to selected religious dignitaries, reincarnated lamas, and geshés. Instead of rendering support in such a selective manner, it would be more beneficial to support the historically grown monastic communities and respecting a donation limit.

In this modern age, the monks and nuns who truly renounce lay life in order to live the life of a renunciant in accordance with the "four contentments of an ārya" are becoming fewer and fewer. The main ambition for most of those who aspire to become geshés seems to be to complete their study curriculum as quickly as possible in order to be able to grab a position in a Western dharma center, or to stylishly renovate the home of their relatives in one of the Tibetan refugee settlements. It would be important to reconsider our role models, such as the monastics in the Theravada and Christian traditions.

When taking a closer look at the Buddhist teachings we can see that they are composed of the canonical scriptures and the pith instruction for the path of practice. Nevertheless, it would not be right to consider that the scriptures only explain philosophy, and that the instructions are the actual guidelines and methods on to how attain buddhahood. The Tengyur, the Kangyur, and Nāgārjuna's six works on Madhyamaka reasoning all contain the methods and instruction on how to progress on the path of enlightenment. To regard practice instructions as separate from those three scriptural collections bears the risk going down a wrong path of practice.

Another important topic that this chapter explores is the denigration of women, a reality that still persists in Tibetan religion and politics. Males are considered to be superior and more capable. Obviously, such an outlook does not agree with Buddhist thought.

In the *Heart Sutra* the Buddha declares that "any son or daughter of the lineage who wishes to practice the profound perfection of wisdom" is alike. This states very clearly that every sentient being equally has the same spiritual potential, regardless of whether male or female. In the same way, the eighteen qualities of a precious human rebirth are identical for men and women. Similarly, when we engage in practice commitments according to either the sutras or the tantras, with regard to the manner of taking vows no differentiation is made on the basis of gender. In fact, the tantric teachings even say that denigrating a man is merely a downfall whereas denigrating a woman is considered a root downfall. It is also considered a tantric downfall if a man, whether he is a lay person or monk, does not prostrate to a woman and circumambulate her out of respect, whether in reality or in a visualized form.

There is no point denying, though, that in some Buddhist scriptures the inequality of men and women is quite clearly the subject under discussion, and that these authors did not shy away from describing the faults of women in detail. These contradictions go so far as to say that if a man becomes a monk it benefits Buddhism whereas if a woman, such as Mahāprajāpati, takes monastic vows it degenerates the Buddhist tradition. That taking monastic precepts in the Buddhist tradition might lead to degeneration directly contradicts the assertion that all the qualities of the Buddha are virtues and so they cannot have a negative impact on society.

This paradox is oftentimes reflected in superstitious behaviour one can still find today. Some Buddhist temples deny entrance to women or refuse to allow them to touch statues or relics. During religious ceremonies where monks, nuns, and laypeople gather together, precedence in terms of seating order is always given to the monks and the male practitioners. Considering that in reality the potential of a male or a female is the same, we have to identify those as faulty traditions.

Besides the spiritual potential of both genders being the same, a stronger ability to generate compassion is attributed to women. This being the case, it is important that women expand their influence in society and assume more responsible positions. If numerous countries were to elect female presidents, this would create the causes for a more peaceful political climate.

The eighth chapter concludes with the biographies of prominent female personalities. From the time of the Tibetan Empire, from 127 BCE onward, there were numerous Tibetan women who excelled through their talent and achievements in the fields of politics, trade, religion, and culture, and thus attained a certain degree of fame.

Combining those of the Tibetan Bön and Buddhist traditions, there were around 125 yoginis who were not just leading experts as far as scriptural understanding, but also outstanding practitioners. How these yoginis entered into Tibetan history by excelling in their achievements in listening, contemplating, and meditating is elucidated.

Glossary

acquired and discarded (*blang dor*). The fundamental practice of Buddhism of acquiring virtues and good qualities and discarding nonvirtues and unworthy traits. It is a practice of accumulating and purifying.

arhat (*dgra bcom pa*). Someone who has achieved the final goal of the Śrāvaka and Pratyeka Vehicles. It is the attainment of nirvana, where all mental afflictions and their causes have been destroyed, never to return.

awareness (*rig pa*). Generally, this refers to the "knowing" aspect of consciousness. On a deeper level, all consciousnesses are pervaded by and arise from this fundamental awareness. Being able to make manifest this awareness in Dzokchen practice is to realize that all phenomena of samsara and nirvana are the play of this awareness, which equates, according to the Dalai Lama, to the Prāsaṅgika understanding of emptiness.

base reality (*gzhi dngos po'i gnas tshul*). All phenomena that constitute the basic realities of existence, which can be established through direct experience and reasoning, and on which the Buddhist paths and results are built.

bodhicitta (*byang chub kyi sems*). A transformation of mind characterized by the desire to attain the full enlightenment of a buddha, motivated by the strong wish to be of benefit to all living beings.

bodhisattva (*byang chub sems pa'*). Someone who has developed bodhicitta.

channels, winds, and drops (*rtsa rlung thig le*). Ordinary or conceived constituents of the human body that are manipulated to precipitate rapid progress along the path in the completion stages of tantric practice.

Cittamātra (*sems tsam pa*). A philosophical school of the Great Vehicle, whose core belief is that all existence is undifferentiated from the mind, and thus they do not accept the existence of external phenomena. Hence, they are known as Mind Only.

clarity and knowing (*gsal rig*). The two fundamental components of consciousness. Clarity refers to the ability of consciousness to take on the aspect of its object, much in the same way as a mirror naturally reflects whatever is placed in front of it. Knowing is the intrinsic awareness consciousness has of that object.

clear light (*'od gsal, prabhāsvara*). A term that essentially refers to the fundamental nature of mind. It is the clarity aspect of the two characteristics of consciousness. As this entity of mind is untouched by adventitious defilements, it also known as the primordial mind. This primordial mind is manifest during the death process, where it is known as death clear light. In tantra it is made manifest through completion stage practice. When this primordial mind is used to cognize emptiness, "clear light" can also refer to the object of emptiness.

coexisting cause (*lhan cig byed rkyen*). A phenomenon whose entity does not undergo a fundamental change when functioning as a cause, as with water used to help a seed to grow.

cognition (*blo*). The innate characteristic of the mind to "know" its object. It can refer to both conceptual and nonconceptual perception. When combined with "mind" (*yid*) it often refers to mental cognition.

conceptual construct (*don spyi*). Literally "a universal of an actual phenomenon." That which is conceived by a valid conceptual cognition is a representation of an actual existence. A conceptual construct is a universal because it conceptualizes all instances of that phenomenon into one construct, such as when you think "trees." Alternatively, it does the opposite and conceptually deconstructs a phenomenon for the purposes of analysis, such as when contemplating the impermanence of a particular phenomenon.

consciousness (*shes pa*). The nonmaterial part of a sentient being's makeup that has the ability to know and to take on the aspect of the objects it apprehends. As a continuum it has both coarse and subtle levels.

crossing over (*thod rgal*). A Dzokchen practice of bypassing the graded steps of realization.

cutting through (*khregs chod*). A Dzokchen practice in which the continuum of mental delusion is severed by coming into direct contact with nondualistic awareness.

dependent imputation (*brten nas btags pa*). Existence as understood by the Buddhist Madhyamika school; anything that exists, despite the way it appears, is dependent on other factors for its existence, the most subtle of which is mental imputation through conceptualization.

deprecation (*skur 'debs*). A denial of something existing where it evidently does.

designation (*rtha snyad*). The labeling of phenomena either verbally or conceptually in keeping with convention.

Dharma (*chos*). As used in this book, it means religion, and more specifically the Buddhist religion.

dharma body (*chos sku, dharmakāya*). One of the four bodies of an enlightened being. Strictly speaking, this is the mind of an enlightened being. It is a body in the sense of being a collection of enlightened qualities. Sometimes it can refer to the ultimate nature of the mind of a buddha, and sometimes to the ultimate nature of any being's mind. In Dzokchen it is the space-like empty nature of the naturally arisen gnosis.

dharmadhātu (*chos dbyings*). A term meaning realm or sphere of reality, and usually referring to a particular perception of the ultimate truth.

Dzokchen (*rdzogs chen*). The essential practice of the Nyingma and other Tibetan Buddhist traditions, where the primordial awareness is brought out in its clarity and nakedness as the naturally arising gnosis.

emanated body (*sprul sku, nirmāṇakāya*). One of the four bodies of an enlightened being, it is emanated from the dharma body and appears to the perception of ordinary beings, where it goes through the birth, aging, and death process. In Dzokchen it is the all-pervading compassion of the naturally arisen gnosis.

emptiness of other (*gzhan stong*). There are varying definitions of this kind of emptiness and its counterpart, "emptiness of self" (*rang stong*). The Gelukpa sect describes one such understanding as a conceptualized entity that is completely empty of all phenomena existing on the level of deluded appearance—that is, conventional existence. It is therefore, according to its adherents, an ultimate truth but not a nonaffirming negation.

enjoyment body (*longs sku, sambhogakāya*). One of the four bodies of an enlightened being, it is a form that is able to "enjoy" or make use of the complete range of the Great Vehicle. It emanates from the dharma body and is only visible to advanced practitioners. In Dzokchen it is the clear light nature of the naturally arisen gnosis.

entity body (*ngo bo nyid sku, svabhāvakāya*). One of the four bodies of an enlightened being, it is the emptiness or the very entity of the mind of a buddha. In tantra it can be composite or noncomposite.

five paths (*lam lnga*). The path from the beginning of entering one of the three vehicles until its completion, divided into five parts: path of accumulation, path of preparation, path of seeing, path of meditation, and path of no further practice.

five sensory consciousnesses (*dbang shes lnga*). Visual, aural, nasal, gustatory, and bodily consciousnesses. These five, unlike conceptual consciousnesses, rely upon sense organs, or powers, in order to be manifest.

generation and completion stages (*bskyed rim rdzogs rim gnyis*). The two main stages of tantric practice. The initial generation stage involves a conceptualization of an inner and outer divine world intended to ripen the practitioner's mind for the subsequent completion stage, in which the inner bodily winds, channels, and drops are utilized and manipulated to transform that conceived divine world into a reality.

geshé (*dge bshes, kalyāṇamitra*). Literally "spiritual friend." Originally a general title for Buddhist teachers and mentors, these days it is a degree or title awarded to monks, and recently to nuns, who have passed a rigorous examination of their studies. It is of varying grades, the highest of which is lharampa, awarded to those who have successfully sat in debate in all three monastic seats. Lower grades are karampa, tsokrampa, lingsé, and dorampa.

Great Vehicle (*theg chen, mahāyāna*). The Buddhist path whose destination is the buddhahood that is the complete perfection of insight, compassion, and ability to be of benefit to all beings without exception.

imputed (*brtags pa*). A phenomenon conceived by conceptualization.

insight (*lhag mthong, vipaśyanā*). Generally, any realization of hidden truths developed through meditation, but specifically used here to describe a conceptual or nonconceptual comprehension of the ultimate truth or reality of phenomena.

Jetsun/Jetsunma (*rje btsun/rje btsun ma*). A title of great reverence, often translated as "venerable." "Je" means lord in the sense of having authority. Secularly it is applied to those who have power and authority over others, while in a religious sense it means possessing the authority of insights and qualities. "Tsun" means having control over all faulty conduct of body, speech, and mind.

Jonang (*jo nang*). Indigenous Tibetan Buddhist tradition of philosophy and practice, popularized in the thirteenth century by Dölpopa Sherap Gyaltsen. It is a proponent of the "emptiness of other" tenet and is renowned for maintaining the practice of the six-branched yoga of the *Kālacakra Tantra*.

Kadampa (*bka' gdams pa*). A lineage of Buddhism that appeared in Tibet by way of the teachings of the Indian master Atiśa, who traveled there in the eleventh century. It focuses on practice and was the initiator of mind-training practices.

Kangyur (*bka' gyur*). The teachings of the Buddha that were translated from Sanskrit, and occasionally from Chinese, into Tibetan. It consists of about one hundred volumes.

lama (*gu ru*). A title informally given by disciples to their master. A tulku is a formal title of recognition given to an incarnation, whereas a lama is a title of devotion and does not have to be a tulku. Also, as the Dalai Lama often points out, not all tulkus are lamas. In some traditions in Tibet the title "lama" is awarded to those who have completed particular meditation retreats.

Lokāyata (*rgyang 'phen pa*). An ancient Indian school of thought; philosophically materialist, not subscribing to any law of cause and effect, believing instead in the natural or random arising of existence, and not accepting consciousness as an entity distinct from matter.

love (*byams/byams brtse*). The genuine wish for others to be happy.

Madhyamaka (*dbu ma pa*). A proponent of the Buddhist philosophy who rejects the true existence of all phenomena.

Mahāmudrā (*phyag rgya chen mo*). A direct practice of realizing the nature of mind, commonly found in the Kagyu tradition.

material cause (*nyer len*). Also called a substantial cause, this is a composite phenomenon whose very entity undergoes change when functioning as a cause—like a seed becoming a sprout, for example.

meditative absorption (*bsam gtan, dhyāna*). An advanced meditative state often associated with a level of concentration required to be reborn into the form and formless realms, where an absorption into form as antidote to desire and into formlessness as an antidote to attachment to form is a prerequisite. In Buddhism it is the fifth of the six perfections.

meditative concentration (*ting nge 'dzin, samādhi*). A state of mind able to remain on its object without distraction. At a basic level it is a mental factor commonly employed to aid analysis. As an advanced state of mind developed through concentration it becomes mental quiescence focused upon emptiness.

mental affliction (*nyon mongs, kleśa*). Defined as states of mind that adversely afflict the mental continuum, arising as they do from a basic state of ignorance. They include thoughts, attitudes, and emotions.

mental cognition (*yid blo*). The part of the mind that is primarily cognitive by way of thought, analysis, and so on, together with resultant feelings, as opposed to direct sensory cognition and its associated feelings.

mental consciousness (*yid shes*). A consciousness that does not require the direct presence of the sense faculty and objective conditions but arises primarily by way of the immediate condition. (See **three conditions.**)

mentally constructed (*kun brtags*). When juxtaposed with "innate" it refers to the apprehension of a "self" that has been deliberately conceived through philosophical contemplation, as with the theory of atman, for example. Otherwise, it is one of the three categories of existence posited by Cittamātra philosophy.

nonaffirming negation (*med 'gag*). Conceptual cognitions of existing phenomena can be arrived at by affirmation or by a process of negation. The latter is of two types: those that do not affirm other phenomena and those that cognize solely by negation.

nondeceptive (*mi bslu ba*). As used here, it is the essential characteristic of valid cognition, in the sense that such a cognition can be relied upon, is trustworthy, incontrovertible, and infallible. It can also be used to describe speech and persons that exhibit the same qualities.

obscurations to omniscience (*shes bya'i sgrib pa*). A category of mental obscuration that has to be eliminated on the path to buddhahood. According to Prāsaṅgika Madhyamaka these obscurations are imprints of mental affliction that prevent the direct perception of the two truths simultaneously.

Prāsaṅgika Madhyamaka (*dbu ma thal 'gyur ba*). A Great Vehicle follower who as well as rejecting the true existence of all phenomena also negates the intrinsic existence of all phenomena even conventionally.

psycho-physical aggregates (*phung po, skandha*). The physical and material components of a sentient being. Usually enumerated as five, they can be condensed into body and mind.

quiescence (*gzhi gnas, śamatha*). A stillness of mind gained through prolonged focus-based meditation as a way of gaining control over the mind to the point where practitioners are capable of focusing the mind to their own volition with ease and without distraction.

rainbow body (*'ja' lus*). An attainment in Dzokchen practice whereby the physical constituents of the practitioner's body dissolve into light at the time of death.

Sautrāntika (*mdo sde pa*). A realist Buddhist philosophy based upon sutra tenets rather than the Abhidharma.

sense faculties (*dbang po*). The five organs of sight, hearing, smell, taste, and touch that act as dominant conditions for the arising of the sense consciousnesses.

seven features (of union) (*kha sbyor yan lag bdun*). This is a synonym for Vajradhara, the Buddha as the teacher of tantras, and refers to seven constantly present characteristics:

1. *Body of complete enjoyment*: Being endowed with the thirty-two major and eighty minor marks of complete enlightenment.

2. *Union*: Being in meditative union with consort.

3. *Great bliss*: Experiencing great bliss through the winds entering, abiding, and dissolving in the dhūtī.

4. *No inherent nature*: Understanding the noninherent nature of the mind dwelling in pure bliss.

5. *Unbroken continuum*: Never entering nirvana but remaining until the end of samsara.

6. *Filled with compassion*: Never straying from working for others by way of nonapprehending compassion.

7. *Unending*: An endless and continuous stream of enlightened activity.

Shijé (*zhi byed*). Literally "pacifying." A Buddhist doctrine introduced to Tibet by Phadampa Sangyé in the twelfth century. It is a practice based upon the perfection of wisdom designed to pacify mental afflictions.

six perfections (*phar phyin drug*). Six categories of practice essential for accomplishing the bodhisattva goal: the practice of giving, ethics, patience, effort, absorption, and wisdom.

spheres and sensory sources (*khams dang skye mched*). In the categorizing of phenomena as found in the Abhidharma literature, the eighteen spheres comprise the six types of consciousnesses, the six sense faculties such as the faculty of the eye, and the six objects of those consciousnesses. This division is based upon each of these eighteen occupying its own "sphere," or entity. The twelve sensory sources are the six faculties paired with the six objects. This division is made on the basis of each pair being a source of a corresponding apprehending consciousness.

superimposition (*sgro 'dogs*). An exaggeration or imputation of something existing where it does not.

ten levels (*sa bcu*). The path from the path of seeing of either of the three vehicles up to the final goal, divided into ten parts.

ten nonvirtuous acts (*mi dge ba bcu*). The restraint from or abandonment of these ten constitute the basic morality or ethical behavior of someone who has entered the Buddhist path. They are divided into physical, verbal, and mental acts: killing, stealing, sexual misconduct, lying, harsh words, divisive speech, idle gossip, malice, covetousness, and wrong view.

Tengyur (*bstan gyur*). Treatises and commentaries written by Indian masters that were translated from Sanskrit and other Indic languages, and in some cases Chinese, into Tibetan. It consists of about two hundred volumes.

three appearances (*sngang ba gsum*). (1) An emptiness pervaded by a whitish appearance like moonlight on an autumn night (*snang ba*); (2) an emptiness pervaded by a reddish appearance like sunlight on an autumn day (*mched*); and (3) an emptiness pervaded by darkness like a moonless autumn night (*nyer thob*). These three occur sequentially during the death process and precipitate the dawning of death clear light.

three categories (*mtshan nyid gsum*). A division of existing phenomena posited by Cittamātra philosophy: mentally constructed phenomena, dependent phenomena and absolute reality.

three conditions (*rkyen gsum*). As used in the book these are the conditions necessary for a sense consciousness to arise. The objective condition is the accessible sense object of form, sound, and so on. The empowering condition is a functioning sense faculty. The immediate condition is a preceding moment in the continuum of consciousness.

Three Jewels (*dkon mchog gsum*). A Buddhist goes for refuge to the Three Jewels: the Buddha, Dharma, and Sangha. The third of these initially referred to monastics who had attained the noble, or ārya, levels. The Tibetan term is *gendun* (*dge 'dun*) and also refers to the monastic community generally.

three vehicles (*theg pa gsum*). Great Vehicle, Śrāvaka Vehicle, and Pratyeka Vehicle.

treasure text (*gter ma*). A teaching that was written down and hidden away at an earlier time, to be revealed at a later time by special treasure-revealers (*gter ston*). Some treasure texts are not revealed in written form but are received in meditation by advanced practitioners.

tulku (*sprul sku*). Literally "emanated form." Originally a term applied to a type of emanation of an enlightened being or buddha that is visible and accessible to all. In Tibetan religious terminology it is a title given to someone who has been formally recognized as the reincarnation of a great spiritual adept. This incarnation can of course reincarnate again, and in this way tulku lineages are formed.

Vaibhāṣika (*bye brag smra ra*). A realist Buddhist philosophy based upon general Abhidharma tenets.

Vajra Vehicle (*rdo rje theg pa*). Another term for the path of tantra or mantra.

valid cognition (*tshad ma, pramāṇa*). A cognition whose primary characteristic is one of being nondeceiving, reliable, and authoritative with regard to the object it apprehends. In Buddhist contemplative analysis it is often produced through systematic reasoning in order to apprehend phenomena not accessible to sense consciousnesses.

wrong cognition (*log shes*). A cognition whose conceived object has no correspondence in reality.

Notes

1. This is an indication that not every word in the book was actually spoken by His Holiness. See introduction.

2. The controversy over this supernatural figure is well known among Tibetans and Western Buddhists and is described in detail in Gavin Kilty, *Understanding the Case against Shukden* (Boston: Wisdom Publications, 2019).

3. The information in this paragraph has been drawn from the Gaden Phodrang preface, which has not been translated for the book.

4. That is, he became a monk.

5. Adhering to the bare necessities of food, clothing, place, and bedding.

6. Gathering disciples by way of giving, gentle and skillful speech, good conduct, and acting in accordance with what they teach. There are many variants on the last two.

7. One of the three wheels; the other two are the wheel of the meditative concentration by way of abandoning and the wheel of activity through deeds.

8. This quality together with three other qualities listed in the following three paragraphs (enclosed in quotation marks) are the four great qualities of studying the stages of the path literature, as described by Tsongkhapa in his *Extensive Exposition on the Stages of the Path to Enlightenment*.

9. The "great fault" is that of abandoning the Dharma, whereby some practices are seen as essential while others are ignored. Having the first two qualities, described above, means that this fourth quality will naturally be present.

10. These are the seventeen pandits, or masters, who studied at Nālandā Monastery, beginning with Nāgārjuna in the first century CE up to the Indian master Atiśa, who traveled to and passed away in Tibet in the eleventh century. Nālandā was an ancient Indian Buddhist monastery in the present-day Indian state of Bihar and flourished between the fifth and eleventh centuries. The prayer to these seventeen masters, composed by His Holiness, is included later in the text.

11. A critique of a text's content, purpose, essential purpose, and the internal connections between them.

12. A large yak is difficult to kill, and therefore requires a skilled butcher.

13. An epithet of Jé Tsongkhapa.

14. A Tibetan exclamation of wonder.

15. A common saying, meaning that scholars are only recognized as such in the presence of their peers.

16. Tsongkhapa, *Praise of Dependent Arising*, verse 28. In the last line "this" refers to dependent arising.

17. Tsongkhapa, *Praise of Dependent Arising*, verse 34.

18. The first two volumes of this work have been translated and published separately by Wisdom Publications as *Science and Philosophy in the Indian Buddhist Classics*, vol. 1, *The Physical World* (2017); and vol. 2, *The Mind* (2020).

19. A labrang is the monastic household of an incarnated lama.

20. Although this title (literally "spiritual friend") has been used in Tibet over the centuries as a term of veneration, under the Thirteenth Dalai Lama it became a specific academic degree awarded to those monks who had completed the recognized monastic curriculum and passed the appropriate examination. The suffix "-ma" feminizes the term.

21. The five sciences are arts and crafts, medicine, grammar and language, logic, and philosophy.

22. "A friend of no acquaintance," a term often applied to the Buddha, meaning that unlike ordinary people, he does not need to be acquainted with someone in order to be their friend. He is a friend to all, irrespective of whether he knows them or not.

23. These four bodies are explained in chapter 7.

24. Rinpoché gives weapon builders as an example.

25. *Mngon mtho*, which usually refers to birth in the realms of gods and humans.

26. The chapter titles are as follows: "Rethinking Secularism"; "Our Common Humanity"; "The Quest for Happiness"; "Compassion: The Foundation of Well-Being"; "Compassion and the Question of Justice"; "The Role of Discernment"; "Ethics in Our Shared World"; "Ethical Mindfulness in Everyday Life"; "Dealing with Destructive Emotions"; "Cultivating Key Inner Values"; "Meditation as Mental Cultivation."

27. Common paths are those traveled by Buddhists of all tenet systems. Exclusive paths are the Great Vehicle paths.

28. Also known as buddha nature. Sugata (*bde gshegs*), literally "one gone to bliss," is an epithet of a buddha. "Essence" refers to the fact that the possibility or potential to become a buddha exists in every living being.

29. The Buddha is venerated because he taught the Dharma, but the actual refuge is the Dharma. This refers to the truth of cessation and the truth of the path as insights within the mind.

30. The trainings in ethics, concentration, and wisdom. These are explained later.

31. "Ripened" in the sense of these qualities being karmic fruits of past actions.

32. There are 112 prime and secondary physical features found in a buddha or enlightened being.

33. This point about being attractive in order to win people over has brought some criticism of His Holiness when he has mentioned it in public. This is not a dismissal of the disabled or of those who do not conform to modern standards of "beauty." It is a recognition that if someone wants to be of benefit to the world, it is advantageous to possess some degree of attraction. If anything, such a wish says a lot about the conventional perception of the world. If everyone was even-handed and did not judge others by their appearance, such a wish to be attractive would not be necessary.

34. The four close contemplations, the four perfect abandonments, the four branches of magical powers, the five powers (or strengths), the five forces, the seven branches of enlightenment, and the eightfold path of the āryas collectively make up the thirty-seven facets of enlightenment.

35. The mind-training teachings of the Indian pandit Atiśa were summarized into seven key points.

36. "Merit" is an Asian and particularly Buddhist concept of a beneficial force accumulated as a result of good deeds, acts, or thoughts in previous lives. "Good karma" is a popular, if imperfect, rendering of the concept.

37. Songtsen Gampo, Tri Songdetsen, and Tri Ralpachen, who ruled Tibet in the first millennium.

38. The Sakya period was from the thirteenth to the fourteenth century.

39. The figures of 30 million, 6.4 million, and 6 million are taken from a Tibetan book on its population by Tsering Wangchuk, *Bod kyi mi 'bor sa ya drug skor lam tsam dpyad pa* (Dharamsala: CTA Department of Information and International Relations, 1989). The first figure is explained as including the population of all the territories Tibet conquered. The other two figures of about six million do not include these territories because they were calculated after the dissolution of the Tibetan empire. The figure of ten million is not from the book and is an estimation by His Holiness.

40. Some Tibetan thinkers have said that Tibet was lost to the Chinese invasion because religious standards had declined, and the Dharma could no longer protect it.

41. In this paragraph, the phrase, "fearful of death" does not refer solely to being afraid of one's death or being scared of dying. It refers more to an abhorrence or horror of death as a general event.

42. This information is from Wikipedia.org/wiki/Major _religious groups. The numbers here have been updated from the original Tibetan text, as per Wikipedia.

43. As discussed above, the first is promotion of human values and the third is the welfare of the Tibetan religious culture and environment.

44. This is the general definition of faith found in the standard Buddhist literature on mental factors. Faith is a mental factor whose presence in the mind actively works to dispel the habitual lack of faith, which is also a mental factor.

45. Haribhadra, *Abhisamayālaṃkāra*. Toh 3793, shes phyin *ja*, 79a2.

46. The śrāvaka and pratyeka were non–Great Vehicle disciples of the Buddha. The practitioners known as śrāvaka (literally "listener") relied heavily upon the Buddha's words. The pratyekas preferred to meditate on their own.

47. *Ṛṣi,* a Sanskrit term of reverence meaning "sage."

48. The enlightened mind of a buddha.

49. An epithet traditionally used for the ordained monks of the Buddha.

50. This refers to a logical fallacy commonly discussed in works on Buddhist dialectics and epistemology. For example, by seeing that the rice at the top of the cooking pot is cooked, we declare that all the rice is cooked. This is an example used by the seventh-century Indian Buddhist logician Dharmakīrti. In truth we simply see that rice is cooked in one place and do not see any uncooked rice elsewhere.

51. These four will be explained in more detail in chapter 8.

52. These are the two main philosophical schools of Great Vehicle Buddhism.

53. This is the verse accompanying a ritual offering of the universe, which is depicted as a mandala-like world dominated by a huge central mountain called Meru. Around this mountain the sun, moon and planets revolve, and at its four compass points are found the four great continents of the world. The Dalai Lama encourages his followers to not take this ancient and traditional flat-earth cosmology literally.

54. These are known as the Mind and Life Dialogues.

55. These are composite phenomena that are neither consciousness nor form.

56. This was an ancient Indian materialistic school of thought that did not accept past and future lives or the existence of consciousness.

57. This would be meditation on the impermanent nature of phenomena, for example.

58. The four truths are explained in chapter 8.

59. Method and wisdom are the two main categories of practice. Method involves aspiration and is linked to bodhicitta practices such as the cultivation of compassion. It is the vastness of the path. Wisdom involves penetrating the nature of reality through meditation. It is the depth of the path. Together they are described as the two wings needed to fly to enlightenment. The ultimate resultant attainments of method and wisdom are the two enlightened forms—the body and mind of a buddha.

60. "Form affording visibility" (*mngon par skabs yod kyi gzugs*) is a type of "form" that is the space between things, allowing us the capability to perceive far-off objects. This is not the same as noncomposite space, which is an absence of obstructing form. "Not a source of visible form" means that is not the kind of visible form that acts as a cause for a visual consciousness to arise, as is the case with coarse forms. "Form as a mental phenomena source" means that it is form cognized by the mental consciousness. The Abhidharma system speaks of twelve "sources" (*skye mched, āyatana*), or causes, whose function is to create and increase sensory and mental cognition. The five sense powers or faculties, such as the eyes, and the five sense objects, such as sound, make up ten of these sources. Very subtle form, for example, not visible to the naked eye, and the mental cognition that conceives it make up the last two. Therefore, these particles act as mental phenomena sources, and are known as "mental phenomena."

61. Buddhist cosmology speaks of cycles of existence followed by destruction and a period of "nothingness." These cycles are measured in eons.

62. "Clarity" refers to the mirror-like or sky-like quality of consciousness, able to take on and reflect objects without hindrance. It does not refer to the clarity of an unconfused mind, for example. "Knowing" is its characteristic of awareness. It does not refer to knowing in the sense of correctly understanding.

63. A mind of hatred can become a mind of kindness and compassion, but both are in the nature of clarity and knowing.

64. The Tibetan term used throughout this section (*klad rtsa*, literally "nerves of the brain") has been translated as "neurons." The Tibetan term as used here might be an umbrella term covering related neural phenomena, but I have chosen the single term "neurons" after consultation with Tawni Tidwell, TMD, PhD, postdoctoral research associate, Center for Healthy Minds, University of Wisconsin–Madison, and Tsondue Samphel, international program coordinator, SEE Learning, Center for Contemplative Science and Compassion-Based Ethics, Emory University. I am very grateful for their help in this matter.

65. An "afflicted desire" is one that is tainted by mental affliction or deluded perception.

66. This refers to a particular kind of meditative concentration—found in Buddhist and non-Buddhist practitioners—in which the qualities of the higher realms of existence, such as those of the form and formless realms, are regarded as desirable to attain, while those of the lower realms are seen as coarse.

67. *Mimosa pudica*. Also known as the "sensitive plant," or "touch-me-not."

68. The full quote is "As the bodily sense power pervades the body, so ignorance pervades all," and comes from *Four Hundred Verses*, a work on Buddhist practice and philosophy by the Indian master Āryadeva (third century).

69. *Mi bslu ba*. This term, often translated as "valid," is also rendered as "incontrovertible," "infallible," "trustworthy," "undeceiving," and so on.

70. In the example of seeing a tree, the tree is the objective and external condition. The sense faculty of the eye is the empowering or determining condition, and the immediately preceding continuum of consciousness is the immediate condition.

71. In the Buddhist philosophical manuals on types of knowing, these three are presented as being synonymous.

72. This is the highest of the four classes of Buddhist tantra.

73. This is the Tibetan reading. Querying this, Dagyab Rinpoché says that maybe it should read, "or that consciousness is created from no cause," as has been stated previously.

74. *Prakṛti*, the central tenet of the Samkhya Hindu philosophical school, referring to a universal and unchanging source from which all things become manifest.

75. *Lokāyata* literally means "far flung."

76. This oft-cited verse is not found in the original sutra but is cited in *Stainless Light*, for example.

77. *Tshad ma'i skyes bu*. Literally "valid person." Epistemologically the term "valid" can be applied to cognition, speech, and persons. Valid cognition is the main subject in epistemological works, which seek to explain which type of cognition is valid in the sense of being nondeceptive and trustworthy. The same criteria apply to persons.

78. According to Abhidharma philosophy, nighttime is the shadow cast by Meru as the sun travels behind it.

79. *Miśraka-abhidharma-hṛdaya-śāstra*. This appears to not have been translated into Tibetan.

80. At this point in the Tibetan text there begins a section of about fifty pages on cosmological description translated into Tibetan from Western sources. This is for Tibetan readers and so has been omitted here.

81. The Tibetan term is *bsnyen* (Sanskrit *seva*). This is a retreat the length of which is often determined by a specific number of mantras to be completed. The Sanskrit seva is cognate with the English "service," thus having the meaning of devoting oneself as a way of becoming close to the object of devotion. The "accomplishment" is not an actual unity with the deity but a result of the devotions whereby one is almost in contact with the deity.

82. Kullu is a district in the northern Indian state of Himachal Pradesh.

83. These four will be explained below.

84. See glossary for a brief description of these four tenet systems.

85. The fundamental tenet of this school is that phenomena arise naturally without the need for causes. Therefore, nothing has a beginning, because a begin-

ning would require a cause, and a cause would imply a continuum of that cause either by substance or type. Conditions coming together to produce the world, self, and so on preclude the need for a previous continuum.

86. Literally "the later treatise." Sometimes translated as *The Sublime Continuum.* See bibliography: Maitreya, *Uttaratantra.*

87. According to Buddhist texts, the Tibetan term *mir chags pa* ("becoming a human being"), translated here as "embryo," refers to the first four or five weeks after conception, up to the development of limb protrusions. Western medical terminology says that an embryo becomes a fetus after the eleventh week. In stages of the path teachings, the object of killing is "a sentient being that possesses life."

88. Here and elsewhere "nonsentient" means "without mind." The Tibetan literally reads, "If mind can be created from matter that is without mind."

89. These "demons" are personifications of obstructions and hindrances. The fourth, Devaputra, is somewhat akin to Cupid.

90. This is from *Fundamental Wisdom of the Middle Way,* 18:5. The whole verse is often cited by His Holiness. Here, only the second line is quoted.

91. *Tshul min yid byed.* This is a technical term used to describe the conceptualizing of objects as desirable, undesirable, and so on, which gives rise to the afflictions of desire and aversion.

92. The pilgrimage place of Buddha's enlightenment in the Indian state of modern-day Bihar.

93. By "blessed" His Holiness means that the Buddha was in control of his lifespan but chose to pass away in order to teach impermanence.

94. Here, the term "countless" is not literally beyond number but the name of a very long eon.

95. According to the tantra tradition, many tantra teachings and even whole tantras appeared in the minds of special disciples after the Buddha had passed away.

96. Dagyab Rinpoché notes that there are many differing assertions on the dates of the Buddha, but that this, the Theravada tradition, is widely accepted.

97. *Prayer of Good Conduct.* Toh 1095, gzungs, *vaṃ*, 263b.

98. These three are the categories of monastic discipline, sutra, and abhidharma. Different editions have different numbers of volumes.

99. A section of the Kangyur, primarily devoted to mantra-based rituals for accomplishing certain aims.

100. A hill near the ancient city of Rajgir, in the Indian state of Bihar.

101. Near Amrāvatī, capital of the Indian state of Andhra Pradesh.

102. The first three of these places are in present Bihar state; the last is in Punjab, Pakistan.

103. Also known as Ba Salnang, author of an influential work on the history of Buddhism.

104. Lekdrup died on the way back to Tibet.

105. These men were known as "the seven men to be tested," in the sense of seeing if they could keep the vows of a Buddhist monk.

106. "Pure perception" is the seeing of the divine in certain people and objects. In some advanced practitioners it arises naturally and acts as a support for further insight. At other times it is cultivated in order to strengthen faith and to receive blessings. Used unwisely it can be a barrier to seeing the reality of a situation.

107. The fivefold self-arisen statue is a statue of eleven-faced Avalokiteśvara in a chapel of the Jokhang Temple in Lhasa. It contains within it a self-arisen sandalwood statue of the same deity. Emperor Songtsen Gampo and his two brides were said to have also dissolved into the main statue, hence its name.

108. See note 21.

109. This is stated in *Research on Nālandā*. Other sources say he was the abbot or the incumbent of the Buddha's Throne in Bodhgaya.

110. A town southwest of Lhasa.

111. Apparently, this mammoth creation was destroyed.

112. At this point, Dagyab Rinpoché has inserted a list of the most important compositions of the seventeen pandits. These are reproduced in the appendix at pp. 455–64 of the present volume.

113. Abbot Śāntarakṣita, Emperor Tri Songdetsen, and Ācarya Padmasambhava, as mentioned previously.

114. A siddha is a practitioner with great powers and insight.

115. These are Sachen Künga Nyingpo, Sönam Tsemo (1142–82), Drakpa Gyaltsen (1147–1216), Sakya Pandita Künga Gyaltsen (1182–1251), and Pakpa Lodrö Gyaltsen (1235–80).

116. This is a rather cryptic paragraph, according to Dagyab Rinpoché.

117. Panchen Losang Chögyen, *Geluk Kagyu Tradition of Mahamudra*, p. 4.

118. Previously this phrase was translated as "clarity and knowing" but "awareness" is preferred by Nyingma translators.

119. These are referred to as the four yogas of Mahāmudrā.

120. In each of these three isolations, the winds are brought into the central channel in order to manifest the clear light consciousness.

121. A set of completion stage practices that differ from the usual five stages. The six-branch yoga is found in the *Kālacakra Tantra* and in the eighteenth chapter of the *Guhyasamāja Tantra*.

122. This refers to the progression of four appearances at the time of death as all conceptual minds gradually absorb and dissolve into the clear light.

123. Conceptual cognitions of existing phenomena can be arrived at by a process of negation. Those that do not affirm other phenomena and those that do are nonaffirming and affirming, respectively.

124. Drigung Palzin was a fourteenth-century scholar of the Drigung Kagyu school who claimed that the Nyingma tantras were written by Tibetans.

125. The eight main deities of Mahayoga practice with their corresponding tantras and sadhanas.

126. Dzokchen tradition established by Aro Yeshé Jungné in the tenth century.

127. The source of this verse is unknown.

128. This exchange is found in Gyalwang Chöjé Losang Trinlé's *Great Biography of Tsongkhapa*, p. 622.

129. This refers to seven texts on this genre by the seventh-century Indian Buddhist logician Dharmakīrti.

130. Chapa Chökyi Sengé was a Tibetan scholar credited with creating the format and structure of the Geluk monastic debate curriculum.

131. The original Shechen Öntrul Gyurmé Thutop Namgyal (b. 1787) was a well-known Nyingma lama of Shechen Monastery.

132. For example, hoisting prayer flags and holding offering ceremonies to the gods are not strictly Buddhist practices but they do no harm, can even be beneficial, and are embedded in the culture with which the people identify.

133. This first paragraph is taken from Ngawang Nyima's *A Religious History*. The remainder mainly consists of the Dalai Lama's own words, with extra detail such as dates inserted by His Holiness's Private Office.

134. These place names are some of the thirteen Tibetan administrative districts existing at that time.

135. Chögyal Phakpa was the fifth throneholder of the Sakya school and the first "imperial preceptor" of Kublai Khan's dynasty, who was given administrative control over Tibet.

136. Ütsang, Domé, and Dotö.

137. This seems to refer to the reported annual execution of Chinese citizens for population control. By offering it to Phakpa, he was effectively putting a stop to it.

138. *Guoshi* in Chinese, or *goshri* in Tibetan.

139. Kharngön is a city in Inner Mongolia that is now called Hohhot.

140. The Mongolian Khalkha prince also known as Choghtu Khong Tayiji.

141. Phuntsok Namgyal was the ruler of Tsang province, in western Tibet.

142. The author etymologizes this title to mean "Palace of a Hundred Joys."

143. Dagyab Rinpoché concedes that Tibetan histories, like many others, are subject to bias and that the events related here are told differently by different sides.

144. Still standing in Beijing and known as the White Dagoba.

145. See note 21.

146. This is the famous Yonghe Temple, or "Lama Temple," in Beijing.

147. Both places are in Inner Mongolia.

148. Da Khüree, in Mongolian; present-day Ulaan Baator (Ulan Bator), the capital city of Mongolia.

149. Along with Dākhural, Ikhural (Ikh Khüree) is another old name for present-day Ulaan Baator.

150. Possibly Baldan Braibun in Buryatia.

151. This account of the Sixth Dalai Lama can be found in *Religious History of Mongolia* (*Hor chos 'byung*) by Dharmatala, composed in 1889. In this account the Dalai Lama did not die in mysterious circumstances at the age of twenty-three in Qinghai, as is commonly reported, but lived a long life in Mongolia.

152. The Ninth Jetsun Dampa was recognized in 1936 by the regent of Tibet but was kept a secret because of this Russian declaration made in 1929. With the secret still intact, he came to India in 1959.

153. Earth, water, fire, wind, and space, within and without the body.

154. Modern scholars claim that Ölmo Lungring is west of Tibet in the land of Tazik, or is Tazik itself. Although it is tempting to identify Tazik with Tajikistan in Central Asia, scholars are wary of doing so. Shangshung is said to be east of Tazik and might be part of Tibet itself, with Mount Kailash as its center. The great contemporary scholar and master Namkhai Norbu Rinpoché says that Ölmo Lungring is in the center of Shangshung.

155. Yungdrung (*g.yung drung*) is the Tibetan version of the swastika, and refers to the eternal nature of these Bön teachings.

156. The word *bön* refers to reality or an unchanging doctrine. Thus, for the Bönpo it has the same connotations as *chos* (dharma) in Buddhism. Therefore, the term "Bön form" (*bon sku*) is equated with the term "dharmakaya," as part of the threefold form of an enlightened being.

157. *Drang srong.* Here the term refers to monastic practitioners, and this vehicle describes monastic discipline.

158. Some of these kings and translation of their names can be found in Chögyal Namkhai Norbu, *The Light of Kailash* (Merigar, Italy: Shang Shung Publications, 2009), pp. 130–33.

159. Phuk (*phugs*) and Bar (*bar*) clearly mean inner and middle, and so it is reasonable to assume that Gopa (*sgo pa*) refers to Outer Shangshung.

160. *Srad ma ka lig.* Also written as Semakar (*sad mar dkar*).

161. This is not an entirely serious comment. Clearly Tibet did have the knowledge to produce their silver coins and paper currency. The practice refers to holding aloft a leg of a sheep as part of an elaborate ritual to produce wealth.

162. This paragraph comes from Kunsal Nyingpo's *Explanation of Shang Religion and Culture*, p. 111.

163. Here and in the following two paragraphs, the term "secondary mental affliction" does not refer to the standard set of twenty secondary mental afflictions found in Abhidharma literature, but are used in terms of being secondary to the three poisons.

164. From the three trainings of ethics, concentration, and wisdom, as described below.

165. Viewing the impure as pure, suffering as happiness, the impermanent as permanent, and no-self as self.

166. The Buddhas teachings are not always direct and definitive. Many are provisional and have an intent other than the literal meaning.

167. These are states of meditative concentration (samadhi), gained in this life by a progressive rejection of attachment to desire and form, and which after death will lead to rebirth in one of the many form or formless realms.

168. Here the term "conceptual construct" is not a literal translation of the Tibetan technical term (*don spyi*). That which appears to a conceptual cognition is created by that cognition and is a representation or a "universal of the actual phenomenon," which would be closer to the literal translation. A conceptual construct of chocolate is not chocolate because you cannot eat it. Nevertheless, it engages with the actual phenomenon of chocolate and therefore is valid and useful.

169. This refers specifically to those ascetic practices found in ancient India that involved the mortification of the body and so on. It does not refer to all non-Buddhists.

170. The three kinds of suffering are (1) the evident suffering that all humans and animals recognize as suffering; (2) the suffering of change, which is the ordinary pleasure that is experienced, sought after, but ultimately destined to fade; and (3) a more subtle all-pervading suffering, which is always present as long as samsaric existence lasts.

171. The powers and the forces constitute graded degrees of faith, effort, mindfulness, concentration, and wisdom.

172. Each of the four truths have four main characteristics that define them.

173. Mental afflictions are usually described as states of mind that disturb the mental continuum. Most of these are innate in the sense that they have not been learned or taken on by recourse to a philosophical system.

174. Peak of existence is the highest of the worldly realms. It has an equivalent meditative state, or absorption, that can be attained without actually taking birth in that realm. The degrees of subtlety of the eliminations of the path of

meditation are determined by these absorptions. The coarsest are those of the desire realm, as mentioned.

175. Lamas who are to have disciples should exhibit genuine qualities and possess conduct that attracts disciples. These can be categorized into four types.

176. The four close contemplations, the four perfect abandonments, the four branches of magical powers, the five powers (strengths), the five forces, the seven branches of enlightenment and the eightfold path of the āryas collectively make up the thirty-seven facets of enlightenment.

177. The fetters are what bind one to acts that perpetuate samsara. These three are (1) the view of holding the aggregates to be self, (2) holding one's ethics to be supreme, and (3) afflicted doubt.

178. This is the actual antidote and is "uninterrupted" because nothing will obstruct it until its resultant wisdom arises.

179. Obscurations are veils preventing insight, which have been produced by afflicted imprints planted on the mental continuum over many lives. Some of these prevent the attainment of freedom from suffering, or nirvana, and others prevent the attainment of omniscience, or full enlightenment.

180. *Aṣṭasāhasrikāprajñāpāramitā*, Toh 10, shes phyin, *ka*, 73a.

181. This is explained below.

182. Cited in Nāropa, *Commentary on Short Teaching on Initiations*, Toh 1351, rgyud, *na*, 222a8.

183. A mandala, as described here, is a divine residence with divine features used in the practice of tantra. The residents are the deities that dwell within it.

184. One of the twelve months in the Kālacakra calendar. Assigned to the sun's occupation of Aries, it is usually the first month of the year.

185. The ascertainment of the emptiness of all phenomena.

186. These first two branches refer to meditation on oneself as a deity and meditation on the deity as other than oneself.

187. In tantra, enlightenment is often described as the union of the two truths, method and wisdom, illusory body and clear light, and so on.

188. The completion stage consists of five stages: body and speech isolations as one, mind isolation, illusory body, actual clear light, and union. Body isolation and the yoga of "a little control over wisdom" are found on both generation and completion stages.

189. The "state of Vajradhara" is enlightenment.

190. This "level" refers to the imprints that are obscurations to omniscience.

191. The difference between a cooperating cause and a material or substantial cause is that the cooperating cause does not have to change its entity to produce the effect and is thus not in the same material continuum of the effect.

192. This citation is from an Indian tantric text by the Guhyasamāja master Buddha

Śrījñāna and is often quoted by Tibetan masters, especially by Tsongkhapa in his *Great Exposition of Secret Mantra*.

193. Not apprehending a truly existing giver, giving, or recipient, for example.

194. Panchen Losang Chögyen, *Geluk Kagyu Tradition of Mahamudra*, p. 4.

195. The enlightened body, speech, and mind.

196. *Pañcakrama*, chapter 3, Toh 1802, rgyud, *ngi*, 52b4.

197. The ultimate basis of imputation of sentient beings is the primordial clear light, and on that basis the animate world is regarded in that way.

198. Earth, water, fire, air, space, and consciousness—meaning all human beings and animals.

199. In tantra, "bodhicitta" often refers to semen.

200. Certain insects that seemingly appear in wood, water, and so on were deemed to be born from those substances.

201. The causal motivation is generated before commencing the act, and the contemporaneous motivation is generated for the duration of the act.

202. The "pure basis" is the pure mind, and the "temporal basis" is the ordinary mind.

203. "Dependence" indicates emptiness because arising negates any intrinsic existence. "Arising" indicates existence.

204. In tantra the subtle consciousness apprehending emptiness and the emptiness itself are both referred to as clear light.

205. The Kadampa practitioners were known for keeping their practice of tantra hidden. It was said that you only knew a Kadampa master practiced tantra when you found his vajra and bell hidden under his bed after he had passed away.

206. This is how the term "tantra" is usually rendered in Tibetan.

207. The "something else" is the illusory body achieved on the completion stage, and which in tantra is designated as the conventional truth. The bliss and emptiness of the first kind of union is designated as ultimate truth.

208. The "innate form" here refers to the pure and impure illusory bodies developed from the innate subtle wind.

209. Tsongkhapa, *Great Exposition of Secret Mantra* (*Sngags rim chen mo*; Mungod, Karnataka, India: Je Yabse Sungbum Project, *a*; Drepung Loseling Education Society, 2019), vol. *ga*, p. 413.

210. Ibid., pp. 458–59.

211. Ibid., p. 462.

212. *Hevajratantra*, chapter 5. Toh 417, rgyud 'bum, *nga*, 25a1. Tilottamā (*thig le mchog ma*) is a goddess well known in Hindu mythology.

213. Nāgārjuna, *Pañcakrama*, 50a4. Sutra reference: *Lalitavistarasūtra*. Toh 95, mdo sde *kha*, 125a4. All the following lines are in sequence.

214. Ibid., 50b1.

215. Ibid., 50b2.

216. Abhayākaragupta, *Mañjarī*. Toh 1198, rgyud, *cha*, 34b1.

217. *'Og min stug po bkod pa*. Akaniṣṭha is the highest of the form realms.

218. *Mngon par byang chub, abhisambodhi*; refers to the clear light fourth stage.

219. *Hevajratantra*, chapter 9. Toh 417, rgyud 'bum, *nga*, 10b7. The "purity of self-perception" is the great bliss perceived by the yogi on the tantric path.

220. *Guhyasamājatantra*, chapter 17. Toh 442, rgyud 'bum, *ca*, 146a.4.

221. Śāntarakṣita, *Essence of the Reality of Valid Cognition. Tattvasiddhiprakaraṇa*. Toh 3708, rgyud, *tsu*, 26b.

222. Tripiṭakamala, *Nayatrayapradīpa*. Toh 3707, rgyud, *tsu*.

223. That is, bodhisattvas, śrāvakas, and pratyekas.

224. Candrakīrti. *Entering the Middle Way. Madhyamakāvatāra*, chapter 8, verse 2.

225. *Vajra Canopy Tantra. Vajrapañjaratantra*. Toh 419, rgyud 'bum, *nga*, 64b6, chapter 1.

226. *Hevajratantra*. Toh 417, rgyud 'bum, *nga*, 13b.3.

227. Channels are subtle material avenues within the body for the passage of winds and drops. The main channel is the central channel, which in most tantras remains obstructed by knots until completion stage practices loosen the knots and wind flows within it.

228. Nāgabodhi, *Analysis of Activity. Karmāntavibhaṅga*. Toh 1811, rgyud, *ngi*, 146b3. Some versions of this citation have the conditional "if" and place the consequence of not purifying the appearances in the future (that is, "If the appearances are not purified, it will not bring the fruit of enlightenment"), whereas Tsongkhapa, in his *Lamp to Illuminate the Five Stages*, associates this citation with the path taken by the historical Buddha and the consequence can be interpreted as being in the past.

229. Dalai Lama Kalsang Gyatso, *Elucidating the Reality of the Empowerments*, pp. 115a–121a.

230. From the *Perfection of Wisdom Sutra in Eighteen Thousand Verses*, as cited previously.

231. This work is widely regarded in the Tibetan tradition as the most important work of this genre and forms the basis for the subsequent development of the dialectical curriculum in the monastic tradition.

232. Cessation, peace, excellence, and emancipation.

233. Āryadeva, *Cittāvaraṇaviśodha nāmaprakaraṇa*. Toh 1804, rgyud, *ngi*.

234. A figure that some in the Gelukpa tradition revere as a protector of Tsongkhapa's teachings but others, including the Dalai Lama, regard as a harmful spirit. See Gavin Kilty, trans., *Understanding the Case against Shukden* (Boston: Wisdom Publications, 2019).

235. In depictions and visualizations of various assemblies, the figures are placed in rows according to importance.

236. Immeasurable love, compassion, joy, and equanimity.

237. A kind of offering made in tantric rituals, usually made of dough and shaped according to instructions in the text. *Torma* is a Tibetan word and is often left untranslated.

238. Concerns of fame, notoriety, gain, loss, praise, criticism, pain, and pleasure.

239. Renunciation, bodhicitta, and the view of emptiness.

240. In Buddhist philosophy, permanence refers to phenomena not produced by causes and therefore not subject to the transitory nature that characterizes impermanence.

241. In his *Compendium of Abhidharma, Abhidharmasamuccaya*. Toh 4049, sems tsam, *ri*.

242. The mere presence of cause and condition is sufficient to cause production. The presence of a creator is not necessary.

243. *Sutra of the Rice Seedling. Ārya-sālistambha-nāma-mahāyānasūtra.* Toh 210, mdo sde, *tsha*, 116a.

244. The mind at death is subject to becoming virtuous or nonvirtuous for as long as it is a coarse state. At the end of the death process the mind becomes a very subtle perception and is neutral in the sense that it cannot apply itself to any developed virtue. This is confirmed by a citation in Tsongkhapa's *Great Exposition on the Stages of the Path*. I am grateful for the input of Yangten Rinpoché and Samdhong Rinpoché on this point.

245. Not suppressing someone when necessary is a breach of a bodhisattva's secondary vow.

246. By "separate isolates" His Holiness means the conceptual isolation of a feature or phenomenon from other similar or dissimilar phenomena for the purposes of examination, communication, and so on. Phenomena are empty by nature, but that emptiness does not appear to general conceptualization of phenomena.

247. The Tibetan term *mya ngan las 'das pa* is often translated as "nirvana," but as its etymology is being discussed, the more literal "beyond sorrow" is preferred here. The Tibetan here translated as "sorrow" (*mya ngan*) is not that common, whereas "suffering" (*sdug bsngal*) is a far more common term.

248. *Rational System of Explanation. Vyākhyāyukti.* Toh 4061, sems tsam, *shi*, 36a4.

249. "Dharma" has the root meaning of "hold," and it is in the sense of holding that these ten are given. They are not exact equivalents. Merit, path, and nirvana, for example, "hold" one from falling into samsara.

250. Nirvana is "fearful" for the bodhisattva because it is a state of self-absorbed peace that hinders working for others.

251. Also, to remake, improve upon, correct, modify, and so on.

252. This verse is untraced.

253. Analysis to ensure noncontradiction by direct evident perception, inferential perception, and valid scripture.

254. "Branches" here refers to the topics of the preceding eight chapters of the book, which are primarily the first five perfections—giving, ethics, patience, effort, and concentration.

255. *Guhyasamājatantra*, chapter 2. Toh 442, rgyud 'bum, *ca*, 98b2. The complete verse:

> Devoid of all phenomena,
> aggregates, constituents, sources,
> apprehending and apprehended all abandoned
> with the no-self of phenomena and equality,
> your mind, unborn from the beginning,
> is the nature of emptiness.

The Dalai Lama is also referring to the succeeding verses.

256. Tsongkhapa, *Great Exposition*, vol. *ga*, p. 58.

257. This refers to the practice of inviting members of the monastic community to households in order to perform rituals.

258. Gungthang Tenpa Dronmé, *A Jeweled Garland: A Short Exposition of the Difficult Points of Vinaya*, Collected Works, vol. 2, p. 22.

259. Gendün Chöphel, *Grains of Gold. Gser gyi thang ma* (Bod Lhasa: Bod ljongs bod yig dpe rnying dpe skrun khang, 1990), p. 332.

260. Ibid., p. 333.

261. The monasteries of Drepung, Sera, and Ganden, all on the outskirts of Lhasa.

262. These three together with the Lingsé degree are lesser titles than the Lharampa degree and are named according to the place or circumstance of the final exam.

263. The two paragraphs on awards are taken from a book (p. 6) consulted by Dagyab Rinpoché called *The Legacy of Chapa Chökyi Sengé* by Sherab Gyatso.

264. This term refers to students of the Geluk tantric colleges who did not previously complete a course of philosophical study at one of the monasteries.

265. These dates are the new, half, and full moon days in a lunar month and are regarded as auspicious.

266. That is to say, different from the rest.

267. These are five classical works of Yogācāra: *Abhisamayālaṃkāra*, or *Ornament of Realization*; *Mahāyānasūtrālaṃkāra*, or *Ornament of Great Vehicle Sutras*; *Madhyāntavibhāga*, or *Distinguishing the Middle from the Extremes*; *Dharma-*

dharmatāvibhāga, or *Distinguishing Dharma and Dharmata*; and *Ratnagotravibhāga* (*Uttaratantra*), or *Lineage of the Three Jewels*.

268. A general contentment with food, clothing, dwelling place, and possessions, all of which are conducive to developing the insights of an ārya being.

269. Several passages in this section on the status of women are translated excerpts from Resa Könchok Gyatso's Tibetan-language volume *Stories of Tibetan Women* (*Gang ljongs skyes ma'i lo rgyus spyi bshad*; Lhasa: Bod ljongs mi dmangs dpe skrun khang, 2003). Sometimes whole passages are cited verbatim (noted where possible) and at other times passages have been condensed and paraphrased. The biographies in the section that follows ("Great Women of Tibetan History and Literature") are almost all from the book, with the Dalai Lama's voice absent.

270. These are found in the Vinaya, or monastic discipline sutras, and are categorized into four groups of two: those that nurse on the lap, those that nurse at the breast, those that clean the child, and those that play with the child.

271. A human form possessed of eight freedoms and ten endowments is said to be a "precious" human form because of the opportunity it provides for practicing Buddhism. These eighteen are readily sourced elsewhere in stages of the path literature.

272. These titles are mentioned in *Stories of Tibetan Women*, p. 177.

273. In tantra the categories of practice known as method and wisdom, from the aspects of their main characteristics, are assigned gender.

274. I cannot find any record of this sutra in the various Kangyur editions.

275. Mahāprajāpati was the maternal aunt of the Buddha, and the first Buddhist nun.

276. The specific source for this well-known episode from the Buddha's life is untraced.

277. The sutra citations are taken from *Stories of Tibetan Women*, p. 155.

278. These eight can be found in Tsongkhapa's *Great Treatise on the Stages of the Path to Enlightenment* in the section on karma and its effects (see Kilty, trans., *A Lamp to Illuminate the Five Stages*, p. 243).

279. It has been prophesized that buddhas in this world would have two chief female disciples and two chief male disciples in their entourage. These were the nuns Kṣema and Uppalavana and the monks Śariputra and Maudgalyāyana.

280. A sect founded by Dharmagupta, who was a disciple of Maudgalyāyana. Its monastic tradition was influential in China.

281. This paragraph is taken from *Stories of Tibetan Women*, p. 185.

282. The Tibetan word itself has no derogatory etymology. It is in usage that it has become derogatory.

283. The old Kadampa tradition began with the arrival of the Indian master Atiśa

in the eleventh century. The new tradition began with the Tibetan master Tsongkhapa.

284. Tibetan text focusing on Avalokiteśvara, the deity of compassion, attributed to Emperor Songtsen Gampo and revealed as a treasure text (*terma*).

285. *Dri med gzi brjid*, a twelve-volume biography of the Bön master Tönpa Shenrab.

286. Orgyen Lingpa. *Five Chronicles. Bka' thang lnga.* New Delhi: International Academy of Indian Culture, 1982. Beijing: Mi rigs dpe skrun khang, 1986. Delhi: Tibetan Cultural and Religious Publication Centre, 2007.

287. *Be'u bum sngon po.* A compilation of early Kadampa teachings.

288. This list is taken from *Stories of Tibetan Women*, p. 163.

289. I have not been able to source this citation, but it is cited in *Stories of Tibetan Women*, p. 183.

290. Gendün Chöphel, *Grains of Gold*, trans. Donald S. Lopez and Thupten Jinpa (London: University of Chicago Press, 2014). Butön is referencing women as demonesses, whereas the tantric vows forbid the denigration of women. Also cited in *Stories of Tibetan Women*, p. 155.

291. *Rgyal rabs gsal ba'i me long*, compiled by Lama Dampa Sonam Gyaltsen (1312–75). Translated by Per K. Sorenson as *Mirror Illuminating the Royal Genealogies* (Wiesbaden: Harrassowitz Verlag, 1994).

292. This injunction is one of sixteen codes of conduct attributed to Emperor Songtsen Gampo.

293. *Zhal lce bcu gsum.* Set of laws introduced by Karma Tenkyong Wangpo (1606–42), who was the last Tsangpa *desi*, or ruler, from the Tibetan province of Tsang.

294. Page number not available.

295. Most of the document and scriptures found at Dunhuang on the Silk Road were from the early propagation beginning around the eighth century.

296. The Tibetan consort of Padmasambhava who was also said to have been a wife of Tri Songdetsen.

297. Taksham Nuden Dorjé, *Biography of Yeshé Tsogyal*, pp. 119–20. Cited in *Stories of Tibetan Women*, p. 169.

298. An eleventh-century heroine from Gyangtsé in Tibet, whose life is described in a Tibetan folk opera of the same name.

299. Wife of the legendary King Gesar.

300. These proverbs are taken from *Stories of Tibetan Women*, pp. 167–68.

301. The suffix *-ma* indicates female.

302. Majestic mountains regarded as gods and invoked in song as protectors by the Tibetan emperors.

303. These are mountains traditionally associated with the abodes of guardian spirits.

304. These places are abodes of guardian spirits. Gar was a renowned minister of Songtsen Gampo.

305. All feature in the famous epic of King Gesar.

306. A genealogy of the Lang lineage, which rose to political power in eastern Tibet in the fourteenth century.

307. As quoted in *Stories of Tibetan Women*, p. 9.

308. The first seven kings, beginning with Nyatri Tsenpo, were said to be "divine," because they descended from the god realms to rule on earth, and returned there when they died. The eighth king, Drigum Tsenpo (fourth century), is believed to have been the first king to have remained on earth after he died.

309. *Smad kyi lde gsum.* Three sons of the ruler Tashi Tsekpa (tenth century), who were all called Dé.

310. Said to be a Bön text describing how the first Tibetan heavenly kings descended from the god realms.

311. *Spur/spu/pur rgyal.* The old name for Tibet, a period sometimes said to begin from the time of the eighth king, but here taken to begin earlier.

312. *Brtan ma bcu gnyis.*

313. These five sisters are known as the five long-life sisters or goddesses.

314. Biographies of many of these women can also be found on The Treasury of Lives (treasuryoflives.org). Where they appear under a different name, and when extra information from The Treasury of Lives is relevant, these have been annotated.

315. The son, Dusong, also died young and so his mother ruled the kingdom a second time.

316. *Sba ra na.* He was one of the first seven monks ordained in Tibet.

317. Few, if any, of these women are documented historically.

318. This last sentence is by Dagyab Rinpoché, commenting on the text of *Stories of Tibetan Women*.

319. Mentioned in *Stories of Tibetan Women* as a consort of the Ācarya.

320. These two sentences echo the idea held by some that Ralpachen's religious rule was detrimental to the power of the Tibetan empire.

321. The period of decentralization of power stretches from the assassination of Langdarma in 842 to the advent of Sakya rule in the thirteenth century.

322. Cemeteries and other fearful places were common sites of practice for tantric yogis. The horrific, ugly, and unpleasant is used to challenge and transform conventional perception. It is not clear whether she used the corpses as companions or whether their flesh was part of the "feast."

323. *Delok* (*'das log*) are those who die and return to life within the same body. Sometimes, as in the case of Nangsa, it is because their karma for this life is not exhausted.

324. See *Tales from the Tibetan Operas*, trans. Gavin Kilty (Boston: Wisdom Publications, 2019).

325. *Ané* is the vernacular and, these days, is a rather disparaging term for a nun. It means "aunt." *Stories of Tibetan Women* says that in some operas she is portrayed as a nun but that this is incorrect.

326. These hindrances and their cure are described in Gö Lotsāwa Shönu Pal, *Blue Annals*, trans. George Roerich (Delhi: Motilal Banarsidass, 1976), p. 222.

327. There are conflicting assertions for her dates and for other details of her life. Here only the short biography from *Stories of Tibetan Women*, as compiled by Dagyab Rinpoché, is used. There is a lot of interest in Machik Labdrön among Western Buddhists and much has been written about her life and achievements. Therefore, more detail and differing accounts can be found elsewhere; notably *Women of Wisdom* by Tsultrim Allione and *Machik's Complete Explanation* by Sarah Harding, both listed in the bibliography.

328. *Mchod gnas.* According to Harding (p. 330) Thrangu Rinpoché explains that this term refers to Machik's work of reciting the scriptures.

329. This is the Tibetan funeral tradition of disposing of a corpse by cutting it up and offering it as carrion to birds of prey.

330. *Gcod.* Detailed explanations of this profound practice can be found in Harding and Allione. In essence it refers to cutting (*gcod*) attachment to the notion of self and pacifying the "four demons" by the visualization of offering parts of your body to others. The philosophy behind the practice is that of the perfection of wisdom sutras.

331. As quoted in *Stories of Tibetan Women*, pp. 61–62.

332. Majo (*ma jo*) seems to be synonymous with Jomo (*jo mo*), which, as explained later, can mean nun, aristocratic wife, and female lama. Other accounts of the twenty-four use "Jomo." Also, "Jomo" is the title prefixed to many of the twenty-four. According to *Blue Annals*, "Majo" is a term for an ordained nun. But some of the twenty-four were married. *Ma* and *mo* are both common suffixes denoting female, while *jo* means lord or master.

333. The accounts here are compiled from *Stories of Tibetan Women* and in most cases are abridged.

334. *Blue Annals* (p. 915) has "without returning to her native place."

335. This Jomo is not listed in *Blue Annals* as one of the twenty-four but is mentioned as one of the four dakinis (p. 984). The list of the four in *Blue Annals* does not include Shelmo Gyajam.

336. The "I" here and below is Resa Könchok Gyatso, the author of *Stories of Tibetan Women*.

337. As quoted in *Stories of Tibetan Women*, p. 73.

338. According to Cyrus Stearns in *Luminous Lives* (Boston: Wisdom Publications,

2001), p. 60, Machik Shachungma is the same as Machik Shama, and was one of the twenty-four disciples of Phadampa (p. 239).

339. According to Stearns (pp. 21 and 257) she was the first wife of Sachen Kunga Nyingpo.

340. According to *Blue Annals* (p. 443) she was born in Oyuk.

341. Excerpts that follow are as quoted in *Stories of Tibetan Women*, p. 78.

342. "Sutra" here refers to the *Sutra Amassing Every Intention* (*Mdo dgongs pa 'dus pa*), the primary tantra of the Nyingma Anu Yoga system.

343. As quoted in *Stories of Tibetan Women*, p. 80.

344. Chapa Chökyi Sengé was abbot of Sangphu Monastery and is the founder of the structured debating tradition commonly used in the Tibetan monastic curriculum. This is based on a number of texts compiled as *Collected Topics*, which in turn have their origins in the epistemological works of the Indian masters Dignāga and Dharmakīrti.

345. The kind of sharp, back and forth monastic debate where positions are challenged by playing devil's advocate in an attempt to get the opponent to contradict themselves.

346. Meaning "Has she traveled a long distance? Did she have to fend off wild dogs on the way?"

347. Meaning "Has he bestowed the Vajra Garland empowerments widely, such that he has covered the earth with vow breakers and created a sure entrance to hell?" That is, if he has given the empowerments, then there will be many who will break the tantric commitments and therefore fall to hell.

348. The Trophu Kagyu tradition was established by Kunden Repa and developed by his nephew, Trophu Lotsāwa.

349. Meaning that her realizations were complete and there was nothing more to be known, like a knife and a sharpening stone that have both been worn away.

350. A sacred mythical place venerated by Tibetan traditions for the development and dissemination of tantric teachings and inaccessible to ordinary beings. It is conventionally placed in the Swat District of Pakistan.

351. Tsewang Gyal, *Lhorong Religious History* (*Lho rong chos 'byung*; Lhasa: Bod ljongs bod yig dpe rnying dpe skrun khang, 1994), p. 752.

352. As quoted in *Stories of Tibetan Women*, p. 85.

353. This refers to Götsangpa, of whom Yangön was a disciple.

354. As quoted in *Stories of Tibetan Women*, p. 86.

355. "Karmapa" probably refers to the Second Karmapa, Karma Pakshi.

356. Sometimes, practitioners who live in remote places would forgo ordinary food and rely upon specially prepared "essence pills," or elixirs (*bcud len*). These pills relieved the need for cooking food and produced a lightness in

the body, which was conducive for meditation. They took many forms, one of which was consecrated water.

357. A story of these four geomancers is found at sorig.net: When they arrived at Manasarovar, a cow suddenly emerged from the waves of the lake and charged against the supply yak. One of the geomancers hit the cow and they followed it back to the shore. There a nāga girl appeared, whose name was Dorjé Lumo. They apologized and brought her offerings of gold and sand. They asked her to teach them about earth and nature. Through playing with the sand she transmitted to them the knowledge of geomancy. Playing with the sand she transmitted to them the knowledge of geomancy by forming hills and mountains, and placing stones to let them see the rivers and lakes.

358. Dudjom Rinpoché, *The Nyingma School of Tibetan Buddhism*, trans. Gyurme Dorje and Matthew Kapstein (Boston: Wisdom Publications, 2002). This information is found on p. 771.

359. This fact is pointed out in an endnote in *The Nyingma School of Tibetan Buddhism*.

360. Tāranātha, *Places of the Jonang* (*Jo nang gnas bshad*; Beijing: Krung go'i bod rig pa dpe skrun khang, 2008), p. 151.

361. As quoted in *Stories of Tibetan Women*, p. 91.

362. Many of the biographies describe her and her husband as nomads.

363. A fourteenth-century master, also of the Nyak clan.

364. Tāranātha, *Places of the Jonang*, p. 152.

365. Like the other periods into which this section is divided, the dates are somewhat arbitrary, but are given to provide a time frame for women described.

366. *Gnas sgo phyes pa.* Rinpoché explained this term (literally "opening the gate") to mean that a particular place is designated by a great practitioner to be a sacred place, after which it becomes a place for pilgrimage.

367. The text lists more places but only by their first syllables, making them difficult to identify.

368. Her biography, as related almost verbatim here, can be found in Kongtrul Yontan Gyatso's *Great Treasury of Rediscovered Teachings*, vol. *ka*, pp. 547–49.

369. A particular form of the deity Yamāntaka.

370. Famous siddha, founder of the Tibetan folk opera tradition, and bridge builder, whose dates are said to be 1361–1485.

371. Tibetans used to believe that occasionally a child could change sex naturally.

372. General teachings, as opposed to specific (red) instructions for retreat.

373. *Gnam lcags ur mo.* Some sources refer to this as a deity, while for others it is meteoric iron.

374. Tsampa is roast barley flour. "Measure" (*bre*) here is one for a dry goods mea-

sured by volume. One measure is the volume taken by about two pints of water.

375. Elsewhere she is known as Kuntu Sangmo.

376. *Stories of Tibetan Women* references this citation as appearing on p. 134, but I am unable to locate the source book. Information on the block print edition is in bibliography.

377. This refers to a meditation posture formed by binding with cord the two knees, the two elbow crooks, and the two shoulders, which collectively form the "six stoves."

378. In the thirteenth century the Mongols divided Tibet into thirteen territories, or myriarchies (*khri skor*), ruled by an administrator, or myriarach (*khri dpon*). Drigung was one of these territories. At this point the text adds, "Goma (*sgom ma*) is usually a title with a religious connotation, but here it was the custom to call the administrator of the Drigung myriararchy the *gopa*. The administrator of the Sakya territory is called *pönchen* (*dpon chen*). Therefore, they are titles specific to an administrated territory."

379. At least two biographies of this practitioner exist in Tibetan: One is an auto-biography (*Rje btsun rdo rje rnal 'byor ma'i sprul pa skal ldan phrin las dbang mo'i rnam thar gsang ba'i ye shes*) and the other (*Kha skong bde chen nyin byed*) is a supplement to the autobiography. Both can be located at Buddhist Digital Resource Center (https://library.bdrc.io/). Also see Michael Sheehy's excellent article on Jetsunma, "Materializing Dreams and Omens: The Autobiographical Subjectivity of the Tibetan Yoginī Kun dga' 'Phrin las dbang mo (1585–1668)," *Revue d'Etudes Tibétaines* 56 (October 2020).

380. Ngawa Prefecture in Sichuan, and especially Dzamthang County, is home to many Jonang monasteries. Although the first Jonang monastery was built there in the fourteenth century, many Jonang followers migrated there in the seventeenth century when their tradition was all but outlawed by the Tibetan government.

381. Entry not found.

382. Pholha(né) was a powerful figure and military leader in Lhasa during the turbulent times of the eighteenth century.

383. Pemakö is a mysterious and hidden land in southeast Tibet, sought out by many Nyingma lamas, such as Chöjé Lingpa and Gampowa mentioned above, to escape the ravages of the Dzungar Mongols in the seventeenth century, who had a hatred of the Nyingma school. Pemakö in terms of spiritual geomancy is said to be a physical representation of the female meditation deity Vajravārāhī (or Vajrayoginī). Several geographical features correspond to parts of the deity's body. The Rinchen Pung ("Heap of Jewels") area is one

of these. See Hamid Sardar Afkhami, "An Account of Padma-Bkod: A Hidden Land in Southeastern Tibet," *Kailash* 18, no. 3: 3–21.

384. The text says that the biography can be found in the Mirik Phodrang Library in Beijing.

385. A small town and pilgrimage lake in Himachal Pradesh, whose local name is Rewalsar.

386. These were itinerant storytellers who would set up a large scroll painting as a backdrop and a mandala in front of them. They attracted a crowd by blowing a conch shell and intoning the mantra *om maṇi padme hūṃ*.

387. These are bodhicitta, deity form meditation, devotion, the nature of reality, and dedication.

388. According to The Treasury of Lives: *Gangs shug ma ni lo chen rig 'dzin chos nyid bzang mo'i rnam par thar pa rnam mkhyen bde ster.* Snga 'gyur rnying ma'i gsung rab series 22 (Gangtok, India: Sonam Topgay Kazi, 1975).

389. Most other sources give her dates as 1892–1940. Her biography presented here is not from *Stories of Tibetan Women* but from the introduction to her autobiography written by the Golok Governmental Office for the Publication of Ancient Texts, in vol. 1 of her Collected Works: *A Jeweled Mirror of Excellent Writing* (*Zab gsang theg mchog gi rnal 'byor ma chen po dbus bza' mkha 'gro kun bzang bde skyong dbang mo bde ba'i rdo rje'i gsung 'bum legs bshad nor bu'i me long*; Sichuan: Si khron mi rigs dpe skrun khang, 2009). The autobiography itself (*Dbus mo bde ba'i rdo rje'i rnam par thar pa nges 'byung 'dren pa'i shing rta skal ldan dad pa'i mchod sdong*) is 537 pages and is followed by a versed synopsis.

390. The root text *Buddhahood without Meditation* is by Düjom Lingpa and was translated by Richard Barron (Junction City, CA: Padma Publication, rev. ed. 2002) and by Alan Wallace in *Dudjom Lingpa's Visions of the Great Perfection* (Boston: Wisdom Publications, 2016).

391. This and the previous paragraph are taken verbatim from the introduction to her Collected Works.

392. An elegant way of saying that she passed away.

393. *Klo pa.* A forest-dwelling ethnic tribe in the southeast regions of Tibet.

394. According to The Treasury of Lives, her year of passing could have been 1973.

395. A religious title, similar to Shapdrung.

396. According to Treasury of Lives, this refers to removing cataracts (*mig 'byed*, literally "opening the eyes").

397. Ailments or illnesses are those of the three humors: wind, bile, and phlegm. Wind ailments benefit from good food, warm clothing and so forth.

398. Dorjé Phakmo (Vajravārāhī) is a tantric meditation deity traditionally portrayed with a sow (*phag mo*) above her right ear.

399. A school named after the great master Bodong Panchen Chöklé Namgyal

(1375–1451). As the author of 135 volumes, he is one of the most prolific writers in Tibet. Bodong is a place near Shigatsé in Tsang, and the location of E Monastery, which was the seat of Bodong Panchen.

400. The dates given in the Tibetan text for all twelve incarnations mainly come from *Stories of Tibetan Women*. They are at odds with dates elsewhere, although it should be said there is no unanimous agreement on the dates, especially for the earlier incarnations. However, the dates of her birth and death in the text also seem to conflict internally with dates of other figures and events mentioned. For example, both of the dates given for the founding of Samding Monastery by the first incarnation occur before she was even born. The dates of her birth and death given in Hildegard Diemberger's *When a Woman Becomes a Religious Dynasty: The Samding Dorje Phagmo of Tibet* (New York: Columbia University Press, 2007) tally much more with other dates in the text and therefore both dates are given, with the Tibetan text date given first.

401. Untraced.

402. Jikdral (*'jigs bral*) is Bodong Panchen, although his name, with no change of meaning, is usually written Jikmé (*'jigs med*).

403. Untraced.

404. Composed by someone only identified as Khedrup. See bibliography for publication details.

405. Other sources give her name as Yeshé Tsomo. Clearly neither of her dates tally with those of the fourth incarnation.

406. Ritual involving the arrangement of thread upon a frame, designed to lure in harmful forces adversely affecting a person's body.

407. Although a Mongolian word, *hothokthu* is a title originally bestowed upon great lamas by the Manchurian emperors. The Dalai Lamas and Panchen Lamas also have the authority to grant this title.

408. Other sources such as *Dungkar's Dictionary* state that Losang Chödrön was the second incarnation, with the first being an aristocratic woman from Lhasa known as Lhatsi Pönmo.

409. Dagyab Rinpoché cites from *Dungkar's Dictionary* (p. 254) on this person: "Depa Kyishö Tenzin Losang Gyatso was the first incarnation of Gungru Kyishö Shabdrung. He received empowerments and permission initiations from the Fourth Dalai Lama, Yönten Gyatso, and Panchen Losang Chögyen. His Kyishö estate was seized by the Tsang forces, and he had to flee to Kokonor in Amdo. He visited most monasteries in Domé and contributed greatly to the propagation of the teachings."

410. Thirteenth-century Indian master who received direct teachings from the deity Avalokiteśvara.

411. Other sources give her dates as 1935–2011.

412. Nāgārjuna, Āryadeva, Asaṅga, Vasubandhu, Dignāga, and Dharmakīrti, plus
      Guṇaprabha and Śākyaprabha.

Bibliography

SUTRAS AND TANTRAS

Guhyasamāja Tantra. *Guhyasamājatantra*. *Gsang ba 'dus pa'i rgyud*. Toh 442, rgyud 'bum, ca.

Hevajra Tantra. *Hevajratantra*. *Kye'i rdo rje'i rgyud/Brtags gnyis pa*. Toh 417, rgyud 'bum, nga.

Perfection of Wisdom Sutra in Eighteen Thousand Verses. *Ārya-Aṣṭādaśasāhasrikā-prajñāpāramitā-nama-mahāyānasūtra*. *Shes rab kyi pha rol ti phyin pa khri brgyad stong pa*. Toh 10, dbu ma, ga.

Prayer of Good Conduct. *Ārya Bhadracaryāpraṇidhānarāja*. *'Phags pa kun tu bzang po spyod pa'i smon lam gyi rgyal po*. Toh 1095, gzungs, 263b.

Sutra Explaining the Intent. *Ārya-saṁdhinirmocana-nāma-mahāyānasūtra*. *'Phags pa dgongs 'grel pa shes bya ba theg pa chen po'i mdo*. Toh 106, mdo, ca.

Sutra of the Four Truths. *Catuḥsatya-sūra*. *Bden bzhi'i mdo*. Toh 316, mdo, sa.

Sutra of the Rice Seedling. *Ārya-sālistambha-nāma-mahāyānasūtra*. *'Phags pa sā lu'i ljang pa zhes by aba theg pa chen po'i mdo*. D210, mdo, tsha.

Sutra of the Ten Levels. *Daśabhūmikasūtra*. *Sa bcu pa'i mdo*. Chapter 31 of the *Avataṁsaka Sutra*. Toh 44, phal chen, kha.

Sutra Requested by the Householder Ugra. *Gṛhapati-ugraparipṛcchā*. *Khyim bdag drag shul can gyis zhus pa*. Toh 63, kon brtsegs, nga.

Tattvasaṁgraha Tantra. See *Vajradhātu Tantra*.

Vairocana Enlightenment Tantra. *Vairocanābhisaṁbodhitantra*. *Rnam snang mngon byang*. Toh 494, rgyud 'bum, tha.

Vajra Canopy Tantra. *Ārya-ḍākiṇīvajrapañjaratantra*. *'Phags pa mkha' 'gro ma rdo rje gur zhes bya ba'i rgyud kyi rgyal po chen po brtags pa*. Toh 419, rgyud 'bum, nga.

Vajradhātu Tantra. *Sarvatathāgatatattvasaṁgraha*. *De bzhin gshegs pa thams cad kyi de kho na nyid bsdus pa*. Toh 479, rgyud, nya.

Vajra Garland Tantra. *Vajramālābhidhānatantra*. *Rdo rje phreng ba mngon par brjod pa rgyud*. Toh 445, rgyud, ca.

Vajra Peak Tantra. *Vajraśekharatantra*. *Rdo rje rtse mo rgyud*. Toh 480, rgyud, nya.

INDIC TREATISES

Abhayākaragupta. *Sheaves of Instructions, Mañjarī. Man ngag gi snye ma.* Toh 1198, rgyud, *cha,* 34b1.

Āryadeva. *Cittāvaraṇaviśodha nāmaprakaraṇa. Sems kyi sgrib pa rnam par sbyong ba zhes bya ba'i rab tu byed pa.* Toh 1804, rgyud, *ngi.*

Āryadeva. *Four Hundred Verses. Catuḥśatakaśāstra. Bstan bcos bzhi brgya pa zhes bya ba'i tshig le'ur byas pa.* Toh 3846, dbu ma, *tsha.*

Āryadeva. *(Lamp of the) Compendium of Practice. Caryāmelāpakapradīpa. Spyod pa bsdus pa'i sgron ma.* Toh 1803, rgyud, *ngi.*

Asaṅga. *Compendium of Abhidharma. Abhidharmasamuccaya. Chos mngon pa kun las btus pa.* Toh 4049, sems tsam, *ri.*

Asaṅga. *Summary of the Great Vehicle. Mahāyānasaṃgraha. Theg pa chen po bsdus pa.* Toh 4048, sems tsam, *ri.*

Bhāviveka. *Blaze of Logic. Madhyamakahṛdayavṛttitarkajvālā. Dbu ma'i snying po'i 'grel ba rtog ge 'bar ba.* Toh 3856, dbu ma, *dza.*

Bhāviveka. *Essence of Madhyamaka. Madhyamakahṛdayakarikā. Dbu ma'i snying po'i tshig le'ur byas pa.* Toh 3855, dbu ma, *dza.*

Buddhaśrījñāna. *Oral Teachings of Mañjuśrī. Dvikramatattvabhāvanāmukhāma. Rim pa gnyis pa'i de kho na nyid bsgom pa'i zhal gyi lung/'Jam pal zhal lung.* Toh 1853, rgyud, *di.*

Candrakīrti. *Autocommentary on Entering the Middle Way. Madhyamakāvatārabhaṣya. Dbu ma la 'jug pa'i bshad pa.* Toh 3862, dbu ma, *'a.*

Candrakīrti. *Clear Words. Mūlamadhyamakavṛttiprasannapadā. Dbu ma rtsa ba'i 'grel pa tshig gsal ba.* Toh. 3860, dbu ma, *a.*

Candrakīrti. *Entering the Middle Way. Madhyamakāvatāra. Dbu ma la 'jug pa.* Toh 3861, dbu ma, *ah.*

Dharmakīrti. *Commentary on Valid Cognition. Pramāṇavārttikakārikā. Tshad ma rnam 'grel tshig le'ur byas pa.* Toh 4210, tshed ma, *ce.*

Dignāga. *Compendium of Valid Cognition. Pramāṇasamuccaya-nāma-prakaraṇa. Tshad ma kun las gtus pa zhes bya ba'i rab tu byed pa.* Toh 4203, tshad ma, *ce.*

Haribhadra. *Ornament of Realization. Abhisamayālaṃkāravṛtti. Shes rab kyi pha rol tu phyin pa'i man ngag gi bstan bcos mngon par togs pa'i rgyan zhes bya ba'i 'grel pa. 'Grel pa don gsal.* Toh 3793, shes phyin, *ja.*

Maitreya. *Ornament of the Sutras. Mahāyānasūtālaṃkāra-nāma-kārikā. Theg pa chen po mdo sde'i rgyan zhes bya ba'i thsig le'ur byas pa.* Toh 4020, sems tsam, *phi.*

Maitreya. *Uttaratantra/Mahāyānottaratantraśāstra/Ratnagotravibhāga. Theg pa chen po rgyud bla ma'i bstan bcos.* Toh 4024, sems tsam, *phi.*

Maitripa. *Ten Verses on Reality. Tattvadaśaka-nāma. De kho na nyid bcu pa.* Toh 2236, rgyud, *wi* 112b.

Nāgabodhi. *Analysis of Activity. Karmāntavibhaṅga. Las kyi mtha' rnam par 'byed pa.* Toh 1811, rgyud, *ngi.*

Nāgārjuna. *Compendium of Sutra. Sūtrasamuccaya. Mdo kun las btus pa.* Toh 3934, dbu ma, *ki.*

Nāgārjuna. *Five Stages. Pañcakrama. Rim pa lnga pa.* Toh 1802, Tengyur, rgyud, *ngi.*

Nāgārjuna. *Fundamental Wisdom of the Middle Way. Mūlamadhyamaka-kārikā. Dbu ma rtsa ba'i tshig le'ur byas pa shes rab.* Toh 3824, dbu ma, *tsa.*

Nāgārjuna. *Precious Garland of Advice for the King. Ratnāvalī/Rājaparikathāratna-mālā. Rgyal po la gtam bya bar in po che'i phreng ba.* Toh 4158, spring yig, *ge.*

Nāgārjuna. *Sixty Verses of Reasoning. Yuktiṣaṣṭikākārikā. Rigs pa drug cu pa'i tshig le'ur byas pa.* Toh 3825, dbu ma, *tsa.*

Nāropa. *Commentary on a Short Teaching on Initiations. Paramārthasaṁgraha-nāma-sekoddeśaṭīkā. Dbang mdor bstan gyi 'grel bshad don dam pa bsdus pa.* Toh 1351, rgyud, *na.*

Puṇḍarīka. *Kālacakra Great Commentary / Stainless Light. Vimalaprabhā-nāma-mūla tantrānusariṇīdvādaśasāhasrikā-laghukālacakratantrarājaṭīkā. Bsdus pa'i rgyud kyi rgyal po dus kyi 'khor lo'i 'grel bshad rtsa ba'i rgyud kyi rjes su 'jug pa stong phrag bcu gnyis pa dri ma med pa'i 'od ces bya ba.* Toh 845, rgyud 'bum, *śrī.* P2064 (Dro Lotsawa translation, found in Kangyur). Toh 1347, rgyud, *da.* P2064 (Shong Lotsawa translation).

Śāntarakṣita. *Essence of the Reality of Valid Cognition. Tattvasaṃgrahakārikā. Tshad ma'i de kho na nyid bsdus pa.* Toh 4266, tshad ma, *zhe.*

Śāntideva. *Engaging in Bodhisattva Deeds. Bodhicaryāvatāra. Byang chub sems pa'i spyod pa la 'jug pa.* Toh 3871, dbu ma, *la.*

Tripiṭakamala. *Light of the Three Ways. Nayatrayapradīpa.* Toh 3707, rgyud, *tsu.*

Vasubandhu. *Treasury of Abhidharma. Abhidharmakośa. Chos mngon pa mdzod,* Toh 4089, mngon pa, *ku.*

Vasubandhu. *Rational System of Explanation. Vyākhyāyukti. Rnam par bshad pa'i rigs pa.* Toh 4061, sems tsam, *shi.*

TIBETAN SOURCES

Agon Rinpoché, ed. *Drigung Treasury Biography of Milarepa. Mi la re pa'i rnam thar mdzod nag ma.* Lhasa: Drigung Mthil Dgon, 2004.

Biography of Lama Phak Ö. Bla ma 'phags 'od kyi rnam thar. Publication details not found.

Dalai Lama Kalsang Gyatso, Seventh. *Explanation of the Mandala Ritual of Guhyasamāja Akṣobhyavajra: Elucidating the Reality of the Empowerments. Dpal gsang ba 'dus pa mi bskyod rdo rje'i dkyil 'khor gyi cho ga'i rnam par bshad pa dbang don de nyid yang gsal sngang ba rdo rje sems dpa'i zhal lung.* Collected Works, vol. *ga.*

Dalai Lama Ngawang Losang Gyatso, Fifth. *Heavenly Raiment: An Illusory Play of the Appearances in the Life of the Zahor Monk Ngawang Losang Gyatso Presented as a Biography. Za hor gyi ban de ngag dbang blo bzang rgya mtsho'i 'di snang 'khrul pa'i rol rtsed rtogs brjod kyi tshul du bkod pa du kū la'i gos bzang.* 3 vols. Woodblock edition, Lhasa edition. Vol. 1 has been translated by Samten G. Karmay as *The Illusive Play.* Chicago: Serindia, 2014.

Dalai Lama Ngawang Losang Gyatso, Fifth. *Oral Transmission of Mañjuśrī. 'Jam dpal zhal lung.* Collected Works, vol. *na.*

Dalai Lama Tenzin Gyatso, Fourteenth. *Beyond Religion: Ethics for a Whole World.* Boston: Houghton Mifflin Harcourt, 2011. London: Rider, 2012.

Dharmatala. *Religious History of Mongolia. Hor chos 'byung.* New Delhi: Sharada Rani, 1975.

Dodrup Jikmé Tenpai Nyima. *Overview of Guhyagarbha Tantra. Gsang ba snying po'i spyi don.* Collected Works, *ka.*

Dokharwa Tsering Wangyal. *Biography of Miwang Sönam Topgyal. Mi dbang rtogs brjod.* Chengdu: Si khron mi rigs dpe skrun khang, 1981.

Drigung Resa Könchok Gyatso. *Stories of Tibetan Women. Gang ljongs skyes ma'i lo rgyus spyi bshad.* Lhasa: Bod ljongs mi dmangs dpe skrun khang, 2003.

Drukpa Kunlek. *Autobiography of Drukpa Kunlek. 'Brugs pa kun legs kyi rnam thar.* Lhasa: Bod ljongs mi dmangs dpe skrun khang, 2005.

Dungkar Lobsang Trinlé, *Dungkar's Dictionary. Dung dkar tshig mdzod chen mo.* Beijing: China Tibetology Publishing House, 2002.

Gendün Chöphel. *Grains of Gold. Gser gyi thang ma.* Lhasa: Bod ljongs bod yig dpe rnying dpe skrun khang, 1990. Translated by Donald S. Lopez and Thupten Jinpa. London: University of Chicago Press, 2014.

General Compilation of Treasure and Tantra. Gter rgyud spyi 'dus. Publication details not found.

Geomancy: A Precious Garland of the Earth Spread Out and Amassed. Sa dpyad brdal spungs rin chen phreng ba. Publication details not found.

Gö Lotsāwa Shönu Pal. *Blue Annals. Deb ngon po.* Translated by George Roerich. Delhi: Motilal Banarsidass, 1976.

Götsangpa. *Biography of Rechungpa. Rje btsun ras chung rdo rje grags pa'i rnam thar rnam mkhyen thar lam sal wa'i me long ye shes snang wa.* Translated by Peter Roberts as *Rechungpa: A Biography of Milarepa's Disciple.* Crestone, CO: Namo Buddha Publications, 2002.

Götsangpa. *The Heart of the Sun Illuminating the Vajrayana: A Biography of Tsangnyön Heruka. Gtsang snyon he ru ka'i rnam thar rdo rje theg pa'i gsal byed nyi ma'i snying po.* New Delhi: Sharada Rani, 1969.

Gungthang Tenpa Dronmé. *A Jeweled Garland: A Short Exposition of the Difficult Points of the Vinaya. 'Dul ba'i rgya mtsho'i dka' gnad mdor bsdus pa nor bu 'phreng ba.* Collected Works, vol. 2. Beijing: Mi rigs dpe dkrun khang, 2003.

Guru Tashi Ngawang Lodrö. *Religious History.* Beijing: Krung go bod kyi shes rig dpe skrun khang, 1990.

Gyalwang Chöjé Losang Trinlé. *The Great Biography of Tsongkhapa. Rje'i rnam thar chen mo.* Sarnath, India: Mongolian Lama Guru Deva, 1967.

How the Gods Were Divided. Yo ga lha gyes can. No author and publication details found.

Jakhyung Incarnations. Bya khyung gdan rabs. Mtsho sngon mi rigs dpe skrun khang, 1984.

Ju Mipham. *A Dance to Move the Hearts of the Ḍākiṇīs: A Great Bliss Whorl of Joy. Ḍā ki'i snying bsgul gyi glu gar bde chen dga' 'khyil pa.* Collected Works, vol. 32.

Ju Mipham. *Courier of the Four Joys: A Song to Recall the Queen of Passion. Chags pa'i rgyal mo rjes dran gyi glu dbyangs dga' bzhi bya ma rta.* Collected Works, vol. 32.

Ju Mipham. *Hook to Attract the Heart Essence of the Host of Ḍākiṇīs. Ma tshogs ḍā ki'i snying gi dwangs ma 'gugs pa'i lcags kyu.* Collected Works, vol.32.

Ju Mipham. *Pleasing Smile of Sarasvati: A Brief Description of the Yoga of the Mudra of Bliss and Emptiness. Bde stong phyag rgya'i rnal 'byor gyi tshul mdo tsam brjod pa mtsho byung dgyes pa'i 'dzum dkar.* Collected Works, vol.32.

Karma Chakmé. *Biography of Dakpo Lhajé. Dwags po'i rnam thar.* Collected Works, vol. 1.

Karma Chakmé. *Instructions Given to Jomo. Jo mor gdams pa'i zhal gdams.* Publication details not found.

Kathok Situ. *Guide to Central Tibet and Tsang. Dbus gtsang lam (gnas) yig.* Chengdu: Si khron mi rigs dpe skrun khang, 2001.

Khachö Gyepa Dorjé. *Biography of Dampa Sangyé: A Sun that Blazes with the Rays of a Thousand Siddhis. Dam pa Sangs rgyas kyi rnam thar dngos grub 'od stong 'bar ba'i nyi ma.* Darjeeling: Rdor gling dpe mdzod khang, 200?

Khedrup. *A Suckling Dowry: The Religious History of Lhokha. Lho kha'i chos 'byung skyes ma'i nu rin.* Beijing: Mi rigs dpe skrun khang, 2005.

Khedrup Gelek Palsang. *Dispelling the Darkness of Wrong Views. Lta khrid mun sel sgron me.* Collected Works, vol. ja.

Khenpo Kunpel (Kunzang Palden). *Elixir of Faith: A Biography of Patrul Rinpoché. Rdza dpal sprul gyi rnam thar dad pa'i gsos sman bdud rtsi'i bum bcud.* New Delhi: Konchhog Lhadrepa, 1997.

Kongtrul Yonten Gyatso/Lodrö Thayé. *Great Treasury of Rediscovered Teachings. Rin chen gter mdzod.* Delhi: Shechen Publications, 2007.

Kongtrul Yonten Gyatso/Lodrö Thayé. *Treasury of Knowledge. She bya kun khyab mdzod.* 4 vols. Delhi: Shechen Publications, 1997.

Kunsal Nyingpo. *A New Dawn: Explanation of Shang Religion and Culture. Zhang bod chos dang rig gnas skor gyi legs bshad skya rengs gsar pa.* Beijing: Mi rigs dpe skrun khang, 2004.

Lelung Jedrung. *Life Stories of Myriad Ḍākinīs. Mkha' 'gro rgya mtsho'i rtogs brjod.* Publication details not found.

Lelung Jedrung. *Prayer of the Magic Vajra Key. Smon lam rdo rje'i 'phrul mig.* Publication details not found.

Lelung Jedrung. *Prayer of the Treasure House of the Four Joys. Smon lam dga' bzhi'i bang mdzod.* Publication details not found.

Lhatsün Rinchen Namgyal. *Meaningful to Behold the Extraordinary: A Roughly Complied Biography of Tsangnyön Heruka. Gtsang snyon he ru ka'i rnam thar rags btus ngo mtshar mthong ba don ldan.* Publication details not found.

Ngawang Kunga Sonam. *The Sakya Lineage. Sa skya'i gdung rabs.* Sakya Monastery, Tibet: Sakya par khang, n.d.

Ngawang Lodrö Drakpa. *Jonang Religious History. Jo nang chos 'byung zla ba'i sgron me.* Beijing: Krung go'i bod kyi shes rig dpe skrun khang, 1992.

Ngawang Nyima. *A Religious History: A Beacon of Reason and Scripture. Chos 'byung lung rigs sgron me.* Varanasi: Sanskrit University, 1966.

Nyak Chronicles. Gnags rabs. No author or publication details found.

Panchen Losang Chögyen. *Geluk Kagyu Tradition of Mahamudra. Dge ldan bka' brgyud rin po che'i phyag chen rtsa ba rgyal ba'i gzhung lam.* Delhi: Rgyud stod dpe mzod khang, 2014. Translated by Alexander Berzin. Ithaca, NY: Snow Lion Publications, 1997.

Pawo Tsukla Trengwa. *The Religious History of Lhodrak. Lho brak chos 'byung.* N.p., n.d.

Protecting Oneself: Taming the Seven Planets. Rang srung gza' bdun kha chings. No author or publication details found.

Rikzin Kunsang Ngé Dön Longyang. *Jewel Necklace of Biographies. Gsangs sngags snga 'gyur gyi bstan 'dzin skyes mchog rim byon gyi rnam thar do shal.* Dalhousie, India: Damchoe Zango, 1976.

Sakya Paṇḍita Künga Gyaltsen. *Treasure of Reasoning. Tshad ma rigs pa'i gter.* Collected Works, vol. 2.

Sangyé Lingpa (revealer). *Compilation of the Guru's Intent. Bla ma dgongs 'dus.* Buddhist Digital Resource Center Core Collection 1.

Sharza Tashi Gyaltsen. *The History of Bön: A Treasury of Explanation. Legs bshad bshad rin po che'i gter mdzod.* Beijing: Mi rigs dpe bkrun khang, 1985.

Sönam Öser. *Biography of Siddha Orgyen. Grub chen u rgyan gyi rnam thar.* Lhasa: Bod ljongs bod yig dpe rnying dpe skrun khang, 1997.

Songtsen Gampo (attr.). *Maṇikabüm. Ma ṇi bka' 'bum.* Delhi: Trayang and Jamyang Samten, 1975.

Tai Situ Jangchup Gyaltsen. *The Single Volume of Lang. Rlangs kyi po ti bse ru.* Lhasa: Bod ljongs mi dmangs dpe skrun khang, 1986.

Taksham Nuden Dorjé (revealer). *Biography of Yeshé Tsogyal. Mkha' 'gro ye shes mtsho rgyal gyi rnam thar.* Chengdu: Sikhron Mi-rigs Dpe-skrun Khang, 2015. Translated by Padmakara Translation Group as *Lady of the Lotus-Born.* Boston: Shambhala Publications, 2002.

Tāranātha. *Places of the Jonang. Jo nang gnas bshad.* Beijing: Krung go'i bod rig pa dpe skrun khang, 2008.

The Sand Spread Out and Amassed: A Presentation of the Correct Practices of Geomancy. sa dpyad legs nyes kyi blang dor rnam gzhag bye ma brdal spungs. No author or publication details found.

Tibetan Religious and Cultural Society, compiler. *Necklace of Precious Jewels: A List of Indian Pandits Who Visited Tibet and Tibetan Scholars Who Traveled to India between the Seventh and the Seventeenth Centuries, Their Dates and Brief Description of Their Activities.* Dharamsala: Sherab Parkhang, 1968.

Tsangnyön Heruka. *Biography of Milarepa and Guide to Liberation and Omniscience. Mi la re pa'i rnam thar rnam thar dang thams cad mkhyen pa'i lam ston.* Translated by Andrew Quintman as *The Life of Milarepa.* New York: Penguin Books, 2010.

Tsewang Gyal. *Lhorong Religious History. Lho rong chos 'byung.* Lhasa: Bod ljongs bod yig dpe rnying dpe skrun khang, 1994.

Tsongkhapa. *Essence of the Excellent Explanation on the Provisional and Definitive. Drang ba dang nges pa'i don rnam par 'byed pa legs bshad snying po.* Mungod, Karnataka, India: Je Yabse Sungbum Project, Drepung Loseling Education Society, 2019. Vol. *pha.*

Tsongkhapa. *Great Exposition of Secret Mantra. Sngags rim chen mo.* Mungod, Karnataka, India: Je Yabse Sungbum Project, *a.* Drepung Loseling Education Society, 2019. Vol. *ga.*

Tsongkhapa. *Great Exposition on the Stages of the Path to Enlightenment. Byang chub lam rim chen mo.* Mungod, Karnataka, India: Je Yabse Sungbum Project, Drepung Loseling Education Society, 2019. Vol. *pa.*

Tsongkhapa. *Lamp to Illuminate the Five Stages. Rim lnga gsal sgron.* Mungod, Karnataka, India: Je Yabse Sungbum Project, *a.* Drepung Loseling Education Society, 2019. Vol. *nga.* Translated by Gavin Kilty as *A Lamp to Illuminate the Five Stages.* Boston: Wisdom Publications, 2013.

Tsongkhapa. *Praise of Dependent Origination. Brten 'brel stod pa.* Tibetan and English translation found in *Splendor of an Autumn Moon* (Gavin Kilty, trans.). Boston: Wisdom Publications, 2001, p. 247.

Wangdu Tsering. *The Stainless Mirror: A History of Translation in Tibet and Biographies of Translators. Bod kyi sgra sgyur lo rgyus dang lo tsā ba rim byon gyi mdzad rnam gsal ba'i me long.* Beijing: People's Printing Press, 2001.

Yangönpa Gyaltsen Pal. *Mountain Dharma Miscellaneous Writings. Ri chos zhal 'don thor bu.* No publication details found.

Zhijé Ripa. *The Biography of Mila: A Lamp of Sunlight and Moonlight. Mi la'i rnam thar nyi zla'i 'od zer sgron ma.* No publication details found.

WORKS CONSULTED BY THE TRANSLATOR

Allione, Tsultrim. *Women of Wisdom.* London: Routledge and Kegan Paul, 1984.

Chögyal Namkhai Norbu. *The Light of Kailash.* Merigar, Italy: Shang Shung Publications, 2009.

Diemberger, Hildegard. *When a Woman Becomes a Religious Dynasty: The Samding Dorje Phagmo of Tibet.* New York: Columbia University Press, 2007.

Dudjom Rinpoché. *The Nyingma School of Tibetan Buddhism.* Translated by Gyurme Dorje and Matthew Kapstein. Boston: Wisdom Publications, 2002.

Harding, Sarah. *Machik's Complete Explanation.* Ithaca, NY: Snow Lion Publications, 2003.

Jamgon Kongtrul Lodro Taye. *The One Hundred Tertons.* Translated by Yeshe Gyamtso. Woodstock, VT: KTD Publications, 2011.

Kyesar Ludrup. *Research on Nālandā. Nālandā zhib 'jug.* Dharamsala, India: Library of Tibetan Works and Archives, 2009.

Lamotte, Etienne. *History of Indian Buddhism.* Louvain La Neuve: Institut Orientaliste, 1988.

Sheehy, Michael. "Materializing Dreams and Omens: The Autobiographical Subjectivity of the Tibetan Yoginī Kun dga' 'Phrin las dbang mo (1585–1668)." *Revue d'Etudes Tibétaines* 56 (October 2020).

Shakabpa. *Tibet: A Political History.* New Delhi: Paljor Publications, 2010.

Stearns, Cyrus. *Luminous Lives.* Boston: Wisdom Publications, 2001.

Thuken Chökyi Nyima. *Crystal Mirror of Philosophical Systems.* Translated by Geshé Lhundub Sopa, edited by Roger Jackson. Boston: Wisdom Publications, 2009.

Index

A Short Biography of His Holiness
the Fourteenth Dalai Lama

HIS HOLINESS THE DALAI LAMA is the spiritual leader of the Tibetan people and is a beacon of inspiration for Buddhists and non-Buddhists alike. He has persistently reached out across religious and political lines in his mission to advance peace and understanding in the world. In doing so, he embodies his motto "My religion is kindness."

He was born in 1935 in the northwestern Tibetan province of Amdo and enthroned as the Fourteenth Dalai Lama in 1940 in Lhasa, the capital of Tibet. He was educated in a traditional manner in the Potala Palace, the official residence of the Dalai Lamas. In 1950, at the time of the Communist annexation of Tibet, he assumed his responsibilities as head of state. He traveled to Beijing in 1954 to negotiate Tibetan autonomy with Mao Zedong and other Communist leaders.

In 1959, in the wake of the failed Tibetan uprising, shortly after completing his traditional *geshé* degree, he sought exile to India and set up his exile government. The next year he initiated the exile government's transition to democracy.

For his efforts to ensure the survival of the Tibetan people and their culture, and for his advocacy of peaceful resistance to Communist rule in Tibet, in 1989 he was awarded with the Nobel Peace Prize.

He has traveled globally to minister to Tibetan exile communities, advocate for peace, teach kindness and compassion, meet with religious and political leaders, and explore with scientists the many ways in which Buddhism and science can learn from each other.

His Holiness stepped down from his role as head of state in 2011, following the inauguration of the first democratically elected Tibetan president. Since then he has dedicated himself to his four commitments:

1. As a human being, he is committed to developing the intrinsic and fundamental qualities of goodness that exist in all of us.
2. As a Buddhist monk, he is committed to encouraging harmony among the world's regions.
3. As a Tibetan he is committed to working for the welfare of the Tibetan people.
4. As a follower of the Indian Nalanda tradition of Buddhism he is committed to preserving this ancient Indian knowledge tradition.

Readers are encouraged to learn more about His Holiness's life through his autobiographies and biographies.

Dalai Lama. *Freedom in Exile*. San Francisco: Harper Collins, 1991.

Dalai Lama. *My Land and My People*. New York: McGraw-Hill, 1962.

Dalai Lama and Sofia Stril-Rever. *My Spiritual Journey*. New York: HarperOne, 2011.

Norman, Alexander. *Dalai Lama: An Extraordinary Life*. Boston: Mariner Books, 2020.

Tenzin Geyche Tethong and Jane Moore. *His Holiness the Fourteenth Dalai Lama: An Illustrated Biography*. Northampton, MA: Interlink Books, 2020.

A detailed biography of His Holiness the Dalai Lama is being published by the Norbulingka Institute in Dharamsala, India, under the title of *Rgya chen snying rje'i rol mtsho*. The publication began in 2009. Twenty-four of a planned fifty volumes have been released, covering through to the year 1995.

A Short Biography of His Eminence
Dagyab Kyabgön Rinpoché

HIS EMINENCE Loden Sherab Dagyab Kyabgön Rinpoché was born in 1940 in Minyak, eastern Tibet, into a peasant family. At the age of four was recognized as the Ninth Kyabgön (patron) of the Dagyab region. He belongs to the third ranking of tulkus in Tibet and holds the honorary title of Hothokthu Nomanhan.

Rinpoché studied the major and minor subjects, such as the Buddhist psycho-ethical philosophy and grammar, poetry, and astronomy, at the monastic university of Drepung, earning a geshé degree and the reputation as an exceptional scholar.

In 1959 Rinpoché fled to India with His Holiness the Fourteenth Dalai Lama. Since that time, the two have established a tight and personal bond. His Holiness has full confidence in Rinpoché, as is shown by his asking Rinpoché to compile the present work based on His Holiness's teachings given over the past several decades.

In 1964 His Holiness appointed Rinpoché as first director of Tibet House New Delhi. This developed into an internationally recognized institute for the preservation and promotion of Tibetan culture.

In 1966 he accepted a position at the University of Bonn, Germany, as a Tibetologist at the Institute of Central Asian Studies. He served as an international research fellow and lecturer for thirty-eight years, until his retirement in 2004. His main field of research was Buddhist art, symbolism, and iconography. He is the author of several books. A list of publications can be viewed at www.dagyab-rinpoche.com.

In the 1980s he was asked by a group of Germans interested in

Buddhism to become a spiritual teacher, and in response he founded a Buddhist community, Chödzong, in southern Germany. Since then he has also taught in other European countries, North and South American, and Asia.

Rinpoché is the founder of Tibet House Germany (Tibethaus Deutschland), which is under the patronage of His Holiness the Dalai Lama. As the successor organization of Chödzong, it was established in Frankfurt in 2005 as the Tibetan Buddhist Cultural and Educational Institute Tibet House Germany. Rinpoché still serves as its spiritual director together with H. E. Zong Rinpoché. The institute has five departments: Buddhism, Personality and Society, Art and Culture, Medicine, and Science.

Rinpoché mainly teaches at Tibet House Germany and its rural retreat center, Berghof, where he gives sutra and tantra teachings as well as talks on Tibetan culture, in both the German and English languages. Since 2000 he has visited Singapore yearly to teach at Gaden Shartse Dro Phen Ling. He has also taught in Tibetan monasteries in Tibet and India. Since 2020 he has been giving online teachings to participants from many Eastern and Western countries, including China.

H. E. Dagyab Kyabgön Rinpoché is known to hold a large number of transmissions of the Geluk lineage, as well as many Sakya and Kagyu lineage transmissions, and he teaches the full range of Tibetan Buddhism, beginning with the cultivation of the basic human values—which His Holiness has emphasized for many years as the foundation of all religions—up to the two stages of Highest Tantra. His ability to transmit the rich tradition in all its diversity and depth, and at the same time teach according to the human needs and realities of today's time and culture, is greatly appreciated by his students. With encouragement, without pressure or coercion, he always emphasizes the benefits of changing one's mind, the taking of daily life as the main field of spiritual practice, and the strengthening of one's capacity to be a good human being.

He and his wife, Norden, moved from Bonn to Berlin after his retirement to be close to their two children and five grandchildren. Rinpoché continues to focus on writing on Buddhism, Tibetan history and language, and biographies, as well as on teaching in different countries. His dedication to pass on as much of his inexhaustible knowledge as possible, and otherwise to be of service, still guides his activities.

Also Available from the Dalai Lama and Wisdom Publications

Buddhism
One Teacher, Many Traditions

The Compassionate Life

Ecology, Ethics, and Interdependence
The Dalai Lama in Conversation with Leading Thinkers on Climate Change

Essence of the Heart Sutra
The Dalai Lama's Heart of Wisdom Teachings

The Essence of Tsongkhapa's Teachings
The Dalai Lama on the Three Principal Aspects of the Path

The Good Heart
A Buddhist Perspective on the Teachings of Jesus

Imagine All the People
A Conversation with the Dalai Lama on Money, Politics, and Life as It Could Be

Kalachakra Tantra
Rite of Initiation

The *Library of Wisdom and Compassion* series:

Volume 1. Approaching the Buddhist Path

Volume 2. The Foundation of Buddhist Practice

Volume 3. Saṃsāra, Nirvāṇa, and Buddha Nature

Volume 4. Following in the Buddha's Footsteps

Volume 5. In Praise of Great Compassion

Volume 6. Courageous Compassion

Volume 7. Searching for the Self

Volume 8. Realizing the Profound View

The Life of My Teacher
A Biography of Kyabjé Ling Rinpoché

Meditation on the Nature of Mind

The Middle Way
Faith Grounded in Reason

Mind in Comfort and Ease
The Vision of Enlightenment in the Great Perfection

MindScience
An East-West Dialogue

Opening the Eye of New Awareness

Practicing Wisdom
The Perfection of Shantideva's Bodhisattva Way

Science and Philosophy in the Indian Buddhist Classics, vol. 1
The Physical World

Science and Philosophy in the Indian Buddhist Classics, vol. 2
The Mind

Sleeping, Dreaming, and Dying
An Exploration of Consciousness

The Wheel of Life
Buddhist Perspectives on Cause and Effect

The World of Tibetan Buddhism
An Overview of Its Philosophy and Practice

About Wisdom Publications

Wisdom Publications is the leading publisher of classic and contemporary Buddhist books and practical works on mindfulness. To learn more about us or to explore our other books, please visit our website at wisdomexperience.org or contact us at the address below.

Wisdom Publications
199 Elm Street
Somerville, MA 02144 USA

We are a 501(c)(3) organization, and donations in support of our mission are tax deductible.

Wisdom Publications is affiliated with the Foundation for the Preservation of the Mahayana Tradition (FPMT).